A COMMON GOOD
APPROACH TO
DEVELOPMENT

A Common Good Approach to Development

Collective Dynamics of Development Processes

Edited by
Mathias Nebel, Oscar Garza-Vázquez
and Clemens Sedmak

OpenBook
Publishers

https://www.openbookpublishers.com

ISBN Paperback: 9781800644045
ISBN Hardback: 9781800644052
ISBN Digital (PDF): 9781800644069
ISBN Digital ebook (EPUB): 9781800644076
ISBN Digital ebook (AZW3): 9781800644083
ISBN XML: 9781800644090
ISBN Digital ebook (HTML): 9781800646742
DOI: 10.11647/OBP.0290

Cover image: Cuetzalan, Puebla (2008). Photo by Oscar Garza-Vázquez.
Cover design by Anna Gatti

Contents

Acknowledgements

This book is the result of a research process that involved many people over four years. We want to express here our gratitude to the friends and colleagues as well as the institutions that made this journey possible. First we would like to thank all the authors that took part in this project for their excellent contributions contained in this volume. This book would not be possible without your commitment, patience, and dedication throughout this process. Each one of you made this project better. We also must acknowledge our debts to the local research group based in Puebla, Mexico. Thank you Antonio Sánchez, Jorge Medina, Valente Tallabs, Ignacio Arbesu, Juan Pablo Aranda, Roy Nuñez, José Luis Ávila, Juan Martin Castro, María del Rosario Andrade, and Viviana Ramírez for the many, many hours of debate and discussion that gave way to the matrix and metrics of common good dynamics. This time of academic friendship was precious and your insights invaluable. Similarly, we would like to thank the many researchers that took part in one or more of the three research seminars in Puebla, Barcelona, and Notre Dame between 2017 and 2018. Again, to be able to share and debate very widely the ideas shaping this book ensured not only its coherence but also the academic quality of each part. Thank you especially to Oscar Martínez Martínez (REMIPSO's President), Roberto Vélez Grajales (CEEY's Executive Director), Graciela Teruel Belismelis (EQUIDE's Director), Gerardo Leyva Parra (INEGI's Research Director) and Luis Felipe López-Calva (UNDP Regional Director for Latin-America) for their illuminating comments. Finally, we would like to express our appreciation to the two anonymous reviewers. Their helpful comments helped us improve the overall structure of the book and gave us the opportunity to clarify further the main arguments in it.

Then, we are also in debt with institutions: first the *Universidad Popular Autonoma del Estado de Puebla* (UPAEP) and its *Instituto Promotor del Bien*

Común (IPBC). They were the ultimate driver of this journey, granting the needed funds for our research. Thank you also to the *University of Notre Dame* and its *Center for Social Concern*, and to the *Institut Químic de Sarrià* at *Universitat Ramón Llull* for hosting one of the three research seminars. Thank you also to Elizabeth Rankin for her thorough proofreading and suggestions to several of the chapters in this book. Likewise, thanks to Andrea Cuspinera for her technical assistance in the final steps of the book edition. Finally, we would like to express our appreciation to Open Book Publishers for making the whole publishing experience as efficient and agreeable as it can be (thank you Alessandra Tossi, Melissa Purkiss, Anna Gatti, and Luca Baffa).

Introduction

Mathias Nebel and Oscar Garza-Vázquez

1. The Research Question

'[A] misconceived theory can kill', wrote Amartya Sen more than two decades ago (1999, p. 209). Certainly, the terrible (and unequal) human cost of the COVID-19 pandemic and its associated crushing economic impact, which has pushed thousands of people into subsistence levels (or worse), painfully reminds us that the ideas we use to organise our societies can result in an unbearable toll of human lives. We could also consider the millions of lives that are threatened everyday by injustices such as extreme poverty, rampant inequality, discriminatory practices; the continuing deterioration of natural life due to our climate irresponsibility; and the disproportionate burden that populist rhetoric, technocratic recommendations, 'development' policies, and power imbalances, pose for many. In line with Sen's quote, our failure to address the systemic and interdependent nature of all these concerns threatening our common humanity does suggest that our current development thinking does not seem to be fit for purpose. Yet, this rather crude and dismal verdict should not be one of defeat, but one of hope. We may change and enrich mainstream ideas about development or envision new ones to face our current social ailments and procure a better future for all (see Chapter 9). This is what this book is about.

It proposes an alternative way of assessing our social realities that we conceive as 'a common good approach to development'. We certainly maintain that development is about people, and about how each person is able to live, but we contend that it is also—and more importantly for

 https://doi.org/10.11647/OBP.0290.16

today's problems—about how we are able to live together with others. It is about cooperation, about the common goals that we pursue together and about the kind of social life that we are constantly creating and sustaining. In a nutshell, our approach to development is about how systems of commons are generated and maintained over time.

The common good traditions are multifarious.[1] For centuries they were the main frameworks for understanding social processes and shaping policies. As an architectonic concept, the common good articulated the practice of government, law, tax administration, and merchant guilds, as well as monastic communities. The concept was not considered theoretical, but rather practical. It was a way to understand and govern the many 'commons' around which societies gathered. Gradually, the emergence of the modern state, coupled with the shift toward social contract theories, displaced the concept to the sidelines of political philosophy and of development thinking—so much so that today the notion of the common good appears to most people as outdated, fuzzy, and ambiguous, and certainly not something that would help us move toward a more efficient development practice. It is this understanding that our book wants to challenge. It focuses on the *practical relevance* that a common good perspective can have for development issues.

Our research question is quite straightforward: *How can we assess and measure common good dynamics?* This question obviously involves several others: What do we understand by 'common goods'? Is it meaningful to adopt a common good perspective on development? Should we really add a new metric to the ever-growing list of development indicators? What are we really looking for through a common good indicator, and what advantages can we expect from such a perspective? This book can't possibly answer all these questions and does not pretend to do so. It rather starts a discussion we hope may lead to new insights in questions of development, both from a theoretical and from a practical perspective. In particular, we defend a common good approach that aims at assessing *the quality of a given system of common goods — what we call 'the nexus of common goods'—at the local level.*

---

1   The historical development of the notion is now better understood than previously, see for example, Kempshall (1999), Hibst (1991), Lecuppre-Desjardin and Van Bruaene (2010).

This book is the result of a research project that has spanned over four years, gathering together a group of international researchers to try to build both a robust matrix and a metric of common good dynamics. The *Instituto Promotor del Bien Común* (IPBC) at the UPAEP University (Puebla, Mexico) founded the project. The IPBC is a research institute dedicated to the notion of the common good and furthering the capability to use the concept as a robust analytical tool. The UPAEP officially launched this effort in December 2017, and three research seminars took place in Puebla, Barcelona, and Notre Dame between December 2017 and October 2018. Each meeting gathered around twenty-five invited scholars to work on the design of a matrix of common good dynamics. An IPBC discussion paper would focus the debate during the two-day seminars and lead to a revised proposal for the next one. In February 2019, a first version of the matrix and metric of common good dynamics was presented at an international conference organised by the UPAEP (a revised version of it provides the content of Chapter 2). In the following months, the IPBC research team came up with a questionnaire, which was discussed in regular meetings of the local committee, tested during cognitive interviews, and verified in a pilot project involving 180 residents of Atlixco, Mexico, in May 2019 (see Chapter 3). The questionnaire was then duly revised and successively applied in three municipalities between July and December 2019. The results of these empirical applications were published in the form of a special issue on the common good approach at the end of 2020 (Rivista Internazionale di Scienze Sociali). In contrast, the content of this book investigates the theoretical and practical foundations of our common good approach and discusses its expediency for development topics.

The book is divided in three parts. Part I presents the conceptual framework that the IPBC proposes for operationalising a common good approach to development. This theoretical part introduces and justifies the rationale of a matrix of common good dynamics composed of five key normative drivers (collective agency, justice, stability, governance, and humanity) (Chapters 1 and 2). It then presents a possible metric for capturing common good dynamics in municipalities and considers the extent to which this can give us an edge in policy-making and governance (Chapter 3). This conceptual framework serves as the backbone of the book, with all other contributors referring to it. In Part II several scholars of different academic backgrounds discuss how each of the five elements composing the common good matrix can be justified, enriched or criticised from their own discipline (Chapters 4, 5, 6, 7, and 8). Finally, Part III explores the relevance of a common good approach through different case studies (Chapters 9, 10, 11, and 12).

The uniting theme throughout the book is the shared recognition of the need to devise an alternative framework to understand the interdependency of our lives, the collective nature of the social world in which we experience our lives, and the transformatory potential of human cooperation. Given the rich interdisciplinary outlook on these urgent matters, this book should be of interest to a wide audience dealing with development issues. Despite its strong theoretical orientation, we believe this book to be equally relevant for academics and researchers involved with development issues, as for practitioners and policy-makers looking for a new approach to inform their actions.

2. Why Do We Need a Common Good Approach?

The world as we 'knew' it is no longer the same. The COVID-19 pandemic came to disrupt our everyday reality and its apparent normality. It unveiled the social structures and collective dynamics that underlie the functioning of what seems to be the natural order of the world. It revealed that our societies are built around some essential goods, and it forced nations and individuals out of their illusion of autonomy towards a recognition of our radical interdependency. It awoke our dormant sense that something was wrong with our beloved normality, an awareness of our unpreparedness to face the challenges of an interconnected world, and the need to recognise our shared social reality.

Throughout our recent history, we have been told an incomplete story about who we are, about how the world works, and about how we ought to solve humanity's problems (Bruni 2008). This is a story that starts and ends with individuals. It starts by conceiving of people as individuals whose interest can be reduced to their own self-interest, who live in a world of—and ignited by—individual competition, and whose common problems (including the satisfaction of individual human needs) are solved mainly through market interaction and individual efforts. Distilled from this individualistic outlook, social progress was thought of as an increase in individual achievements, usually aggregated at a certain moment in time (either in terms of income, resources, utility, freedoms, rights, etc.). Social progress and development were to be measured as an increase in the autonomy of individuals.

In this fictitious world, the common good rhetoric tends to disappear. Even inherently collective goods are thought to be better appraised—so the argument goes—through the language of individual human rights. Social choice theories replaced the common good discourses in development economics, with the provision and distribution of public goods becoming the main concern, while in general the focus of political philosophy and public discourse shifted toward procedural justice and liberal democracy.

Of course, this is an oversimplification. But it highlights the fact that this dominant narrative curtails part of who we are as human beings, of our common life, of the collective goods we produce and enjoy together, and of our belonging and interdependency. We are also social/ relational beings who care, share, interact, and cooperate with others. We define who we are, and experience wellbeing, in relationships. We inhabit a social world, we belong to groups, we share identities and goals with others; our whole existence as individuals is embedded in a web of collectively-generated meanings, values, and goods. Even market production is a collective enterprise, which is in turn embedded in an institutional arrangement of formal and informal institutions (e.g., judicial systems to enforce contracts, property rights, reputational effects, coordination and routines between economic agents, social norms, etc.).

These are all relational and common goods which are central to the dynamics of our social reality and to development processes. The effect of omitting these elements from the story goes beyond a simple misrepresentation of human life. It limits our capacity to fully grasp the nature of a true *human* development, and more importantly, it limits our way of thinking about how we do development (e.g., see Andreoni et al. 2021). Hence, although there are excellent reasons to account for individual goals of development, the narrow individualistic approach has non-negligible shortcomings. It fails to tell us anything about *how* and *why* development happens, and thus about how to solve our common problems. This would require an understanding (1) of the commonality of meanings, (2) of common behaviour and shared practices—the way people cooperate and coordinate to produce something collectively—and (3) of the interdependent and systemic nature of results.

(1) *Commonality of meanings*. As early as 1983, criticising John Rawls' *Theory of Justice* (1971)—one of the main theoretical arguments along the mainstream line of thought in justice and development—Michael Walzer (1983) highlighted the importance of collective goods. According to Walzer, the production and distribution of any social good entails a preexisting shared understanding of the value of this good by the community involved. In India, for example, beef can't be produced and distributed in the same way as in the United States. The communal meaning given by the Hindu faith to animals—and especially to cows—does not allow it. Good distribution is embedded in the historical reality of a living community and heeds the social meaning of the good itself. That is, development goals *are only* common goals as long as they build upon the shared meaning and value given to some *social* goods.

(2) *Common behaviour and shared practices*. Elinor Ostrom's pioneering work (1990) revealed the ubiquitous existence of commons such as collective pasture grounds, irrigation systems, or cooperative fisheries, whose sustainable efficient management could not be properly understood from a self-maximising individual rationality. Her work made clear that the economic dichotomy between state and market—between public goods provided by state institutions and private goods produced by a free market economy—was definitely too narrow. We were missing something important, namely the strength and capacities of civil society, the social capital imbedded in society (Putnam 2000; for an overview of social capital theories, see Joonmo 2020). The very existence of these common pool resources implied some forms of collective collaboration framing competitive individual behaviours so that they may not threaten the very existence of the common pool resource (Ostrom 1990, pp. 8–17). Indeed, commons are frameworks of governance mechanisms, rules, and roles commonly agreed upon and collectively managed. They set the ground for economic behaviours that allow for a sustainable use of the common-pool resource by all and its preservation for future generations.

All in all, Ostrom's work pointed toward our obliviousness and ignorance of the many *practices of commoning* existing in our societies.

How do commons arise in a society? How can they be sustained? How do they change and adapt through power struggles? How do we 'do' commons? These are no trivial questions limited to local pastures and fisheries, but also relevant queries for global issues like climate change, education, or human development.

Climate change may indeed serve as an example to illustrate the two previous points. Part of the difficulty in addressing this urgent matter is that the international community needs to agree not only on the goals and procedural elements of a technical solution to CO_2 emissions, but on the very *meaning* and *value* of the environment. The latter is not a question that can be sidelined forever, for it is precisely the meaning and value given to the environment that commands the very social practice sustaining the constant increase of CO_2 emissions. If climate change has to be effectively addressed, it necessarily entails a change of our social and economic practice, which in turn means that we will need to review the way we collectively conceive of and value the environment. Let us stress this point: It is *we* who have become acutely aware that *our* patterns of production and consumption must change if *we* want to avoid a catastrophic increase of greenhouse gases in the atmosphere.

(3) Interdependence and systemic nature of results. The previous example puts into sharp relief the systemic and interconnected nature of our lives. For climate change unveils first that our freedom is not an individual trait at all: it is a shared good. We are not safe until everyone is safe. Our life depends on others and the lives of others depend on us, literally. Fighting climate change requires us to reconsider the way we behave collectively, that is, how we enter into institutionalised cooperation with others. What is more, climate change is not a challenge that can be resolved without at the same time considering other social issues. We certainly need to address it, but without undermining other commons, such as the economy, human rights and freedoms, or solidarity. Likewise, it also implies that we cannot pretend to offer a proper solution to a specific problem if we isolate it from the multiple factors that—in conjunction— produce a certain result. As Beretta and Nebel recognise (2020), it is not enough to acknowledge the multidimensionality of development through a list of goals or objectives, we also need to understand how these interrelate as an '*integrated process* of this multidimensionality'. Development is a systemic, 'dynamic process unfolding in time and

space. It cannot be reduced to checking whether basic preconditions are in place, nor to measuring achievements on a predefined list of desirable outcomes.' (both quotes p. 372; emphasis in original).

Models based on aggregated individual rationalities are not well equipped to account for the social, interconnected world in which we live. Crucially, they cannot provide proper solutions to real-world problems and more often than not have 'unforeseen' and 'unintended' adverse effects (Tirole 2016). We need therefore new ideas to guide our actions. Neither the states, nor markets, nor the international community have been able to give a convincing answer to this necessary change of social and economic practice. We think that a common good perspective is not only pertinent, but may hint at another model of society, another way to understand development. In particular, the common good approach we advance takes up these points: that questions of justice and development are linked to the meaning and the shared value given to social goods; we understand development as a process embedded in communities and in how people produce and distribute social goods like security, education, and mobility.

Thus, the common good approach we defend here focuses on the *processes* through which local communities create and maintain a specific set of social or 'common goods'. It understands these goods as *irreducible social goods*. As Taylor (1990) argues, these are good that are immanent to the *cooperation* of people in a community; immanent to *collective organisation* that allows the achievement of a social good; immanent to the *shared understanding* of their value. However, taking the local community as the locus of the development process does not mean that a common good approach sacrifices the universal to the particular. Rather, such an approach understands the universal common good as a dialectic that progressively sees the many systems of common goods becoming larger in scope and deeper in humanity, in an eschatological hope that the universal common good can be real and possible.[2] Similarly, we will sustain that the three features

---

2   The French Jesuit Gaston Fessard (1944) introduced three distinctions in the vocabulary of the common good that have inspired most of the reflections in this book. Fessard distinguishes between the *'good of a community'* (le bien de la communauté), the *'community of the good'* (la communauté du bien) and the *'good of communion'* (bien de la communion), which is the universal and eschatological

identified above underlie any development dynamics at any level (from household dynamics, organisations, communities, states, nations, to global issues). Wherever there are people interacting with each other to produce something—as is the case in every development process—these elements are present to a greater or lesser degree. Each of these processes implies a shared background of action, a coordination and cooperation, and an interdependency.

Therefore, the question of the commons and how we produce, sustain, and govern them is one of the crucial questions of the twenty-first century. We can state it this way: while the twentieth century focused on the protection of individual rights and capabilities, the big challenge of the twenty-first century may well be communal life. How can we build a shared, common, human future for all? This seems to us a sufficiently important question to dedicate a book to.

3. A Common Good Approach to Development. Where Do We Stand?

The notion of the common good is enjoying a kind of resurrection. It almost died out, suffering constant decline during the nineteenth century and a brutal rejection after the sixties. The notion however now finds itself back at the forefront of discussions. We may quote, among others, the works of Michael Sandel (2020), Alain Badiou (2019), Robert Reich (2019), Daniel Finn (2017), Jean Tirole (2016), Christian Blum (2015), Catherine Hudak Klancer (2015), Patrick Riordan (2014; 2008; 1996), Hans Sluga (2014), Axel Kahn (2013), Tim Gorringe (2014), Robert K. Vischner (2010), Dennis McCann and Patrick Miller (2005), David Hollenbach (2002), Herfried Munkler and Harald Bluhm (2001–2004), Inge Kaul, Isabelle Grunberg, Marc Stern (1999), and Elinor Ostrom (1990).[3] Together these authors have decisively added to the sense that the notion of the common good is not only pertinent for the twenty-first century, but that it offers a real and complementary way forward.

---

common good. He therefore shapes the common good as a dialectical dynamic toward the universal common good (2015, pp. 83–85, 102–105, 123–129).

3 Still very relevant are older thinkers such as Fessard (1944) and Maritain (1949). In addition, a whole set of studies has been dedicated to the history of the notion: Kempshall (1999), Hibst (1991), Lecuppre-Desjardin and Van Bruaene (2010), and Collard (2010).

Its revival seems closely linked to three topics: (1) The limits of *political liberalism* (Blum 2015, pp. 7–9; Hollenbach 2002, pp. 3–16), (2) the definition of *new public goods* (Kaul et al. 1999, Deneulin and Townsend 2007, pp. 19–36) and the rediscovery of *'economies of the commons* (Felber 2015, Bollier 2003, Bollier and Helfrich 2015, Ostrom 1990), and (3) a need to reassert the *goals of governance* beyond technical criteria and mere democratic procedures (Crowther et al. 2018, Giguère 2004, Whitman 2009). All in all, it is a pragmatic revival, linked to the preservation or the creation of 'common goods' whose social value is essentially intangible, such as health, education, and enjoyment of cultural heritage, wellbeing, or the environment. This is remarkably evident when the World Bank proposes to define good governance as the traditions and institutions by which authority in a country is exercised for the common good (World Bank 2004) or when UNESCO suggests using the paradigm of the common good to understand education (UNESCO 2015).

As we briefly mentioned in the previous section, in her landmark book Ostrom proposes a set of guidelines needed for commons to exist and be sustained. *Governing the Commons* (1990) is about cooperation to achieve and sustain common pool resources. It is about the agency or freedom of a group. It is about organising this agency through roles, rules, sanctions, and goals. Her work highlighted some key elements for a dynamic of the commons to be sustained over time. While highly focused, her practical research revealed a blind spot in economic and political literature for which she would ultimately be awarded the Nobel Prize in Economic Sciences in 2009.[4]

First, she highlighted the *political dimension* of the commons, that is, the fundamental decision made about the *value* of a common (Ostrom 1990, pp. 38–45). The local community would hold 'in common' that the pastures, irrigation systems or fisheries had a value that exceeded the private individual interest. It was vital for the community to reach an agreement on the way these resources could be used *by all* while preserving at the same time their very existence in the long run. Such agreements, held at the local level, are political in nature but eschew the logic of the free market or state institutions. They are agreements

---

4   See https://www.nobelprize.org/uploads/2018/06/ostrom_lecture.pdf.

about the collective meaning and value of commons to each and every member of a community. This process is complex. It entails at least two steps: (1) the determination by a polity about how it *understands itself* and (2) how it defines *legitimate use* and *handles resources* in accordance with this self-understanding.

Second, Ostrom's work put into sharp relief a 'world of commoning' that neither the state nor the market recognised (1990, pp. 7–28). Mainstream conceptions of the polity and the market take the commons as a given, with their existence supposed to be unlimited and stable, like natural resources. Yet the 2008 financial crisis, for example, revealed this notion to be delusional. The crisis shone a light on the fact that financial markets need trust to function but do not produce it themselves. Two major blind spots distorting the lens of modern politics and economics are therefore the understanding of commons as a given and the failure to understand the political dimension of the same.

A wide range of development practices have enthusiastically built on her findings ever since. For example, the World Bank finances the so-called 'Community-Based or Community-Driven Programs', which are structured around three elements: (i) adopting processes that strengthen the capacity of a community to organise and sustain development; (ii) supporting community empowerment through user participation in decision-making, and (iii) reversing control and accountability from central authorities to community organisations (Narayan 1995). These Community-Driven Development (CDD) projects are thought to (a) increase the efficiency, cost effectiveness, and sustainability of development projects; (b) increase the empowerment of the local population; and (c) change the behavioural patterns of the population. These three points are intuitively tied together; you can't achieve results if you don't get the population to participate in the project, and the project doesn't last long if consistent patterns of behaviour do not sustain the result.

These efforts already highlight the importance of expanding development thinking to include collective goods and to involve the local community in this process. Yet, while this revival of the commons for development is welcome, it is also problematic: *welcome* because it proves the practical need for such a notion (as the common good cannot be reduced to individual interest or utility) but *problematic* because the notion of 'commons' is too narrow, and it still lacks a systemic approach.

First, Ostrom's conception of commons inherited by CDD projects focus on tangible things (e.g., construction of roads, schools, or health clinics, collective resources such as irrigation systems, fisheries, pastures, etc.). However, commons go well beyond these material goods to include intangible goods such as cultural goods, knowledge, language, and the like. We ought therefore to understand commons as a social construct inherently related to the social practice underpinning it (Helfrich 2012). Second, the revival of the commons still lacks an overall coherence that would link specific 'common goods' (education, health, governance, etc.) into a system or nexus of common goods. In other words, the dynamic *coalescence of common goods into a shared striving for the common good* is lacking as these approaches tend to see each common good in isolation, as detached from other social goods and detached from the social structure holding all of them together.

Hence, a common good approach to development (see Chapters 1 and 2) extends previous efforts to revive the commons. It focuses on social action and is radically practical, starting with a community and the common goods it values and produces. It sees development as a process; as a systemic equilibrium of collective values, meanings, and actions embodied in social institutions and social practices that together generate a social dynamic that co-creates and sustains a particular way of social life—this is what we call 'a nexus of common goods'. Therefore, the approach we investigate here centres mainly on the equilibrium created by that community among the many social goods and tries to capture the way this equilibrium—'the nexus of common goods'—is generated, maintained, and enriched over time. The research question framing this book is therefore as practical as possible, focusing on the quality of this nexus and the possibilities of assessing it empirically.

4. Does a Common Good Approach to Development Undermines the Plurality of Modern Societies?

Anyone who wishes to advance a common good approach to development faces an uphill battle and must confront a series of widely held assumptions pushing back against any attempt to do so. Some of these objections are justified, other less so. Let's briefly review some of the arguments usually held against the use of the common good language in development studies.

Two major claims are regularly made against revivals of a common good approach. The most usual is that the concept is lofty, mostly rhetorical, and certainly not precise enough to be practicable. It is said to be an empty shell, a meta-discourse used to cover other, usually darker, intentions. What is the common good? Everything and nothing in particular, say skeptics. A concept meant to show that one's intentions are noble and generous, rather than selfish and self-interested. But then certainly a mere protest of altruistic intentions does not add up to a vision of society or a set of public policies. Thus, to reason on the ground of the common good is at best naïve, at worst deceitful—or at least so say the skeptics.

This rhetorical use to justify one's intentions is well attested and can't be denied. Most politicians do sooner or later fall into this self-justified protest of altruistic intentions. But this can hardly be considered an argument against the common good. Few words have been more misused by crooked politicians than 'freedom,' 'democracy,' or 'solidarity' but nobody argues in response that the value of such concepts is thus null and void. Misuse by itself is not enough to discard a concept.

A second claim frequently made against the common good is that it is rooted in theology or metaphysics. And according to this argument, this can't be tolerated anymore. Do we not live in a pluralistic society? Why should we want to relapse to any forms of theocracy? For these critics, to argue from a worldview in which groups and collectivities take a central role is a practical rejection of pluralism. A widespread assumption is that whoever picks up the discourse of the common good is thus trying to impose on the rest of the society a religious or metaphysical view of the good. To defend the pluralism of the public square, to defend both religious minorities and agnostic citizens alike, we therefore ought to avoid a discourse based on the common good, preferring either a Habermassian or Rawlsian approach to democracy.

This whole argument is however based on a double assumption: (1) that any conception of the common good is paramount to a comprenhensive and metaphysical conception of the good; and (2) that liberal views of the polity are free of similar preconceptions and can accommodate pluralistic views of the good. Both statements can be challenged. Nebel (2018) addresses the second claim at length in a previous publication and will not be repeated here, but we will briefly state why our approach does not contradict the pluralism of our societies nor its focus on individual freedom. First, we will propose in Chapter 1 to understand the common good as an *open* and *dialectical political process, inherently plural and conflictual*, that requires a constant political debate to discern which commons we may value together and how to achieve them. By differentiating between the universal common good as a normative horizon of politics and the many, complex, and ever-changing historical systems of common goods, we open the space needed for pluralism to exist.

Second, the common good perspective introduced here is as practical as possible. It puts its emphasis on the empirical fact that development outcomes (good or bad) and the social order of a particular society are always the result of social and collectively sustained practices. It is these collective dynamics that the conceptual framework proposed in Chapters 1 and 2 aims to grasp. Bringing these collective *processes* into our assessment of development need not be incompatible with individual-based notions of development (Chapter 4); it can complement it and render it more truly human—as we briefly argue in the subsection below. Our main interest is to shed light to the *common* aspect of our social lives—which is often obfuscated in mainstream development literature—and not on a metaphysical *good* that ought to be pursued universally. The common good perspective developed hereafter, is that there is not a 'one size fits all' universal system of common goods, but a necessary and legitimate plurality of common good systems, within the limits of the normative key drivers of common good dynamics.

5. Why Measure Common Good Dynamics?

There is no shortage of metrics that try to measure development. Yet, most development approaches capture development through a list of items for which they provide indicators and metrics relying on individual-level data. These may be the extent to which individuals succeed to satisfy a list of basic needs, human security, capabilities, human rights, or selected features of human flourishing. But most of them focus on either *preconditions* of wellbeing development or a selected set of *achievements* or *functionings* (see Chapter 2 and Chapter 3).

While a common good approach recognises the need and value of individual-based indicators, we contend that they do not fully explain the social processes involved in development. They leave out the *structural dimension of development*, i.e., how a social environment shapes these individual functionings or achievements. As mentioned, a growing literature argues that we also need to include group or community data in order to grasp and measure 'collective achievement' of goods or services that are essentially 'shared' or 'common.' Indeed, different approaches to development, including social capital (Putnam 2000), public goods (Kaul et al. 1999), the commons (Ostrom 1990), social rights (Ulrike 2013), and collective capabilities (Ibrahim 2017, Ibrahim 2016), are currently making advances in this direction. Moreover, many development indicators try to capture what are best regarded as collective goods, like health and education, through individual data.

Our approach is different. It adopts the point of view that development is not first and foremost a matter of individuals but of groups, communities, or nations. It is only together that development can be achieved, not only as a means to an end, but as an end in itself; there is no human development without a shared, common development process. Only development attained in common can be truly called *human* development. Hence, we focus on the *commons* and the social *process* through which a community achieves common goods and the way these build up in society to create a system or *nexus of common goods*. By concentrating on this 'common good dynamic', our aim shifts from focusing on outputs and results (i.e., a set or list of basic common goods) to the social drivers of this dynamic equilibrium.

Indeed, a focus merely on outputs would have led us to verify the delivery of a list of basic common goods and whether or not they exist. While interesting, such an approach fails to answer the *why* question. *Why* do precisely this set of common goods exist? *Why* are they arranged in this specific equilibrium, and not some other one? *Why* did such dynamic equilibrium emerge, and how is it maintained? The *why* question is under-addressed in development literature. We are usually much more interested in the provision of specific common goods— education, work, housing, mobility, etc.—leaving open the question of how (and by whom) these specific common goods will be arranged and of how they will work together. Generally, development literature assumes that providing income, housing, education, and health to a population will somehow add up to trigger development and raise people out of poverty. This is rather naïve. Complex social systems do not function under a logic of mere aggregation. To tackle the question of how common goods 'build up' to form a "nexus of common goods" we have to focus on the process rather than the outputs, on the dynamic of the nexus rather than on its components.

In particular, we focus on the social *drivers* of this dynamic. Chapters 2 and 3 will argue, as the literature on the commons does, that *drivers* must include justice, governance, sustainability, and what we can call 'collective agency freedom'. It will then be argued that the quality of a nexus must allow people to live together as human beings, thus *humanity* should be recognised as the normative horizon of common good dynamics. This normative horizon is understood here as a set of *habitus,* describing our shared, common humanity through a set of collective practices. This is not a naïve regression to Aristotle, but rather builds on Bourdieu and Giddens's reciprocity between social structures and practice. Each nexus commands a certain set of *habitus*, which will allow us to discern if the dynamic is heading toward a more human coexistence, or elsewhere.

6. Structure of the Book

Part I–A Common Good Approach. The first part of the book drafts the theoretical argument on which the matrix and metric of common good dynamics is based (Chapters 1 and 2). It also presents a specific metric of common good dynamics meant for municipalities (Chapter 3). These chapters will be of use for scholars interested in the theoretical background of a common good approach to development. They will however also be of interest to policy-makers and practitioners searching for new ways to address social realities.

Chapter 1 elaborates a possible understanding of a common good for the twenty-first century. Building on Foucault, Arendt, Bourdieu, Giddens, Ostrom, Taylor, and Riordan, Mathias Nebel proposes to understand the common good from the perspective of the interactions structuring our communal life. The chapter borrows from many of the antique and medieval insights into the notion but then reframes the concept from the perspective of a philosophy of action, which epitomises the way we approach the concept. The common good is essentially linked to how our social interactions generate and thrive. A common good perspective on society is therefore neither totalitarian, nor conservative as some people assume. On the contrary, it is creative, and capable of novelty and inclusiveness; it embraces not only justice and law, but also the good life (*eudzen*) as the purpose of politics. For the sake of clarity, the chapter structures its theoretical insights around a vocabulary of the common good, which is then used by all other authors in this book. We distinguish between the many *specific common goods* existing in a society and coin the term *nexus of common goods* to explain the dynamic system of specific common goods in a given society. Specific common goods and the nexus of common goods are then differentiated from the *universal common good*, which is in itself a goal and a task, and whose content is our common humanity.

Chapter 2 proposes a matrix of common good dynamics that tries to capture the quality of the nexus achieved at the local level. Jorge Medina and Mathias Nebel build on the previous chapters and set the foundation for the metric that will be presented in Chapter 3. Most importantly, we decided to focus on a *metric of the nexus*. There are other measures or proxies for specific common goods such as health, education, or associative life; what is lacking is a metric of *how specific common goods link to one another—along a common good dynamic—to form a nexus of common goods*. We are thus interested in processes: the conditions required for a positive dynamic to exist within such a nexus. The descriptive and normative dimensions of this dynamic make up our matrix of the nexus. Grounded in empirical studies and the theoretical background, it identifies five key normative drivers of common good dynamics at the local level: *collective agency freedom* as the engine of common good dynamics; *justice, governance,* and *stability* as the social functions needed to drive the complex equilibrium of specific common goods toward an ever-more-human coexistence; and *humanity*, as the systemic outcome of common good dynamics.

Chapter 3 uses the theoretical developments provided in previous chapters to present the metric and indicators proposed to capture the quality of the common good dynamic at the municipal level. The chapter reflects on the challenges, and lessons, of translating the theoretical framework into a practical instrument of measurement in order to guide policy efforts. Oscar Garza-Vázquez and Viviana Ramirez begin by discussing the importance of developing a metric to operationalise a common good approach and how such a metric may contribute to development practice. They argue that this metric adds insight to development practice by making visible and tangible two factors that have been neglected in traditional measures of development: (a) the socio-structural aspect of development and (b) the relational dynamic processes underlying social change. They then present and discuss each of the dimensions and indicators used to bring to life the matrix of the common good dynamic presented in Chapter 2. They conclude by pointing out future challenges if the metric is used to guide policy and decision-making at the local level.

Part II—Discussing the Normative Elements of Common Good Dynamics. This part sees experts discuss and reflect on each of the five dimensions identified as the normative pillars of our matrix of common good dynamics from their own discipline and area of expertise. They do this in a critical way, showing the strengths as well as the difficulties of such an approach to development. This second part critically situates our approach within this field, and will therefore be of interest to scholars and students familiar with current development debates.

Chapter 4 situates "agency freedom" as a normative element of development that recognises people as active subjects capable of forming, revising, and pursuing their own goals. Drawing on insights from the first part of the book and on Sen's conceptual framework, Oscar Garza-Vázquez looks at people as agents capable of shaping their own development. He argues, however, that approaching development from a common good perspective brings to light some caveats related to the literature on Sen's notion of agency: that (a) it tends to focus on the freedom of people to achieve goals unconnected to wellbeing; (b) it is primarily discussed at the individual level; and (c) its conceptualisation reflects this bias by over-emphasising the ability of individuals to make choices. Accordingly, Oscar proposes the notion of *collective agency freedom*, which can be broadly understood as the opportunity of a given population to self-organise and to act as a collectivity to achieve common goals. Finally, he proposes three possible dimensions to appraise the proposed conceptualisation of collective agency freedom: (a) *the freedom to imagine things together;* (b) *the freedom to organise around a common goal,* (c) *the freedom to achieve things in unison.*

In Chapter 5, Clemens Sedmak addresses the difficult task of appraising the quality of our shared humanity. He first reminds us that the concept of humanity is at the same time pervasive and evasive in development literature. What does it mean to be human? Evident as it may be, the concept is nonetheless difficult to define in a positive manner. He assumes therefore a negative approach, through the experience of beings who are infrahuman or definitively not human. Four pairs of qualities can express our humanity, he says: (a) uniqueness and complexity; (b) vulnerability and socialness; (c) agency and the power to transform; and (d) equality and existential closeness. He translates these four points into the idea that living a life according to one's human dignity means living a life that allows for a range of experiences: the expression of uniqueness, the pursuit of complexity, the protection and cultivation of proper vulnerability, the fostering of relationships, the experience of agency, the cultivation of the potential to transform the world into a better place, and the experience of equality. He closes by proposing four practices as possible indicators for the 'humanity' dimension: (a) practices of reconciled pluralism; (b) practices of deep inclusion; (c) habits of integral ecology; and (d) patterns of permeability.

To grasp the polycentric governance of a nexus of common goods, in Chapter 6 Tom de Herdt and Denis Augustin Samnick focus on *reflexive governance* and the rule-setting processes that control commoning practice. There is a multiplicity here that is unavoidable, with each common good having its own dynamic and its own rule setting. However, based on the results of Ultimatum Game experiments, they suggest that recognition and 'cognitive empathy' appear as key aspects of a governance of commons within a set of institutions. Yet, following Sandel's *civic approach* and the notion of *commoning*, they shift from the question of which entitlements governance should secure to the question of *how* citizens secure entitlements and *who* participates in these processes. They identify voice and accountability mechanisms as key features of an indicator of nexus governance.

In Chapter 7, Rodolfo de la Torre explores a possible metric for the justice component of the common good matrix. He structures his reflection by elucidating three main points. First, justice cannot be reduced to a separate dimension of its own, isolated from the agency, humanity, governance, and stability components of the common good. It does, however, make sense to distinguish this dimension for analytical and measurement purposes. Second, it is convenient to conceptualise the justice component of the common good as dealing with fair production of social goods and the possibility of shared benefits. Procedural and distributional aspects of justice are and must be involved. Finally, freedoms and rights offer ways to approach the procedural aspects of justice. Equality of results and equality of opportunity are key to its distributional aspects. Both elements play a role in the concept of justice and should therefore be the feature on which indicators for the justice dimension are based.

In Chapter 8, Flavio Comim starts with a conceptual discussion about 'stability', exploring its links with similar constructs such as sustainability and resilience. He then examines the normative character of stability, echoing Anand and Sen's critique of the use of the sustainability concept, to assess the positive and negative aspects of stability. Next, he investigates measurement possibilities for this dimension, such as the issue of intertemporal rates of discount and the use of RBM (Results Based Management) to link common objectives to a single framework. Finally, he puts forward a tentative classification of stability indicators according to their usefulness in empirical common good nexus models.

Part III—Case Studies and Applications. This last part of the book presents different case studies showing how the matrix of common good dynamics may contribute to an understanding and assessment of different social realities. This part of the book will be of interest to development practitioners and social scientists wondering how to work from a common good perspective in practice.

Chapter 9, written by Helen Alford, introduces this last section of the book, bridging the previous theoretical part, and showing how it may translate to practical cases. Helen Alford shows first the relevance of a shift toward a common good approach to development, and how this can change our understanding of social realities. She then introduces her own work with business leaders, and considers the change in mindset brought about by the discussion of and agreement on a "blueprint for better business".

In Chapter 10, Patrick Riordan offers a case study of Bangsamoro, a new autonomous region in the southern Philippines, from the perspective of common good dynamics. The common quest for autonomy must accommodate a complex reality in Bangsamoro, with an indigenous population composed of Muslims and animists and new, usually Christian, settlers. This case study analyses the construction of a complex equilibrium of common goods from the perspective of the five key drivers identified in the matrix. It shows that the quest for autonomy can be seen as the creation of a nexus of common goods, with the matrix highlighting the processes' strategic political and social priorities.

In Chapter 11, Valente Tallabs and Mathias Nebel apply the matrix of common good dynamics to a study of the municipality of Atlixco, in Mexico's Puebla state, as mentioned above. They identify and aggregate quantitative data to build each of the five key drivers of the matrix and then proceed to assess the dynamics of the Atlixco nexus in terms of a simple 'traffic light' for each of the dimensions of the matrix. The case study highlights the possibility of framing the socio-political analysis of a municipality in terms of a common good dynamic, pointing out some deep structural deficiencies as well as the municipality's strengths.

Chapter 12 summarises Simona Berretta's research on micro-social relations, discussing how they can contribute to our understanding of the nexus of common goods. Do transformative micro-social relations also generate a dynamic of the common good, and if so, how? What can we learn about the inner dynamics of the common good at the macro level by looking at the micro-dynamics of personalised relations of care involving vulnerable people? The author studies a faith-based rehab community in Italy and a programme for prisoners in the US. She shows that the common good matrix may help us understand the building blocks of sociality.

References

Andreoni, A., Chang, H.-J., and Estevez, I. 2021. The Missing Dimensions of the Human Capabilities Approach: Collective and Productive, *The European Journal of Development Research* 33 (2021), 179–205. https://doi.org/10.1057/s41287-020-00356-y

Badiou, A. and Engelmann, P. 2019. *For a Politics of the Common Good*, Cambridge: Polity Press.

Beretta, S. and Nebel, M. 2020. "Introduction", in Beretta, S. and Nebel, M. (eds), A Special Issue on Common Good, *Rivista Internazionale di Scienze Sociali 4*, 367–381.

Blum, C. 2015. *Die Bestimmung des Gemeinwohls*, Berlin and Boston: De Gruyter. https://doi.org/10.1515/9783110379020

Bollier, D. 2003. *Silent Theft. The Private Plunder of Our Common Wealth*, London: Routledge. https://doi.org/10.4324/9780203821855

Bollier, D. and Helfrich, S. (eds) 2015. *Patterns of Commoning*, Jena: The Common Strategies Group.

Bruni L. 2008. *Reciprocity, Altruism and the Civil Society*, London: Routledge. https://doi.org/10.4324/9780203926666

Collard, F. (ed.) 2010. *Pouvoir d'un seul et bien commun (VIe XVIe siècle)*, Numéro thématique de la *Revue Française d'Histoire des Idées Politiques 32/2*, https://doi.org/10.3917/rfhip.032.0227

Crowther, D., Shahla, S., and Moyeen, A. (eds) 2018. *The Goals of Sustainable Development: Responsibility and Governance*, Singapore: Springer Verlag. https://doi.org/10.1007/978-981-10-5047-3

Deneulin, S. and Townsend, N. 2007. Public Goods, Global Public Goods and the Common Good, *International Journal of Social Economics 34/1–2 (2007)*, 19–36. https://doi.org/10.1108/03068290710723345

Felber, C. 2015. *Change Everything: Creating an Economy for the Common Good*, London: Zed Books.

Fessard, G. 2015 (1944). *Autorité et bien commun*, Paris: Ad Solem.

Finn, D. K. (ed.) 2017, *Empirical Foundations of the Common Good*, Oxford: Oxford University Press.

Giguère, S. (ed.) 2004. *New Forms of Governance for Economic Development*, Paris: OCDE.

Gorringe, T. 2014. *The Common Good and the Global Emergency*, Cambridge: Cambridge University Press.

Helfrich, S. 2012. "Common Goods Don't Simply Exist–They Are Created", in Bollier D. and Helfrich, S. (eds), *The Wealth of the Commons: A World Beyond Market and State*, Levellers Press: Amherst. http://wealthofthecommons.org/essay/common-goods-don't-simply-exist-—they-are-created

Helfrich, S. 2012. "The Logic of the Commons and the Market: A Shorthand Comparison of Their Core Beliefs", in Bollier, D. and Helfrich, S. (eds), *The Wealth of the Commons: A World Beyond Market and State*, Levellers Press: Amherst. http://wealthofthecommons.org/essay/logic-commons-market-shorthand-comparsion-their-core-beliefs

Hibst, P. 1991. *Utilitas Publica–Gemeiner Nutz–Gemeinwohl*, Frankfurt: Peter Lang.

Hollenbach, D. 2002. *The Common Good*, Cambridge: Cambridge University Press. https://doi.org/10.1017/cbo9780511606380

Ibrahim, S. 2006. From individual to collective capabilities, *Journal of Human Development 7/3*, 397–416. https://doi.org/10.1080/14649880600815982

Ibrahim, S. 2017. How to Build Collective Capabilities: The 3C-Model for Grassroots-Led Development, *Journal of Human Development 18/2*, 197–222. https://doi.org/10.1080/19452829.2016.1270918

Joonmo, S. 2000, *Social Capital: Key Concepts*, Cambridge: Polity Press.

Kahn, A. 2013. *L'homme, le libéralisme et le bien commun*, Paris: Stock.

Kaul, I., Grunberg, I., and Stern, M. A. 1999. *Global Public Goods*, Oxford: Oxford University Press.

Kempshall, M. 1999. *The Common Good in Late Medieval Thought*, Oxford: Clarendon Press.

Klancer, C. H. 2015. *Embracing Our Complexity. Thomas Aquinas and Zhu Xi on Power and the Common Good*, Albany: State University of New York Press.

Lecuppre-Desjardin, E. and Van Bruaene, A. L. (eds) 2010. *The Discourse and Practice of the Common Good in the European City*, Turnhout: Brepols. https://doi.org/10.1484/m.seuh-eb.6.09070802050003050209090801

McCann, D. and Miller, P. 2005. *In Search of the Common Good*, New York: Clark International.

Maritain, J. 1949. *La personne et le bien commun*, Paris: Desclée de Brouwer.

Münckler, H. and Bluhm, H. (eds) 2001–2004. *Gemeinwohl und Gemeinsinn*, Vols 1–4, Berlin: Akademie Verlag. https://doi.org/10.1515/9783050079639

Narayan, D. 1995. *The Contribution of People's Participation: Evidence from 121 Rural Water Supply Projects*, Environmentally Sustainable Development Occasional Paper, Washington, DC: World Bank Press.

Nebel, M. 2018. "Searching for the Common Good", in Nebel, M. and Collaud, T. (eds), *Searching for the Common Good. Philosophical, Theological and Economic Approaches*, Baden-Baden: Nomos Verlag, 111–148.https://doi.org/10.5771/9783845283012-110

Ostrom, E. 1990. *Governing the Commons*, Cambridge, Cambridge University Press.

Putnam, R. 2000. *Bowling Alone: The Collapse and Revival of American Community*, New York: Simon and Schuster. https://doi.org/10.1145/358916.361990

Reich, R. B. 2019. *The Common Good*, New York: Penguin Random House.

Riordan, P. 2008. *A Grammar of the Common Good*, London: Bloomsbury Academic.

Riordan, P. 1996. *A Politics of the Common Good*, Dublin: Institute of Public Administration Press.

Riordan, P. 2014. *Global Ethics and Global Common Goods*, London: Bloomsbury Academic. https://doi.org/10.5040/9781474240062

Sandel, M. 2020. *The Tyranny of Merit. What´s Become of the Common Good?* New York: Farrar, Straus and Giroux.

Sen, A. 1999. *Development as Freedom*, New York: Alfred A. Knopf, Inc.

Sluga, H. 2014. *Politics and the Search for the Common Good*, Cambridge: Cambridge University Press. https://doi.org/10.1017/CBO9781107705920

Solomon, D. and Lo P. C. (eds). 2016. *The Common Good: Chinese and American Perspectives*, Dordrecht: Springer.

Taylor, C. 1990. "Irreducibly social goods", in Brennan, G. and Walsh, C. (eds), *Rationality, Individualism and Public Policy*. Canberra: Centre for Research on Federal Financial Relations, Australian National University, 45–63.

Tirole, J. 2016. *Economie du bien commun*, Paris: PUF. https://doi.org/10.3917/rimhe.023.0101

Ulrike, D. 2013. The Rise of the "Global Social" Origins and Transformations of Social Rights under UN Human Rights Law, *International Journal of Social Quality 3/2*, 41–59. https://doi.org/10.3167/IJSQ.2013.030203

UNESCO 2015. *Rethinking Education. Towards a Global Common Good?* Paris: Unesco Press. https://www.unesco.org/new/fileadmin/MULTIMEDIA/FIELD/Cairo/images/RethinkingEducation.pdf

Walzer, M. 1983. *Spheres of Justice: A Defense of Pluralism and Equality*, New York: Basic Books.

Vischner, B. K. 2010. *Conscience and the Common Good: Reclaiming the Space between Person and State*, Cambridge: Cambridge University Press. https://doi.org/10.1017/S0748081400001260

Whitman, J. 2009. *Advances in Global Governance*, New York: Palgrave Macmillan.

World Bank 2004, The Public Sector Governance Reform Cycle: available diagnostic tools, *PREM Notes 88*, 1–8.

PART I
A COMMON GOOD APPROACH TO DEVELOPMENT

Introduction to Part I

Aim of Part I

This first part aims at clarifying the common good vocabulary we will use throughout the book and outlines a common good approach to development (Chapter 1). We will claim that a society can be approached and described as a *dynamic system of common goods*. This system may be arranged in different ways according to the specific history, culture, and circumstances of its people.

It is this concern for common goods that seperates our discussion from mainstream development theories, which focus on individuals' entitlements, achievements or capabilities and analyse societies as an aggregation of the same. A common good perspective of development focuses on two elements. First, what are the *basic common goods* a people *must share* to live together as human beings? Secondly, what are the *normative key drivers of the dynamic equilibrium of common goods*? Therefore, our approach does not focus so much on actual achievements of development goals. Rather, we place an emphasis on the *quality of development process*, which makes these goals sustainable.

Hence this first part proposes a theoretical framework that identifies basic common goods and shows how they may combine to create a dynamic system conducive to development. Chapter 1 deals with the concept and vocabulary of the common good. Chapter 2 presents a matrix of common good dynamics. Chapter 3 then elaborates on the two previous chapters and proposes a metric of common good dynamics for municipalities.

To Whom Is it of Interest?

This first part will be of interest to social philosophers, political scientists, and development thinkers. In the following pages, they will find the

 https://doi.org/10.11647/OBP.0290.01

theoretical backbone of a common good approach to development, one, however, which is carefully grounded in action. Chapter 2, from theory to practice, reinstates operationality to the concept of the common good and offers an original way to deal with development questions. Academics will find it useful for understanding the precise conditions under which development goals may, when combined, trigger a development process. They may also find it convenient as a means to address development questions that can't be solved at the level of individual rationality (game theories) and require an understanding of group or community behaviours (social choice theory). In turn, students will find this part useful for its explanation of the concept of the common good in a modern and straightforward way. In contrast to the widespread impression that this concept is outdated, largely rhetorical, and even dangerous for democracy, they will see that it more accurately describes the *real* functioning of societies, sustains rather than undermines democracy, and is downright practical. Finally, practitioners will find in this first part a roadmap for triggering common good dynamics in development projects.

Why Does it Matter?

Most development theories are based on a conception of society as an aggregation of individual characteristics. This can be an aggregation of will, of interests, of rights, of entitlements, functionings or capabilities, and so on. But in all cases, the rationality of the social system is said to be grounded in the rationality of individuals. Accordingly, most development data are based on information that refers to individuals. Data on income, years of studies, adequate housing, access to health systems, and social mobility, among others, are all based on some kind of aggregation of individual characteristics. Our approach is different. It starts with the commons we create and share together; it seeks to understand a society through the commons that effectively bind individuals together as a functioning whole. Our approach refers therefore to a different informational space and addresses some of the blind spots of more conventional approaches to development, namely the structural and systemic dimensions of development.

1. The Theoretical Framework

Common Goods and Systems of Common Goods

Mathias Nebel

Reasserting the Notion of the Common Good in the Twenty-First Century

My goal in the following pages is to propose a possible understanding of a common good approach to society for the twenty-first century. This is certainly not a full-fledged theory of the common good, but rather the scaffolding for one. We apply many insights of antiquity and medieval times to the notion but then reframe the concept from the perspective of a philosophy of action.

This reframing is actually our main shift in our approach to the concept. The common good has to do first and foremost with action, and not so much with metaphysics. In essence, the concept is linked to how our social interactions are generated and thrive. A common good perspective on society is therefore neither totalitarian nor conservative. On the contrary, it is creative, capable of novelty and inclusiveness; it embraces not only justice and law, but also the purpose of the good life in politics.

I will proceed in two stages. The first section lays the foundation for a reinterpretation of the various traditions of the common good. The second considers the common good's dynamics, structure and essential elements.

    https://doi.org/10.11647/OBP.0290.02

1. The Common Good Belongs to the Sphere of Action

I. A Notion Implicit in All Public Action

My main intuition here is that the common good is not only or even primarily a metaphysical concept—it is an ethical principle, a principle that governs action and remains implicit in all action undertaken in the public realm. The common good is not first and foremost a question about the good itself, or about the hierarchy of human goods, or even about whether the whole or the part has priority. It is not primarily a comprehensive view of the good—some complex, splendid architecture in which each part fits into the whole, as in a cathedral. My conviction is that the common good is based on the logic of common action and cooperation (Sherover 1984, pp. 475–498; Sluga 2014, pp. 155–167).

The essential input from scholastic authors on the common good was metaphysical, focusing on the quality of the 'good' in the term 'common good' (Kempshall 1999, pp. 76–101). But in the order of action planning, it is the 'common' generated by our interaction that is the crucial question (Arendt 1985, p. 50; Bollier and Helfrich 2015). How a community rallies around a goal, and congregates in the pursuit of that goal, is the key element of the common good. This is Thucydide's conviction: the most precious and primary common good is our common freedom (Palmer 1992, pp. 15–37), a thought that Aristotle would further develop in his assertion that the *entelechia* of a city is our common humanity, emerging in the form of shared practice or virtue (Aristotle 1094). A widely shared assumption among philosophers of antiquity is the idea that the common good has to do with the expression of the human *logos* and, more specifically, with the glory of the deeds of freedom (Palmer 1992, pp. 111–114).

That is why the question of the common good is far more prosaic and specific than is usually thought, for it is implicit in all interaction. As soon as common action is *wanted*, it carries a hope, the hope of a common good; and as soon as it is *conceived of*, the interaction reveals the structure of a dynamic, the dynamic of the common good (Nebel 2006, pp. 7–32). The issue of the common good can be extended to all public or political action, for it is its principle and its driving force.

Of course, this assertion can be seen to conflict with warfare, which grows out of the constant wish throughout history to appropriate other people's goods by force, subterfuge, or lies.[1] It seems almost laughable to claim that the basis of public action is the common good, for experience seems to show that private interests and power plays are the *true* basis for politics. This is an old argument. Machiavelli framed it in a treaty; Ludwig von Rochau coined a name for it: *realpolitik* (Machiavelli 1995, Von Rochau 1972). Yet it is not the only reasonable, prudent option, nor does it reflect the whole experience of politics.[2] It is a narrow understanding of the common good, sized down to fit the interest of a prince, a social class, or a nation. It sees the common good of others as inherently antagonistic to its own and therefore discounts the possibility of a universal common good. Sound politics are then reduced to the protection of our own interests and renounce the search for something bigger—namely the universal common good.

Maintaining that the common good is based on action means asserting that it can be grasped and understood only *through action*. If the common good is a normative concept, it is dynamically so, as a duty to act and a horizon for action. For in action, as Blondel once remarked (Bondel 1893, p. 326), we may recognise something similar to the Kantian categorical imperative (Nebel 2013 pp. 151–163). There is a need to act. There is a duty to act. And since antiquity this duty in the public sphere has been named and framed through a concept: the common good.

II. The Need to Act in Common: The Community Created by Common Action

Whenever you have a mass of people, it tends to organise itself through a combination of shared history, common needs, or primary forms of human solidarity. Certain goods emerge spontaneously as being useful to all, and appreciated by all. Producing such goods, organising their distribution, and obtaining them—this is what will organise the masses; this is what forms the basis of society; this is what makes a fluid group of

---

1   This tension is indeed forcefully presented by Thucydides in the Melian dialogue. See Thucydides 2010, paragraphs 64–74.

2   Public action has never been only conflict, subterfuge, and lies. On the contrary, a lasting community on a human scale—one that is able to welcome, recognise, and protect fragile human dignity—cannot be constructed on conflict, subterfuge, and lies.

individuals gradually create a common way of life, shared institutions, and a culture whose social goods mold collective habits.[3]

This is not a vision of the mind, but an empirical fact, as state-building practices have shown (Weller and Wolff 2005, pp. 1–23, 230–236). It can be seen whenever war, poverty, or misfortune force a whole population to flee. What forms the rationality of everyday life—family, work, friends—is now lost. War and/or poverty have destroyed the former structure of society, and its culture, standards, and institutions no longer operate. In fleeing imminent danger, refugees are a mass of individuals united by misfortune, the hope of a refuge, and the desperate urge to survive. And it is these common features that generate the embryos of society: on the road you have to keep eating, find water and shelter for the night, plan the next day's journey. The importance of these primary goods is the basis for *collaboration*. People work together to meet these basic needs; they will collaborate and organise, for it is easier to obtain them together.[4] It is this shared action, this organisation in common to achieve a social good, that the notion of the common good describes.

The common good is linked to these interactions that forming the basis of community life. The notion can't be properly grasped without referring to these common needs, these shared goals, and the primordial forms of care and solidarity that tend to unite us. Wherever there is a community, the question of the common good arises at this *practical level*. What are our common needs? What goods do we need? What shared benefits may we get by seeking a specific goal together? The question of the common good is specific, not speculative.

The question arises again and again in every community or society because of the innumerable interactions that take place and then must be continued, recast, or abandoned. None of these interactions is spontaneous or natural. Societies are not mushrooms. They do not grow in the dark through some kind of systemic autopoiesis (Luhmann 1997), repeating some given, 'near biological' pattern of organisation. On the

---

3   I rely for this paragraph more on the French tradition than on the Anglo-Saxon one, more on Lévi-Strauss and Bourdieu than on McIntyre.

4   Similarly, archaeologists distinguish the advent of the first great Mesopotamian civilisations by their major agricultural works, their creation of law, their ability to make military plans, and their development of trade. All these features point to the importance of agricultural production, law, trade and security as specific social goods. Cf. Ostrom (1990).

contrary, they are free, fragile, and conscious. And so the question of the common good keeps returning to the forefront, requiring public decisions to be made and political governance to be exercised. Political governance, most specifically, is at the core of the common good question. It is the place where the question should arise, be debated, and settled, as we will see later on.

III. The Elements of Common Action

What are the elements of common action? With Mounier (1949, pp. 15–29) and Ricœur (1990, pp. 86–89, 109–110, 167–179), we may distinguish the following: the *subject* of the action, the *object* of the action, and the *social stage* on which the action unfolds. The subject is, of course, the 'who' that performs the action, in this case a collective subject, a group of people sharing a common intentionality and linked together in pursuing the object of the action. The object describes the purpose of an action, the goal it aims for and gradually achieves, while the social stage is the cultural environment 'enabling' the action, the environment where it 'makes sense' (Ricœur 1986, pp. 168–178, 184–197).

The action keeps the subject and the object together on the social stage (Ricœur 1986, p. 193). What is more, action is the specific form through which the subject appears to others on the stage: the unique way they exist for others in this environment. What appears on the social stage is not the subject 'in itself,' but an 'acting subject.'[5] Similarly, the goal of an action is 'present' in our social environment mainly through the very action achieving it.[6] It is present on the social stage as an 'object being realized.' Finally, there is the 'world of the action' (Ricœur 1986, pp. 168–172), i.e., the cultural context giving coherence and meaning to

---

5   This recalls the Arendtian conception of action as the vehicle of thought and the place where interiority is revealed to others—action that constructs the common artefact, action that constitutes the common world. See Arendt (1958, pp. 73–78, 175–188).

6   *Ibid.*, 175–176. The object's independence and otherness in contrast to the subject only apply to material objects. Most objects involved in a common action are immaterial: education, peace, stability. Although they have a material dimension, these goods are essentially common meanings that are inseparable from the subject that carries them out and the community to which they have meaning. It is in the action that creates it that the object will then be chiefly present on the stage—as an object being created.

the action. The action is thus never a mere machine that mechanically transforms an intention into some output, but the main way in which both the subject and the object exist on the social stage (Ricœur 1990, pp. 86–92). There, the subject and object of the action are coextensive, united by the very process of their interaction.

On the social stage, the subject is never *neutral*. It is in-formed by the cultural context. The subject of a common action is always a situated subject, regulated by the social stage in its language and the shared rationality used by the group's members, and limited by the larger cultural assumptions structuring this community. As Walzer (1983, pp. 6–10) indicates, there are no pure, timeless, or a-cultural subjects. It is on a distinctive social stage that both the 'acting subject' and the 'achieved object' will acquire a specific meaning and be appreciated as having a value and representing a good (McIntyre 1984, pp. 206–210).

What strikes us then is the great fragility of action, and indeed its impermanence (Arendt 1958, pp. 188–191). Action must constantly renew itself in order to endure. It must constantly retrieve its intention and reinvent itself to face unforeseen events, while making sure to maintain the commitment of the people involved. The miracle of action is that it exists! Its main hazard is that it may lose its dynamism and be dispersed. Action is maintained as a tension—an *in-tention* to achieve something—that is constantly threatened by the fragility of human commitment and the tribulations of time.

This perspective affects how we perceive subjects as different and external to the action. They are not. They are part and parcel of the action, and the main question is then how the subjects may remain themselves while changing through the action. How can the subject's intention and commitment be maintained for the long term? We are talking here about the subject's unity and stability while acting.[7] Similarly, this perspective changes the way in which the object of the action is perceived. The question becomes how to maintain the unity of the object pursued by the action while the action is taking place.

I will therefore study the notion of the common good by transposing the question from the metaphysical level to the ethical level of public action—in the hope that this will re-emphasise the practical dimension of the common good.

---

7   This, of course, is the essence of Ricœur's thinking about his notion of narrative identity (1990, p. 167).

2. The Vocabulary of the Common Good

The notion of the common good is an old one and its lexical field is broad.[8] Through the ages, and through various translations, many terms have been added to this field, either to establish distinctions that were deemed necessary or to express specific aspects. The use of the same term by different writers should, therefore, always be treated with caution. More often than is realised, a notion may be understood in quite different ways by different authors. It is this polysemous vocabulary that I will address in this section, specifying each of the terms that will subsequently be used in the next chapter.

I. The Social Good and the Shared Value of the Common Benefit

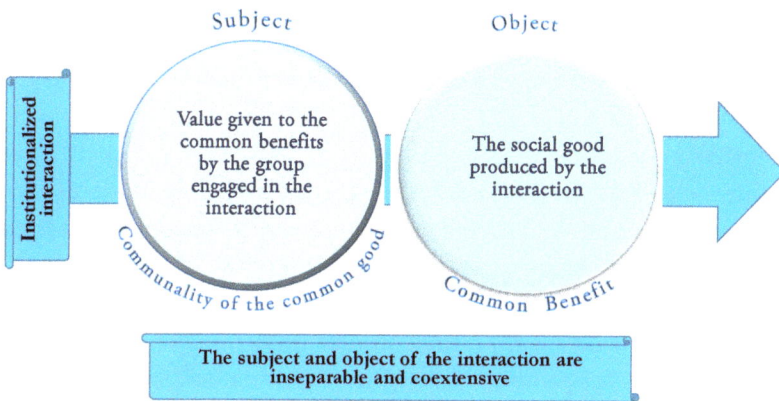

Figure 1. A common good as shared interaction producing a given social good.

As we see in Figure 1, every interaction has a certain object and gradually achieves it, unless the interaction is in vain. I will call this goal of interaction the '*social good.*' We must remark first that the social good is not just the result of an interaction, but is coextensive to the interaction itself. Secondly, the term 'good' is not used here in an explicitly moral sense; it simply means that the community of people engaged in its

---

8   We now have a series of modern studies of this history: Hibst (1991), Jehne and Lundgreen (2013), and Kempshall (1999).

achievement usually assigns a positive value to this good. Finally, the social good adds something to the community: a collective capability whose distribution we will call the '*common benefit*' shared among the community (see Chapter 4).

The relationship between involvement in the interaction and sharing in the common benefit is one of the main features of a common good approach to society. Yet the criterion for distributing the benefit is not necessarily equality, nor even complex equality. For instance, someone may be illiterate but still involved in the collective effort to build a village school and pay a teacher so that the children can receive an education. What is shared is the valuation of the common benefit itself. Thus, a community that gathers around a social good is more than just a community of interests. It is not necessarily united by a correlation of individual interests, as social contract theories would have us believe. That is why the people who create the social good are not always, or necessarily, the same people who benefit from it. The community that benefits may be larger, or smaller, than the one doing the creating.

This is not to say that the common benefit need not be distributed fairly. When the hoped-for benefit is unduly diverted or appropriated by a person or group, people's anger and indignation are reactions based on their sense of fairness. However, what is claimed is not necessarily one's own share, but respect for the meaning of the social good in itself, i.e., for the value assigned to it by the community. It is the common nature of the benefit, linked to the shared recognition of its value, that is negated by undue appropriation. Returning to the previous example, if a local shopkeeper offers to rent an 'unoccupied' classroom as a storehouse for his goods, then takes advantage of this agreement to gradually turn the whole school into a storehouse, forcing the teacher to teach out on the playground, the community of people who have built the school and who pay the teacher will have been swindled out of their social good. They will feel robbed of the common benefit created by their interaction. They will claim that this is 'unfair'! Not primarily because they are denied their 'due,' but rather because there is a conflict with the meaning and shared valuation of the social good. They will say, 'we didn't build a school for it to be used as a storehouse!' It is the meaning of the social good—the school and the children's education— that is diverted and then negated by the shopkeeper's action. Being well aware of this, the shopkeeper will take good care to avoid claiming that the building is not a school, but will argue speciously that 'he has a fully legal contract,' that 'the children can be taught in the open air anyway during the dry season,' or even that the 'whole thing is an emergency measure' and that he will 'soon stop using the premises.' He will never say, 'the building isn't a school any longer—it's my storehouse.'

So the social good can't be detached from a *'communality of meaning.'*[9] What this neologism means is that the social good does not only exist materially—in the school's walls, tables, and chairs—but also as a meaning shared by the people involved in the interaction. The community that gathers around the meaning of this social good makes it exist as such, and imposes this meaning on anyone who seeks to misuse it. Therefore, an inherent feature of every social good is a community to whom it has a particular, normative meaning.[10] This is what the village blames the shopkeeper for, and it is this meaning that the shopkeeper knows he has violated. And thus the villagers will reject the shopkeeper's specious arguments 'in the name of the common good.'

II. The Good of Order and the Common Rationality it Creates

When a number of people want to get something done, they organise themselves. The good we want to achieve together, the object of the interaction, will have to be planned. If we want to build a school, we need a site, plans, and funding; we have to persuade the families and children, find a teacher, and agree on the school timetable. To cooperate is to organise. There is no way to efficiently provide a certain social good without some immanent 'good of order' that organises our cooperation.[11]

---

9   Riordan (2014, pp. 83–96) proposes to understand the 'common sense' associated to a common good as one of its crucial elements.

10 To understand the distribution, we must therefore first understand the value given to the social good by the population. It is this normative meaning—shared by the population—that will be the base of the more or less equal distribution of the benefits, which is basically the central point made by Walzer against Rawls in 1983 (pp. 3–31). Now, regarding normative meaning, we do not refer to the discussion in analytic philosophy about the normativity of language, but to Ricoeur's understanding of meaning as convening to action (1986, pp. 184–197). See also Sherover (1989, pp. 27–52).

11 This section builds on the old, scholastic notion of 'good of order', but revisits the notion through the sociology of organisation and social structures developed by Friedberg (1993) and Giddens (1984).

This organisation of interactions generally involves determining the shared goal, each person's status and role,[12] and responsibilities in our interaction, and the rules that will govern our cooperation. The fact is that the 'communality of meaning' comes along with a specific organisation of the community, which, once internalised by people, is the shared rationality that makes sense of each individual action as part of the interaction. One person is responsible for finding and purchasing the future site; another draws up the plans for the school; masons supervise the volunteers who are to build it; and someone else will look for a teacher. Any interaction that seeks to produce a social good efficiently will necessarily produce a specific organisation, a shared rationality (ever more so when an interaction increases in complexity). This 'good of order' describes the organisation of a community so that it can achieve and then maintain a given social good.

The 'good of order' derives its *raison d'être* or its value from the object of the interaction, the social good it seeks to achieve. It therefore has an instrumental value, and its quality can be judged by: (a) how it coheres to the meaning of the social good; and (b) whether the good is achieved efficiently.

Finally, with the 'subject,' we describe a community that shares the same understanding of the social good. Each and every member of this group will have internalised the 'good of order' as the 'common rationality' of their interaction. Indeed, any given organisation—in order to be efficient—defines a set of standard statuses and rules that are *rational* in this specific context. Two chess players, for example, are bound by the rules of the game and the moves that can be made by the various pieces. They analyse their opponent's strategy and devise their own on the basis of these rules. The rationality of each move on the chessboard depends thus on the logic of the game. The more the players have internalised this rationality, the more they will manage to play well and predict their opponent's next moves. It is the logic of the game that explains the opponents' strategies. However, just like the good of order,

---

12   The *status* describes here the powers, duties and responsibilities attributed to a position in the interaction while the *role* refers to the way a specific person enacts this status. The first is unpersonal and refers to a position in the interaction, for example the striker in a soccer team. The second refers to a person, acting as *the* striker of this team. Following the example, not every striker has the genius of a Diego Maradona or Lionel Messi.

the value of this rationality is instrumental, and is assessed through its consistency with the social good and its ability to achieve it efficiently.

III. A Specific Common Good

Together, the 'social good' (communality of meaning), the 'common benefit' (shared valuation), and the 'good of order' (common rationality) form what I will call a 'specific common good' (the communality of a common good). The common good created by an interaction is made up of these three features: the 'social good', the 'common benefit,' and the 'good of order.' Correspondingly, the common good will be upheld by the subject as 'shared valuation,' a 'common rationality,' and a 'communality of the common good,' as Figure 2 shows:

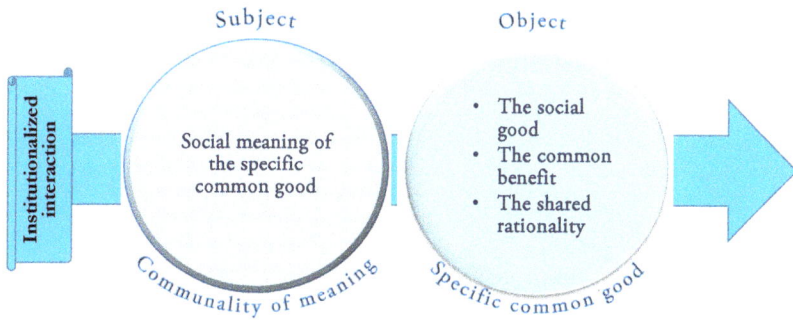

Figure 2. The core elements forming a specific common good.

It is now time to bring up what I have thus far ignored for the sake of clarity. The subject and the object are held together in the dynamic of the action. The common good cannot be reduced to its objective dimension (the production of a social good), but nor can it be reduced to its purely subjective dimension (a communality of meaning and habitus).

The common good creates a social dynamic whereby a community exists and asserts itself. It is a specific community, as specific as the social good that gathers its members together. Let's reconsider the previous example. Among the people of the village, there is a group who wanted to create the school and organised themselves to do so. This group is very specific. It enables the social good to exist and be maintained. Yet its boundaries are hard to draw. At the centre there will be a number of people who are clearly part of it: the parents, the teacher, the children. Further away, there will be those who helped to build the school and whose work for the project is now over, and even further away, the broad circle of those who support and approve of the project without benefiting from it or being actively involved in it. So the boundaries of this community are essentially the boundaries of the *communality of meaning*, that is, the meaning given by the community to the social good. In contrast, those who are not part of this community are those who, for some reason, can't or don't commit to this conception, and whose practical actions may conflict with the coherence of the common meaning—as the shopkeeper's did.

Seeing the common good as a dynamic process also means that none of its embodiment can be considered as settled once and for all. To be preserved, the common good must be constantly reinvented over time. It is an interaction, and as we have seen, no interaction is spontaneous: it is the result of a certain communality of meaning and continuity of will. Thus, a specific common good will have to be readopted and reinvented by each generation if it is not to be lost and disappear—which also effectively means that the community gathered around a common good is not itself natural, but the result of a real sharing of a communality of meaning, which can easily be lost. Over time, the village in our story may become a nearby city's smart suburb, whose children attend other schools. The village school, and what it once meant to the original population, would then gradually lose its meaning. Common goods may change or transform over time, which is only natural. But they will do so only if the meaning given to the social good radically changes.

IV. The Nexus of Common Goods

It goes without saying that every society is built on an often very broad set of common goods that only partially overlap. There is a whole series of relationships between these specific common goods; most of the relationships are complementary, superimposed, and mutually reinforcing. This is not to say that all these specific common goods are uniform or equally important. There are tensions, or sometimes even contradictions, between them that make it hard for them to coexist within the same society. I will use the expression '*nexus of the common good'*[13] to denote the real relationships between these various specific common goods in a given society.

Such a nexus does not appear of its own accord, as a kind of spontaneous self-organisation of society (Luhmann 1984, p. 15). On the one hand, it is the result of a shared history—centuries of common experience that have gradually brought various social goods together and created a hierarchy among them—and on the other, it is a result of the constant efforts of the present generation to reframe and to some extent reinvent them. This is a shared responsibility, a political task *par excellence*. A nexus of the common good results from exercising this political responsibility. That is why nexuses vary considerably in quality, with substantial gradations. Their quality partly depends on this shared history and partly on the present generation's commitment and wisdom.

This commitment usually takes the form of a specific interaction seen as a particularly important social good: contributing governance to the 'nexus of the common good.' It is political power itself that is here valued and constructed as a common good, and one which is of crucial importance to any society. Indeed, the task given to governing bodies is to pursue an ever richer, deeper, and more inclusive nexus of the common good. Their task is to work out a real conjunction between the many specific common goods existing in the society, so that their nexus may be more humane.

Such a need for 'collective wisdom' appears frequently after terrifying or traumatic man-made events such as war, revolution, or genocide. The 1789 Declaration of the Rights of Man, for example, emerged from a rejection of the structural injustice upon which the *ancien régime* was built. It was an explicit effort to learn to live by another standard of humanity. It encompassed and enshrined hard-earned wisdom about what it means to live together as human beings.

Now, we should not think of the 1789 Declaration of the Rights of Man as the *ultimate* expression of such wisdom. A document like this should be constantly reassessed and renewed by each generation, as

---

13 Rather than the terms 'network' or 'web'—now overused because of the Internet and globalisation—I prefer the Latin term 'nexus', which means 'relationship, intertwining or linkage of causes, connection, bond,' a term linked in Roman law to that of responsibility or duty. It is derived from the verb *nectere*, which means 'to tie together, to unite, to link.'

indeed has been the case for the Declaration after the Second World War in 1948, and again in 1976. And this is precisely where wisdom comes back into politics. In my framing, the sole and purest goal of governance can't be justice. The most pressing political question does not concern distribution, but rather coherence of meaning embedded in the nexus— the coherence of what it means to be human. We can summarise the point easily enough: does the nexus—in all its complexity—provide a social system where we can *all* live together as human beings? Or does this nexus only permit such standard of living for a restricted part of the population? Or even worse, does the nexus thrive by considering some of its population useless and redundant—the poor, for example? Even if this question obviously implies a notion of justice, it does start with an insight into what it is to be human. It starts with a wisdom whose legitimacy is only as strong as the collective experience that validated this 'truth' in the public square—war, genocide, systemic humiliation, etc. It starts, in other words, with an understanding of humanity as a shared, common humanity (see Chapter 5).

What is ultimately at stake in political governance is the humanity of our coexistence; no political entity can escape this question forever. As Aristotle said long ago, a polity, to be recognised as such, has to serve the common good.

Now, this wisdom is not formal. It can't be enshrined in a declaration or a constitution. Real wisdom is linked to real behaviours. Along with authors as different as Bourdieu (1980), Giddens (1979),[14] or McIntyre (2007, p. 187), we may recognise that social structures entail social practice, or, as Bourdieu (1980, pp. 88–89) would have it, collective habitus.[15] These normative social practices are standard expectations of behaviours directly linked to the overall rationality of a nexus. These are the social practices needed to access and play along with the

---

14   Social structures are for Giddens dual in the sense of 'both the medium and the outcome of the practices which constitute social systems.' See also Giddens (1981, p. 27).

15   Bourdieu develops a rich understanding of the duality existing between social structures and practice. To quote his impossible French, habits are for him a « *système de dispositions durables et transposables, structures structurées disposées à fonctionner comme structures structurantes, c'est-à-dire en tant que principe générateurs et organisateurs de pratiques et de représentations qui peuvent être objectivement adaptées à leur but sans supposer la visée consciente de fins et la maîtrise expresse des opérations nécessaires pour les atteindre* ».

institutional framework of a society. They are objective and not a matter of individual choice. You can obviously disagree and reject them at a personal level; but not to follow them entails a cost not limited to public shame or underground culture. Being excluded from the basic social goods controlled by the nexus may be tantamount to death. Social goods like work, citizenship, or education are so important that the person will usually abide by the practices directing the work ethic, citizenship, or intellectual integrity in higher education. Not all collective habitus in a nexus are relevant to humanity. However, at a systemic level, there is no nexus that does not present a number of normative practices regarding the way we should behave with fellow humans in the nexus (outside of close family and friends).

Indeed, a frequent error is to believe that the nexus of the common good is a given, a natural state of affairs. On the contrary, the nexus is fragile and changes constantly. Its humanity is the result of a collective wisdom painstakingly acquired through history about what is *more* and what is *less human* in the organisation of society. It is always a patchy and imperfect wisdom. More often than not, a nexus will also carry some form of collective blindness to and tolerance of structural injustices. That is why its political governance needs more than legislators to determine what is just. It needs public actors who can assign a value to the coherence between many specific common goods, and understand their limitations and the tensions that both separate and unite them—in other words, public actors who endeavour to judge the moral quality of the nexus. This essential exercise of judging largely depends on the horizon of the universal common good.

Finally, it is important to underline that the nexus of the common good is what lends societal coherence to the communality of meaning. The communality of meaning is what binds together a society or a culture, providing it with some degree of identity and unity—a fragile and dynamic identity, to be sure, but an identity nonetheless. Perhaps even more importantly, the stability and resilience of the nexus derives from its quality (see Chapter 10). The richer in connections and more coherent the nexus is, the better it will be able to withstand shocks and reinvent itself. The poorer and more superficial it is, the more blindly it will focus on its supposed identity, and the more likely it is to be destroyed when confronted with a different social ethos (see Figure 3).

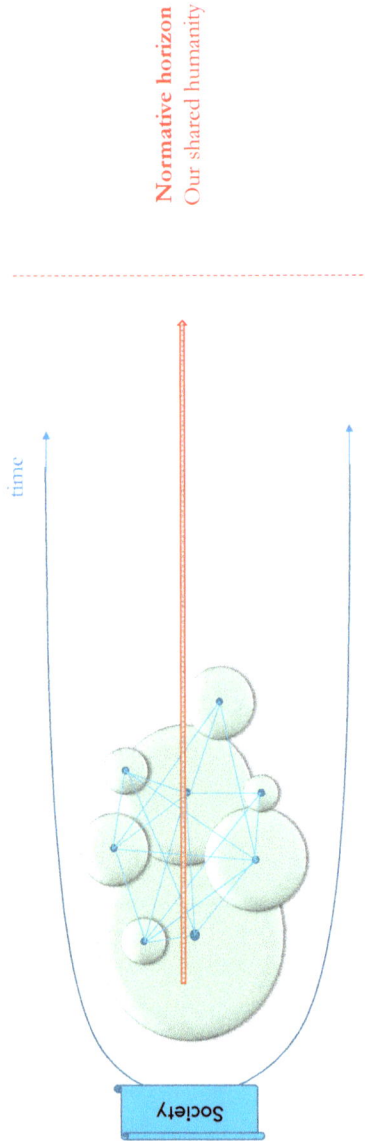

Figure 3. A nexus of common goods.

Using this vocabulary, the next sections of this paper will attempt to explain the specific features of this nexus and its dynamic tendency towards the universal common good.

3. Aspiring to the Universal Common Good

Arendt (1983, pp. 175–176) famously stated that human freedom crafts itself into being through action. Freedom of thought—this utterly internal freedom—only becomes historical to the extent that it is expressed in history, shaping its human environment through its radical novelty (Ibid., p. 177). Freedom that rejects action is freedom that rejects itself. To Arendt, freedom only achieves the radical novelty it carries insofar as it engages in action. Action is thus the place where human freedom is actualised and comes to fruition.

That is why, to Arendt, political society results from action (Ibid., p. 199). It is born of shared action, free interaction between human beings. A polity is not the result of a sum—an aggregation however complex of individual acts—but rather the interplay of these actions as they produce an environment, a sphere in which each action is not only recognised as achieving a utility, but as the revelation of a thought and a freedom (*novum*). What she calls politics is thus the only space in which human action is recognised as human through its involvement in social interaction. Politics is the space in which an agent's action is recognised; the space in which the various agents' inputs construct a common world whose primary feature is humanity: accepting the fragility of humanity, making it possible, deepening and continuing it. In Arendt, this recognition does not initially assume the form of law, which remains formal. This recognition is only real where the interaction directs and develops it (Ibid., pp. 230–235). Thus the humanity of society is not so much to be sought in the various meta-discourses that supposedly legitimise it,[16] but in the very specific way that interactions operate and favour a real, present recognition of our common humanity.

The paradox of society is that, born of possible cooperation between freedoms, born of deliberate interactions, it is constantly *undone* by the

---

16 *Ibid.*, 294 ff. Although Arendt does not use the term 'meta-discourse', she lays the groundwork for analyses such as Foucault's of the relationship between truth and power.

conflicts that undermine it. Conflict and violence are so co-extensive with society that they may be considered as the primary evidence of political philosophy. This is the whole Augustinian current of thinking, which sees in the power of political authority the necessary remedy for the violence that original sin induces in social relationships (Gilson 1954, pp. 47–80). It is on this skepticism that British philosophers, at the dawn of the modern age, based their view of the need for state power. As Hobbes saw it, the natural and insurmountable conflict of individual passions required a Leviathan state that would mandate prioritising the general interest over private interest. This, supposedly, is the price to be paid for a minimal threshold of peace, justice, and wellbeing to exist. And yet the vitality of society and its continuous historical reinvention bears witness to something different. It displays a deeper truth than conflict and violence as the basis of a polity. It bears witness to a hope: *the hope of a possible and real conjunction between personal good and the good of the community*. In other words, the hope is that my good and your good are not forever in opposition, but will eventually enrich each other. It is the hope that my good and your good are augmented by each other, as our freedoms do not so much clash, but empower us both. This hope that our freedoms are not ultimately diminished by that of the other, but augmented and enriched, drives the search for the common good (Nebel 2007, pp. 217–232).

By no means does this hope deny the conflict inherent to social relationships. What it refuses is to posit violence and war as the basis of the polity (Rousseau). An anthropology of the common good states that even though conflict exists, it is no more 'natural' or 'original,' or even more dominant, than the hope for the common good. Rather, such an anthropology states that the incompatibility that frequently arises between the private good and the good of the community will be one of the specific features of the search for the common good. To desire and aim for the common good will thus be marked by *conflict*; and this is why the *hope* of the common good must be backed by a *will* for the common good in order for it to be achieved. This is also why any historical achievement of the common good is but a transient stage of an ever-ongoing process.

Always specific, the *will* for the common good will also be limited by time and space. And hence, because it excludes from the achieved good the people who are beyond the boundaries of the interaction, any achievement of the common good will always be partial and will always entail a potential conflict linked to its very limitations. The common good is thus a *dialectical* concept[17] whose horizon is *the hope of a future humanity in which each person's good would finally coincide with the good of all* (Arendt 1983, pp. 305–308). This is why the hope of the common good is ultimately based on a transcendent hope: that of an *eschaton* of human history in which the good of the whole of humanity would coincide with that of each of its members. The hope of the common good thus depends on a belief—secular or religious—in the eschatological advent of a reconciled humanity.[18] The political conviction at the root of a common good approach may thus be framed as believing that the unity and solidarity of humanity can be real and possible.

Reclaiming Aristotle's statement in the *Politics* (1979a), we may thus recognise the common good as the overarching goal of any polity. As a hope and a common endeavour, our *shared humanity* is the core of this goal. In other words, wanting to live together is not just a matter of wanting to survive, but of wanting to live well (Ricœur 2001, pp. 55–67). The good life—*the hope of a future humanity in which each person's good would finally coincide with the good of all*—is the normative horizon founding the aspiration to the common good. Without this hope, the conflicts that mark the pursuit of the common good could no longer be seen as part of an ascending dialectic, but as evidence that pursuit of the common good is irrational. The obstacles to the broadening of the common good could then finally exhaust the hope that drives political action, for, once the dialectical pendulum is broken, the hope that dwells in the will to live together would seem little more than a naïve illusion or a theological relic from which we should be 'brave' enough to break free. 'Political realism' then withdraws to a minimum: limiting conflicts, preserving public order and peace, maintaining the rule of law. Yet the hope of the common good is constantly reborn, over and over again, and no historical failure seems able to destroy it. Though defeated,

---

17   Fessard (1944, pp. 96–98) is the one that identified the dynamic of the universal common good as a dialectical dynamic. Unfortunately, his Hegelian reinterpretation of the common good has widely been overlooked by the Anglophone literature on the topic.

18   The introduction of this historical tension into the notion of the common good is specifically Christian. See Hibst (1991, pp. 144–157).

conquered, and bruised, it is always reborn. The hope that drives social action is invincible—and this is the paradox! The common good is not just any hope; it is the eschatological horizon onto which all political action is projected. Therefore, a reinterpretation of the common good must, in my view, account for this paradox driving the political dynamic.

4. The Common Good as the Dialectic of Politics

I have identified the elements of the common good, and mentioned the hope that dwells in its pursuit; but I have not yet specified the nature of this hope. This final section will attempt to do so.

I. The Conjunction of the Individual Good and the Good of the Community

Historically, the concept of the common good refers to the relationship between *the good of an individual* and *the wider community to which he belongs*. So it is not a particular good that is fixed and determined once and for all, but the *dynamic coincidence of two or more goods* that fluctuate over time.[19]

It is an interaction that combines these two goods, for every interaction is simply the organised collaboration between different freedoms, united around the achievement of a given social good. It is people who collaborate in the intention and creation of a social good; it is people who share a common benefit and a certain practical rationality derived from the good of order and therefore find their own good in this collaboration. The social good that they produce together is thus both the good of all and the good of each one of them.

Here we must bear in mind how profoundly our thinking is marked by materiality (Bergson 1896). We spontaneously think about sharing a good as if what is obtained by one person is lost to another, as if we were sharing a biscuit. But the material element of social goods is only part of what is shared, and not the most important part. Of course, interaction does usually produce a material, tangible good, but its creation, and even more so its existence, depend, as we have seen, on a communality

---

19   Writing from a different perspective, Hans Sluga arrives at the same conclusion. See Sluga (2014, pp. 231–250).

of meaning: a common intention and will, a common benefit and communal rationality. All of these elements are intangible, but still real. And the sharing of intangible goods is marked by the fact that what is given to one person does not diminish what others receive. On the contrary, a broader distribution base, to a greater number of people, tends to increase the total good. The classic example is a mother's love for her children. The birth of another child does not reduce her love for the previous ones.

The expression 'basic social goods' is used in development literature to designate the minimum goods that should be available to all, such as food, housing, safety, and all the fundamental human rights.[20] Each of these basic social goods is what is referred to in this book as a specific common good. What my analysis adds to this literature is first an understanding of all the intangible elements that structure the actual existence of these goods, and second, a focus on the social process through which they exist. The lasting creation of a 'basic social good' depends on the existence of a communality of meaning. None of these goods—decent work, formal education, adequate housing or the right to food—can be created on a lasting basis unless they are collectively seen as common goods that we want to create together.

Indeed, it is clear that even in the case of food the problem is not merely a question of production. Of course, in a famine there may be a real shortage of food; but, as Sen (1981) has pointed out, famines are not so much due to the lack of food as to the lack of will to distribute it to everyone. It is rare to have food crises under democratic regimes. What prevents the implementation of the right to food is the widely held belief that food is *only a private good*. Ultimately, it is because there is no communality of meaning surrounding the notion that no one in a community should die of hunger that some people still do. Food production and distribution is organised on such a fundamental consensus.[21] This is even truer of education, in which the distribution of the intangible element—knowledge—does not involve any reduction of

---

20 A basic needs approach to development was proposed by the Bariloche Foundation in 1976 and adopted later on by CEPAL, the UN, and many other organizations. Cf. Amilcar et al. (1976).

21 Recognition of the right to food as a human right is a first step towards the recognition of food as a common good. But in terms of the nexus of the common good, this human right clashes with other requirements, especially legal and economic ones.

shares. Teachers do not lose or forget what they impart to their pupils; on the contrary, their knowledge is enriched by being passed on to others.

It is because common goods are essentially intangibles that the good of the individual and the good of the community can overlap in interaction. One person's good increases another's, even though it is shared.

II. Wanting the Common Good

This conjunction of individual and community, even though it is an intrinsic part of our social condition, does not occur without us. We have to *want* the common good. We have to work out how it *must* occur, and *can* occur, in the present circumstances. We have to work at wanting to live together, in order to maintain, reinvent, and increase the common goods around which we gather together as a community. Although already found in their most basic forms within the family, clan, or ethnic group,[22] actions for the common good are bound to become increasingly conscious and free, i.e., political (Sherover 1991, pp. 55–60, 89–90). It is this process—this common good dynamic—that must determine which goods unite us, which ones we want to create together, and how to design, share, or distribute them.

But since the conjunction achieved at the level of the nexus must be wanted and given the fact that different equilibriums between specific common goods may be possible, this conjunction should be the central object of political deliberations. We must discern exactly what the conjunction consists of, what it requires in the present circumstances, determine the goods that bring us together as a community and what we want to promote in common (for example, appreciation of common goods, formation of hierarchies, coherence, resolution of conflicts of meaning/production/distribution). The forms that political agencies of deliberation and decision-making take are many, but in contrast to the now prevailing idea, democratic institutions are not the unique or even

---

This goes to show the complexity of this nexus, and why political governance is so essential.

22   The conjunction of the common good is based on a certain logical and empirical correspondence between the existence of the individual and the existence of a community. The existence of an individual is always a social existence. This is self-evident in practice; it can be challenged in theory, but not in terms of action.

prevalent source of this *order of the common good*. More often than not, democratic governance does not invent, but inherits, the order of the common good and is only called on to frame and develop it.

Take customary law, which in all civilisations is one of the oldest forms of the common good nexus. The reciprocity of customary rights and duties organises a community. Custom coordinates individual goods with the good of the community, preexisting positive law formulated by a legislature. The order of the common good is thus primarily a practical matter, and its political dimension only emerges gradually. The same applies to the executive, which in the vast majority of cases is in much more of a position to manage the nexus of the common good than to create it. The daily bread of the executive is to assess and settle the many possible *conflicts* emerging between individual good and that of the community. The origin and then the slow flourishing of the nexus of the common good thus escapes the republican ideal: that of an omnipotent, sovereign assembly that decrees the form of the state, decides the general interest, and promulgates a constitutional order. The fact is that these decisions are not usually the result of an assembly, but of far longer processes, age-old experiences that form the wisdom of a people and ground its political culture. That is why a common good approach, while acknowledging the important role of democratic governance, does not reduce governance to a parliament or state bureaucracy.

III. The Dialectical Dynamic of the Common Good

Yet the quality of different nexuses of the common good may vary significantly. Some will be more human, others less human. Some will be organising the social relationship binding us together in a more human way, while others will be degrading it with violence, injustice, and oppression. Not every nexus of the common good is equally valuable. Some are basic, reduced to the simplest common goods; others are more complex and, like modern society, include many specific common goods. Yet it is not complexity that determines the quality of the nexus of the common good, but the *quality of the relationships it creates between people*. The freer these relationships, the more they will enhance our dignity. The truer they are, the more universal they will be. The more they are focused on values of the spirit, the more they will be able to accommodate our desires for the good life.

Deepening and broadening the common good often involves a paradoxical stage in which the quality of the previous nexus is lost in order to broaden its base. The lost quality will then have to be reconstructed among this broader base of people. But this is a perilous undertaking that may also fail. Without the lost quality, the new equilibrium may be worse than the previous one. Aiming for the universal common good takes thus the form of a dialectic. Its progress is not linear. Any deepening or enlargement will come at a cost and will trigger resistance. Creative destruction can't be totally avoided. It is part and parcel of the progress of the common good dialectic.[23]

The construction of Europe is a good example of a common good dialectic. It began with a wish to integrate Europe's various countries, i.e., to broaden and deepen the nexus of the European common good. The attempt to do so is remarkable, brave, and makes sense. It responds to the call of the common good. But will it succeed? The question remains entirely open. European integration was first seen in terms of economic integration, the free movement of goods, services, and people through a single market. But such integration is only one aspect of the common good—the creation of economic wellbeing—and it is quite clearly insufficient. Everyone is aware of this: the quality of the nexus of the European common good cannot be reduced to just an economic good. The difficulty is that the pursuit of integration, the deepening of a nexus of the European common good, entails transferring sovereignty to the European Commission and the European Parliament. It is the very nation states involved in integration that are putting the brakes on and rejecting it. The success or failure of Europe will depend on nation states' ability to forge a European nexus of the common good of a quality similar to those they have created at the national level. If in the long term the quality is not the same—or, worse, if European integration reduces the quality of national nexuses of the common good—it is a fair bet that the democratic process in some countries will encourage a

---

23 Fessard's Hegelianism is but the translation of a much older, theological intuition of the patristic era: the movement of the common good is essentially that of God's Spirit or Charity leading humanity toward its ultimate reconciliation with the Father in Christ. Thus, its movement necessarily involves a kenotic moment (2015, pp. 96–98). The cross is not a part of a reconciliation that can be avoided altogether. This idea of a kenotic moment is not exclusively religious, however. Marx used it to frame the dialectic struggle between capital and labour.

nationalist withdrawal, wreck the European project, and contribute to the slow decline of the various national nexuses.

Indeed, every determination of the nexus of the common good is historical, and hence incomplete and unfinished. First of all, the nexus is dynamic, and the equilibrium achieved in recent decades cannot claim to respond to all future challenges. Populations change, economies are transformed, technologies develop; and the nexus of the common good must respond to these changes. Second, the size of the reference community varies and tends to keep increasing. The common good of a family is not that of a nation, or of the whole of humanity. The nexus of the national common good is too narrow to cope with the various processes of globalisation. The national nexus *must expand*, for many of the interactions of the nexus are nowadays beyond the governance of the nation state, like the regulation of transnational corporations, financial flows or CO_2 emissions. If the dynamic of achievement of the common good tends towards universality, it is not just with reference to a moral imperative, but also to a gradual movement towards global integration of communities (Hollenbach 2002, pp. 212–229).

If every historical determination of the common good is never more than partial and incomplete, destined to be revised and transformed, and if every achievement of the common good is characterised by conflict, we can only say that what drives the wish for the common good is *hope—hope that this conjunction* of the individual good and the good of the community *is possible* and *will one day be real*. This hope is at the root of politics and political commitment. Should it ever be lost, the community will collapse. If the hope of the common good disappears, the institutions that make up a society can, depending on their resilience, do no more than delay the gradual dissolution of the nexus.

Conclusion: The Quality of Common Good Dynamics

Let me conclude this chapter with something that will be developed more thoroughly in the next one. One key open question is that of whether we can assess the quality of the nexus. Can we? The complexity of a social system is enormous. Can we really think that we may be able to assess the quality of the common good dynamic in terms of humanity? It seems a daunting prospect at best, and at worst a hubristic and morally dangerous endeavour.

However, even the most unsophisticated person knows for sure that some nexuses are undeniably more human than others. It is obvious to any refugee: poverty, oppression, injustice, persecution, and war make for a less human nexus than peace, wellbeing, justice, rule of law, and political freedom. Why can't academics understand what any refugee knows for sure? This book tries to formulate an answer. Can we find some normative anchors that may work to assess dynamics of the common good?

We noted in the previous section that nexuses are dynamic equilibria moving toward an ever deeper and broader humanity: a humanity we described as -embedded in the collective practices or habitus that govern the relationship to others in this nexus. This means basically two things. First, that the main normative anchor will be humanity, not a formal humanity acknowledged through rights and duties, but a real one, embodied in the practices that define our coexistence. Humanity describes the *overall direction*, or the *compass* indicating the North Pole of common good dynamics. Second, if a nexus is a dynamic equilibrium, we may also identify some permanent features required for the equilibrium to move toward more humanity. The next chapter will propose that we recognise four such *drivers* of common good dynamics, namely: agency freedom, governance, stability, and justice.

We could also think of a minimal threshold of basic common goods inherent to any nexus of the common good, including for example culture, solidarity, education, the rule of law, etc. While the *drivers* refer to the dynamic of the equilibrium as it moves toward humanity, an inexhaustive list of basic common goods might describe the core elements needed for any sort of nexus. Such a list would include common goods deemed so essential to human society that any nexus that does not include them would be considered below a minimal threshold of humanity. The next chapter will describe each of these elements and present a matrix of common good dynamics.

References

Arendt, H. 1958. *The Human Condition*, Chicago: Chicago University Press.

Aristotle. 2009. *Politics* (trans. Barker, E.), Oxford: Oxford University Press.

Bergson, H. 2012 (1896). *Matière et mémoire*, Paris: Presses Universitaires de France.

Blondel, M. 1893. *L'action*, Paris: Alcan.

Bollier, D. and Helfrich, S. 2015. *Patterns of Commoning*, Amherst: The Commons Strategies Group.

Bourdieu, P. 1980. *Le sens pratique*. Paris: Editions de Minuit.

Bourdieu, P. 1977. *Outline of a Theory of Practice*, Cambridge: Cambridge University Press.

Ostrom, E. 1990. *Governing the Commons*, Cambridge: Cambridge University Press.

Fessard, G. 2015 (1944). *Autorité et bien commun*, Paris: Ad Solem.

Friedberg, E. 1993. *Le pouvoir et la règle. Dynamique de l'action organisée*, Paris: Seuil.

Giddens, A. 1981. *A Contemporary Critique of Historical Materialism*, vol. 1, London: Macmillan.

Giddens, A. 1979. *Central Problems in Social Theory: Action, Structure and Contradiction in Social Analysis*, Berkeley: University of California Press.

Giddens, A. 1984. *The Constitution of Society. Outline of the Theory of Structuration*, Cambridge: Polity.

Gilson, E. 2005 (1954). *Les métamorphoses de la cité de Dieu*, Paris: Vrin.

Herrera, A. O. (ed.) 1976. *Catastrophe or New Society? A Latin American World Model*. Ottawa: IDRC, https://idl-bnc-idrc.dspacedirect.org/bitstream/handle/10625/213/IDL-213.pdf?sequence=1&isAllowed=y

Hibst, P. 1991. *Utilitas Publica—Gemeiner Nutz—Gemeinwohl*, Frankfurt: Peter Lang.

Hobbes, T. 2014 (1651). *Leviathan* (ed. Malcolm, N.), Oxford: Oxford University Press.

Hollenbach, D. 2002. *Christian Ethics and the Common Good*, Cambridge: Cambridge University Press. https://doi.org/10.1017/CBO9780511606380

Jehne, M. and Lundgreen, C. (eds) 2013. *Gemeinsinn und Gemeinwohl in der römischen Antike*, Stuttgart: Steiner. https://doi.org/10.1515/hzhz-2014-0343

Kempshall, M. 1999. *The Common Good in Late Medieval Political Thought*, Oxford: Clarendon Press.

Luhnmann, N. 1984. *Soziale Systeme: Grundriss einer allgemeinen Theorie*, Frankfurt: Suhrkamp.

Machiavelli, N. 2008 (1532), *The Prince* (trans. Bondanella, P.), Oxford: Oxford University Press.

McIntyre, A. 1984. *After Virtue*, South Bend: Notre Dame University Press.

MacIntyre, A. 2007. *After Virtue: A Study in Moral Theory*. South Bend: Notre Dame University Press.

Mounier, E. 1949. *Le personnalisme*, Paris: Presses Universitaires de France.

Nebel, M. 2006. "El bien común teológico: ensayo sistemático", *Revista Iberoamericana de Teología 1*, 7–32.

Nebel, M. 2007. "Espérance et bien commun", in Gavric, A. and Sienkiewicz, G. (eds), *Etat et bien commun*. Berne: Peter Lang, 217–232.

Nebel, M. 2013. "Action de Dieu et actions de l'homme", *Transversalité 128/4*, 151–163.

Palmer, M. 1992. *Love of Glory and the Common Good: Aspects of the Political Thought of Thucydides*, Lanham: Rowman & Littlefield Publishers.

Ricœur, P. 1986. *Du texte à l'action*, Paris: Seuil.

Ricœur, P. 1990. *Soi-même comme un autre*, Paris: Seuil.

Ricœur, P. 2001. "De la morale à l'éthique et aux éthiques", in Ricoeur, P., *Le juste II*, Paris: Esprit.

Riordan, P. 2015. *Global Ethics and Global Common Good*, London: Bloomsbury. https://doi.org/10.5040/9781474240062

Rousseau, J.-J 2009 (1762). *Discourse on Political Economy and The Social Contract*, (trans. Betts, C.), Oxford: Oxford University Press.

Sen, A. 1981. *Poverty and Famines*, Oxford: Oxford University Press.

Sherover, C. 1984. The Temporality of the Common Good: Futurity and Freedom, *Review of Metaphysics 37/3*, 475–497.

Sherover, C. 1989. *Time Freedom and the Common Good*, New York: New York University Press.

Sluga, H. 2014. *Searching for the Common Good*, Cambridge: Cambridge University Press.

Von Rochau, L. 1972 (1859). *Grundsätze der Realpolitik,* Frankfurt am Main: Ullstein.

Walzer, M. 1983. *Spheres of Justice*, Oxford: Blackwell.

Weller, M. and Wolff, S. (eds) 2005. *Autonomy, Self-Governance and Conflict Resolution: Innovative Approaches to Institutional Design in Divided Societies*, Routledge: New York. https://doi.org/10.5040/9781474240062

2. From Theory to Practice

A Matrix of Common Good Dynamics

Mathias Nebel and Jorge Medina Delgadillo

The goal of this chapter is to propose a matrix of common good dynamics allowing us to measure the quality of the nexus achieved at the local level.[1] It builds on the previous chapter, which laid out the foundation for this matrix of common good dynamics. Most importantly, we decided to focus on a *metric of the nexus*. Other measures or proxies for specific common goods such as health, education, or associative life already exist, while measures for the universal common good remain elusive. What is lacking is a metric of *how specific common goods build up—along a common good dynamic—into a nexus of common goods*. We are thus interested in processes: the conditions required for a positive dynamic to build up within a nexus of common goods. The descriptive and normative dimensions of this dynamic make up our matrix of the nexus. The metric itself, which will be presented in the next chapter, is intended as a diagnostic tool aimed at assessing local-level development priorities.

This chapter is divided into two parts. The first revises the empirical foundations on which the matrix can be built. The second introduces

---

1   This chapter benefitted from the discussion and exchanges during several sessions of the IPBC research committee and at the second IPBC research seminar in Barcelona (2018). We are grateful for the substantial remarks made by our colleagues in these occasions, many of which are now integrated to the text. We would particularly like to thank Clemens Sedmak, Patrick Riordan, Cécile Renouard, Simona Beretta, Helen Alford, Antonio Sánchez Díaz de Rivera, Valente Tallabs González, Oscar Garza Vázquez, José Luis Ávila Valdez, Ignacio Arbesu, and Viviana Ramírez Ramírez.

and describes the five *normative dimensions* constitutive of any common good dynamic. We suggest that the density and the quality of the relationships between the five normative elements can be taken to be a measure of the common good achieved at the local level. Only the integration and coherence of the different normative elements within the nexus can give us an accurate account of 'how human' our social interactions actually are.

Part I: The Empirical Foundations of the Matrix

In addition to the theoretical foundations of the matrix outlined in the previous chapter, we need to empirically ground our new matrix of common good dynamics. Fortunately, two large sets of studies are at hand. The first is related to the work done by Elinor Ostrom (1990) and the International Association for the Study of the Commons (IASC) which she helped found. Its extensive literature on present-day commons reviews cases from all over the world, reaching back into history as well.[2] With a social science approach to the topic, this literature is heavily dependent on case studies and has formalised a set of stable, empirical features of commons. Ostrom's results have been confirmed by the research done since by the IASC, as we discuss later in this chapter. However empirical research has also highlighted some limits of her approach, shifting the interest to the community engaging in commoning practices. Proper attention was not given by Ostrom to the role of the group or community in the definition of the common as a common. Her attention was instead concerned with the description of the collaboration mechanisms. The second set of empirical studies that we draw on in building the matrix are the so-called Community-Based or Community-Driven Development Programs (CBD and CDD). Over the last thirty years, such programmes have become a major instrument for further development projects, attracting billions of dollars of investments all over the world. This approach emphasises the importance of local participation and the value of being embedded in the community. To be sustainable and efficient, development programmes need to be locally

---

2   See the IASC 'digital library of the commons' https://dlc.dlib.indiana.edu/dlc/ (hundreds of articles) as well as the International Journal for the Commons (https://www.thecommonsjournal.org/).

constructed and managed. The knowledge of development experience gained from both sets of empirical studies was instrumental in the creation of our matrix of common good dynamics.

I. Commons and Commoning

What do we understand by commons? Elinor in her seminal work started the present use of the term. She describes a *common* as a resource system held by a group and managed in such a way that individual 'appropriation' by members does not undermine the system's sustainability. A common could be the high mountain meadows of a Swiss alpine village or irrigation systems in Spain, which are managed in common (Ostrom 1990, pp. 61–70). In both cases there is a *common pool resource*[3]—the mountain meadows, the irrigation system—whose economical rationality is outside the free market or the state management of public goods. A common pool resource implies the capacity of competitors to collaborate so that individual use of the meadow or the irrigation system does not lead to the collapse of the whole resource system. Commons, in Ostrom's understanding, involves the sustainable use of a resource by a group of commoners. We can define commons, as Ostrom does, as 'long-enduring, self-organized, and self-governed' common pool resources (Ostrom 1990, pp. 58).

It is important to understand that Ostrom builds on the classical distinction in economics between 'private' and 'public' goods. In 1954, Samuelson proposed to ground the difference between the two in their respective *competitiveness in consumption*. A private good can be 'parceled out among different individuals' for their private consumption, whereas a public good can be enjoyed in such a way 'that each individual's consumption of such good leads to no action from any other individual's consumption of that good.' (p. 387) For Samuelson, public goods are non-competitive in consumption, while private goods are comptetitive. Soon after, Buchanan (1965, pp. 1–14) added to the 'competitiveness in consumption' a second element of difference: *excludability*. Some goods are—by their very nature or by public decision—non excludable. On this basis, public goods differ from private ones in the sense that it is

---

3   Ostrom uses the terms 'commons' and 'common pool resources' almost as synonyms.

difficult or even illegitimate to impede anyone's access to a public good. In contrast, private goods—whether by nature, force, law or public decision—can be exclusively possessed or enjoyed. The production and distribution of private and public goods are also different. While the free market produces and distributes private goods, the state provides and regulates access to public goods. The distinction was a hugely successful one in economics, and a critical tool in delineating the boundaries and respective responsibilities of the market and the state in liberal, capitalist societies. It was so elegant: two sorts of goods, two actors, two institutions, two different logics or rationalities.

Ostrom's investigation of common pool resources highlighted the limits of Samuelson's model. First, there were not just private goods on the one hand and public goods on the other, but a third sort of good, namely common goods. It also meant that a third economic actor, namely civil society, composed of groups and communities, would be recognised as important. Finally, it supposed that beyond state management and market mechanisms another sort of economic organisation and activity that allowed for *collaboration in competitiveness* had to be recognised. This theoretical breakthrough won Ostrom the Nobel Prize (2009).

However, her main contribution, perhaps, is to have described in detail the practical mechanisms required to govern commons as commons. On the basis of her empirical studies, she highlighted eight principles specific to the governance of common pool resources:

- Define clear group boundaries;
- Match rules governing the use of common goods to local needs and conditions;
- Ensure that those affected by rules can participate in modifying the rules;
- Make sure the rule-making rights of community members are respected by outside authorities;
- Develop a system, carried out by community members, for monitoring members' behaviours;
- Use graduated sanctions for rule violators;
- Provide accessible, low-cost means for dispute resolution;

- Build responsibility for governing the common resource in nested tiers from the lowest level up to the entire interconnected system (Ostrom 1990, pp. 91–102).

The list is built on an analysis of the commons as composed of an *actor* (the group), an *output* (the common pool resource system) and *shared governance mechanisms* (the principles). Good governance requires: 1. a clear definition of *who belongs* to the group; 2. *rules* to structure collaboration so that they match the context and needs of the local community; 3–4. local community authority to revise the rules and to eventually change them; 5–7. a locally embedded monitoring system, capable of implementing sanctions (albeit progressive ones) and resolving conflicts; 8. a mechanism that counters the capture of the commons by elites and enforces the participation of the lower tiers of the group. These empirical principles for the governance of commons led to a flourish of research that verified the presence of these elements in the management of common pool resources (Van Laerhoven and Berge 2011, pp. 1–8). Practitioners quickly and widely adopted the list as a way to induce efficient local governance of commons.

However, it soon became clear that Ostrom's understanding of commons was too limited (Linebaugh 2009, De Angelis and Harvie 2013, pp. 280–294). One early critique was that most of the commons she studied were natural resources, which suppose a subtractability of use. But commons may also be intangible, like knowledge, language, or culture.[4] In these cases, consumption by one individual does not usually limit that of another, but rather will increase the existence of a body of knowledge, a language or a culture along the lines of 'the more we share, the more we have.' These early critiques, however, quickly shifted toward the social and political definitions of commons. Commons 'don't simply exist—they are created,' states Helfrich (2012, pp. 61–67). What a common is or is not ultimately depends not on the good itself, but on the way a society understands this good and acts accordingly. A common depends on what a community defines as being one. The study of the sociological and political process by which commons are defined as such, as well as governed, is absent from Ostrom's detailed analysis of common pool resources.

---

4   Hence the term 'new commons' to describe them. See Hess 2008, pp. 1–75.

Along with this second group of critiques, it became necessary to give more importance to: (a) the group or community united around the re-production of commons; (b) the interaction underpinning the commons; and (c) the definition of the legitimate use of commons. Let's develop these three points:

First, a commons always implies a community. There is no commons without a community holding it as such, without a community creating the commons and using it. This community is *more* than a mere 'productive unit'; it is a complex social system (Fournier 2013, pp. 433–453; De Angelis and Harvie 2003). How it values and defines the commons is crucial to understanding the collective organisational arrangement created to govern the commons. The public assessment and political definition of commons is thus a key factor in its very existence.

Second, a definition of commons should therefore put more emphasis on the activity itself and less on the output of this activity, the common pool resource system. Linebaugh puts it straightforwardly: 'the commons is an activity and, if anything, it expresses relationships in society that are inseparable from relations to nature. It might be better to keep the word as a verb, an activity, rather than as a noun, a substantive' (2009, p. 279). According to Helfrich (2012b, pp. 35–36), we may better understand commons and their institutional arrangements if we think of them first as *social practices* shaping a society. The *process* by which commons are produced and maintained is not only important for their sustainability. The process shapes the community, or as Euler states using the old scholastic distinction, it 'in-forms' the community (2018, pp. 10–16). We can't correctly understand commons without thinking of the *social practice* underpinning the reproduction of the common (Giddens 1986).

Thirdly, a definition of commons must consider the *diversity of use* of resources (De Angelis and Harvie 2013, Fournier 2013). The social meaning of a common is not fixed and may change according to the evolution of a society. Thus, the *legitimate use* of a certain good will have to be defined. In line with the two previous critiques, a resource's diversity of use underscores the cultural and political nature of commons. Their organisational arrangements may not be driven only by questions of subtractability of use and sustainability, as Ostrom proposed, but also by the meaning given to a common from which the *legitimate use* defined for it by a society derives.

Hence, commons may be better *defined* as an 'institutionalized, legal and infrastructural arrangement for a practice—commoning—in which we collaboratively organize and take responsibility for the use, maintenance and production of diverse resources' (Acksel et al. 2015, p. 135). Commons can be *understood* in terms of the social systems through which communities share resources and define the modalities of use, production and circulation of these resources (De Angelis and Harvie 2013, pp. 289–291). Our matrix of common good dynamics will adopt this definition.

II. Community-Based or Community-Driven Development Programmes

Ostrom's principles were swiftly picked up by the World Bank, which in the 1990s launched a new sort of development project called Community-Based or Community-Driven Development (CBDs and CDDs). The importance of gathering the right political will needed for projects to achieve results was acknowledged (Kaufmann et al. 1999). Equally important and related was the need to embed development practice in local communities whenever possible (World Bank 1996). These CBD and CDD programmes became a growing trend in the following years (Mansuri and Rao 2004, pp. 1–77; 2013).

Why were they so popular? CBDs and CDDs stem from a wide recognition of the failure of a top-down, provider approach to development.[5] To be sustainable and meaningful, a development programme needs to be embedded in the local community, studies have shown. This evidence called for a participatory approach to development. CBDs and CDDs answer that call to embed development practices. They emphasise community control over planning, decision-making, and investment resources. Central to these programmes are three key endeavours: 'Adopting processes that strengthen the capacity of a community to organize and sustain development; Supporting

---

5   As Narayan wrote in 1995 (pp. 1–2): 'From time immemorial, societies have organized themselves to take care of collective and individual needs. Why then have so many attempts at getting people to participate and take responsibility for community-based development failed in the last fifty years? One reason is that never before in the history of humankind has there been such a massive experiment to induce change through the infusion of external ideas, management, funds and technology, all controlled from places far distant from the site of development.'

community empowerment through user participation in decision-making; Reversing control and accountability from central authorities to community organizations' (Nayaran 1995, p. 5).

It was thought that this sort of radical turn would bring about an increase in the *efficiency, cost effectiveness and sustainability* of development projects, while at the same time increasing the *empowerment of the local population* and changing *behavioural patterns*. These three actions were intuitively tied together; you can't achieve results if you don't get the population to participate in the project, and the project doesn't last long if coherent patterns of behaviour do not sustain the result.[6]

After more than thirty years of practice we can assess the effectiveness of these claims. Results have been varied.[7] The World Bank assessment by Susan Wong (2013, pp. 1–16) of its own CDD programmes shows they have had a positive impact on provision of and access to services and goods. Compared to other modes of service delivery, CDDs achieve a higher cost-effectiveness and rate of return. On the negative side, they have had almost no impact on social capital and behavioural change. The emphasis on the participation mechanisms is also ambiguous, as they have frequently been captured by local elites or have offered new possibilities for rent seeking and corruption (Baldwin et al. 2016, pp. 1–40). A broader study by Mansuri and Rao (2013) on the impact of participatory programmes is much harsher. It analyses the results of over 500 studies covering decades of development projects. Empirical results do not sustain two main assumptions widely held as true: (1) that involving communities in the design and implementation of development will automatically increase adequate delivery of goods and services; and (2) that participatory practice results in higher levels of local cooperation and governance and builds social capital (Mansuri and Rao 2013, pp. 7–8). Mansuri and Rao successfully argue that civil society failures occur just as frequently as government and market failures do (2013, pp. 59–79). Does participation improve development

---

6   This is basically Ostrom's point: the building of a local irrigation system does not last long if the local population is not involved in its governance and does not behave according to rules that are consistent with the preservation of the irrigation system (1990, p. 157).

7   See Bennet and D'Onofrio (2015, pp. 1–14), Mansuri and Rao (2013), King (2013, pp. 1–55), Wong (2013, pp. 1–16), Baldwin et al. (2016, pp. 1–40), Mansuri and Rao (2004, pp. 17–47).

outcomes? Modestly, and then usually to the advantage of higher tiers of the population. Does participation strengthen civil society? Not really, at least not in the long term (Mansuri and Rao 2013, pp. 221–224, 275–277). Participation *alone* is not sufficient.

Two other key findings of the report are noteworthy. First, participatory interventions work better and last longer when they are embedded in the wider social system and supported by the state (Mansuri and Rao 2013, p. 288). This relationship to the context is of such importance that the authors recommend that projects always be flexible, i.e., that they have built-in mechanisms of learning and adaptability. Second, the authors note the difference between building bridges or roads and seeking social change. The former may be planned, and the results assessed in terms of production costs and access to services, but social change is complex to achieve, and must contemplate the long term. 'Repairing civil society and political failure requires a shift in the social equilibrium that derives from a change in the nature of social interactions and from modifying norms and local culture. *These much more difficult tasks require a fundamentally different approach to development*—one that is flexible, long-term, self-critical and strongly infused with the spirit of learning by doing.' (Mansuri and Rao 2013, pp. 12–13).

Mansuri and Rao's review does not condemn the participatory approach. It denounces some simplistic assumptions made by development planners and pinpoints the need to rethink some of the theoretical tenets of CBDs and CDDs. Among the theoretical elements in need of clarification, Bennet and d'Onofrio (2015, pp. 1–4) highlight two as crucial: (a) there is a fundamental ambiguity about the goal of participatory development. What are we really aiming for when we seek to implement participatory development? And, (b): how do we conceptualise social change interventions? Both remarks point us toward questions of *teleology*. What do we seek development for? Is justice the goal of development? Or is it rather the freedom to live the life we have reason to value? Or is it about a sustainable and harmonious relationship with the environment? Why should we seek participation in development—to impose external goals on a local population or to help people discover their own development priorities?

III. Empirical Elements of the Matrix of Common Good Dynamics

These two sets of empirical studies—the IASC research and the CBDs and CDDs projects—can help us identify the key drivers of common good dynamics.[8]

The first characteristic we notice is the constant insistence on the importance of 'local actors' and on the 'embeddedness' of local development practice for commons to exist. A common implies a community that values and engages in a shared practice. As we have seen, this is one of the latest shifts in commons studies, along with the importance given to the public 'meaning of commons' and the definition of 'legitimate use.' Both Ostrom's list of governance principles and the World Bank development practice show the importance of the participation mechanism. To be real, participation must be organised, supervised, and seek inclusion. Thus, *collective agency*, the capability to freely organise together, seems to be a key driver of common good dynamics. Without collective agency, there is simply no capacity to recognise the meaning and value of the nexus's common goods and neither is there the ability to change them. We therefore select collective agency freedom as the first of our normative dimensions for the nexus. Without collective agency freedom, no long-term systematic dynamic of common goods can be sustained.

Participation in itself is not enough. This much has been made empirically clear by CBD and CDD projects. We thus need to think carefully about local governance. How to discuss the local needs and account for the specificities of a particular context? What about the decision-making process, and how to set priorities? What rules should we set to coordinate our action in an efficient way? Who will supervise

---

8   However we ought to be cautious when reviewing some of these studies' empirical conclusions. Most of the practical cases analysed by IASC as well as the CBDs and CDDs are at the micro level. They focus on one commoning practice or a common pool resource but do not study the complex equilibrium of commoning practices and common goods in a given society, as we will be doing. The nexus is a *system* of common goods and will have therefore features that may not be identified at the local level. But as the governance of the nexus' equilibrium is itself a kind of commoning practice, we may assume that micro key drivers will still be found to be true at the macro level. However, it is an assumption that we will have to verify through the application of the metric.

compliance with the rules and how? How can we avoid elite capture and include the most vulnerable among us? With no governance, no commoning practice is stable, and no commons pool resource system can be sustained in the long run. The same must hold true for the nexus of common goods. The specific equilibrium of commons in a society requires the existence of some *governance capability* at the level of the nexus. If it failed to exist—if governance of the nexus failed to be efficient and well-organised—then the relationships between the society's common goods would not be driven to evolve and adapt to the circumstances. The connections would not hold together under the strain of time and events and would eventually fall apart, leaving behind the marginalised. One of the key empirical findings of CBDs and CDDs is that the relationship to the wider context, especially higher governance authorities, is crucial to the success of such projects. We will select *governance* as the second normative dimension of common good dynamics.

Justice also appears as an essential feature of commons. The group engaging in a commoning practice assumes some form of equality between its members, an equality of participation that entails at least some claim for a fair share of the common benefits. The empirical study of commons reveals the importance of justice; indeed, the claim of justice is at the root of the commons' perspective. Take, for example, the very idea of common pool resources. These are organised in such a way that each of the group members may have a fair share of resources, from the common pool system. It's a question of complex equality and distributive justice. Take also the insistence on gradual sanctions for rule breakers, inclusion mechanisms, and efficient, local conflict resolution systems. Each of these distinctive features of commons point toward the deep structuring role of justice in commoning practice. Without some sense of justice, the cooperation among members apparently can't sustain itself. We believe that justice must take the same role at the level of the nexus. Why should it be different? The more unjust a nexus is, the less collaborative it will become. *Justice* is the third normative dimension of common good dynamics.

Another key empirical driver emerging from studies of the commons is the importance of *sustainability*. In Ostrom's seminal work, the whole governance process focused on the preservation of the common pool

resource system. Governance must ensure a sustainable use of the
common, taking a long-term perspective and making sure that short-
term gains do not undermine the very existence of the resource (Ostrom
1994, pp. 1–33). Later studies showed that what was true for the output
was also perhaps even more relevant for the community engaged in the
commoning practice (Fournier 2013, pp. 433–453). A common concern of
a community, and the requirement that it be a stable one, lies at the root
of the insistence on the common's sustainable use. In fact, the stability
of commoning practices is key to achieve the stability of the community
itself. The reciprocity between both elements, community and commons,
is therefore of utmost importance. Indeed, it is another key lesson of
CBDs and CDDs: good results can't be achieved if the population doesn't
participate in the project, and the project doesn't last long if coherent
patterns of behaviour in the local community don't develop to sustain
the result. Stability, like justice, infuses the very structure of commons
because they are all about community, and communities work for the
long term, not the short. Social change must contemplate the long term.
Stability, this capability to think and work for the long term, is the next
normative dimension of common good dynamics.

Finally, we ended the previous section by mentioning some important
questions about the importance of a clear understanding of development
goals. The critical question arises again and again in development
practice: what are we seeking development for? Development is about
real people, not just ideas. Development must matter for them; it must
be meaningful to them. If it can't, then it easily becomes an imperative
imposed on a local population by far-away authorities. Worse still, it
may become something that the local population rejects as disrupting
their own nexus of common goods. To *make sense*, development goals
must align with the local context, and even if development practitioners
strive to change that context, they must acknowledge it. In addition, the
local community must be able to validate the social change proposed
in a development programme, not only by querying during a formal
approval process, but by weighing the programme to see how it fits into
the local nexus. Can we *make sense* of this project within our traditions,
history, and community life?

At the same time, development can't be restricted to the wishes and
wills of local communities. Systemic injustice, poverty, and exclusion

may be part of the current nexus. Adaptative preferences might then lead to rejection of positive development projects as incompatible with the current appalling socio-political system. The resilience of various mafias in Italy or drug cartels in Mexico proves how difficult it is to further change when criminal organisations co-opt political governance. Development is also about universal ends. Hence, the question of the development goals also involves anthropological and metaphysical strands, such as reason, passion, or freedom, to name a few. Several classical answers frame the present debate. We may argue that development is about justice as fairness, about capabilities and human flourishing, or about democracy and human rights. To leave it open—as academics like to do—is not a real alternative at the level of practice. The theoretical dilemma has to be resolved when deciding this or that specific option on the ground. Not doing so impedes action and becomes a seed of organisational incoherence in the long run. We argued in the previous chapter that the normative horizon of such dynamics is our own common humanity. The goal of development, then, is to further our humanity: a task and a goal we may only achieve together. *Humanity* will therefore make up the last of the normative dimension by which we assess common good dynamics.

Part II: Toward a Matrix of Common Good Dynamics

This second part of the chapter presents a matrix of common good dynamics (CGD) that merges the theoretical approach developed in the previous chapter with the empirical elements we just reviewed. We will argue here that the combination of the five normative dimensions selected for the matrix can provide a fair insight into the quality of CGD. The strength of each dimension, and the coherence and integration of their mutual relationships, will be considered as a proxy for CGD quality.

As we argued earlier, a society can be described as a complex and dynamic equilibrium of common goods. Specific common goods do not just float around in a society, but are organised in a specific way—a nexus of common goods—unique to each society (see Chapter 1, Figure 3). It is crucially important to remember that such an equilibrium is dynamic and must evolve constantly to adapt to internal and external pressures.

We seek to design a matrix that describes the normative drivers that will lead the nexus dynamic toward a deeper and richer humanity. If we now incorporate the conclusions of the earlier section into Figure 1, we get the following matrix of common good dynamics.

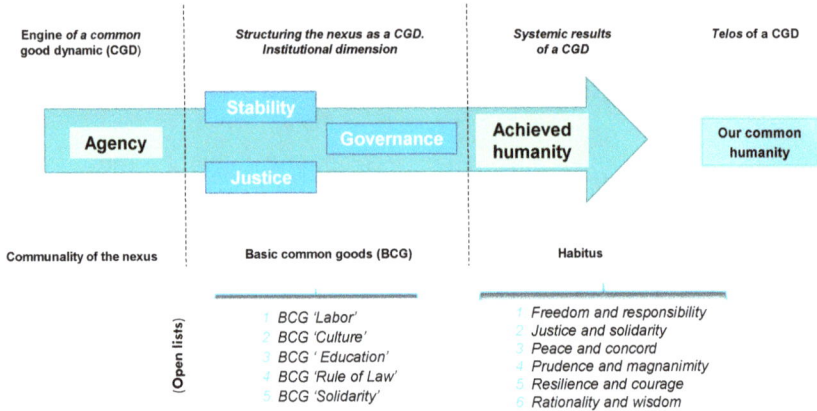

Figure 1. The normative drivers of common good dynamics.

We will describe in the following sections this representation of the matrix in detail, beginning with (1) what it is intended to capture; and (2) what is understood by each of the five normative drivers; then explaining (3) how we intend to measure humanity; and closing with (4) the relational nature of matrix.

I. What Does the Matrix Capture? A Few Preliminary Remarks

First, we intend through the matrix to capture the strength and quality of a *process*, not a mere outcome. The matrix illustrates how a nexus of common goods may change, either for the better or for the worse. This is why the information we are looking for is not the kind that provides us with a static picture of the nexus. We are looking for *key normative drivers* that may help us to identify and record the direction taken and the transformations made by the nexus, or to put it another way, to understand how the nexus moves, and if it moves in the right direction. With the expectation that it will inform the user about the strength and direction of a CGD, the matrix thus gives crucial information that few other indicators provide about the *quality* of a development process.

Second, ethical norms do not obligate in one and the same way, so the normativity of each dimension must be differentiated. Humanity stands for the *telos* or *normative horizon* of development. It functions as the key normative aspect of the nexus, its polar star, indicating the overall direction we should aim for as well as giving us a rough idea of the distance that is still left to travel to reach the port. But it also provides a yardstick with which to gauge the overall systemic outcome of a specific nexus. In contrast to humanity, the other drivers—governance, justice, and stability—are not teleological norms, but deontological ones. These are instrumental norms that inform, structure, and regulate the relationships between specific common goods contained in the nexus in order to lead it toward a more human society, a more complete humanity. Finally, 'agency' functions normatively as the engine of common good dynamics, the normative element required to infuse the nexus with freedom. It is the force that flows through the nexus, transforming it, either for the better or for the worse. That's why agency must be informed by justice, good governance, and stability in order to strive for a more human society.

Our third comment flows naturally from the two earlier ones. The five normative drivers of common good dynamics cannot be considered independent elements. They are relational, by which we mean that the normativity of each one relates to that of all the others. As we've said, agency is not sufficient in itself. It must be concomitant with the deontological requirements of justice, good governance, and stability, exactly as justice won't generate common good dynamics if it does not foster agency, stability, and governance *at the same time*. The following image may help understand the importance of this point.

Let's imagine that a nexus is like a big ship. The rear engine is agency, while several smaller, mobile engines situated at the front (good governance) and the sides (stability and justice) are used to steer the ship. All engines must point in the same direction—toward humanity—for the ship to advance along a straight line. If one of the engines doesn't function well or is not aligned with the other three, the ship will slowly lose its heading. Worse still, if none of the engines works together, then the ship's movement will become chaotic, going in circles or stalling altogether. The appropriate balance of the engines and the ship's speed as the vessel advances toward more humanity is the information provided by the matrix.

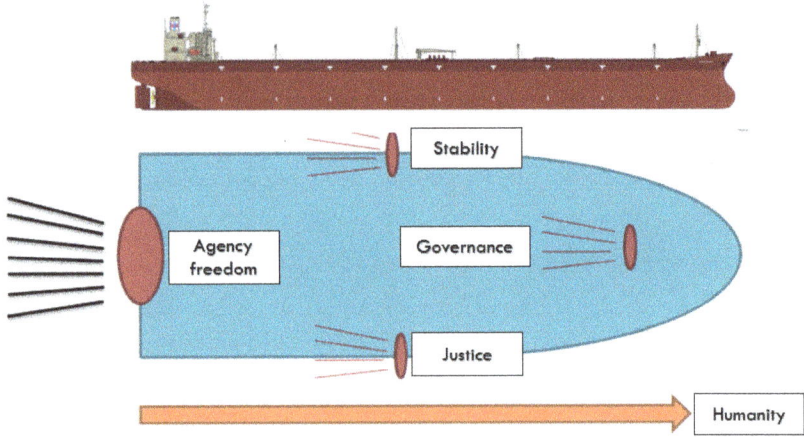

Figure 2. Common good dynamics. The analogy of a boat.

Our ship metaphor brings up a fourth comment. Up until now, we have spoken about the normative dimensions of the matrix as if they were concepts. They obviously are, but they are not only that. We will see below that by 'justice' or 'agency freedom,' we indeed do refer to some abstract universal features essential to identify and recognise as what we call 'justice' or 'agency.' But concepts become concrete by becoming specific. Justice becomes real as it is institutionalised in the practices of a judiciary system. Collective agency freedom becomes real and effective when democratic institutions make political participation possible. The point is that each specific realisation of a concept is radically limited and incomplete. It does not embody the full, universal meaning of the concept. Therefore, when we speak here of normative dimensions commanding common good dynamics, we speak about a universal matrix that allows us to investigate the inherent diversity of reality. But at the same time, it must be clear that what we will be looking for in these normative dimensions are the very concrete institutions and social practices making them real. Ethical principles must be embedded to become effective.

A fifth clarification concerns the purpose of the matrix. The metric, it may be feared, could easily become too rigid, its claim to universality squashing the *inherent diversity* we should expect to find at the local level. The present chapter is highly sensitive to this danger. We think that our focus on processes rather than outcomes allows us to respect the huge diversity of nexuses existing all over the world. What is important to us is not so much the specific composition of the nexus, but the fact that it is moving in the right direction, that there *is* a common good dynamic furthering its coherence, integration, and humanity. The normative framework only fixes the instrumental conditions (agency, justice, good governance, and stability) for such a dynamic to exist, as well as fixing the normative horizon (humanity) by which we may value the progress of the whole. Under this framework, the diversity of possible nexuses is almost infinite, each village, town, or nation having its own specificities. But whatever the elements making up a nexus, the question will be the same: does the present equilibrium move along a common good dynamic or not, and if so, how quickly?

But what about the telos then? Is humanity not defined and imposed by the matrix? Is it not a fixed concept? Not really. Humanity is a normative horizon, something we are meant to seek and slowly discover in doing so. Our common humanity is a task as well as a quest. We can't renounce the seeking but its meaning is still to be fully discovered. What it means to be 'human together' is a question each generation will have to answer anew and in an incremental way. Nonetheless, we already know that humanity is not without boundaries. Humanity is like a space with borders, circumscribed by the possibility of the nonhuman. The matrix adopts this second form of framing 'humanity' by describing its boundaries through two open, incremental lists: one of *basic common goods* and another of *core habitus*. Lists are necessary. Without becoming specific, humanity is but an empty word. But by allowing for the list to be added to, we escape the trap of an ideological conception of humanity.

Finally, as we said previously, the matrix's normativity is relational. Each normative dimension is assessed through its relationships to all the others and therefore opens the way for *partial orderings*. That means it is possible to have many specific orders of priorities emerging from an application of the matrix. The matrix does not impose one and the same solution onto each situation, but allows for a plurality of solutions within a specific, normative framework. With these preliminary comments set out, we can now turn to the description of the five normative dimensions.

II. The Five Dimensions of the Matrix

The Definition and Systemic Function of Each Dimension

The normative role of each dimension is specific. Agency may be understood as the *systemic precondition* of common good dynamics, i.e., the efficient causality of the nexus. Justice, stability, and governance describe key *systemic social functions* that organise the dynamic and are required to lead the nexus toward the universal common good—social functions, in other words, that are normatively bound up with the achievement of the common good (formal causality). Finally, humanity refers to the *systemic achievement* of common good dynamics (end causality).

'*Collective agency freedom*[9] refers to the overall capacity of the nexus population to *engage with others and act together freely, cooperating to the sequencing of social goods* (Arendt 1958, pp. 82–115). It is the collective capability to act together to solve common problems, a capability embedded in various formal and informal institutions structuring the nexus. Three systemic social functions include the following: (a) *Governance* describes the capacity to lead the nexus toward an ever broader and deeper human integration. It is polycentric and abides by an organic subsidiarity; (b) *Justice* contemplates the fairness of the processes by which people take part in the consecution of the social goods produced by the nexus and take part in their benefits, i.e., the fair generation of different social goods and the just distribution of the common benefits among the people; and (c) *Stability* describes the social institutions preserving and enriching the achieved humanity of the nexus into its long future. These are the institutions that preserve, transmit, and reinvent the nexus's humanity, providing it with resilience and sustainability. Each of these three key social functions are correlated, subsequently checking and correcting the other two. Together, they structure the nexus and bring about a common good dynamic. Finally, *Humanity*, the *systemic achievement* of a common good dynamic, denotes the human quality of our coexistence in the nexus: how we relate and act together as human beings in that particular society. More precisely,

---

9   On agency and collective capability, see: Ibrahim and Alkire (2007, pp. 379–403), Deneulin (2008, pp. 105–124).

we characterise 'humanity' as the achievement of a set of basic common goods and core habitus.

What Do We Mean by Collective Agency Freedom?

We understand this freedom not in terms of rights, but as the real freedom to engage with others and act together freely, cooperating in the consecution of social goods (see Chapter 4). Basically, collective agency freedom describes how a given population engages in common issues, drafts solutions, and achieves some social good (commoning) (Euler 2018, pp. 10–16). It is first and foremost a positive freedom. How accustomed are people to discussing common issues and solving them together? In other words, the term describes how much agency freedom is embedded in a particular culture. But it also describes a negative freedom. Are people free to take part in such initiatives? Does the legal and administrative framework of the state make it possible for them to organise around common issues? Is there a space left between the market and the state for people to strive toward a commons? The more robust this collective agency freedom is in a given population, the more energy will power the nexus of common goods. The less agency freedom there is, the more violent, unstable, fragmented, and inhuman the nexus will be. Collective agency freedom accounts for the inventiveness and creativity existing in the nexus, and for the collective capability to generate commons in the nexus.

Agency as a positive collective freedom. We consider agency freedom as one of the normative conditions for the existence of common good dynamics in a society. The importance of freedom for the common good is nothing new. The proud defense of freedom by Pericles in Thucydides' work is a precise recognition of our collective agency freedom as a valuable social good (Sherover 1984, pp. 27–52). In Pericles' speech, freedom is either real and effective or it is neither (Thucydides 2010, §2.34–2.46). Consequently, freedom is seen as a *collective achievement and duty*—you are called on by all the others to behave as a free person—not an individual right. We are free together, because we together value that freedom, live and organise our lives according to it, and, if necessary, fight in common to defend it (Palmer 1992, pp. 15–37).

We are no longer accustomed to thinking about freedom in this sense. Indeed, social contract theory postulates that collective agency freedom will somehow derives from the recognition of equal individual rights. As a social good, agency freedom is seen as a consensus among free individuals defining equal formal rights for all. This arrangement leaves to the state the duty to protect and promote the formal rights of each citizen. But how will these rights collaborate with one another? How will they grow to be more than an aggregate of individual freedoms? The question of individual rights versus collective rights has always been a difficult one for liberal democracies. We propose a different approach. We don't start thinking about society's freedom from a formal set of universal rights, but from the *effective capability to freely act together*. We think of agency freedom as a positive collective freedom through which each member of the group actualises his or her own liberty. As such, individual and collective agency freedoms are considered concomitant. Empirically, we are born into social relationships that shape the acquisition of our own personal freedom. It seems consequently relevant to recognise collective agency freedom as a telling indicator of the quality of the engine of the common good dynamic in a society.

Agency freedom as a negative freedom. The importance given to positive freedom does not mean that we don't appreciate the importance of the negative freedom requirement of such collective agency freedom. In the long run, the rule of law, administrative requirements, and economic restrictions deeply shape our collective agency freedom. Thus, any measurement of agency freedom will have to assess it as both a *positive freedom* and a *negative freedom*. Our focus on the quality of the nexus of the common good absolutely requires both. The real, effective agency freedom displayed by a population is the mix of the positive capability and the constraints of the wider institutional context.

And What about Governance?

A definition of 'governance.' If agency freedom can be seen as the engine of the nexus, then governance is its steering wheel. The nexus is not an autopoietic system but a human construct, slowly knotted together and modified by each passing generation. As a complex and dynamic equilibrium, the web of social goods and communities that makes up the nexus is never a given. Its inherent fragility requires constant care. It needs governance *to preserve itself, to adapt and project the nexus toward an ever-more-human common future.* It is this key social function of the nexus that we call governance.[10] *Good* governance is therefore governance for the common good,[11] i.e., *governance aiming at an ever more universal and human nexus of common goods.*

'*Governance goals.*' As a systemic social function, governance propels the existing nexus of the common goods toward deeper and broader integration, moving the whole nexus in the right direction, toward the universal common good. Governance does so not only by furthering integration, but by addressing conflicts and imbalances, seeking coherence in the commons, and preparing for incoming challenges. Governance is not just the present administration of the nexus, but the driving force that prepares and invents the future of our coexistence. We may thus distinguish two goals for the governance of the nexus. The first aims to project the nexus's dynamic into the foreseeable future. In this goal, governance is an act of *prevision*, of *reinvention*, and of *transmission* of the nexus. Beginning with the *prudent prevision* of future events or situations that may affect the existing nexus and of how to adapt to them, governance then embraces a *creative reinvention* of the nexus, tackling its many limitations and directing it toward the universal common good. The second goal aims to further the existing nexus of the common good and focuses on the present of the dynamic. According to this second objective, governance aims to promote a deeper integration of the nexus.

A fragmented and polycentric social function. Governance is by no means a single, all-encompassing social function, but rather a fragmented and polycentric one (Van Zeben 2019, pp. 38–49). In addition, governance of the nexus can't be reduced to one formal institution since it is

---

10   As such, governance can also be thought of as a specific common good, but one arising from the necessity to forge a dynamic of the common good between the existing social goods. It is out of the need to drive the social goods toward an ever-deeper nexus of the common good that governance exists. Without it, the existing system stagnates, becomes rigid, and decays.

11   'Governance consists of the traditions and institutions by which authority in a country is exercised. This includes the process by which governments are selected, monitored and replaced; the capacity of the government to effectively formulate and implement sound policies; and the respect of citizens and the state for the institutions that govern economic and social interactions among them'. World Bank Governance Index Definition (2019) (https://info.worldbank.org/governance/wgi/). An early version of the definition of governance held that governance is: 'traditions and institutions by which authority in a country is exercised for the common good' (World Bank 2004).

implemented by a wide array of organisations, which can be divided into several groups. The first group of social processes concerns the generation of commons (Ostrom 1994, pp. 1–33; Tosun et al. 2016, pp. 1–12): the many processes that allow questions of the common good to emerge to be answered and implemented. What do we value together? What do we want to achieve in common? How can we achieve it together? Mostly these are associations and interest groups from the civil society. A second group is made of the institutions projecting the nexus into the foreseeable future, anticipating and preparing for social changes, political power plays, technological developments, and economic shifts, for example universities, think-tanks or international organisations (Mayntz 2002, pp. 15–27). Finally, a third group of institutions deals with the management of the public square. But for all the importance and authority of this last group of largely state institutions, they can't possibly cope alone with all facets of the governance of the nexus.[12] Indeed, the all-important tasks covered by the first and second group of institutions are usually rather poorly performed by the administrative bodies of modern states.

Organic subsidiarity. A common good perspective will also insist that governance doesn't trickle down from the top (De Rougemont 1949, pp. 59–72, 95–96). Rather, it grows from the local level up toward the national level. As a complex cooperative game, common good dynamics start with local people and real problems that must be solved in common. Then, when a solution requires taking it to the next level of collaboration (mezzo/macro), power is delegated further up, to a wider level of cooperation and governance. This movement through delegation can be called an *organic subsidiarity* (De Rougemont 1970, p. 124), where final decisions are kept as close as possible to the people they will affect, with decisions transferred to a higher level of governance only when they can't be resolved at the present level. Only respect for this organic subsidiarity engenders both the authority *and* the efficiency of governance. Top-down, centralised forms of governance may well be more efficient in the short term, but in the long term they tend to rely more on coercion than public support. Indeed, the authority of governance is for De Rougemont directly linked to the communality of the common good, i.e., the capacity for people to exercise their

---

12   See for example Kautay (2016, pp. 47–61), and Weiss (2010, pp. 795–814).

agency freedom through political governance processes (pp. 141–143). Whenever public decisions around public policies are decided elsewhere and without consultation with the people they affect, then the authority of the decision or the policy will decay in the long run. People do not obey a new policy only for the utility it produces or out of a fear of punishment, but because the policy makes sense, generating a common good *they* value (Riordan 2015, pp. 83–96). Hence governance for the common good is federalist in essence. Its ordinary functioning is an organic subsidiarity contemplating the medium and long term.

Justice as a Normative Driver of Common Good Dynamics

A definition of 'justice.' In a common good perspective, justice concerns the fair processes by which people participate in the common goods of the nexus, or, to put it another way, justice is the *fair generation of the different social goods making up the nexus, including a just distribution of its common benefits* (Walzer 1983, pp. 6–10). Justice concerns a complex equality, as we do not start with individuals but with social goods and interactions. Justice then appears as a collective task concerned with the production and distribution of common goods. As we saw in the previous chapter, common goods are 'shared' in many different forms. We may share their *meaning* and their *value* and take part in the *practical rationality* and the *collective habits* needed for their consecution. But we may also have a share in the common *benefit* that common goods create, thus accessing with others a specific service or good (Walzer 1983, pp. 21–25). No distribution of benefits can be thought of without referring to shared consecution and meaning. Our understanding of the complex equality that rules the distribution of common benefits depends largely on the meaning given to a common good (Walzer 1994, pp. 32–36). Moreover, most of the common benefits are non-tangible and do not diminish by having others participate (Hess 2008, pp. 38–40). Focusing on how we share common goods thus significantly widens our conception of justice (Riordan 2015, pp. 159–178), which has to consider (i) shared meaning (communality of the common good), (ii) shared consecution (participation), and (iii) shared benefit (common use).

Justice as a social function of the nexus. A society is composed of the dynamic integration of many common goods. Justice does not arise here as a given. To the contrary, it appears as a hard-won victory: the result of a balancing act between the social meanings of the common goods, the production of these common goods, and the distribution of the shared benefits among the members of a society (Walzer 1983, pp. 31–63). A society's sense of justice builds up slowly through complex social processes that progressively *state what is fair* and implement *just interactions* in the nexus. This dynamic balancing act is what we call the 'social function of justice'.

Indeed, justice, like governance, is a social function, a complex set of processes and institutions required to drive the nexus toward an ever-more-human integration. From a common good perspective, justice has to do with the 'we' of the nexus, with 'our togetherness,' with how people 'hold together' in a differentiated but integrated society (Riordan 2015, p. 179). It illustrates that our existences are deeply interconnected through the many common goods organising our society. In fact, our interactions in the nexus are so tightly intertwined that we can hardly disentangle ourselves from them. Our everyday lives depend on the existence of the nexus, and on the communal life we share within it. Justice from this perspective does not seek societal unity or even a formal equality among the different members of the nexus. Justice focuses on solidarity among the people belonging to the nexus: *a solidarity regarding the generation of social goods and their distribution.* Thus, justice is part of what we have called the good of order, the order needed for a dynamic of the common good to flourish within the nexus. Without justice, such a dynamic will falter and fail, and the nexus will slowly implode along the fault lines of poverty, violence, and exclusion (Lindahl 2013, pp. 1–12).

The tasks of justice. The tasks of the social function of justice are twofold. On the one hand, justice keeps watch over the nexus so it does not *disintegrate.* It fights exclusion, violence, and poverty. It deals with the external limits of this 'we' as well as with its many internal tensions (Lindahl 2013, pp. 39–43, 187–196). On the other hand, justice seeks to *promote a dignified and flourishing life for each and every person in the nexus.* It furthers solidarity through a deeper integration of the nexus (Ibid., pp. 239–248). The first task points to a 'thin understanding of justice,' while the second, to a 'thick conception of justice' (Walzer 1994, pp. 1–19). The tasks are correlated; to look after the excluded, to battle for basic common goods, and to seek human flourishing are part of one and the same process, creating a deeper inclusion in the nexus.

The Dimension of Stability

A definition of 'stability.' While we are familiar with governance and justice as existing social functions, stability is not usually recognised as key to achieving an order conducive to the common good.[13] Stability describes *the preservation and reinvention of the achieved humanity of the nexus and looks to its long future* (Nebel 2013, pp. 131–144; Arendt 1972, pp. 238–251). Providing sustainability and resilience, stability includes the institutions that preserve, transmit, and reinvent the nexus's humanity.

Stability as a social function. Stability is the overall capability of the nexus to ensure the continuity of our humanity. Without such stability, no common good dynamic can be sustained. Stability as a social function describes the capacity to preserve the long human past and to articulate it in the long human future, while maintaining the nexus's dynamic toward the universal common good. Whereas *governance* is responsible for driving the nexus toward the future, and *justice* looks after the nexus's fairness, *stability* is responsible for the long-term 'human sustainability' of the nexus. Stability's currency is time. But not any time: human time, a *duration*, a continuity of time that allows humanity to flourish in the nexus.[14] While governance addresses change, and justice, fairness, stability generates continuity. The social function of stability is responsible for the continuity of our humanity. It is this continuity that gives the nexus its resilience. The length of time coherently encompassed by the nexus—into the past and toward the future—informs us of its human sustainability.[15]

The tasks of stability. We can thus distinguish two tasks of the social function of stability. The first is the transmission of the past,

---

13 It is unusual to think about stability as a social function. To begin with, is stability not an odd attempt to oppose 'social progress' and to further 'traditional values'? Worse still, does it not empower 'reactionary forces' in society? Modernity was largely crafted around a rejection of the past, and some topics, like stability, are still widely rejected as being opposed to modernity or progress. But stability, understood as the sustainability of the nexus's equilibrium, has little to do with the French Revolution. Stability is a permanent, normative, and empirically well-documented requirement of human flourishing.

14 This is the core of Bergson's analysis of human temporality (1950, pp. 100–128).

15 A society needs a certain depth of time, a certain continuity of time to be able to project itself into it. In times of war, pandemic, or crisis, the future become so uncertain that societies are unable to plan or start projects. In a similar way, poverty can be seen as a lack of capacity to plan for the long future, as future incomes are always uncertain.

the necessity for a people to be rooted in a common history of what it means to be human.[16] Human beings need to be rooted. They need to access the living memory of a people to receive from the common treasure of history most of their intellectual, spiritual, and moral life.[17] This collective memory does not mechanically auto-replicate itself. No memory does. As individuals, we select from our past those events we deem meaningful and then knot them together into narratives of the self, narratives that explain who we are (Ricœur 1992, p. 141). Something similar occurs at the level of the nexus. Past collective experiences are knotted together to amplify a collective memory, a common treasure of intellectual, spiritual, and moral life upon which every member of society relies to develop as a human being. The importance of this collective memory is grasped most fully during times in which it can't be transmitted, either because of war, mass migration, or a conscious decision to forgo this collective memory (cultural genocide) (Ricœur 2000). Education, especially family education and public education, have always been recognised as the most important institutions of this transmission (Arendt 1972, pp. 251–252). Therefore, the first task of the social function of stability may be understood as this *transmission of the common memory of what it means to be human*.

The second task derives from the first one. The transmission of culture is not an end in itself. To transmit a memory of what it means to be human serves the capacity of a people to project themselves into the future as a human community (Sherover 1989, pp. 46–52). Thus the second task may be understood as this social crafting of the long-term future. It is a creative process. To transmit is not to reproduce the past in a sterile manner. To transmit is to reinvent in order to create a future for

---

16   We understand history as the accumulated culture of a people that has shaped their understanding of what it is to be a human being and how to behave as such. It is not to be confounded with a history of political power, social organization, or the history of production/distribution.

17   « L'enracinement est peut-être le besoin le plus important et le plus méconnu de l'âme humaine. C'est un des besoins difficiles à définir. Un être humain a une racine par sa participation réelle, active et naturelle à l'existence d'une collectivité qui conserve vivants certains trésors du passé et certains pressentiments d'avenir. Participation naturelle, c'est-à-dire amenée automatiquement par le lieu, la naissance, la profession, l'entourage. Chaque être humain a besoin d'avoir de multiples racines. Il a besoin de recevoir la presque totalité de sa vie morale, intellectuelle, spirituelle par l'intermédiaire des milieux dont il fait naturellement partie. » Weil (1949, p. 61).

all. To transmit is to open up the past to a common future. To transmit is to be open to the newness of otherness. It is to be capable of assimilating what is different and other into our own future identity.

The Humanity Dimension

Humanity as a normative horizon of the nexus. The goal of a society is to be a human society, an ever-more-human society (see Chapters 2 and 4). As a normative horizon, humanity is both a call and a task that can't be renounced without renouncing who and what we are. We are human already, but must still become more fully human; we are human, but are compelled to seek our humanity in order not to lose it. But what does it mean to behave as human beings (see also Chapter 7)? We will assume here that humanity can be approached—yet not enclosed or defined—by a set of *basic common goods* and a core array of *habitus*. By basic *common goods*, we mean the minimal social goods required for a society to be a human society; in other words, these are relational goods, linked to common basic needs[18] like speech, culture, solidarity or work, that are required for us to access our humanity (Nussbaum 2000, p. 84). By *habitus* (Bourdieu 1990, p. 53), we mean the social structures embodied within human practice, and by *core habitus*, what Bourdieu defined as *doxa*.[19] But where Bourdieu sees power plays over conventions and culture without reference to ethics, we see in the progressive identification of certain habitus the cumulative progression of a *prudential wisdom* about which human behaviours are and must be. It is indeed an imperfect wisdom, but nonetheless a wisdom that lays out what is meant by behaving as a human being (Aron 1993, pp. 383–387). These *core habitus* enshrining a wisdom of the human are obviously not free of metaphysical assumptions but their universality is also practical. The relevance of

---

18   Along the line developed early on by Stewart (1985), and later bridged with the capability approach, again by Stewart (1995, pp. 83–96).

19   Doxa refers to the idea of social self-evidence, what is 'taken for granted' without further questioning by a population. 'The adherence expressed in the *doxic* relation to the social world is the absolute form of recognition of legitimacy through misrecognition of arbitrariness, since it is unaware of the very question of legitimacy, which arises from competition for legitimacy and hence from conflict between groups claiming to possess it' (Bourdieu 1977, p. 168). For a complete analysis of the concept, see Deer (2008, pp. 119–130).

these *core habitus* as *human behaviours* has been verified experimentally through the centuries all over the globe.[20]

Humanity as a systemic outcome of the nexus. Humanity is not only a normative horizon, but also a systemic outcome of the nexus. Humanity is not first and foremost a concept. It is a communal life, a shared social practice. According to Giddens, social systems enable, as much as they constrain, social practices.[21] Individual behaviours are not limited by social structures but directed by them toward certain goals. Through social structures, the logic of root narratives informs individual intentions (Ricœur 1983, p. 226; Simmons 2020), and with many tensions and incoherencies, ensures a broad observance of a given set of *habitus*. Humanity can therefore be seen as the systemic result of a social system. Each nexus of common goods is consistent with a *certain set of habitus*, favouring some and rejecting others. What is more, humanity increases or decreases in a nexus according to its common good dynamics. While an imploding nexus will see violence, humiliation, and injustice flare within a negative common good dynamic, an integrating nexus will see more human behaviours flourish within a positive common good dynamic.

Framing humanity through a set of basic common goods and core habitus. Aristotle famously identified what was specifically human by reference to the infra-human (animals) and supra-human (gods) (Aristotle 1159[a], pp. 8–12).[22] We were neither speechless and irrational like animals, nor eternal and autonomous like gods. Within these boundaries lay the space of 'the human.' To cross those boundaries was always possible, but at the cost of losing our humanity and becoming either gods or animals. Aristotle saw this human space not so much as a limit than as a possibility for unlimited progression, a space in which to seek the perfection of the art of being human: a space for human flourishing. The space of 'what is human' in Aristotle is thus defined by rationality,

---

20   See, for example, on world religions the Global Ethic Project (https://www.global-ethic.org/the-global-ethic-project/) or academic approaches like Schwartz's Value Survey or the European Values Study (https://europeanvaluesstudy.eu/).

21   I build here on Giddens's understanding of agency as built into social structures that in turn are substantiated by social practice (1986, pp. 5–28). Giddens defines social structures as: 'Rules and resources, recursively implicated in the reproduction of social systems. Structure exists only as memory traces, the organic basis of human knowledgeability, and as instantiated in action', *ibid.*, p. 377.

22   See also Nussbaum's reinterpretation of the same argument (1995, pp. 86–131).

speech, and collective autonomy while human flourishing is captured as the 'higher deeds of freedom.'

Our approach is inspired by Aristotle's, which frames a space for humanity without limiting any progression in it. The set of basic common goods acts as the lower limit, the minimal threshold below which a nexus is not human anymore. The *core habitus* functions—imperfectly—as a header or upper limit, beyond which behaviours are not human any more (see Figure 3). Within the space thus defined, an unlimited progression of our humanity is not only possible but is our common task.

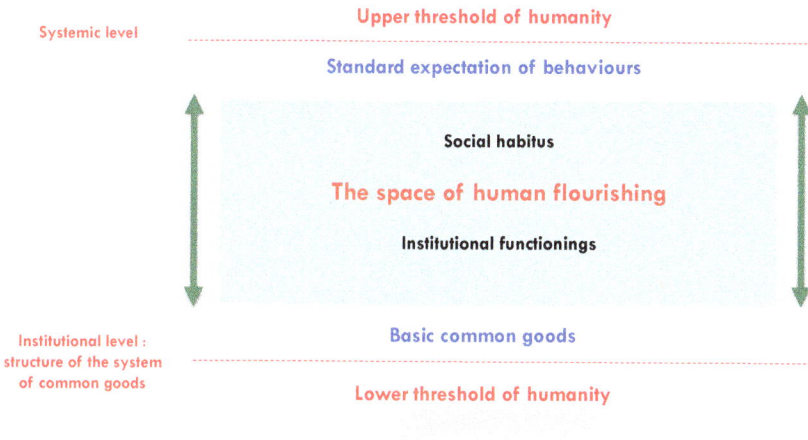

Figure 3. Humanity as a space.

III. A List of Basic Common Goods and Core Habitus

A List of Basic Common Goods

As we noted earlier, by basic common goods we mean the relational goods linked to common basic needs and required for us to access our humanity, like culture, work, education, or solidarity. We should stress that these are not individual or personal basic needs, but *common* basic needs. While individual needs concentrate on what is absolutely required for an individual to survive or access a minimal standard of wellbeing, these common needs focus on what we collectively need to access our humanity.

The International Covenant on Economic, Social and Cultural Rights (1976) may serve as a guide for building such a list. The covenant describes as collective rights those rights whose subjects are not individuals but a community. These rights, like all other human rights, are deemed universal and inalienable, originating prior to positive law and bestowed upon each and every person due to their common human dignity. But as the goods they protect is social in nature, they have come to be seen as 'state obligations.' Collective rights are widely understood today as the duty of the state to provide specific 'public goods.' More precisely, the duty refers to the creation of institutions and public policies to generate and distribute the social goods protected by these rights. One successful example is primary education. States have over time created universal public-school systems so that each and every child can access at least a primary education. But not all collective human rights may be subsumed under the concept of the public good/state governance framework. Culture and language, for example, exist prior to and independently of state institutions. The notion of a public good— either in its Roman-law origins or in Samuelson's economic definition— does not fully match the actuality of these collective human rights. Nor is the state the only actor involved in the production, protection, and development of these rights. We may argue with Ostrom that the social good protected by collective human rights is better approached as commons, or more precisely, as a basic common good (Deneulin 2007). UNESCO made a similar move regarding education in 2015. Such a move is more than rhetorical, letting us understand the provision and distribution of these rights in a different way. It certainly allows us to understand the rights as embedded in community life as commoning practices rather than formal rights guaranteed and provided only by state institutions.

We selected from the ICESCR the following set of basic common goods. As we said before, this is an inexhaustive list. It does not claim to be comprehensive and is open to further discussion. Our selection was guided by the need to create a metric adapted to measure CGD in municipalities. We thus considered as basic common goods: culture, education, solidarity, work, and rule of law. The very existence of these basic common goods in a society can be taken as a fair proxy for a minimal threshold of humanity. Their coherent integration in the nexus's functioning tells us something important about its basic human quality.[23]

Education. As a basic common good, education takes into consideration: a) the community that values and defines it as a common good; b) the formal and informal interactions through which education is conveyed from one generation to the next; and c) the common benefit created by these interactions and how it must be used and shared.

a) As a basic common good, education refers to the way a given population appraises and values the knowledge and wisdom accrued by a society over time and to how important it is to the members of that society to convey this knowledge and wisdom to new generations.

b) As a basic common good, education denotes the formal and informal processes by which a person is introduced to, actualises, and reinvents the common knowledge and wisdom accrued by a society over time. Practically, education refers to the institutions and social structures by which a society actualises and conveys this knowledge and wisdom from one generation to the next.

c) As a basic common good, education covers general knowledge and wisdom as well as the basic intellectual and practical skills with which everybody in a society should be entrusted. Education therefore covers the basic wisdom, knowledge, and skills needed in order to be understood and to function in a society.

Solidarity. As a basic common good, solidarity must take into consideration: a) the community that values and defines it as a common good; b) the formal and informal interactions keeping individuals safe in time of societal need or distress; and c) the common benefit created by these interactions, the legitimate use of solidarity, and its distribution throughout the population.

---

23   Beyond existence, the crucial questions are: How are they structured in the nexus? Which ones are considered the most basic? Which are considered important? Which ones are considered at odds with others? How many are problematic? Which ones are a practical priority in the present context? The point is to see if they contribute to the growth of the nexus.

a) As a basic common good, solidarity refers to the determination of a given population to keep individuals safe from the worst forms of human need and distress. Implicit in solidarity is a strong sense of belonging to a human community that will not let one of its members fall behind without helping. Solidarity describes the value given by a community to these basic forms of human security.

b) As a basic common good, solidarity denotes the formal and informal processes by which these basic forms of human security are enacted.

c) As a basic common good, solidarity refers to a safety net of reciprocal help. The rules governing the access and use of this safety net are of crucial importance: they include rules determining the access to the safety net; rules defining distress, need and the conditions of reciprocity under which help will be provided.

Culture. As a basic common good, culture must take into consideration: a) the community that values and defines it as a common good; b) the formal and informal interactions by which their common memory and traditions, language and values are inhabited by a given population; and c) the common benefit created by these interactions.

a) As a basic common good, culture refers to the value given by a specific community to the common memory, traditions, language, and values forming their shared world. A culture is alive as long as people value it.

b) As a basic common good, culture refers to the many and mostly informal interactions by which a community inhabits and actualises its common memory, traditions, language, and values.

c) As a basic common good, culture refers to the shared rationality and understanding created by inhabiting a common world. Culture provides a community with the root narratives by which we understand each other and make sense of our daily lives (Swidler 1986, pp. 273–286). The use and reach of culture are by definition constrained to the sphere of understanding inhabited by a community.

Work. As a basic common good, work must take into consideration: a) the community that values and defines it as a common good; b) the formal and informal interactions by which work is socialised; and c) the common benefit created by these interactions and its distribution among the population.

a) As a basic common good, work refers to the social meaning and collective value given by a population to the set of activities by which we meet our needs and achieve a certain level of wellbeing.

b) As a basic common good, work also designates the institutions that socialise work by: providing it with a *symbolic exchange value* (money); *organising it in an efficient way* (firms; organisations; market); *redistributing* it (taxes; public policies); and *protecting* it (unemployment insurance).

c) As a basic common good, work refers to the level of wellbeing enjoyed by the population, which involves: specifying legitimate forms of work and what amounts to a fair remuneration for work (decent work; minimum salary); looking to create the economic conditions for full employment; and protecting people against unemployment.

Rule-of-law. As a basic common good, rule of law must take into consideration: a) the community that values and defines it as a common good; b) the formal and informal interactions by which a fair recognition of common dignity and freedoms is enacted in a population, and more specifically how a set of basic rights and freedoms is guaranteed, upheld, and enforced by the state; and c) the common benefit created by these interactions.

a) As a basic common good, the rule of law is the value given by a society to universal respect for the law and its fair application. Built on recognition of a fundamental equality of dignity and freedom, rule of law is concerned with the enforcement of law.

b) As a basic common good, the rule of law refers to the formal interactions by which a fair recognition of our common dignity and freedoms is enacted in a population, and more specifically, how a set of basic rights and freedoms is guaranteed, upheld, and enforced by the state.

c) As a basic common good, rule of law refers to justice and freedom as the founding rationality of human behaviours and interactions in a society. Consequently, this common benefit should extend to each and every member of the society.

Which Set of Core Habitus?

Our common humanity is a goal, something we achieve in common. *Core habitus* captures the *values* engendered by the functioning of a nexus (systemic outcome). These are not abstract values, but concrete ones, embedded in the common practices contributing to the humanity of our lives together.

These values represent the 'higher deeds of freedom' that the Greeks saw as the content of the good life and expressed as virtues. We do not fully go along with all of the Greek rationale in this instance, however. Where they saw virtues as personal features mediated through the law, we refer here to Bourdieu's notion of *habitus*. He describes the *permanent internalisation of a given social order in a person*—in our case the nexus—*that does not prescribe any specific actions, but nonetheless orients actors to some specific set of goals.*[24] Habitus are the subjective, internalised representations of a given social order. They are not heteronomous norms to the person, but important features of their own autonomy, and hence they blur the lines of our often-spurious opposition to autonomy and heteronomy. What is key is that habitus, even if they are indeed internalised by individuals, are social in essence: social structures embodied within human practice. Habitus frame individual action just as a nation's narrative frames the specific story of an individual. It is through habitus that a social system normalises and synchronises

---

24   We use here the word in the specific sense given to it by Bourdieu (1990, p. 53): 'The conditionings associated with a particular class of conditions of existence produce *habitus*, systems of durable, transposable dispositions, structured structures predisposed to function as structuring structures, that is as principles which generate and organize practices and representations that can be objectively adapted to their outcomes without presupposing a conscious aiming at ends or an express mastery of the operations necessary in order to attain them.'

individual behaviours; how it produces similar forms of behaviour without pressure on or the restriction of individual freedom. Habitus function through the knowledge and meaning conveyed by social structures (Giddens 1986, pp. 25–27). It is this common, shared meaning that frames the way people understand and project their own specific behaviour, 'naturally' reproducing and reinforcing this narrative each time they act according to it.

But the real force of a habitus lies with the 'standard expectation of behaviour' they create in a society. This is where habitus turns more objective (Bourdieu 1990, pp. 135–142). As root narratives spurned by the nexus and framing individual behaviours (Ricœur 1983, p. 171), habitus also create social expectations of behaviours coherent with them. These are the behaviours that *others expect me to adhere to*, like paying after eating in a restaurant or not jumping on a table in a classroom or not committing murder to solve a conflict with my neighbour. Such behaviours make up the *specific rationality and predictability of the public space*. So habitus, while part of our autonomy, can't be reduced to individual preferences or values.

Now, we are not interested in just any habitus, but in a normative set of social practices with which to compare the habitus created by a specific nexus. The differences will inform us about the humanity achieved by the nexus and complement the information we can receive from our tally of basic common goods. The habitus we have in mind here are not to be confused with the universal common good as such, but mark its progress in a society in the same way that happiness marks the pursuit of human flourishing. Habitus are actually immanent to the research of the common good and may be understood as the moral markers of common good dynamics.

The list of core habitus should not be understood as a static or exhaustive list. Some social virtues may be sensitive to the sort of common goods integrated into the nexus; some will be required in certain circumstances more than others (war and peace do not produce the same sort of common practices); some will be more akin to certain religions than others, etc. This variation is why the relative importance of the virtues on the list, and their positions and arrangement on the list, may change over time and history. As the nexus of the common good is dynamic, the values it achieves may also transform slightly.

However, we can reasonably expect these habitus to be widely shared and to be fairly universal, as expressions of our human condition. The list accounts for values and social practices around which most if not all polities have organised. They reflect a widely shared wisdom of what being human together means in practice.

- *Freedom and responsibility*
- *Justice and solidarity*
- *Peace and concord*
- *Prudence and magnanimity*
- *Resilience and courage*
- *Practical reasoning and wisdom*

The list contemplates six groups of two habitus. The pairing of habitus here is so as to capture two aspects of a single reality through two kinds of behaviour. The polarity arising from the pairing is helpful. First, it serves to narrow the focus of one term by making reference to the other term. Second, it opens a space of flexibility to identify behaviours expressing specific aspects of the pairing.

- The habitus of *freedom and responsibility* frame the capability to act as autonomous persons and to assume responsibility for our own decisions and actions.

- The habitus of *justice and solidarity* frame the capability to respect the dignity and freedom of others and help them in times of need or distress.

- The habitus of *peace and concord* frame the capability to trust others not to use violence to resolve conflicts and to seek cooperation and consensus.

- The habitus of *prudence and magnanimity* frame the capability to seek the truth and foresee the consequences of actions.

- The habitus of *resilience and courage* frame the capability to resist the tribulations of the time and to face difficulties with resolve and determination.

- The habitus of *practical reasoning and wisdom* frame the capability to engage reality through reason and seek to inhabit this reality as human beings.

As noted earlier, this list is not exhaustive and is only very sparingly defined in order to allow for a diversity of interpretations. However, it provides us with a powerful definition of the higher deeds of freedom, and therefore of humanity.

IV. A Relational Normativity: A Tool to Analyse Realities and Tell the Stories of Common Good Dynamics

Each of the normative dimensions implies all the others. They have to be considered together in what medieval thinkers called a *connexio virtutum*. Recalling Ramon Llull's intuition in his *Ars Magna* (Lulle 1517), the normative elements can be rearranged in a pentagon, so that each of the dimensions can be known through their relationships. The result is shown in Figure 4. The normative pentagon of common good dynamics, as we call it, is an analytical tool for understanding and explaining the complexity of common good dynamics, that helps tell the story of a specific community from a common good perspective (Ricœur 1983, pp. 31–51).

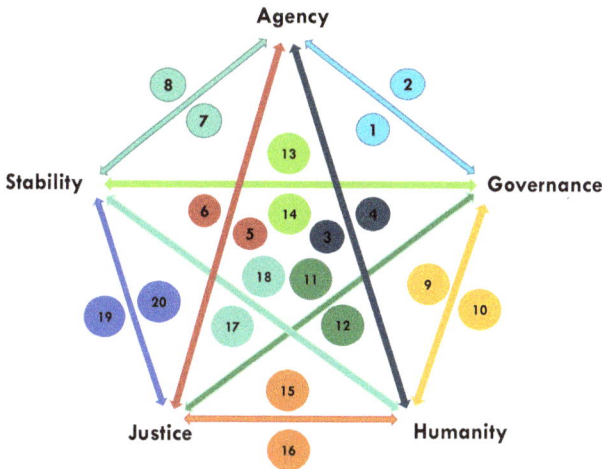

Figure 4. The normative pentagram.

In both the phenomenological and the analytical tradition, there are two ways to approach reality, either directly (*in rectum*) or indirectly (*in obliquo*). We may therefore define agency as we did in the previous section, or account for it through the relationships it builds with the other dimensions. This second approach of studying concepts through their relational dynamics was considered by Rosenzweig as the most effective way to capture their essence (Rosenweig 2005, pp 93–100). Moving forward, we propose such a relational approach to the matrix, showing the twenty relationships across the five dimensions, and offering a core description for each relationship:

1. AG – Participation

2. GA – Empowerment

3. AH – Welfare

4. HA – Social responsibility

Agency: participation, empowerment, welfare, social responsibility, collective habits, capabilities and opportunities, relational quality and resilience of the nexus.

5. AJ – Social practice of justice

6. JA – Just institutions

7. AS – Relational quality

8. SA – Nexus resilience

Governance: participation, empowerment, integration, cooperation, subsidiarity, rule of law, common future and good government.

9. GH – Integration

10. HG – Cooperation

11. GJ – Subsidiarity

12. JG – Rule of law

Humanity: welfare, social responsibility, integration, cooperation, shared rationality, flourishing, human ecology and culture.

13. GS – Common future

14. SG – Good governance

15. HJ – Public rationality

16. JH – Human flourishing

Justice: collective habits, capabilities and opportunities, subsidiarity, rule of law, shared rationality and flourishing, social mobility and democracy.

17. HS – Human ecology

18. SH – Culture

19. JS – Social mobility

20. SJ – Democracy

Stability: Relational quality, resilience of the nexus, common future, good government, human ecology, culture, social mobility and democracy.

Each core description shows aspects of the relationship between the two dimensions. It obliges us to think about the importance of agency for governance (participation) or how justice must inform collective agency (just institutions). It is definitively a creative way to apply the matrix to reality, enriching our understanding of the same.

However, the core descriptions are not universal in the same way as the five normative dimensions. They will depend on the sort of reality to which we apply the matrix, and the context of this reality. This is why a family, a parish community, or a city will have to be accounted for in different ways. The governance of agency is not the same in a parish community, in a family, or in a city. Consequently, Chapter 3 translates the matrix into a metric of common good dynamics in municipalities.

The matrix's relational approach can't serve as the basis for a metric, but may serve as an important *analytical tool* for explaining reality from a common good perspective. It may also be seen as a narrative structure for explaining common good dynamics. How does it function? Each of the five vertices of the pentagon relates to the remaining four.[25] We can speak, for instance, of the relationship between *governance* and *freedom* in two ways. We can look at the 'governance of agency,' and in this sense we may ask how governance institutions inspire, guide, manage or promote collective agency. Or we can look at the 'agency of governance,' that is, how collective freedom infuses and informs governance practice— less in dictatorial regimes and more in democratic systems. This sort of bidirectionality among the five vertices can make the reading of the relationships between the elements more evocative. In that way, the pentagon compels a person telling a story of a particular situation to be open to new, often unexpected elements from the 'story of the common good.' To give an example, the 'storytelling of development projects' usually involves speaking of issues of participation and empowerment (agency-governance) and may include the question of just institutions (just agency), but usually does not include aspects related to the stability of humanity. To go through all twenty normative relationships in a specific situation obliges the storyteller to tell the 'full story' of a common good dynamic.

---

25   Although the five normative dimensions of the pentagon may be read in no specific order, we propose in what follows a narrative of common good dynamics as starting with *doing* (A), in an *orderly* way (G), that *pursues fundamental and sublime goods* (H), *which are to be shared among all human beings* (J), *and endure in a broad horizon* of time (S).

Conclusions

As a conclusion to this chapter, it may be useful to summarise the sort of information we expect to obtain through the matrix, which is intended to capture the strength of common good dynamics in a given nexus. We propose to recognise five normative drivers of these dynamics, namely collective agency, justice, stability, governance, and humanity.

The relational nature of the normative drivers gives way to a diversified and complex account of common good dynamics, especially if you add to the drivers a list of basic capabilities and core habitus. But this very complexity is also an obstacle. Once transposed to a metric, will we be able to understand our results? And if we can, will we be able to explain them in a significant way to others? We anticipate here some of these objections.

An M5 matrix (with five key normative drivers) goes beyond our typical three-dimensional notion of reality. It may be difficult, therefore, to grasp the information the matrix will provide once it is applied. We may better understand it if we collapse the three structural dimensions (governance, stability, and justice) into one and then contrast them in an M3 matrix. This gives us Figure 5.

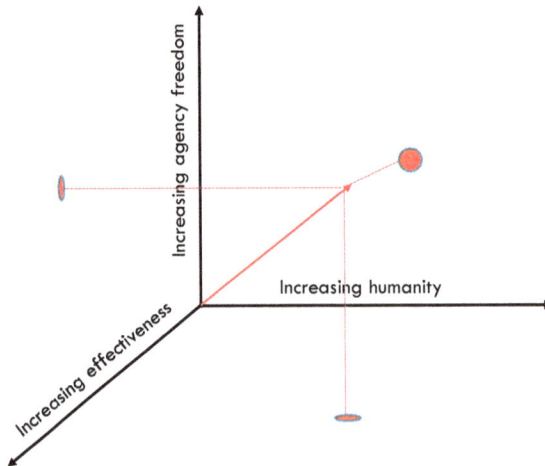

Figure 5. The M3 matrix.

The three axes represent the engine of common good dynamics (agency), the systemic results of the dynamic (humanity), and the structural functioning of the nexus (governance, justice, and stability). The resulting vector shows how free, human, and efficient a given nexus is, as well as all the possible intersections between the three axes.

Two elements of the vector are especially important: its *direction* and its *magnitude*. The common good dynamic results from the coherent behaviour of each dimension, since to move forward, a vessel needs all engines in synchrony. Thus, the equidistant line between the three axes represents the optimum trajectory of the common good dynamic. Each of the points on this line represents the existence, however weak, of a common good dynamic. Each point *not* on this line represents a deviation from the dynamic, a distortion of the nexus that ultimately may lead, if not corrected, to its implosion if the internal tensions become too big. The *magnitude* of the vector gives us an idea of the strength of the dynamic and thus an idea of how much 'steam' for the common good there is in the nexus.

We may still further reduce the complexity of the matrix and collapse agency, governance, justice, and stability onto one axis and contrast it with just humanity. We would then contemplate only how human a nexus it is and how functional it is, from a common good perspective. Figure 6 gives an idea of such an M2 matrix.

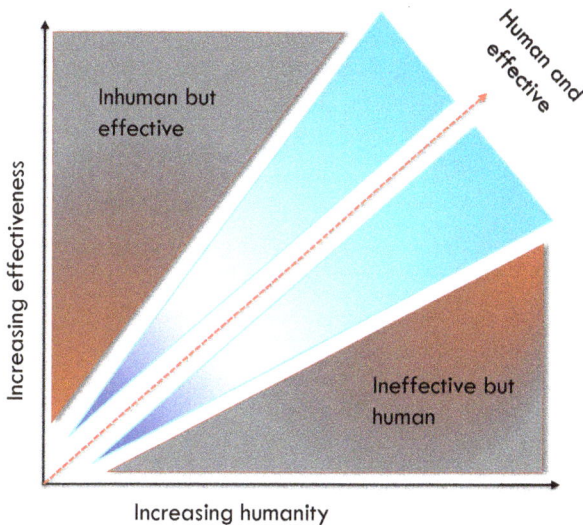

Figure 6. The M2 matrix.

Here, again, we must consider both direction and magnitude as key factors dividing the graph into three quadrants. Each quadrant gives clear and immediate information about the processes at work in the nexus. The dynamic may be human *and* efficient, efficient *but* inhuman, or inefficient *but* human.

However, at this high level of aggregation the finer picture of the dynamic is lost. Much of the important information from the analysis is hidden by the way specific relationships in the M5 matrix are distorted in the M2 matrix, including those specific pieces of information relevant for governance of the nexus, and therefore for development. The metric developed in the next chapters will therefore consider all five elements and attempt to deal with the resulting complexity.

References

Acksel, B., Euler, J., et al. 2015. "Commoning: Zur Kon-struktion einer konvivialen Gesellshaft", in Adloff, F., Volker H. (eds), *Konvivialismos. Eine Debatte*, Bielfeld: Transcript Verlag. https://doi.org/10.1515/9783839431849-010

Arendt, H. 1972 (1954). *La crise de la culture*, Paris: Gallimard.

Arendt, H. 1983 (1958). *La condition de l'homme moderne*, Paris: Calmann-Lévy.

Aristotle. 1999 (1934). *The Nichomachean Ethics* (trans. Rackham H.), Cambridge, Mass.: Harvard University Press.

Aron, R. 1993, "Les antinomies de la politique. Préface au Prince", in Aron, R., *Machiavel et les tyrannies modernes*, Paris: Éditions de Fallois.

Baldwin, K., Karlan, D., Udry, C., and Appiah, E. 2016. *Does Community-Based Development Empower Citizens?*, Abdul Latif Jameel Poverty Action Lab: MIT, 1–40.

Bennet, S. and D'Onofrio, A. 2015. *Community-Driven? Concepts, Clarity and Choices for CDD in Conflict-Affected Contexts*, New York: International Rescue Committee.

Bergson, H. 1950. *Time and Free Will*, London: George Allen.

Bollier, D. and Helfrich, S. 2019. *Free, Fair and Alive. The Insurgent Power of the Commons*, Gabriola Island (CDN): New Society Publishers. https://doi.org/10.1515/9783839445303

Bourdieu, P. 1977. *Outline of a Theory of Practice*. Cambridge: Cambridge University Press.

Bourdieu, P. 1990. *The Logic of Practice*, Stanford: Standford University Press.

Buchanan, J. 1965. "An Economic Theory of Clubs", *Economica 32/125*, 1–14.

De Angelis, M. and Harvie, D. 2013. "The Commons", in Parker M., Cheney G., Fournier V., and Land C. (eds). *The Routledge Companion to Alternative Organisation*, London: Routledge, 280–294. ttps://doi.org/10.4324/9780203725351.ch19

De Rougemont, D. 1949. *L'Europe en jeu*, Neuchâtel: de la Bacconière.

De Rougemont, D. 1970. *Lettre ouverte aux Européens*, Paris: Albin Michel.

Deer, C. 2008. "Doxa", in Grenfell, M. J., *Pierre Bourdieu. Key Concepts*, New York: Routledge, 119–130.

Deneulin, S. and Townsend, N. 2007. Public Goods, Global Public Goods and the Common Good, *International Journal of Social Economics 34/1–2*, 19–36. https://doi.org/10.1108/03068290710723345

Deneulin, S. 2008. "Beyond Individual Freedom and Agency: Structures of Living Together", in Comim, F., Qizilbash, H., and Alkire, S. (eds), *The Capability Approach: Concepts, Measures and Applications*, Cambridge: Cambridge University Press, 105–124.

Euler, J. 2018. "Conceptualizing the Commons", *Ecological Economics 143*, 10–16. https://doi.org/10.1016/j.ecolecon.2017.06.020

Fournier, V. 2013. "Commoning: on the social organization of the commons", *Management 16/4*, 433–453. https://doi.org/10.3917/mana.164.0433

Giddens, A. 1986. *The Constitution of Society. Outline of the Theory of Structuration*, Oxford: Blackwell.

Helfrich, S. 2012a. "Common Goods Don't Simply Exist–They Are Created", in Bollier, D. and Helfrich, S. (eds), *The Wealth of the Commons: A World Beyond Market and State*, Levellers Press: Amherst, 61–67.

Helfrich, S. 2012b. "The Logic of the Commons and the Market: A Shorthand Comparison of Their Core Beliefs", in Bollier, D. and Helfrich, S. (eds), *The Wealth of the Commons: A World Beyond Market and State*, Levellers Press: Amherst, 35–36.

Hess, C. 2008. "Mapping the New Commons", https://ssrn.com/abstract=1356835

Ibrahim, S. and Alkire, S. 2007. "Agency and Empowerment: A Proposal for Internationally Comparable Indicators", *Oxford Development Studies 35/4*, 379–403. https://doi.org/10.1080/13600810701701897

Kaufmann, D., Kraay, A, Zoido, P. 1999. "Governance Matters", *World Bank Policy Research Working Paper No. 2196*, https://ssrn.com/abstract=188568

King, E. 2013. *A Critical Review of Community-Driven Development Programs in Conflict Affected Contexts*, New York: The International Rescue Committee.

Kutay A. 2016. "A Critical Transnational Public Sphere: Bringing Back Common Good and Social Ontology in Context", *Globalizations 13/1*, 47–61. https://doi.org/10.1080/14747731.2015.1037125

Lindahl, H. 2013. *Fault Lines of Globalization*, Oxford: Oxford University Press. https://doi.org/10.1093/acprof:oso/9780199601684.001.0001

Linebaugh P. 2009, *The Magna Carta Manifesto: Liberties and Commons for All*, Berkeley: University of California Press. https://doi.org/10.1525/9780520932708

Lullus, R. 1970 (1308). *Ars generalis ultima*, Frankfurt/M: Minerva Verlag.

Mansuri, G. and Rao, V. 2004. "Community-Based and Driven Development: A Critical Review", *World Bank Policy Research Working Paper 3209*, 1–77. https://doi.org/10.2139/ssrn.501663

Mansuri, G. and Rao, V. 2013. *Localizing Development. Does Participation Work?* Washington: World Bank. https://doi.org/10.1596/9780821382561_CH01

Mayntz, R. 2002. "Common Goods and Governance", in Héritier, A. (ed.), *Common Goods: Reinventing European Integration Governance*. Oxford: Rowman & Littlefield Publisher.

Narayan, D. 1995. "Designing Community Based Development", *Toward environmentally and socially sustainable development 17*, 1–5.

Nebel, M. 2013, "Peut-on éduquer à la charité", *Transversalités 126/2*, 131–144. https://doi.org/10.3917/trans.126.0131

Nebel, M. and Herrera, M. 2018. "Measuring the Meta-Capability of Agency: A Theoretical Basis for Creating a Responsibility Indicator", in Comim, F., Fennell, S., and Anand P. (eds), *New Frontiers of the Capability Approach*, Cambridge: Cambridge University Press, 82–115.

Nussbaum, M. 1995. "Aristotle on Human Nature and the Foundation of Ethics", in Altham J. E. J. and Harrisson, R., *World, Mind and Ethics: Essays on the Ethical Philosophy of Bernard Williams*. Cambridge: Cambridge University Press, 86–131.

Nussbaum, M. 2000. *Women and Human Development: The Capabilities Approach*, Cambridge: Cambridge University Press.

Ostrom, E. 1990. *Governing the Commons*, Cambridge: Cambridge University Press.

Ostrom, E. 1994. *Neither Market nor State: Governance of Common Pool Resources in the Twenty-First Century*, Washington DC: International Food Policy Research Institute, 1–33.

Ostrom, E. 2010. "Beyond markets and states: polycentric governance of complex economic systems", in Grandin, K. (ed.), *The Nobel Prizes 2009*, Stockholm: The Nobel Foundation, 408–444. https://doi.org/10.1257/aer.100.3.641

Palmer, M. 1992. *Love of Glory and the Common Good. Aspects of the Political Thought of Thucydides*, Lanham: Rowman & Littlefield Publishers.

Ricoeur, P. 1992. *Oneself as Another*, Chicago: Chicago University Press.

Ricoeur, P. 2004 (2000). *Memory, History, Forgetting*, Chicago: The University of Chicago Press. https://doi.org/10.7208/chicago/9780226713465.001.0001

Ricoeur, P. 1983. *Time and Narrative*, Chicago: University of Chicago Press.

Riordan, P. 2015. *Global Ethics and Global Common Goods*, London: Bloomsbury.

Rosenzweig, F. 2005 (1921). *The Star of Redemption*, Madison: The University of Wisconsin Press.

Samuelson, P. 1954. The Pure Theory of Public Expenditure, *The Review of Economics and Statistics 36/4*, 387–389.

Sherover, C. 1984. The Temporality of the Common Good: Futurity and Freedom, *Review of Metaphysics 37/3*, 27–52.

Sherover, C. 1989. *Time Freedom and the Common Good*, New York: New York University Press.

Simmons, S. J. 2020. *Root Narrative Theory and Conflict Resolution: Power, Justice and Values*, New York: Routledge. https://doi.org/10.4324/9780367822712

Stewart, F. 1985. *Planning to Meet Basic Needs*, London: Palgrave Macmillan.

Stewart, F. 1995. Basic Needs, Capabilities and Human Development, *Greek Economic Review 17/2*, 83–96.

Swidler, A. 1986. Culture in action: symbols and strategies, *American Sociological Review 51/2*, 273–286.

Thucydides. 2010. *History of the Peloponnesian War*, vols I–II, (trans. Thomas, A.), Cambridge: Cambridge University Press.

Tosun, J., Koos, S., and Shore, J. 2016. Co-governing common goods: Interaction patterns of private and public actors, *Policy and Society 35/1*, 1–12. https://doi.org/10.1016/j.polsoc.2016.01.002

UNESCO 2015, *Rethinking Education. Towards a global common good?* Paris: UNESCO Press, https://unesdoc.unesco.org/ark:/48223/pf0000232555

Van Laerhoven, F. and Berge, E. 2011. "The 20th anniversary of Elinor Ostrom's Governing the Commons", *International Journal of the Commons 5/1*, 1–8. https://doi.org/10.18352/ijc.290

Van Zeben, J. 2019. "Polycentricity", in Hudson, B., Rosenbloom, J., and Cole, D., *Routledge Handbook of the Study of the Commons*, New York: Routledge, 38–49.

Walzer, W. 1983, *Spheres of Justice*, Oxford: Blackwell.

Walzer, M. 1994, *Thick and Thin: Moral Argument at Home and Abroad*, South Bend: Notre Dame University Press.

Weils, S. 1949. *L'enracinement*, Paris: Gallimard.

Weiss, T. G. 2010. Governance, good governance and global governance: conceptual and actual challenges, *Third World Quarterly 21/5*, 795–814. https://doi.org/10.4324/9781315251981-14

Wong, S. 2013. What Have Been the Impacts of World Bank CDD Programs? Operational and Research Implications, *World Bank Social Development Notes 137*, 1–16.

World Bank. 1996. *The World Bank Participation Sourcebook*. Washington DC: World Bank. https://documents1.worldbank.org/curated/en/289471468741587739/pdf/multi-page.pdf

World Bank. 2004. The Public Sector Governance Reform Cycle: available diagnostic tools, *PREM Notes 88,* 1–8.

3. Design and Reflection on the Metric of Common Dynamics[1]

Oscar Garza-Vázquez and Viviana Ramírez

Introduction

Development efforts are increasingly challenging as the world becomes more complex. The interconnectedness of peoples and economies, the diversity of cultures, and the endurance of global development issues demand more than ever approaches that are able to capture this intricacy and multidimensionality both at the global and local levels. In the search for such approaches, development indicators have burgeoned, contributing to the monitoring of the progress of societies and the effectiveness of policy and public decision-making in the last decades. However, most of these efforts focus on measuring progress at the international and the individual levels, overlooking the collective production of progress by people acting together in local contexts. The Institute for the Promotion of the Common Good (IPBC) seeks to meet this gap by proposing a metric of common good dynamics at the municipal level that can capture the shared construction of social goods in order to guide local governments in their development plans.

Although there seems to be a growing interest in moving beyond individualistic narratives, few approaches have ventured to create measures on relational or collective processes. In addition, as explained below, the focus of these approaches either remains at the level of

---

1   Chapter 3 of this book presents a slightly modified version of the article with the same title available in *Rivista Internazionale di Scienze Sociali, Research In Social Science* (2020), vol. 4, published by Vita e Pensiero, Università Cattolica del Sacro Cuore, Milan, Italy. We are grateful to the editors of the journal for granting the rights.

   https://doi.org/10.11647/OBP.0290.04

outcomes or considers a particular dimension in isolation. Instead, the metric presented here adopts a systemic approach within process-oriented dimensions. As such, the contribution of the metric offered here is that it captures the quality of the *nexus of the common good* by analysing how the *structural* and *dynamic* aspects of the production of common goods combine to build a society that lives together. The *structure* of the common good comprises the way in which the social and institutional context in the municipality frames people's opportunity to live well and to achieve collective goals, while its *dynamics* involves the expected patterns of behaviour in which the residents act in the production and distribution of the basic common goods of a municipality over time. The metric examines these aspects of the *nexus of the common good* through the interconnection of five dimensions: *Justice, Stability, Governance, Collective Agency Freedom, and Humanity*.

This article introduces the metric of the common good proposed by the IPBC research group and discusses the steps taken in the construction of the seventy-one indicators that comprise the aforementioned five dimensions, the advantages of this perspective, and the remaining challenges. It is structured as follows. The first section summarises and comments on the pertinence of the common good approach proposed in this book. The second lays out the process of constructing the indicators. This was primarily a dialectic process between experts in the theory of common good, measurement specialists, and local government officials and political actors knowledgeable in the local challenges of the municipalities. This section also reviews the qualities sought in the items as they were designed, as well as the challenges faced. The third section presents the dimensions and the items that comprise them, delineating the specific aspects of the dimension that each item seeks to capture. Before the conclusion, the fourth section discusses the metric's contributions and future challenges if it is to be used to guide policy and decision-making at the local level.

1. The Theoretical Foundations of the Survey

Measuring is never done for its own sake. The collection of data is necessary in order for us to keep track of the evolution of those things that we care about. It provides us with information about how we are doing, whether we have advanced, and how much more we can achieve.

As Székely's (2005) book title states, numbers also move the world; what is measured can be improved. In addition, data allows us to infer things that are beyond our own sight. By learning about how different variables connect with each other we can better understand the world in which we live. We can also learn about some realities which have been ignored by current metrics and of whose complexity and avenues for improvement we have little knowledge. Yet, developing measurements is no simple task. It is always imperfect, and it is always value-laden. Hence, the best one can do is to try to measure what really matters based on people's realities and a sound theoretical framework, and to be transparent about the choices one makes in this process.

Previous chapters in this book have introduced the theoretical foundations of the metric of the common good presented here (see also Beretta and Nebel 2020, Nebel and Arbesu-Verduzco 2020). These chapters offer a rationale for the development of a practical measure of a common good approach as a necessary practical tool to complement existing metrics of 'social' progress. As mentioned, most of these 'social' indicators rely on aggregated individual data as a proxy for the social, and thus they fail to account for the systemic interactions, that is, the interconnection between the common institutions, values, and shared practices underlying the production of individual results. Instead, the matrix of the nexus of the common good aims its focus 'on *commons*', that is, on those things that we value, produce, share, and benefit from, as a collectivity. Likewise, as opposed to these measures, the metric developed here focuses on 'the *process* by which these [collective goods] combine in society to create a nexus–of–commons'.

This move is a major contribution to the conceptualisation of development and to the design and evaluation of social policies to improve people's lives. It responds to the urgent need for measuring things that have long been left outside of our modern conception of development and wellbeing, namely the structural and relational aspects of development, in order to place them in the academic and political agenda.

For a long time, we have given too much importance to what we measure (just because we can measure it) instead of measuring what is important. Indeed, some still justify the use of GDP as a measure of social progress due to its simplicity and its *apparent* exactitude. Yet, even if we assume that GDP indeed offers a precise measure, we may still ask whether it measures the 'right' thing.[2] In the last thirty years, we have seen great advancements in terms of indicators going beyond GDP. Most of these emphasise the need to focus on what really matters, namely, the person and her wellbeing. Nowadays, we know that a GDP measure is simply insufficient (even if necessary), and not the most important indicator of the development of societies, as it does not capture what we truly care about, i.e., people's quality of life. In response, several efforts to measure people's wellbeing have emerged (e.g., Bhutan's Gross National Happiness Index, the Human Development Index, Italian BES, and others). Even if measurements differ, the great majority of them coincide in insisting on the complexity of people's lives, and thus defend the use of multidimensional indicators to assess social realities, and to inform the design, monitoring, and assessment of policies.

This has signified a huge improvement in more directly measuring the relevant dimensions of people's lives. Now, besides income, we have information about health, education, standards of living, and so on. This has also translated into improved poverty measures which now provide a more realistic picture of the many deprivations people face when in poverty (e.g., see the Multidimensionality Poverty Peer Network, www.mppn.org). However, there are also some problems with these measures and with how we interpret them. These issues amount to the fact that these measures rely on the aggregation of individual data, and the fact that we tend to wrongly assume that they are the *only* thing that matters. Indeed, we have come to use these multidimensional measures of individual wellbeing as a new substitute for the supremacy of GDP, as if they were the only relevant information capable of informing development policies. This has the unintended consequence of dismissing as unimportant other features that do not appear in our statistics, even though these are crucial for an integral notion of development and for combating poverty effectively. With the transition from GDP measures to various forms of aggregation through individual wellbeing measures, we have ultimately removed the person and her

---

2   The following paragraphs are inspired by the ideas of two well-known economists: 'We need to stop making important what we measure, instead we need to measure what is important' (Branko Milanovic). Measuring what matters may involve rejecting being 'precisely wrong in favour of being vaguely right' (Hawthorn on Amartya Sen's work: 1987, viii).

experience of life from the social context in which she is embedded and in which her wellbeing is co-constructed.

It is in this sense that, by emphasising the dynamic processes and the socio-structural aspects of development, the common good approach proposed in this volume makes an important contribution. It asks us to reinterpret and broaden the way in which we read the success or failure of social life in at least two areas.

First, it recognises that the processes through which a society generates its outcomes in terms of individual wellbeing are also relevant to our lives. That is, it is not enough to know what kind of functionings people manage to achieve. We also care about other things such as the social arrangements in which we live, people's collective freedom to exercise their agency and responsibilities in society, and the humanity of the processes to achieve them, as these are all part of the complex social dynamic in which we live, and which informs our behaviour. While these concerns are not unique to the common good approach presented in this edited volume, our approach does go further, since these structural aspects are understood as an inherently connected, systemic whole. That is, rather than treating these aspects as isolated dimensions that form part of the development process (e.g., measures of Rule of Law), they are seen as working in a nexus. Justice, for instance, cannot be fully understood without reference to agency freedom, the quality of governance, and so on. Precisely how the latter dimensions (Collective Agency, Governance, and others) work in harmony with others determines how we address justice concerns. It is the quality of these interconnections that the common good approach sets forth, through a matrix of five dimensions—as further explained below. The common good approach does not focus on the function of legal and legitimate authority alone, but also on the total community dynamics within a territorial demarcation.

Secondly, it shifts our concerns from *static* end states of individual functionings to actual *dynamic* patterns of behaviour. The common good approach's primary concern is action rather than accomplishments. As such, it diverts its focus from what people achieve and the quantity in which they achieve it, towards what people—in conjunction with others—actually do in order to achieve whatever they value, and how. Ultimately, it is people's practices and their social interactions that provide us with a richer understanding of the quality of the social development actually experienced by the members of a given community. For instance, from this perspective, to understand the situation of health in the population would imply focusing on whether shared values, goals, and practices lead people in a given community to be healthy, as opposed to measuring only the actual health of each individual (which would disregard the social context in which the results of such a study were produced).

Overall, this stance encourages us to realise that many (if not all) of the things we value, such as agency, humanity, dignity, and other fuzzy concepts, do not reveal themselves dichotomously in our lives. These are not something you either have or do not have. Rather, they are states which are constantly being negotiated and co-constructed in conjunction with others. Therefore, a common good approach affirms that the experience of being agents, of living in a humane way, and so on, can be better appraised through a gradient scale at the social level (i.e., by measuring the extent to which these aspects are present as practices in a given population) rather than as an on/off condition that can then be aggregated for the population as a whole. In fact, both *individual* and *social* achievements are sustained by the recurrence of practices in society, rather than being an on-off condition of individuals within society. Hence, the problem with most measures of social progress focusing on outcomes is that, although they can tell us something about people's wellbeing or agency, for example, the resources that people possess or their internal abilities to make choices (e.g., income, ownership of resources, literacy levels, self-esteem), do not reveal anything about the vitality of practices, nor the extent to which those practices are spread across the population, nor indeed their permanence in the near and distant future.

In sum, a metric of the common good dynamic reveals the fact that although the person and her wellbeing are a central part of development, this is not the *only* concern, as it does not provide the necessary information to tackle the systemic problems we face in the modern world. Operationalising the common good as a nexus, therefore, makes us move beyond individualised, static measures to appraise the dynamic process through which we generate, share and enjoy common goods (including individual enjoyments).

This metric seeks to move beyond a simple description of the state of things (in terms of individual access to education, health, etc.), to allow us to say something about *how* these outcomes are generated. For example, obtaining a desirable outcome through a desirable process that respects human dignity and freedom, is not the same as doing so by means of an undesirable and disrespectful process. Simply stated, we could arrive at similar results in terms of individual levels of wellbeing through very different social dynamics. Therefore, we need to be able to discern between desirable and undesirable development processes, just as we need to know why desirable outcomes are not attained in certain contexts. We need to assess people's behaviours and the processes and social structures in which their actions take place, and understand how these—together—result (or not) in a common good dynamic, in the hope of a freer, more human, more just society. The challenge is to encapsulate this process in a metric. This is precisely the task that the IPBC has set itself, and the subject of our discussion in the following paragraphs.

As has been argued in the previous chapters, and as the metric will show, the questionnaire seeks to capture information through the expected social practices and expected patterns of human behaviours. This is motivated by the idea that every person is deeply embedded in a social context with specific rules that structure their actions and interactions. These socially recognised patterns of behaviour that coordinate our social interactions inform us of whether a particular social dynamic promoting the common good (or a common bad) is being reinforced or transformed. Indeed, when we think, act, and choose, we are not only deciding our way of life, we are also reproducing or confronting social structures that—partly—determine and validate our actions and the processes by which we do things in our common social life (see also Chapter 4). It is through our shared actions with others that we produce, procure, and experience common goods. As such, the metric aims to inform how institutions, behaviours, and groups interact with one another to constitute a nexus of the common good. This will be a necessary tool for informing policies through a more comprehensive view of social dynamics, with the aim of a flourishing community and flourishing individual lives.

The IPBC's team proposes to capture the collective dynamic processes and their interconnectivity through the matrix reproduced below (Figure 1). The model identifies the five normative dimensions deemed minimally necessary for the production of common goods at the local level. It also illustrates the fact that accounting for the presence or absence of each of these dimensions alone is insufficient; for the common good is the systemic outcome resulting from the quality, strength, and density of the interactions between these dimensions—rather than the simple results of their aggregation as separate phenomena. Therefore, the matrix envisions the nexus of the common good as the dynamic resulting from the combination of and interactions between each of these dimensions.[3]

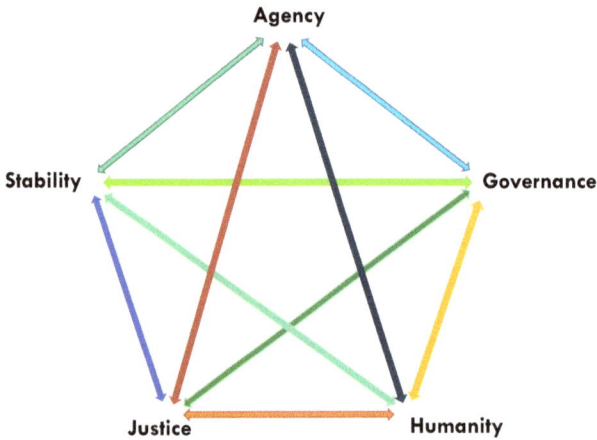

Figure 1. The common good pentagram. Source: Nebel and Medina (in this volume).

2. The Design of the Survey

Anyone who has designed a survey or collaborated in the process knows that it is no easy task. There are too many considerations to take into account in order to stay as close as possible to the original intention of the theoretical framework. Even apparently unproblematic features, such as the wording, response options, and order of questions in a survey can affect the quality of any metric (e.g., Kelley et al. 2003; Brown 2009). Therefore, our metric went through a careful design process, which we can map in relation to recommendations from the literature.

---

3   We provide a brief description of each of these dimensions below, along with the items proposed to measure each dimension.

The construction of the items was primarily the result of an iterative process undertaken in consultation with a number of experts to reflect on how we could operationalise the notion of the common good and to provide advice on the indicators produced. The IPBC, based at the Universidad Popular Autónoma de Puebla (UPAEP), together with other academic institutions, carried out a number of research seminars—Puebla (December 2017), Barcelona (23–24 May, 2018), Notre Dame (22–23 October, 2018) and Puebla (13–14 February, 2019 and 25–26 October, 2019). These meetings sought to bring together a diversity of perspectives, from academics, policy experts, members of civil society and local mayors who engaged in discussions about the conceptualisation and operationalisation of the common good at the municipal level.

In addition to these academic assemblies, individual meetings were held with key specialists such as Flavio Comim (May 2019), Clemens Sedmak (October 2019), and Gerardo Leyva (May 2019), as well as virtual discussions with a large group of academics that have made invaluable comments on the proposal. Finally, the formal production and refinement of the items was achieved through regular meetings of the core research team between March and October 2019. The purpose of these meetings was to integrate the knowledge produced in the aforementioned discussions, while considering the formal requirements of survey indicators and ensuring careful planning and piloting of the survey application.

One of the main difficulties in this process was that many of the items of the metric are completely new in the literature, having been developed for the novel approach presented in this book. For this reason, although the model and the dimensions of the model behind this survey are based on extensive theoretical research, the particular items of the survey were developed through an exploratory process that gave priority to capturing the particular aspects of collective life in Mexican municipalities.

In addition, according to the literature, the process of designing survey questions needs to include some reflection about the qualities that items must follow in order to be selected for the metric. A review of the literature quickly showed that there is a variety of qualities that indicators need to satisfy. In the literature, however, the use of different names to indicate similar qualities is common and, often, the qualities chosen in each study or project are dependent on the final purposes of the scale.[4] Hence, we would be interested in developing items that satisfy the following qualities, which include many of the suggestions of the literature, without losing sight of the particular interest of this metric, i.e., to measure common good dynamics at the municipal level and to diagnose 'development priorities at the local level' through self-reported surveys. For this purpose, the four qualities are: specific, relevant, meaningful, and intelligible.

Specific: Items should be specific in the sense that they capture only the component that they intend to measure, and not any other element within the metric. To achieve this, items should clearly describe and adequately reflect the phenomenon targeted with the measurement. To maximise specificity and the respondents' understanding, it is also important to be clear and unambiguous in the terms included in the item. This is essential to ensure that the data collected is consistent and comparable across municipalities and times. The complexity of the theoretical model behind this metric made achieving specificity particularly challenging. Since the purpose was that each item captured a particular aspect of the nexus of common good—and thus the linkages between dimensions and basic common goods (BCG)—it was sometimes difficult to highlight the aspect that predominated in a statement. To achieve this, the team focused specifically on simplifying the wordiness of the items and being clear about what the particular intersection of the model being measured was. Hence, the team tried (to the extent that this was possible) to avoid items that captured more than one aspect at a time, in order to reduce confusion in the respondent as to what the true purpose of the item was. Yet, this was not always possible and thus some items may not comply perfectly with this requirement. Nonetheless, this was a conscious decision by the team so as to ensure that the survey did not lose its complex systemic approach (which, in the end, is one of the main added values of the approach).

Relevant: To comply with this requirement, items should offer a valid measure of the desired underlying construct. There are a number

---

4   A commonly cited approach is SMART, a methodology used by a number of
     development agencies (e.g., the World Bank and the UN) and governments to
     construct indicators that measure social outcomes and programme results. SMART
     stands for indicators that are Specific, Measurable, Attributable, Realistic and Time-
     bound (for a broader list of qualities see e.g., Brown, 2009).

of ways to assess this, for example the underlying construct might be decided statistically through factor analysis or based on the theoretical framework employed. In this project, relevance was assessed based on the degree to which the item was able to capture the dimensions proposed by the theoretical framework of the common good. Hence, if the item needed to capture, for example, the intersection between a dimension and one of the basic common goods (see section 3 below for further explanation about this), this intersection was first defined conceptually and then the item was construed based on that conceptual definition. Take the intersection between 'Governance' and the basic common good of 'Rule of Law' as an example. To develop the item, this intersection was first defined as the extent to which the law served everyone in the locality, and then the item was construed under this definition. Therefore, the final form of the item was 'In this locality, the municipal administration is at the service of the majority' (see Table 4 below).[5]

Meaningfulness and *Intelligibility*: This means that items must be intelligible and easily interpreted by the average respondent. There are a number of ways to achieve this, and one of them is cognitive interviewing. Cognitive interviewing is a technique that has expanded over the last forty years. It is routinely used by national institutes and research centres and has been recommended as a useful tool for developing quantitative indicators of multidimensional models of wellbeing (Camfield 2016). This tool uses qualitative interviews to test surveys, and it permits observation of the cognitive process that respondents use to answer the survey and evaluation of the quality and effectiveness of the items as well as questionnaire design (see Willis 1999; Forsyth and Lessler 1991).

In the construction of this metric, cognitive interviews were carried out with six individuals who were chosen based on their socioeconomic characteristics that resembled the average population in municipalities in Mexico (e.g., primary or secondary schooling, low- or middle-income households, etc.). The interview process sought to prompt the individual to reveal information about their comprehension of the statement, their response processes and the recall strategies they use to gather the information needed to answer a statement. The core research

---

5   Tables 1 to 4 present the items and the conceptual definition or justification of the indicator for each dimension.

group discussed the findings from these interviews extensively in a series of meetings. These interviews allowed for the identification of those items that were difficult to comprehend or that entailed a complex cognitive evaluation from the respondent. They also helped us to improve response options and item wording, to get a sense of the length of the whole survey and to make a more thorough selection of the final list of items included in the scale.

Ultimately, the resulting version of the survey, including demographic questions, was finally tested in two pilot applications, one in the municipality of Ocotepec (June 2019) and one in the municipality of Atlixco (May 2019). In addition to testing the psychometric performance of the metric, these two pilot studies permitted us to test the entire fieldwork plan. This included, first, identifying the best mode of survey administration for these contexts (either paper-based or electronic surveys), and second, selecting the ideal training for the data collectors. The version of the survey that resulted from these pilot exercises was then used to collect data from stratified and representative samples in Atlixco and San Andres Cholula, results which are reported in the respective articles in a special issue of Rivista Internazionale di Scienze Sociali (RISS 2020).

Based on the previous process, the final items of the survey were designed as statements to ascertain the level of agreement-disagreement of respondents on each issue. A five-point Likert scale was used for response options: (1) strongly disagree, (2) somewhat disagree, (3) neither agree nor disagree, (4) somewhat agree, and (5) strongly agree. The limitations of agree-disagree response scales are well-known as they can be more prone to acquiescence response bias (Krosnick 2012). This bias reflects the common desire of people to be seen as affable and thus tend to agree with the statement regardless of its actual content (see also Nebel and Arbesu-Verduzco 2020 for other limitations). Despite these limitations, this response scale also has noteworthy advantages as it eases the administration of the survey by significantly reducing the duration and increasing comparability across dimensions and indicators to identify underlying constructs. Hence, in this metric this format allows us to reduce the time spent on data collection and other biases that arise as respondent tiredness increases.

The final survey is structured as follows. The first section contains fourteen demographic questions measuring well-known drivers of development and socioeconomic status including neighbourhood, sex, age, education, employment, and ethnicity; and five items that together form an indicator of socioeconomic status (number of bathrooms in the household, number of automobiles owned, access to Internet connection in the household, number of family-members employed, number of people sleeping in the kitchen). The second section of the survey covered the five dimensions of common good measured, through seventy-one items in total; sixteen items for Justice; eleven items for Stability; sixteen items for Governance; eleven items for Collective Agency Freedom; and seventeen items for Humanity. The final version of the survey, along with its content and justification, is presented below.

3. The Dimensions of a Common Good Metric and Its Indicators

The structure of the survey and its characteristics aim at reflecting the theoretical foundations of the metric explained above in two ways.

First, one of the purposes of the metric was to move beyond measuring the simple individual experience, in order to capture the collective processes that structure social life in a municipality. Hence, even though this metric lies at the level of individual perception, (most) items ask respondents to focus and reflect on social goods and the expected social practices of the people in their location. Arguably, these items capture collective (as opposed to individual) doings, in the sense that they refer to the collective action that constrains individual behaviour in the locality (see Chapter 1).[6] The items try to measure the local practices that give structure and dynamism to shared life. This includes aspects such as the way people reproduce, modify, and/or give life to the way institutions work in practice. For instance, the indicator "People take the initiative when they have to solve problems in my locality", in the

---

6   Some items are indeed directed towards the respondent's individual experience as opposed to one's perception about common social practices (e.g., "In my locality, the police protect *me*"). However, we think that in these few cases, the aggregation of responses provides a good proxy about the collective perception of, for example, the effectiveness of the police in the community.

dimension of Collective Agency Freedom, tries to measure the extent to which the population members value self-organising as a group in order to improve something in the locality. This indicator thus aims at capturing, through individual perception, a form of collective agency that goes beyond individuals, as it requires the common volition and shared action in the consecution of something valued collectively.

Second, the items aimed to assess the *structure* as well as the *dynamics* of the nexus of the common good in each of the dimensions (*Justice, Stability, Governance, Collective Agency Freedom*) aside from the dimension of 'Humanity' (which we briefly explain below). As mentioned above, the *structure* is measured by reference to the set of institutions that exist or the quality with which they are perceived to function in a municipality, such as laws, physical buildings, and existing legal support in relation to each of the dimensions. In turn, the *dynamics* of the nexus is gauged through dimensions and items assessing expected social practices in the common good of a municipality for each dimension (again, aside from the dimension of 'Humanity'). Moreover, the degree to which both of these aspects of a common good dynamic are present is, in turn, evaluated in relation to some 'basic social goods', which are considered as a 'minimal threshold [...] inherent to any nexus of the common good'. This minimum set of basic social goods that form part of any nexus of the common good in a municipality are five: Rule of Law, Work, Education, Culture, and Solidarity (see Chapter 1).

Put differently, each dimension has at least one item that measures the combination of the *structure* of the dimension with one or more of the basic common goods. For instance, for the dimension of Justice, the structural aspects refer to people's perception about equal opportunities in participating in the creation, valuation, and access to the benefits of the basic common good in question. In this sense, some items aim at capturing the relationship between the dimension (Justice) and the basic common good of 'Solidarity' in the structural aspect. One item, for example, tries to capture access to institutionalised forms of solidarity ("In my locality, there are places where people can go to get help (DIF, Red Cross, Church, etc.)").

Similarly, each dimension has at least one item that measures the combination of the *dynamic* aspect of the dimension with at least one (or more) of the basic common goods. For instance, for the same dimension

(Justice), the dynamic aspect refers to people's perception in terms of the way people treat each other. To capture the relationship between the dimension (Justice) and the basic common good of 'Solidarity' in its dynamic aspect, one item tries to capture the reciprocity among its members ("In my community, if someone is having a hard time, we organise to help him/her").

Moreover, to address the systemic emphasis of the nexus (even if partially), some items reflect the strength of the relationship between the dimensions and the way each dimension potentialises the other. For this, a number of individual items focus on capturing the two-way relationships between dimensions (e.g., Governance and Stability, Governance and Collective Agency, Governance and Justice, and vice versa). Take, for example, the two-way relationship between the dimensions of Governance and Stability. On the one hand, the governance of stability is measured by one item focused on the capacity of the municipal government to promote a dignified life for everyone in the locality in the long term ("The municipal government works to ensure that everyone can keep living in the community in the long term"). Reciprocally, on the other hand, another item tries to capture the stability of governance ("The programmes implemented by the municipal government have long-term benefits"). Hence, as mentioned before, this multidimensional metric is therefore composed of items that try to capture not only a dimension in isolation, but also the interconnection between dimensions and sub-domains (such as basic common goods).

Now, the Humanity dimension is treated differently (see Chapter 2). For this dimension, the metric drops the *structure/dynamic* division. This dimension is treated differently since it aims at capturing the extent to which the whole structure and dynamic of the nexus results in a socially virtuous way of living together in the community, which makes itself visible through a set of social virtues embodied in people's collective practices in a community. These social virtues include items related to freedom and responsibility, justice and solidarity, peace and concord, and others. Hence, items in the survey ask about the expected behaviour in the community in relation to these.

On the basis of the theoretical framework, the next subsections present the list of indicators of a metric of a common good dynamic.

Each subsection describes one of the dimensions. Each dimension, in turn, presents a table that includes information about: the list of items attributed to the dimension (column 1); and a justification/description of the purpose of each item (column 2).

I. Justice

The dimension of Justice (Table 1) captures the collective processes and institutions at play in a municipality through which people share common goods (in their valuation, production, and benefit). The dimension is measured in terms of equality of opportunity in the five basic common goods (i.e., structure), and in people's expectations about the common practices (i.e., how people treat each other) in the context of the other dimensions of the matrix (Governance, Stability, and Collective Agency Freedom).

Table 1. Justice: items and justification.

Item		Justification/Indicator of
J-I: Basic common good "Rule of Law"		
J1	In my locality, each person's rights are respected.	- The rule of law understood as a basic common good.
J2	In my locality, the police protect me.	- This question investigates the quality of the consensus that exists regarding the rule of law and the effective adherence to legality in the municipality.
J3	In my locality, public officials can be corrupted.	
J-II: Basic common good "Work"		
J4	In my locality, work is valued.	- Work understood as a basic common good, not only referring to the individual who works but to the whole community (both in the benefit created and their organization).
J5	Most people in my locality have work.	- This question assesses the quality of the consensus that exists regarding work as a basic common good. It investigates the possibility of access to work.

Item		Justification/Indicator of
J-III: Basic common good "Education"		
J6	In my community, we value that everyone can study.	- Education understood as a basic common good, that is, as an institution that introduces children to a shared knowledge and a common rationality.
J7	In my locality, anyone can study, should he/she choose to do so.	- This question investigates the value given to education in the community, as well as access to education.
J-IV: Basic common good "Culture"		
J8	My locality's cultural traditions are respected by the majority.	- Culture understood as a basic common good, that is, as a collective identity and a universe of shared meaning.
J9	In my locality, traditional sayings are understood by the majority.	- These questions investigate the value given to culture, as well as the access to the semantic meaning of this culture.
J-V: Basic common good "Solidarity"		
J10	In my community, if someone is having a hard time, we organise to help him/her.	- Solidarity understood as a basic common good, that is, as the needed unity and reciprocity among members of a community.
J11	In my locality, there are places where people can go to get help (e.g., DIF, Red Cross, churches).	- These questions assess the value given to solidarity and the access to institutional forms of solidarity in the municipality.
J-VI Justice and Governance		
J12	In my locality, people are not forced to leave the municipality so as to secure their livelihood.	- This question investigates the extension and distribution of the benefits of government action in the municipality.
J13	Municipal government programmes benefit the majority of the population.	
J-VII Justice and Agency		
J14	In my locality, there are social groups that fail to gain access to power.	- These questions investigate the existence and distribution of a collective agency.

Item	Justification/Indicator of
J15	In my locality, some groups have all the power.	- Measure the way in which power is distributed in the municipality.

J-VIII: Systematic exclusion

J16	In my daily activities in the locality, I am frequently humiliated.	- This question investigates the presence of culturally accepted forms of exclusion and, therefore, invisible to the majority of the population.

Source: IPBC's team elaboration.

II. Stability

The dimension of Stability (Table 2) captures the permanence and transmission of the nexus of the common good. The *structure* of the nexus is measured through items that focus on the extent to which this structure, manifest in the five basic common goods, allows the transmission of humanity in the nexus. The *dynamics* of the nexus, in turn, captures the permanence of the three key elements of the dynamics of common good: Governance, Justice and Collective Agency Freedom. This permanence is measured through (a) the quality of the duration of local institutions (to all, to us, to the majority, or to some); and (b) the time projection of institutions (e.g., one, five, or ten years).

Table 2. Stability: items and justification.

Item	Justification/Indicator of

S-I: Dignity and BCG "Rule of Law"

S17	In my locality, when a thief is caught, we hand him/her over to the police.	- The instance of transmission is the judge which establishes rights and restores the dignity of the victim.
S18	In my locality, when someone is arrested, the police treats him/her with respect.	- The item measures the respect to the rule of law, correspondingly, the usurpation of the role of the judge when the population punishes thieves. - The item measures the capacity of the legal process to respect the dignity of the person arrested.

Item	Justification/Indicator of
S-II: Dignity and BCG "Work"	
S19 — I am proud to talk about my work with others.	- The dignity of work resides in the possibility I have of recognising myself in it, that is, recognising myself as a human in what I do. - The instance of transmission is the way in which the value of work is shared with others.
S-III: Dignity and BCG "Education"	
S20 — Attending school is important to be able to participate in the locality's social life.	- The transmission of dignity in school occurs as the acquisition of the knowledge that is socially valued by the community. - The question measures the importance of the acquisition of basic knowledge to be integrated/respected in the community.
S-IV: Dignity and BCG "Culture"	
S21 — I am proud of my community's culture.	- Culture transfers dignity to the extent that it gives access to a collective memory of our humanity. Culture constitutes a universe of meanings from which individuals construct their own identities.
S22 — The younger generations participate in my locality's traditions, customs, and festivities.	- The question assesses the population's rooting in a culture.
S-V: Dignity and BCG "Solidarity"	
S23 — When a family member or myself seeks help in a local institution, we are treated with respect.	- Solidarity in the form of the institutional support that exists in the municipality. Solidarity transmits dignity to the extent that it prevents the exclusion of vulnerable groups in the community. - The question assesses the way in which vulnerable people are treated in the municipality.
S-VI: Stability and governance	
S24 — The programmes implemented by the municipal government have long-term benefits.	- The question investigates the quality of social time created by the political governance of the municipality in terms of extension. - Measures the time extension of government action.

Item	Justification/Indicator of
S-VII: Stability and justice	
S25 If I buy land or a house, I am confident that the government will respect my property title in the future.	- The questions examine the quality of the social time created by the legal system in terms of extension.
S-VIII: Stability and agency	
S26 Most associations in my locality have existed for a long time (for example: "mayordomía", "jornales", parent association, "ejido" groups).	- The questions investigate the quality of the social time that the population can count on to project collective actions, both in extension and in inclusion.
S27 The members of associations meet frequently (for instance: "mayordomía", "jornales", parent association, "ejido" groups, etc.).	

Source: IPBC's team elaboration.

III. Governance

The dimension of Governance (Table 3) captures whether the basic common goods in a municipality are governed as common goods or not. Put differently, the focus is on whether the basic common goods are placed at the service of the community as a whole (for the good of all and everyone) and not co-opted by certain groups. The structure of the nexus is measured through items that assess the quality of the management, organisation and administration of the common goods by the local authorities and civil society. The dynamics of the nexus is captured through items that evaluate the capacity of political governance to serve the common good. Four areas of quality are studied: authority of the governance, efficiency of the governance, conflict resolution and generation of consensus.

Table 3. Governance: items and justification.

Item	Justification/Indicator of
G-I: Governance of the BCG "Rule of law"	
G28	In this locality the municipal administration is at the service of the majority.	- The governance of the rule of law as a basic common good is verified by the effective guarantee of the legality for all. - The question revolves around: who does the law serve?
G-II: Governance of the BCG "Work"	
G29	In my locality, most people pay taxes.	- The governance of work as a basic common good is verified if individual work also contributes to the wellbeing of the entire community.
G30	The government strives to improve workers' conditions.	- The question revolves around the effectiveness of tax redistribution in the community.
G-III: Governance of the BCG "Culture"	
G31	The government of my locality actively promotes the creation and maintenance of public spaces such as parks, squares and streets.	- Culture characterises, among other things, the way in which we live together. The construction of public space as a space of common use reveals the management of culture as a common good.
G32	In my locality, most people take care of public spaces such as parks, squares, and streets.	- The questions investigate the construction and care of public space in a locality.
G-IV: Governance of the BCG "Solidarity"	
G33	The government provides the conditions for effective solidarity to exist among the citizens of my locality.	- Solidarity in the sense of the forms of mutual help that exist in the community. - Measures the way in which mutual help can extend to all members of the community.
G-V: Governance of the BCG "Education"	
G34	In my locality, the government works so that everyone can finish high school.	- Organisation of education as a common good. - Measures the political will so that all complete compulsory secondary schooling.

Item	Justification/Indicator of
G-VI: Authority of the political governance 1	
G35	In my locality, the government's authority is respected.	- Authority in the sense of immediate and obvious recognition of the power of the government (recognition as something independent from legitimacy). - Measures the degree of authority that the population recognises in the municipal government.
G-VII: Authority of the political governance 2	
G36	The municipal government works for the good of the majority.	- Authority in the sense of the municipal government's efforts to work for the common good of the entire population. - This question investigates if the authority of the government is linked to its search for the common good.
GP-VIII: Governance and efficiency	
G37	When someone takes office, he/she complies with the proposed government plan.	- Efficiency in the sense that the municipal government really reaches the proposed projects. - The question measures the degree of perception by the population of the efficiency of municipal projects.
G-IX: Governance and conflict resolution	
G38	The government has the will to solve conflicts between different local groups.	- Conflict resolution indicates the government's ability to mediate and resolve tensions among the various groups in the municipality, ensuring a minimum cohesion between different social actors (cohesion of the nexus). - The question measures the ability of the government to maintain cohesion between social actors.
G-X: Governance and consensus building	
G39	The municipal government is able to reach agreements that benefit the entire community.	- The creation of consensus indicates the ability of the government to create consensus in view of the common good. - Measures the government's capacity to increase the cohesion of the nexus of common good.

Item	Justification/Indicator of
G-XI: Governance of justice	
G40 The municipal government seeks to ensure that everyone has the same opportunities in the community.	- Active search of justice as a goal of the municipal government. - The question captures the effort placed by the municipal government on promoting equal opportunities.
G-XII: Governance of the stability	
G41 The municipal government works to ensure that everyone can keep living in the community in the long term.	- The active search for stability as a goal of the municipal government. - The question measures the effort placed by the municipal government on the promotion of a dignified life for everyone in the long term.
G-XIII: Governance of agency	
G42 The government of my municipality listens to us.	- Organisation of the political agency as a common good.
G43 I can participate in the decisions of my municipality.	- The question revolves around the way in which effective participation of the population is promoted by the governance.

Source: IPBC's team elaboration.

IV. Collective Agency Freedom

The dimension of Collective Agency Freedom (Table 4) answers the question: 'what determines the quality of collective agency in a municipality?' It measures, on the one hand, the dynamic aspect of collective agency, that is, the capacity of the local population to act together in view of their future. This capacity to self-organise can be captured through (a) the value given to the capacity to self-organise in the community; (b) the legal possibility to self-organise; (c) the capacity to generate consensus around a common goal; (d) the capacity to self-govern in the consecution of a common goal; and (e) the capacity to generate synergy with other organisations to reach a common goal.

On the other hand, it measures the organisation/structure of collective agency, which can be observed through the existence of organisations that give structure to community life and its quality.

Hence, the items related to this aspect measure the capacity of the existing collective agency in the municipality to generate dynamics that promote the common good. This can be inferred through three criteria: (a) the freedom of agency in these organisations; (b) the possibility of universalising the shared benefits generated by these organisations; (c) the quality of the existing relations between organisations.

Table 4. Collective Agency Freedom: items and justification.

Item		Justification/Indicator of
A-I. Agency and the value of self-organization		
A44	In my locality, it is valued that people organise themselves to solve their problems.	- Measures the value given to the act of self-organising in the community.
A45	People take the initiative when they have to solve problems in my locality.	
A-II. Agency and the capacity of consensus		
A46	The neighbours can reach agreements when we have a common problem.	- Measures the capacity to generate consensus around a common goal.
A47	The neighbours know how to organise ourselves to solve a common problem.	
A-III. Agency and the legality of self-organization		
A48	The laws often prevent us from solving local problems.	- Measures the legal possibility of self-organising.
A-IV. Agency and efficient governance		
A49	Most of the time, the neighbours achieve the goals we set for ourselves.	- Measures the capacity to self-organise for the consecution of a common goal.
A-V. Agency and the creation of synergy		
A50	When we face difficult problems, in my community we can get support from other institutions.	- Measures the capacity to generate synergies with other organisations to reach a common goal.

Item	Justification/Indicator of
A-VI. Quality of Agency: Freedom	
A51 I can express my opinions in the groups wherein I participate.	- Measures what degree of personal freedom exists in the common commitment.
A-VII. Quality of Agency: Universalization	
A52 Most of the groups in my community contribute to the common good.	- Measures the possibility of extending to all, the common benefits generated by organisations.
A-VIII. Quality of Agency: Relationships	
A53 Cooperation between the groups in my locality is possible.	- Measures the existing degree of synergy between organisations
A54 The groups in my locality cooperate with the government.	

Source: IPBC's team elaboration.

V. Humanity

The dimension of Humanity (Table 5) refers to the social behaviours and expectations that emerge in the population as a result of the common good dynamics. That is, what are the social expectations in the community about the behaviours that express humanity. These can be assessed through the expectations of standard behaviour in the community, including (a) freedom and responsibility; (b) justice and solidarity; (c) peace and concord; (d) prudence and magnanimity; (e) resilience and courage; (f) rationality and wisdom.

Table 5. Humanity: items and justification.

Item	Justification/Indicator of
H-I. Freedom and responsibility	
H55 The people in my locality demand that I am responsible for my actions.	- Freedom is verified by the collective expectation of responsibility towards oneself, towards their actions and towards others.

| H56 | The people in my locality get upset if I do not keep my promises. | - The question measures the level of standard behaviour required in terms of freedom and responsibility in the municipality. |

H-II. Justice and solidarity

H57	People in my locality get upset if I fail to treat others kindly and respectfully.	- Justice is verified by the collective expectation of honest and just behaviour by others.
H58	People in my locality get upset if I do not do the right thing.	
H59	In my locality, those who do not have solidary with others are frowned upon.	- Solidarity is verified in the collective expectation of solidarity with others.
H60	In my locality, people are honest.	

H-III. Peace and concord

| H61 | In my locality, anyone can go out by day without fear. | - Peace is verified in the absence of violence and reciprocal trust. |
| H62 | People in my locality usually solve conflicts peacefully. | - Concord is verified in the search for harmony and comprehension.
- The questions measure the level of standard behaviour required around peace and concord in the municipality. |

H-IV Prudence and magnanimity

H63	People in my locality get angry if I do not think before acting.	- Prudence is verified in the ability to prevent, as well as in the ability to distinguish and do good.
H64	People in my locality do not tolerate when someone is mean to others.	- Magnanimity is verified in the capacity to constantly expect the best from people.
H65	People in my locality expect the best from me.	- The questions measure the level of standard behaviour required in terms of prudence and magnanimity in the municipality.

H-V. Resilience and courage	
H66	People in my locality expect me to be strong when I suffer some misfortune.	- Resilience is verified as the capacity to withstand the shocks of life.
H67	People in my locality expect others to prove their courage in life.	- Courage is verified as the ability to stand firm in one's duty even in the face of danger. - The questions measure the level of standard behaviour required in terms of resilience and courage in the municipality.

H-VI. Rationality and wisdom		
H68	Most people in my locality express their opinions clearly.	- Rationality is verified in the capacity to explain actions and decisions and the capacity to discuss rationally.
H69	When talking about important topics, the people in my locality ask that it be done in a serious and objective way.	- Wisdom is verified in the capacity to deploy an accurate and intelligent practical judgement.
H70	People in my locality expect me not to make the same mistake twice.	- The questions measure the level of standard behaviour required in terms of rationality and wisdom in the municipality.
H71	People in my locality know how to reconcile after a conflict.	

Source: IPBC's team elaboration.

4. Discussion and Future Improvements

In this section, we would like to offer some general reflections/questions about the metric of the practical common good approach presented above. To begin with, we would like to point out that in a world in which the development of new indicators of social progress/development abounds, this metric has the potential to be much more than a simple alternative to other indicators on progress, wellbeing, or development. In fact, rather than being an alternative, it seems to us that it paves the way towards a new list of indicators interested in processes, actions, and complexity that can complement existing outcome-oriented measures. By shifting the focus of analysis to indicators aiming at capturing institutionalised practices of the local population (in structure and actions), the metric sheds light on the complex social settings within which individuals act, think and choose, and their relevance for understanding the outcomes that societies produce.

People's positive and engaging reactions to the survey in initial pilot applications, as well as their applications to assess different social situations, attest to the significance of this information for people's lives and their localities. Consequently, data produced by this metric will be crucial for informing decision-makers about local social processes, institutions, and their interaction that promote or hinder a common good dynamic. This information cannot but be fundamental for identifying key areas of opportunity and strengths present in the local community (e.g., quality of social ties, organisation skills, knowledge of existing social institutions, etc.) from which to build up a plan of action that promotes a community-driven development towards the common good of living well together.

Despite these welcomed points however, there are some questions, which, although we do not aim to respond to them here, need to be asked and reflected upon to clarify and improve the metric. First, some general questions may arise in relation to the theoretical model and its dimensions. Even if there is a theoretical framework underlying the metric, the criteria for selecting the dimensions are still insufficiently clear. For instance, while we do not dispute the selection of the five normative dimensions already included in the model, one may wonder why other dimensions (or other basic common goods) are not included. One could think that a comprehensive notion of the common good would include, or discuss more explicitly, social concerns such as peace, security, the environment, and the economy, among others. Of course, we grant that the model may indirectly touch upon these concerns and that any metric needs to be as simple and parsimonious as possible, yet an explicit reference to the reasons behind the components of the metric would be welcome.

The second concern is related to the simplicity of the items of the survey. It is desirable that a questionnaire be sure that its items are easy to interpret and clearly understood by the respondent. Although the presented survey already went through a long process of refinement, the survey remains complex in at least five areas. One is the inherent complexity of the statements themselves. The survey asks respondents to think beyond their individual experience in order to reflect on their social world and its common practices (e.g., "In my locality, it is valued that people organise themselves to solve their problems"). While common practices may be identifiable to people after reflection, the dynamics of expected patterns of social behaviour and their influence in the social world tends to be unconscious and difficult to pin down explicitly. A subsequent issue that adds to the inherent complexity of the items is the composition of the statements. Several statements in the metric refer to multiple phenomena at the same time. For instance, the statement "The municipal government is able to reach agreements that benefit the entire community" may direct attention towards both the ability of the government to generate consensus *or* to the resulting benefits of the agreement, *or* to the combination of the two ideas (which is the intention of the question).

This leads to difficulties in interpreting responses. This can be problematic, on the one hand, for composite statements like the latter (is the data shedding light on the ability of the government to generate agreements? Or is it about the benefits in society? Or is it about the ability to generate consensus that at the same time results in a benefit for the entire community?). On the other hand, because even if it is not a composite statement, we do not really know what is behind participants' responses. This is more salient if we want to compare responses between groups. For instance, if we find that women's answers to the statement "Most people in my locality have work" were lower than that of men, we do not know what these lower responses indicate. Are women responding based on their individual experience (i.e., women have less access to work)? Or are they responding based on what women perceive around their community (this is the original intention of the item)? If the latter, do they perceive that there is less work available for women in particular, or in general for the population as a whole (and why might this be different from the men's perception?) In other words, the challenge is that we can only know women perceive this feature differently, but we cannot be sure about what, from their perspective, the exact problem is regarding access to employment in the municipality.[7]

---

7   Note that these concerns may also complicate the statistical analysis of the results.

Second, a related, but somehow distinct concern in relation to the items of the metric is the fact that statements aim at measuring people's perceptions about social phenomena in their localities that contain normative inclinations. In other words, the items are associated with desired common behaviours and processes within the locality, and how individuals perceive these. Although researchers have been testing self-reported items since the 1960s (see Zapf 2000), they have been contested for their potential to be influenced by social desirability biases and adaptive preferences (e.g., Kahneman and Tverskey 1984; Frederic and Loweeinstein 1999; Gasper 2007). Social desirability bias occurs when people answer survey questions based on what they think is expected from them by the researcher or what they themselves think is the ideal behaviour in their locality, instead of what actually occurs in the locality. In turn, adaptive preferences reflect the possibility of people adapting to positive or negative life circumstances. Hence, social desirability and adaptive preferences could result in data that portray the locality more positively than it is actually experienced. This can be especially problematic if the items originally contain normative values of what the desired practice of common good in the locality for a specific dimension is.[8]

Third, when metrics are used as a 'diagnostic tool' to inform social actors about social priorities in the locality, one may also worry about the malleability and the temporality of the phenomena being measured. What we are questioning here is the possibility of changing common social practices, which are established patterns of behaviour embedded in the culture of a certain population, through social policies; and, we could also ask about the timeframe that this change may take. These questions are relevant because they raise the query about the correct time for applying a follow-up survey to measure possible changes in the common dynamic of a municipality, for example. Similarly, when designing metrics to be of use for policy actors, we also need to think about indicators that can shed light on potential courses of action for policy-making and thus on indicators that capture social problems that can be modified by policy interventions.

---

8   For instance, in the application of the survey in two different municipalities (Atlixco and San Andrés Cholula), participants tended to respond more positively to statements related to people's behaviour than to those related to the municipal government's actions (see papers in RISS special issue 2020).

Fourth, this type of comprehensive metrics also makes explicit the tradeoffs associated with the choice of statistical tools available to construct the model, such as Factor Analysis, Principal Component Analysis or Structural Equation Modelling. Statistics such as the latter rely on the amount of variance shared by the items in order to find commonalities between them. Hence, the fact that some of the items of this metric capture different dimensions simultaneously, due to the interconnections of the model, makes it more difficult for these statistical tools to discriminate between dimensions, thereby lowering the quality of the metric based on the reliability analysis offered by these tools. In other words, it is difficult to reconcile the complexity of the metric with the assumptions and requirements behind the statistical tests.[9] However, sometimes these tradeoffs need to be carefully considered and evaluated by researchers when they are interested in constructing more comprehensive, interdependent, and multidimensional measures that capture the complexity of human existence.

A fifth, and last, reflection relates to the difficulty of applying this kind of metric to very diverse audiences. The items of the metric presented here are complex and require a fair amount of cognitive reflection to be answered. Some of them might also require some degree of knowledge and experience about how the local government works, how neighbours interact and act together, and the values of the locality as a whole. Additionally, some items require basic knowledge of the abstract lexicon such as 'laws', 'social programmes', and 'property title'. This could increase the difficulty of applying this survey to individuals who have not participated in different public spheres in their localities, nor kept a household, or those who do not have a certain level of education. This is particularly relevant if the metric will be applied in diverse populations, including those municipalities with indigenous and non-indigenous backgrounds. Translation issues are also relevant here, since the interpretation of the meaning of survey items might vary for people whose mother tongue is not Spanish.[10] Hence, issues of meaning, interpretation and translation need to be taken into account when comparing results across municipalities.

---

9   See e.g., Ramírez (2021) for a similar experience with a multidimensional model of psychosocial wellbeing and a discussion on this.

10   See the Appendix for the Spanish version of the survey.

To close the section, we would like to point out that while these concerns may not be trivial and perhaps more reflection about them is required, we also recognise that the extent to which these previous points are relevant to the metric is a matter of further empirical investigation.

Conclusion

In this chapter, we have presented the rationale, the process, and the structure of the metric developed by the IPBC of Puebla, México to measure the common good dynamics of a municipality. The elaboration of the indicators was the result of a research project that received feedback from prestigious experts, local specialists, NGOs, public officials, and researchers. It was carefully designed to reflect the theoretical framework behind and the common requirements of survey indicators, but also to obtain and include the feedback of potential respondents of the survey through cognitive interviewing. Much reflection has gone into the construction of this metric. We have recognised the many trade-offs involved in the process, and made decisions to the best of our abilities. With this chapter, we wish to make these decisions and their potential implications for the final form of the survey and the resulting data explicit.

We also argued that the new information that this measure of common good will offer to municipal governments, NGOs, researchers, and decision-makers can facilitate the adoption of better-informed policies that take into account the dynamics and structure of the common good produced by the citizens of a municipality. In fact, the initial process of constructing the indicator has already had concrete effects, since it has already encouraged the collaboration of municipal governments in recollecting the data and compromising in order to take the results into account in their municipal development plans.

Overall, we can say that the theoretical framework and the metric presented in this book already provide valuable contributions for the purpose of bettering the measurement of development processes at the local level and the information that governments use to make better policy decisions. However, this is for researchers, governments, policy actors, and, more importantly, for people themselves to decide. Hence, the main intention of this chapter is to promote and encourage more and better discussion in this direction.

References

Alkire, S. 2015. The capability approach and well-being measurement for public policy, *OPHI Working Paper*, No. 94. https://doi.org/10.1093/oxfordhb/9780199325818.013.18

Brown D. 2009. Good practice guidelines for indicator development and reporting. A paper at the Third World Forum on *Statistics, Knowledge and Policy, Charting Progress, Building Visions, Improving Life*, 27–30 October, 2009, Busan, Korea.

Camfield, L. 2016. "Enquiries into Wellbeing: How Could Qualitative Data Be Used to Improve the Reliability of Survey Data?", in White, S. C. and Blackmore, C. (eds), *Cultures of Wellbeing*, London: Palgrave Macmillan, 47–65. https://doi.org/10.1057/9781137536457_2

Deneulin, S. and Shahani, L. 2009. *An Introduction to the Human Development and Capability Approach Freedom and Agency*, London; Sterling; Ottawa: Earthscan. https://doi.org/10.4324/9781849770026

Forsyth, B. H. and Lessler, J. T. 1991. "Cognitive laboratory methods: a taxonomy", in Biemer, P. et al. (eds), *Measurement Errors in Surveys*, New York: Wiley, 393–418.

Frederick, S., Loewenstein, G. 1999. "Hedonic adaptation", in Kahneman, D. (ed.), *Well-Being: Foundations of Hedonic Psychology*, New York, Russell Sage Foundation.

Gasper, D. 2007. Uncounted or illusory blessings? Competing responses to the Easterlin, Easterbrook and Schwartz paradoxes of well-being, *Journal of International Development 19/4*, 473–492, https://doi.org/10.1002/jid.1383.

Kahneman, D. and Tversky, A. 1984. Choices, values and frames, *American Psycological Association, Inc. 39/4*, 341–350.

Kelley, K., Clark, B., Brown, V., and Sitzia, J. 2003. Good practice in the conduct and reporting of survey research, *International Journal of Quality in Health Care 15/3*, 261–266. https://doi.org/10.1093/intqhc/mzg031

Krosnick J. and Fabrigar, L. 2012. "Designing rating scales for effective measurement in surveys", in Lars Lynberg et al. (eds), *Survey Measurement and Process Quality*, Wiley Series in Probability and Statistics, New York, Wiley, 141–164 https://doi.org/10.1002/9781118490013.ch6.

Nebel, M. and Arbesu-Verduzco, I. 2020. "A metric of common goods dynamics", in Beretta, S. and Nebel, M. (eds), *A Special Issue on Common Good*, Rivista Internazionale di Scienze Sociali, 4, 383–406.

Ramírez, V. 2021. *Relational Well-being in Policy Implementation in Mexico: The Oportunidades-Propsera Conditional Cash Transfer*, New York: Palgrave Macmillan. https://doi.org/10.1007/978-3-030-74705-3

Rivista Internazionale di Scienze Sociali. 2020. *A Special Issue on Common Good*, Beretta, S. and Nebel, M. (eds). https://riss.vitaepensiero.it/scheda-fascicolo_contenitore_digital/simona-beretta-mathias-nebel/rivista-internazionale-di-scienze-sociali-2020-4-a-special-issue-on-common-good-000518_2020_0004-370666.html

Stiglitz J. E., Sen A., and Fitoussi, J.-P. 2009. *Report by the Commission on the Measurement of Economic Performance and Social Progress.* Institut national de la statistique et des études économiques (INSEE), Paris. https://ec.europa.eu/eurostat/documents/8131721/8131772/Stiglitz-Sen-Fitoussi-Commission-report.pdf

Székely, M. 2006. *Números que mueven al mundo. La medición de la pobreza en México*, México: Miguel Ángel Porrúa.

Willis, G. B. 1999. *Cognitive Interviewing: A 'How To' Guide. Reducing Survey Error through Research on the Cognitive and Decision Processes in Surveys*, short course presented at the 1999 Meeting of the American Statistical Association. https://www.hkr.se/contentassets/9ed7b1b3997e4bf4baa8d4eceed5cd87/gordonwillis.pdf

Zapf, W. 2000. Social reporting in the 1970s and in the 1990s, *Social Indicators Research*, 51, 1–15. https://doi.org/10.1023/A:1006997731263

Appendix

Instrument's questions to measure the common good dynamics in original language (Spanish).

	Ítem
J1	En mi localidad, los derechos de cada persona son respetados.
J2	En mi localidad, la policía sirve para protegerme.
J3	En mi localidad, se pueden corromper los funcionarios públicos.
J4	En mi localidad, se valora trabajar.
J5	En mi localidad, la mayoría tiene trabajo.
J6	En mi comunidad es importante que todos tengan la posibilidad de estudiar.
J7	En mi localidad, cualquier persona puede estudiar si así lo decide.
J8	Las tradiciones culturales de mi localidad son respetadas por la mayoría.
J9	En mi localidad, los refranes los entienden la mayoría.
J10	En mi comunidad, si alguien la pasa mal nos organizamos para ayudarle.
J11	En mi localidad, hay lugares donde la gente puede acudir para recibir ayuda (DIF, Cruz Roja, Iglesias, etc.).

Ítem

J12   En mi localidad la gente no necesita dejar el municipio para poder vivir.

J13   Los programas de los gobiernos municipales benefician a la mayoría de la población.

J14   En mi localidad hay grupos sociales que no tienen acceso al poder.

J15   En mi localidad hay algunos grupos sociales que tienen todo el poder.

J16   En mis actividades diarias en la localidad, soy frecuentemente humillado.

S17   En mi localidad cuando se atrapa a un ladrón lo entregamos a la policía.

S18   En mi localidad cuando alguien es arrestado, la policía lo trata con respeto.

S19   Me enorgullece hablar de mi trabajo con otros.

S20   Es importante haber ido a la escuela para participar en la vida social de la localidad.

S21   Me siento orgulloso de la cultura de mi comunidad.

S22   Las generaciones más jóvenes participan en las fiestas, costumbres y tradiciones de mi localidad.

S23   Cuando yo o algún familiar buscamos ayuda de una institución en la localidad, somos tratados con respeto.

S24   Los programas del gobierno municipal tienen beneficios de largo plazo.

S25   Si compro un terreno o una casa, tengo confianza que el gobierno respetará mi título de propiedad a futuro.

S26   La mayoría de las asociaciones de mi localidad existen desde mucho tiempo (Por ejemplo: mayordomía, jornales, sociedad de padres de familia, grupos ejidales, etc.).

S27   Los miembros de las asociaciones suelen reunirse con frecuencia. (Por ejemplo: mayordomía, jornales, sociedad de padres de familia, grupos ejidales, etc.).

G28   Considero que en esta localidad la administración municipal está al servicio de la mayoría.

G29   En la localidad, la mayoría paga impuestos.

G30   El gobierno se esfuerza para que los trabajadores tengan mejores condiciones laborales.

G31   El gobierno de mi localidad promueve de manera activa el mantenimiento y la creación de espacios públicos como parques, plazas y calles.

G32   En mi localidad la mayoría cuida los espacios públicos como parques, plazas y calles.

G33   El gobierno crea las condiciones necesarias para que exista una solidaridad efectiva entre los ciudadanos de mi localidad.

Ítem

G34   En mi localidad el gobierno hace el esfuerzo para que todos terminen la preparatoria o bachillerato.

G35   En esta localidad se respeta la autoridad del gobierno municipal.

G36   El gobierno municipal trabaja para el bien de la mayoría.

G38   El gobierno tiene la voluntad de resolver conflictos entre diferentes grupos de la localidad.

G39   El gobierno municipal es capaz de generar acuerdos que benefician a toda la comunidad.

G40   El gobierno municipal busca que todos tengan las mismas oportunidades en la comunidad.

G41   El gobierno crea las condiciones necesarias para que nadie tenga que dejar la localidad para vivir.

G42   El gobierno de mi municipio nos escucha.

G43   Puedo participar en las decisiones de mi municipio.

A44   En mi localidad, se valora que la gente se organice para resolver sus problemas.

A45   La gente toma iniciativas cuando se tienen que resolver problemas de mi localidad.

A46   Los vecinos logramos ponernos de acuerdo cuando tenemos un problema común.

A47   Los vecinos sabemos organizarnos para solucionar un problema común.

A48   Las leyes nos impiden frecuentemente dar solución a problemas locales.

A49   La mayoría de las veces, los vecinos logramos los objetivos que nos proponemos.

A50   Cuando nos enfrentamos a problemas difíciles, en mi comunidad podemos conseguir el apoyo de otras instituciones.

A51   Puedo expresar mis opiniones en los grupos en los que participo.

A52   La mayoría de los grupos de mi comunidad contribuyen al bien común.

A53   Es posible la cooperación entre los grupos de mi localidad.

A54   Los grupos de mi localidad cooperan con el gobierno.

H55   La gente de mi localidad exige que me haga responsable de mis acciones.

H56   La gente de mi localidad se molesta si no cumplo con mis promesas.

H57   La gente de mi localidad se molesta si no trato a los demás de manera cordial y respetuosa.

H58   La gente de mi localidad se molesta si no hago lo correcto.

H59   En mi localidad, se ve mal a la gente que no es solidaria con los demás.

H60   En mi localidad, la gente es honesta.

Ítem

H61   En mi localidad, cualquier persona puede salir de día sin temor.

H62   La gente de mi localidad acostumbra a resolver conflictos de manera pacífica.

H63   La gente de mi localidad se enoja si no pienso antes de actuar.

H64   La gente de mi localidad no tolera que una persona sea mala onda con los demás.

H65   La gente de mi localidad espera lo mejor de mí.

H66   La gente de mi localidad espera que yo sea fuerte cuando sufro alguna desgracia.

H67   La gente de mi localidad esperan de los demás que hagan prueba de valor en la vida.

H68   La mayoría de las personas de mi localidad, expresa sus opiniones de manera clara.

H69   Cuando se habla de temas importantes, la gente de mi localidad pide que se haga de manera seria y objetiva.

H70   La gente de mi localidad espera que yo no cometa dos veces el mismo error.

H71   La gente de mi localidad sabe reconciliarse después de un conflicto.

PART II
DISCUSSING THE NORMATIVE
ELEMENTS OF COMMON GOOD
DYNAMICS

Introduction to Part II

Aim of the Part II

This second part aims at discussing a matrix of common good dynamics. By 'matrix', we understand a model capturing the dynamic equilibrium of systems of common goods. The first part proposed five key drivers as the *necessary conditions* required to trigger common good dynamics in a social system, namely *Agency freedom*, *Humanity*, *Justice*, *Governance*, and *Stability*. In our model, each key driver plays a specific role and answer a specific question: how much freedom does the social system allow to its participants? How human are standard expectations of behaviours created by this institutional framework? Does a basic set of common goods exist? Are they fairly distributed to all members of the social system, and stable over time? And finally: are the basic common goods governed as commons in this social system?

Such a model is quite unheard of in development literature. So, each of these elements was brought into an interdisciplinary discussion with the existing body of research. We asked several leading experts to review how agency freedom, humanity, justice, governance, and stability may indeed trigger common good dynamics. For this purpose, these scholars engaged with and discussed each of these elements on the basis of a discussion paper which included the first version of the matrix and an initial metric of common good dynamics (the revised version of which is now Chapter 2). This second part mirrors the debate we had while discussing the matrix during our research seminars. It will help readers to situate our approach within the existing literature on development. These chapters show both the difficulties and the fascinating aspects brought about by a common good perspective on development processes. They mark the start of a necessary conversation.

© 2022 Book Editors, CC BY-NC-ND 4.0   https://doi.org/10.11647/OBP.0290.05

To Whom Is it of Interest?

This second part will be of interest to academics and postgraduate students who follow the ongoing debates on development. It will show them how a perspective based on commons sheds light on the importance of social processes to development practice. In the capability approach community, for example, an increasing number of authors calls for the recognition of 'social or collective capabilities', which in turns requires an understanding of collective agency freedom itself, not as a given, but as a social process. To take another example, Ostrom's late understanding of polycentric governance of commons naturally leads to the recognition that governance itself may be a common.

Why Does it Matter?

The shortcomings of political and economic liberalism, the polarisation of societies, and the resurgence of populisms and ideologies around the globe require us to explore new ways to understand our world. While the twentieth century can be seen as defending the value and rights of individuals, the great question of the twenty-first century may well be the following: how can we live together, more specifically, how can we live together as human beings? The urbanism of our cities brutally shows how we have shifted toward an ever more individualistic and economic understanding of our coexistence. Modern cities structure social life around malls and supermarkets (consuming together) and sport and leisure facilities (having fun together). This is in strong contrast to the political and religious centres of social life of the previous centuries (to decide and act together; to pray together). A common good approach shows the need to think about the flimsy definition of society defended by political liberalism. What are the social goods we all value? How do we organise to produce and share them?

4. Collective Agency Freedom as the Engine of a Common Good Dynamic

A Conceptual Proposal for Measurement

Oscar Garza-Vázquez

The first part of this book proposes a practical notion of the common good that is dynamic and grounded in people's actions. It sees development as the result of collective processes and collective actions in which people's interactions shape their common destiny. In this sense, agency is posited as the engine of a common good approach to development that is truly human. In this chapter, I focus on this key driver of common good dynamics. My aim here is to reflect on what agency freedom could entail for such an approach by justifying its constitutive role for development and its collective nature, to then identify potential dimensions to measure it.

I identify at least two caveats in how agency is discussed in the literature: first, the notion is primarily discussed at the individual level, and second, existing indicators aiming at capturing this concept generally reflect this bias by over-emphasising the ability of individuals to make choices. Instead, I will argue that it is the collective aspect of agency that provides a more appropriate appraisal of agency for a common good approach, which I present broadly as the opportunity for a given population to identify, organise, and act together as a collective unit to achieve common goals. Three dimensions for its measurement

     https://doi.org/10.11647/OBP.0290.06

are proposed (freedom to imagine things together, freedom to organise around shared goals, and freedom to achieve things together).

The argument develops in three parts. In the first part, drawing on Sen's capability approach, I situate agency freedom as a normative element of development. The second part reviews the literature around agency, and it distinguishes between agency as the process aspect of freedom and agency as the 'freedom to choose'; it also argues that the former is collective rather than individual. The third part justifies agency freedom for the common good as something we do together as a collective. Finally, building on definitions of individual and collective agency, the chapter concludes by suggesting possible dimensions that could be used to appraise the proposed conceptualisation of agency freedom.

1. Agency and Development

Any development project, be it the construction of a road, improving the productivity of rural land, the reduction of any of the dimensions of poverty, or any other objective, necessarily involves taking a stand on what kind of development is appropriate, which processes and strategies are most likely to achieve such goals, and what actors make this progress possible. Therefore, development is about what, how, and by whom. For instance, for a long time, actual development practice was committed to bringing 'development' to 'underdeveloped' areas in the form of higher rates of national income (what), through processes of economic liberalisation, private enterprise, and productivity-raising activities (how), promoted and implemented by non-local technocratic experts (by whom) (Easterly 2013).

Yet, as development scholars and practitioners have repeatedly pointed out, this top-down approach has failed not only in achieving its goals effectively, but also in respecting and taking account of the rights, needs and knowledge of the very same people whose wellbeing was meant to be the main object of concern (Easterly 2013, Malavisi 2019, Mohan 2014). Indeed, there are countless real-life stories all over the world that vividly illustrate these worries; examples range from people being displaced from their livelihoods, the overexploitation of natural resources, direct human rights violations, and the deprivation of people's wellbeing, among other things (e.g., see Chambers 1995, Deneulin 2014, Easterly 2013, Penz et al. 2011). As an alternative, at least since the 1970s onwards, development thinking started shifting towards a more process-oriented participatory approach in which people themselves become active subjects and participants of their own development (Crocker 2008, Mansuri and Rao 2013, Mohan 2014, Pham 2018).

In this context, Amartya Sen's freedom-based approach to development has done a great deal to cement this way of thinking and thus to challenge the limitations of traditional economic technocratic solutions, both in the ends and the means of development (Alkire 2010, Northover 2014, Mansuri and Rao 2013; see also UNDP Human Development Reports). In his framework, development is about expanding people's freedom, and freedom in turn is seen from two distinct but interrelated perspectives, what he calls the opportunity aspect and the process aspect (Alkire and Deneulin 2009). Although both are seen as constitutive of development and interrelated (Sen 1985, 1999a), they aim to capture different ideas. The opportunity aspect refers to real opportunities to choose between different kinds of lives—what Sen understands as people's freedom to achieve wellbeing. The process aspect refers to the process of creating and obtaining those opportunities to live well or to achieve other valuable ends—which captures the notion of agency freedom. The concept of capability captures the former, whereas the concept of agency captures the latter. Together, they offer an alternative account of the what, how, and by whom of development, to wit, people's freedoms are the ends and the means of development.

In this chapter, I am particularly concerned with the agency aspect, people's freedom to take an active role in shaping their own social, political, and economic lives—the whom of development. From this angle, people must be seen 'as active agents of change, rather than as passive recipients of dispensed benefits' (Sen 1999a, p. xiii). This is because even a situation that guarantees high standards of living can still be judged negatively if it 'prevents [people] from speaking freely, or from participating in public debates and decisions' (p. 36), or if it treats people merely as an object whose wants, values, and desires do not deserve attention. Accordingly, development is not only a matter of improving end states, but also of how and *who* makes this improvement (De Herdt and Bastianensen 2008).

As Sen writes: 'The ends and means of development call for placing the perspective of freedom at the centre of the stage. The people have to be seen, in this perspective, as being actively involved—given the opportunity—in shaping their own destiny...' (p. 53). Hence, aside from any other desirable outcome, people's empowerment, their political freedoms, their ability to participate, to influence and shape their social world are 'constituent components' of development beyond their instrumental role (Sen 1999a, pp. 4, 5, 17, 36–37, 291; Alkire 2010). Agency is thus seen as a central component of development. Only people-led development processes are truly human or 'authentic' (Crocker 2008) and the source of common good dynamics (see Chapter 2). However, once agency is established as a normative aspect of development, the challenge is to operationalise it. Although several conceptualisations of the term and of related concepts such as empowerment or autonomy have been proposed recently (e.g., see Alkire 2005, 2007, 2009; Alsop et al. 2006, Ibrahim and Alkire 2007, Samman and Santos 2009), still, what is meant by 'being agents of their own development', what kind of agency best accounts for it, and how it can be measured, remains vague.

Since my intention here is to reflect conceptually on a practical conception of agency freedom for a common good approach, in the remaining of this chapter I take the capability approach and related literature on agency as a starting point (e.g., see Alkire 2005, 2007; Ballet et al. 2007, Classen 2017, 2018; Crocker 2008, D'Agata 2017, Deneulin 2004, 2008; Drydyk 2013, Ibrahim 2008, 2018; Ibrahim and Alkire 2007, Leßmann 2011; Nebel and Herrera 2017, Pelenc et al. 2015). This is because, first, this approach has had a major influence on development discourse and practice around the globe. Second, by rooting his approach in people's freedom, it provides a strong normative anchor for establishing agency not only as a means but also as an end of development. Third, the approach and its collective extensions serve as an inspiration for the common good approach developed in this book. And fourth, as Alkire (2009) recognises, its theoretical framework underpins many of the empirical proposals to measure agency and related concepts.[1] Building on such conceptual work and empirical proposals to assess agency, I will argue that agency for the common good approach must capture its collective aspect; i.e., the extent to which people are free to collectively identify their own objectives, organise, act, and bring about the changes they value.

2. What Is Agency?

Broadly speaking, agency refers to people's capacity to make decisions and act on behalf of their reasoned intentions within specific contexts. In Sen's words, agency has to do with the person's freedom 'to do and achieve [...] whatever goals or values he or she regards as important' (Sen 1985, p. 203), and with 'bring[ing] about the achievements [...] one attempts to produce' (Sen 1992, p. 57), 'which can extend beyond [one's] own interests and needs' (Sen 2009, p. 252). In other words, agency is about taking an active role in the world one inhabits, deciding for oneself and acting towards realising one's own values, objectives, and goals (Claassen 2018, Crocker 2008, List and Pettit 2011). In contrast, a non-agent would be someone who 'may be alienated in their behavior, coerced or forced into a situation, oppressed or simply passive' (Pelenc et al. 2015, p. 227). Thus, an agent is 'someone who acts and brings about [any] change' the person has reason to value (Sen 1999a, p. 19).

In this sense, agency refers to a broad kind of freedom available to people, including the pursuit of self-regarding goals, but also the pursuit of other-regarding goals and social commitments that the person might value (aside from her own wellbeing). That is, agency and wellbeing can interrelate in different ways as agency may lead to personal wellbeing or not. For instance, they may be positively related, as we may use our agency to achieve wellbeing goals (e.g., exercising to promote health) and, at the same time, wellbeing achievements (e.g., being healthy) strengthen our ability to be more effective agents. Likewise, according to Sen, exercising agency may be an integral part of our own wellbeing

---

1   Here I concentrate on the way we currently understand agency as this informs many of the measurements proposed for related concepts as well. For revisions of different conceptualisations of agency, empowerment, and autonomy, and further literature see Alkire (2005, 2007, 2009), Cross Riddle (2018), Ibrahim and Alkire (2007), Kamruzzaman and White (2018), Samman and Santos (2009).

(see also Alkire 2005). Yet, agency and wellbeing may also pull in opposite directions; if one uses her agency to achieve non-wellbeing goals at the expense of her own wellbeing (e.g., when someone joins a protest against injustice even if it might be risky to do so; see Alkire 2009, Crocker and Robeyns 2009, Hamilton 2019, Sen 1985, 2009). Thus, there seems to be no clear-cut distinction between the notion of agency freedom in general and wellbeing freedom in particular.[2]

This interlinkage between the terms, however, has had the unfortunate consequence of representing and measuring agency in much narrower terms. So even if these two aspects of freedom (wellbeing and agency) may sometimes be indistinguishable in practice (Nebel and Herrera 2017), is important to clarify further how these concepts differ as they do account for distinct aspects of freedom and may have different implications for policy (Hamilton 2019). Indeed, this analytical division will prove useful to delineate what we can mean when we talk about (collective) agency freedom.

Sen has tried to clarify the distinction between the terms by emphasising that a 'person's "agency freedom" refers to what the person is free to do and achieve in pursuit of whatever goals or values he or she regards as important.' Consequently, agency-goals are related to, and should be assessed in relation to, the agent's own 'aims, objectives, allegiances, obligations, and—in a broad sense—the person's conception of the good' (Sen 1985, p. 203; see also Sen 1999a, p. 19). In contrast, the exercise of agency related to self-regarding goals strictly connected to one's own wellbeing and the freedom to achieve them is what Sen refers to as 'wellbeing freedom' (Sen 1985, p. 203). In turn, this notion of wellbeing freedom is what the concept of capabilities aims to capture. As stated above, this distinction between "agency freedom" and "wellbeing freedom" implies that, on the one hand, the notion of agency is a more general or broader type of freedom that encompasses the opportunity to achieve a wide variety of goals, whether connected to one's wellbeing or not. On the other hand, wellbeing freedom is a subset of agency, accounting only for those opportunities to achieve personal wellbeing goals.

---

2   Some authors argue that agency precedes and takes preeminence over the conception of capabilities. They suggest that agency might be better understood as a meta-capability (see Crocker 2008, Ballet et al. 2014, Nebel and Herrera 2017).

This distinction is advantageous in that it shows that the notion of agency emphasises that personal goals need not be related only to self-interest; what people value can go beyond purely personal gain. The concept of agency thus extends standard economic theory, which when describing or predicting people's behaviour, characterises persons as purely self-interested maximisers by assuming that a person will engage in an activity insofar as the personal marginal gains exceed the personal marginal costs of performing the action. Certainly, there are countless situations in which people's actions *are* based on improving their own personal situation and nothing else. However, we do not have to think hard to realise that our behaviour responds to much more complex drivers than what narrow economic theory suggests. Just as we do act on self-interest on many occasions, we also do many things where we put others or other goals before ourselves.

For instance, in today's climate crisis, people engage in many non-self-interested actions such as: recycling even if it costs more to do so, or constraining one's own consumption (not buying extra clothes, less driving, less travelling by air, etc.), even if these actions would have had a net positive individual effect. People also protest and put their lives in danger in order to protect the environment from exploitation or over-pollution by corporations. These actions make sense only when we hold to a more accurate portrayal of human beings who are moved—as we are—by a plurality of reasons, and not only self-interest.

Yet, helpful as this distinction between wellbeing and agency freedom may be to clarify the difference between capabilities on the one hand (freedom for the narrower goal of achieving personal wellbeing), and agency on the other (a broader conception of freedom to achieve goals and objectives that transcend one's own wellbeing), it has also created confusion. More clarity is needed in recognising that agency refers to a process and not only to valuable ends separate from one's own personal wellbeing; that agency is built into both the opportunity (consequential) aspect of freedom and the process aspect; and, finally, that agency is therefore a trait of both individuals and collectivities. I briefly touch upon these points below to clarify that when we talk about agency within the process aspect of freedom, then agency should be understood as a kind of a collective freedom.

3. Agency as the Process Aspect of Freedom: Beyond the Goal One Pursues

One issue with the previous distinction between agency freedom and wellbeing freedom (i.e., capability) is that it concentrates *on the goal* the person is aiming for (the wellbeing or non-wellbeing objective), whether she achieves it, and her degree of freedom in the process. Because of this narrow distinction, the concept of agency has been reduced to mean merely freedom of choice and people's success in achieving their goals.

For instance, Crocker and Robeyns (2009) explain that Sen's descriptive version of agency freedom is about 'acting on the basis of what he or she values [...] the freedom to so decide and the power to act and be effective' (p. 75). Likewise, in his reconstruction of agency, Crocker (2008) states, 'persons are agents to the extent that they are able to scrutinize critically their options, themselves decide (rather than have the decision made by someone else or some external or internal force), act to realize their purposes, and have [a positive] impact on the world' (pp. 219–220). In other words, the 'core idea' of Crocker's notion of agency is 'the degree to which one's activities are one's own [... and] autonomous personal involvement in activities' (pp. 252–253). More explicitly, Alsop et al. (2006) define agency as 'an actor's or group's ability to make purposeful choices—that is, the actor is able to envisage and purposively choose options' (p. 11). Similarly, in a more recent account, Claassen (2018) conceptualises agency as 'free and autonomous' individual actions within social practices. As a result, these conceptualisations of agency reduce the meaning of 'agency freedom' to mean simply 'freedom of (autonomous) choice', while 'agency achievement' refers to the actual attainment of the desired or valued goal.

This understanding of agency, however, is only partially accurate. It offers a very 'thin' view of what we may expect from a proper account of agency, which is introduced as 'the process aspect' of a 'broad notion of freedom'. In fact, note that when we associate agency with freedom of choice, we remain within an outcome-oriented approach to development where the outcome stands for having the real opportunity to choose *x* or *y*. From this 'choice' perspective, it not only matters that the person manages to do or be a certain thing (e.g., working out), but also that this doing (exercise) was a real option for the person to freely decide (rather than being imposed upon her). In this example, although information about the process *is* included in the form of the agency involved in reaching a certain outcome (Sen 1999a, p. 27), the focus is nevertheless on an outcome.[3] Thus, we can distinguish that agency plays a role in the *opportunity* (consequential) aspect of freedom by focusing on the process involved in the choosing of any functioning (i.e., whether the person had a real opportunity to choose it or not).[4] It is in this sense that Sen can claim that there is a violation of agency freedom when someone forces you to do whatever you would have chosen anyway (Sen 2004 cited by Crocker and Robeyns 2009; see also Sen 1999a, p. 36; Sen 2009, pp. 229–230).

The problem with interpreting agency in such a narrow way is that it ignores the *processes* through which the freedom to choose (and its subsequent achievement) came about in the first place. A valuable contribution of the notion of agency freedom is (or should be) that it makes us go beyond a narrow concern with outcomes alone—even if outcomes are of a comprehensive kind—to focus instead on the actual process aspect of freedom. From this broader perspective, attention is directed towards whether people themselves are involved in the process of deciding which outcomes/freedoms they want, how they want to generate them, and of organising and producing these real opportunities to reach their (wellbeing or non-wellbeing) goals. These procedural actions matter even if people were ultimately unsuccessful in bringing about a particular opportunity. In other words, in this broader view of agency, the emphasis is not so much on people having a free choice, but on having a voice. It is not so much about deciding to do something or not, but about constructing these opportunities and deciding for ourselves how to do so.

Indeed, when people go out into the streets to protest against unjust economic, social, and political policies, or against an environmentally damaged world, they are not only choosing how to use their freedom.

---

3   This is what Sen calls a 'comprehensive outcome' as opposed to culmination outcomes.

4   I am using here the term 'opportunity aspect of freedom' in such a way that it includes the freedom to achieve both wellbeing and non-wellbeing functionings. This will serve the purpose of distinguishing between the distinct roles of agency that I identify in this chapter.

They are also shaping, transforming, and creating new realities—what, in part, being human is all about. Animals can decide (or are free to choose) whether to eat or not, to run or not, to bark or not at a given time, but only humans can intentionally transform—for good or bad— the dynamics and structures of the world they inhabit. This is a crucial and distinct expression of agency that belongs to the *process aspect* of freedom (as opposed to its role in the *opportunity aspect*). The focus shifts towards the processes that produce social change and transform the current state of the world. In addition to seeing an individual as a free decision-maker, it sees people as agents of change.

Hence, it is important to recognise that agency is part of both:

- In the *opportunity* aspect of freedom, it focuses on whether a person has a choice or not in achieving a particular functioning.

- In the *process* aspect of freedom, it focuses on the process itself of creating, obtaining, and shaping the opportunities to live well or to achieve other valuable ends.

These two roles—one narrower, one broader—embody different understandings of agency, and neither of the two subsumes the other. In this chapter, I am concerned primarily with the latter, the process aspect of agency.

This distinction is crucial since our view of agency informs how we measure it and what the relevant unit of analysis is, i.e., the question of *who* the agent is. In the literature, for example, existing measures tend to associate agency with a person's ability to shape her own destiny in individual terms. Even if indicators are diverse, the focus is primarily on whether individuals are free to decide how to use their freedom. For instance, some emphasise the resources people possess and their internal abilities to act as decision-maker agents; indicators include material assets (income, resources, tools, and ownership of land) and non-material assets (literacy, health, self-esteem, ability to speak in public, etc.) as proxies to measure individual agency. However, these measures have been criticised because they capture prerequisites of agency rather than agency itself, becoming undistinguishable from measures of poverty (Alkire 2009). Instead, other scholars advocate for more direct measures of actual purposeful choices with respect to different goals within crucial spheres of life, such as the economic, political, relational, and familial (e.g., see Alkire 2005, 2007; Ibrahim and Alkire 2007, Samman and Santos 2009). While these proposals offer a more direct measure of agency, the same narrow focus of agency remains. What matters is still whether individuals, especially women, the poor, or the marginalised, are able to make decisions or have control in the areas that affect their own private lives (e.g., see Malhotra et al. 2002, Ruiz-Bravo et al. 2018).

Certainly, these ideas are all important contributions to our understanding of *individual* agency, but these indicators do not tell us anything about the process aspect of freedom—the *processes* through which people together take an active role in determining their circumstances—which is inherently a social-collective process. If anything, these indicators inform us only about whether institutional arrangements and social influences end up facilitating or thwarting individuals' exercise of freedom. This information is useful only insofar as we are interested in looking at individuals' ability to convert their material and non-material assets into their autonomously chosen preferences in a static context, i.e., 'the conversion factor problem' (Otano 2015, p. 115). But such an understanding provides a very static view of social states. It offers no information whatsoever about the processes of how people came to value these freedoms, or the processes that generated one social state or another, or how people envision doing so.

In short, individual indicators of agency do not say anything about how people join efforts to actively shape their social context (Otano 2015). Such indicators do not account for the underlying (ex-ante) *processes* through which people interact, organise, share objectives, and act together towards the consecution of common goals, the production of opportunities to live well, and other social goods. These processes are inherently collective. Thus, when we shift the focus of agency from *choice* to the *process* aspect of development, the relevant actor is primarily the collective and not the individual. In other words, taking the process aspect of freedom seriously implies that agency of a collective kind must figure in our assessments of development. As I explain below, this does not mean that one needs to ignore the moral relevance of individuals' freedom to act as agents in shaping their own lives, nor the relevance of individuals' expression of agency within groups and collectivities.[5] But these other ends of development should not detract us either from recognising the collective nature of agency processes. Therefore, although agency freedom encompasses both individual and collective components, in the next section I will briefly discuss why the collective aspect of agency is the true essence of a common good approach.

4. Collective Agency as the Engine of a Common Good Approach

The common good approach presented in this book begins from the understanding that there are common values, goals, institutions, and practices worth caring about and striving for as a collective, in cooperation with others, and sees these as constitutive goods of our capacity to live well together. It is first and foremost a relational view of development. Hence, the emphasis of the approach is in the 'common' (see Chapter 2). From this perspective, it is the commonality of people's valuation of something (a goal, objective, etc.) that makes that something a *good*, and it is because it is pursued, produced, and enjoyed together that a certain good becomes a *common* good. The approach puts its emphasis on the how (processes) and by whom of development, which it understands as being inextricably linked. Whereas the process of common good dynamics is meant to be captured by the quality of the nexus as a whole, underlying this whole process, the engine that fuels and sets the common good machinery into motion, are people themselves and their shared actions (see Chapter 1).

Since previous chapters of this book have already discussed and justified the profound social and collective nature of the approach, in this section I only briefly highlight two contributions that this approach

---

5   Several studies address the 'individualistic' tendency in the capability approach and aim at expanding its scope to account for the institutional and collective aspects directly (e.g., see D'Agata 2017, Ballet et al. 2007, Deneulin 2008, 2011; Deneulin et al. 2006, Evans 2002, Giraud et al. 2008, Ibrahim 2006, Pelenc et al. 2015, Raushmayer et al. 2018, Stewart 2005, 2013; Stewart and Deneulin 2002; for responses to critiques, see Alkire 2008, Davis 2015, Sen 2002, Volkert 2013). Below, I rely on some ideas within this debate to illustrate my point (for general reviews, see Ibrahim 2018, 2019; HDCA 2013; for brief reviews, see Garza-Vázquez and Deneulin 2019, Robeyns 2005, 2017).

can make to the theory and practice of development. Both points show why agency for a common good approach is collective rather than individual.

First, a common good approach goes beyond individual achievements by directing our attention to the socio-structural aspect of development that enables, facilitates, and co-constructs people´s freedom to live well. In this regard, several scholars have long advocated to recognise and account for the pervasive influence of social and historical institutions on people's reasoning, their values, objectives, and on the way they exercise their agency (Claassen 2018, Deneulin 2008, 2011; Evans 2002, Gore 1997, Stewart 2005, 2013; Stewart and Deneulin 2002). They have argued that, although it is individuals' actions and interactions that reinforce or undermine certain institutions and social practices, this process occurs within a specific social and historical structure that provides meaning to their actions (Deneulin 2008, Raushmayer et al. 2018, Sewell 1992). As such, from this view, people's agency is inherently social in the sense that individuals are always situated within a socio-cultural context (Chapter 1).

However, the social embeddedness of agency is not the only place where the collective aspect of agency lies in the common good approach. Rather than taking the social nature of individual agency as its primary object of study, the common approach focuses directly on the (collective) processes through which people produce and maintain the socio-institutional reality as such. Indeed, the nexus of the common good can be broadly understood as the interconnected web of formal and informal institutions in which individuals are situated that give life to our coexistence. Since this institutional arrangement is the result of shared social practices and the joint efforts of people acting together, coordinating and cooperating with each other, agency for the common good can only be a collective agency.

Second, it understands this process-focused approach to development as a dynamic process that is always in the making. This dynamic process is the result of people acting together organised around a set of shared values and practices. This view is in line with several studies that recognise the potential opportunity that groups, or collectives, provide for successfully acting together in the consecution of shared objectives (e.g., see Giraud et al. 2013, Giraud and Renouard

2009, Ibrahim 2006, 2017; Ostrom 1990, Stewart 2005). These scholars highlight the fact that social progress—transforming unjust structures, opening up new spaces for action, attaining new rights and freedoms, and creating an enabling social environment in which to live well—is the result of people pooling their resources and acting together as agents of their own development. From this perspective, it is through self-help groups, neighbourhood assemblies, social movements, co-operatives, civil society, or other specific groups that people strengthen their voices and attain new freedoms and other valuable goals (see Ibrahim 2006, 2017; Ibrahim and Alkire 2007, Murphy 2014; see Gammage et al. 2016 for more references). As Raushmayer et al. (2018, p. 359) put it, it is by cooperating with others through collective action that 'a group creates a collective potential beyond any individual's capability and may provide a vehicle for increased agency' (see also Evans 2002, Ibrahim 2008, 2018; Volkert 2013).

Similarly, a practical notion of the common good understands development as a dynamic, relational process in which people's actions and their shared practices are protagonists. From this perspective, human development is something we do together. Accordingly, these two features (the focusing on the shared social practices underlying the dynamics of the social world) illustrate that, from a common good perspective, it is agency of a collective kind which is at the root of any common good dynamics. As such, to assess and promote 'authentic' development—to use Crocker's term—in which people are agents of their own development, our measures must account for the shared freedom of people to act together as a collectivity. In the next and final section, I shall offer some thoughts about what measuring collective agency might imply. But before going in that direction, first it is important to address some of the concerns raised in the literature regarding the adoption of a collective view of freedom.

Broadly speaking, for a collective notion of agency, there are two potential challenges that deserve attention (see Ibrahim 2019 for a summary of this debate). On the one hand, some worry about the possible tension between collective and individual freedoms, and instead advocate for an 'ethical individualist' view, i.e., holding 'individuals and only individuals [as] the units of moral concern' (Robeyns 2005, p. 107). As many have pointed out, placing the collective as the unit of concern may overlook existing or potential heterogeneities, inequalities, oppression, and power relations *within* the group (e.g., see Alkire 2008, Robeyns 2005, Sen 2002), and *towards* the members of other groups (Kosko 2019; see also Cleaver 1999, Godfrey-Wood and Mamani-Vargas 2017 cited in Ibrahim 2018). On the other hand, pointing out the possibility of collective failures, others wonder whether group action and inclusive collective agency is possible at all, especially in unequal contexts. For instance, empirical work on participatory development has found that some members of the community (usually the poor, women, or members of disadvantaged groups) are often less able to participate and form groups; that not all members participate or use their voices equally; and that development processes and benefits can be skewed towards the interest of the elite (Boni et al. 2018, Mansuri and Rao 2013, Mohan 2014).

There is no doubt that these are all extremely relevant concerns that we should all care about. But, for the purposes of this chapter, one should note, first, that here I am concentrating on process freedoms only; and advocating for acknowledging its collective feature does not imply ignoring individual (process and opportunity) freedoms. As recognised above, agency is relevant for both the individual (being able to choose how to use one's freedom) and the collective (freedom to collectively shape the social world), and both are part of a true human development. While there are excellent reasons to care about the extent to which individuals are able to control their circumstances or are freely and autonomously 'participating in and within' social practices (Claassen 2018), analysing the way in which people's shared values and collective practices are able to generate such possibility or not also deserves normative attention. Depending on the particular development problem at hand, one of these expressions of agency may take a more prominent role. Despite their potential flaws and difficulties, collectivities may still be the best way for the deprived and the marginalised to change their situation and attain individual freedoms that they value (Ibrahim 2019, Murphy 2014, Stewart 2005).

Second, more importantly, a practical notion of collective agency freedom must be concerned with what the community is actually able to do to act together, it must inform us about the processes through which people interact, organise, and pursue their objectives. That is, the notion of collective agency freedom includes but is not exhausted by the way in which the community participates in specific development projects. And aside from hermits or those completely excluded from social life, people of different socioeconomic backgrounds coordinate to act with others around a common goal, i.e., they exercise collective agency even if at varying degrees of opportunity. In short, development processes *are* collective processes. People's actions and their acting together in a shared institutional framework are the drivers or impediments of development. In this sense, Beretta and Nebel (2020) write:

> Understanding (and measuring) development is (or ought to be) an intrinsically dynamic endeavor. It mirrors the process of generating development, where actual people, in the here and now of history, mysteriously drive history. In other words, development is a practical, intrinsically dynamic process where people are protagonist. (p. 372)

Hence, as I argued above, in so far as the process aspect of freedom is intrinsic to development, then our normative assessments must include information about the freedom to act collectively. This does not mean that people's shared practices, collectivities, or collective agency for that matter, always produce positive social dynamics. But it does ask us to recognise that social ailments such as the subjugation of women, climate change, poverty, inequality, or corruption, among other issues, can only change through the coordination of multiple people acting together, joining efforts with others, constructing, and adapting shared objectives, values, actions, and narratives about the (social) good they wish to establish. Notwithstanding the possibility of extraordinary individual acts, common goods are first and foremost the product of solidarity and cooperation among people (although not without conflict) (see also Biggeri et al. 2018). It is in this sense that collective agency freedom is the precondition for a dynamic notion of the common good approach. Agency for the common good is thus collective agency.[6]

In sum, advocating for a collective view of agency does not imply ignoring the many issues involved in making collectivities a unit of

---

6   The reader should also note that collective agency is only one of the normative aspects of development processes. The common good matrix includes four other normative components aside from collective agency, namely, governance, justice, stability, and humanity. The quality of the development process with the nexus of the common good as proxy is determined by the interrelation and coherence of these five drivers (see Chapter 2).

normative analysis, or the difficulties of generating free and inclusive collective action. Rather, it highlights that our discussions and measures need to go beyond the narrow view of agency in the form of individual choice to also account for the more significant and broader understanding of agency which sees people as doers and makers of the common world we inhabit, and of our shared role in generating (or not) individual and social improvements.[7] In fact, this is in line with Sen's own writings when he talks about 'the *public* not merely as "the patient" whose wellbeing commands attention, but also as "the agent" whose actions can *transform* society' (Drèze and Sen 1989, p. 279 cited by Alkire 2006; emphasis in original, italics are mine). Individual expressions of agency do not exhaust people's exercise of agency freedom; agency matters concern both individual and collective freedoms (Alkire 2010, Biggeri et al. 2018, Crocker 2008, Crocker and Robeyns 2009, Deneulin 2008, 2014; Murphy 2014).

A practical notion of the common good, then, must aim at capturing empirically the political reality through which people exercise collective agency: the degree of shared freedom that people actually enjoy to together be the engine of opportunities to live well, and to generate and attain objectives valuable to them and to others.

5. Measuring Collective Agency for the Common Good

So far, I have argued that from a common good perspective, we need to understand agency in its transformative social sense, and that this role is a collective rather than an individual enterprise. However, in drawing this conclusion I have also used the term rather loosely. In this section I offer, first, some thoughts on the conceptualisation of collective agency to then, second, identify *potential* dimensions and indicators to operationalise it.

---

7   Of course, this understanding of agency as the process aspect of freedom is not foreign to the capability literature. However, Sen's language on agency is vague, and when he refers to it, he does it without explicitly distinguishing the distinct roles that agency plays within his whole framework. Overall, the point that I want to make is the following: most of the literature has concentrated on 'the choice aspect' of agency—especially the literature on measurement—and this limits our view of development. Instead, in this chapter I put the emphasis on the broader—grander—role of agency, the process aspect.

One of the first difficulties of moving towards measurement is that the notion of collective agency has been little theorised in the development literature.[8] Although many scholars recognise the need to go beyond individual indicators of agency to account for its collective aspect (e.g., Ibrahim and Alkire 2007, Samman and Santos 2009), they do not undertake such a task. The reality is that the vast majority of references to any sort of collective agency are made in a rather general way and mainly to defend the existence and the significance of people's collective capacities to improve their (and others') lives for the better.

This is the case, for example, of scholars who try to integrate groups and collectivities into the capability approach through the concept of 'collective capabilities.' They argue that collective capabilities account for those freedoms that are unattainable by an individual acting alone and which, once generated, have irreducibly social benefits in that they are open to the collectivity as a whole and not only to individuals (e.g., Evans 2002, Ibrahim 2006, 2008; Murphy 2014). However, this concept of collective capabilities conflates in its definition both the collective nature of the process and whatever achievement results from it, which may be problematic (e.g., see Sen 2002, HDCA 2013). In contrast, here I am interested in the agency aspect only, i.e., the freedom of the process, and not so much in what comes out of it (Drydyk 2013); not because the content of the goal is unimportant, but for analytical and practical reasons (Raushmayer et al. 2018).[9]

---

8   Some efforts within the literature on participatory development point in this direction when they direct our attention to the quality of the *process* through which local people participate and engage in *group* decision-making, which in turn is taken as a proxy of collective agency or empowerment or both (e.g., Drydyk 2005, Crocker 2008; Kosko 2013; see also Kamruzzaman and White 2018 for a summary of similar approaches). However, these discussions on the *forms* of participation tend to focus on how specific development projects ought to interact with or engage with the local population (see also Mansuri and Rao 2013). Hence, participation in this sense accounts only for a 'limited expression of agency' (Alkire 2006, p. 53). Although insights from this literature will be relevant, in the remainder of this chapter, the aim is to reflect on the conceptualisation of agency in a broader, more general way for the purpose of assessing the actual degree of collective agency embedded in the collective dynamics of a given population.

9   Note that the evaluation of end states is also a matter of collective choice. Thus, rather than imposing the notion of collective capability, we should leave space for collective agents to determine for themselves how the generated outcomes should be judged, either from the perspective of wellbeing freedom or from the point of view of other social concerns.

The question of interest is: How can we conceptualise collective agency and what should we focus on when assessing the degree of collective agency freedom in a population? In answering this question, I take existing analyses of the notion of (individual and collective) agency as starting point. In principle, there is no reason to think that the notion of agency would be radically different when the actor is an individual or a group. After all, when defining agency, it is sometimes implied that such a definition also applies for a group, even if the explanation of what agency entails revolves around the *individual* (e.g., Crocker 2008, Crocker and Robeyns 2009). But as we will see, when thought of in collective terms, the content of agency (what should one focus on) takes a very different form.

Starting, for example, with the basic trait of agency—seeing people as active subjects towards the consecution of valued goals—from a collective angle, the focus is no longer on *individuals* exercising their own agency, but on collective action; on how people act together to achieve a certain goal as a group or collectivity (Ibrahim 2006, Stewart and Deneulin 2002). Thus, we can start with Ibrahim's (2008) definition which suggests understanding collective agency '*as an exercise of human freedoms whereby a group/or a collectivity seeks to pursue goals collectively that go beyond their individual well-being concerns*' (p. 6; emphasis in original). The usefulness of this definition is that it already captures the fact that people can join forces with others to bring about a variety of objectives that 'can only occur via collective action of one sort or another' (Stewart and Deneulin 2002, p. 69) (e.g., rendering the government accountable, protecting their rights, providing a service, or challenging market forces and corporate power). But, we also need to say something about how such collective action happens.

What matters when assessing collective agency is not only the opportunity of 'joining and participating in a group' to pursue goals (Ibrahim 2006, p. 405). Though an important individual freedom in itself, it does not shed light on the actual possibility and the mechanisms of *acting together* 'in concert with others to achieve goals' (Ballet et al. 2007, p. 199). Simply finding and joining others with similar objectives does not automatically render a group of people able to act collectively in an effective and beneficial way (Mansuri and Rao 2013). The group also needs to have the capacity to *organise themselves*, which involves, among other things, being able to devise and agree on a common strategy, coordinate, and cooperate with others (Ostrom 1990, Ostrom et al. 1999; Ibrahim 2006, 2008; see also Chapter 2). That is, as I briefly expand below, the possibility of people coming together *to organise themselves* and *act together* to pursue a common objective are important elements of a practical notion of collective agency. As such, one could argue that the degree of collective agency is greater the more a given population is able to organise itself to act together.

However, a successful organisation to achieve goals does not *fully* capture the notion of collective agency in the sense discussed above. Seeing people as social change actors and as masters of their own common development means that our conceptualisation of collective agency must be broader. Agency is not only about acting in the world but about acting autonomously, i.e., people themselves deciding what is of value to them (Claassen 2018, Crocker and Robeyns 2009, Drydyk 2013, Ibrahim 2017). In the context of collective agency this requirement can be associated with group self-determination and the process through which people are able, and empowered, to participate in setting their own development goals. Despite some differences, scholars within this area agree that simply executing or playing an instrumental role in bringing about a pre-chosen objective within pre-existing institutional settings entails a limited expression of agency. In contrast, the greater the control of local people to determine their own needs, priorities, objectives, and rules, the greater the degree of collective agency they enjoy (Crocker 2008, Drydyk 2005, Kamruzzaman and White 2018, Kosko 2013, Mohan 2014, Murphy 2014).

By putting the emphasis on the prosecution of goals, Ibrahim's definition, as well as Ostrom's empirical studies, concentrate only on a subsection of what collective agency entails, namely on people's coordination capacity to achieve a given objective. But there is no reference to the selection of the objective around which people organise, nor about whether that objective is commonly held as valuable by that group of people. Therefore, our conceptualisation of collective agency must go beyond to also capture people's freedom to together identify, form, and agree on a variety of *collective* goals and objectives that they seek to pursue. Since different people care about different things, a community of people needs to be able to decide what they value together and what they want to achieve together, as a community (Ibrahim 2017). For example, people could collectively decide to transfer control of a natural resource they used to manage in common to a private or centralised entity to concentrate instead on other shared objectives, such as developing other sectors of their community. That is, aside from determining how to organise themselves around a common concern, people must also collectively decide which objectives they value together as commons and which they do not.

We can then define collective agency as 'the capacity of the group to define common goals and the freedom to act to reach the chosen goals' (Pelenc et al. 2015, p. 229). This definition is more complete in the sense that it recognises that prior to people's organisation in the form of collective action, they must be able to form shared objectives and a shared vision of what they wish to change together and how. This does not mean that people will always reach a unanimous agreement, or that life in the community should see them become a group homogenous in their values, beliefs, and objectives. On the contrary, it means that it is possible for people to get together, discuss ideas and share their views with others in order to influence their social reality (Drydyk 2005, UNDP 2002). As Sen argues, collective deliberation and democratic practice can have a 'constructive role' by facilitating the reformulation of people's values, preferences, and priorities (Sen 1999a, 1999b). Yet, in so far as we are interested in collective agency, it is not enough to account for the person's civil and political freedoms (e.g., electoral rights, freedom of expression) and her ability to exercise them (Drèze and Sen 2002, p. 10). The focus should be on the group's capacity and their mechanisms to engage in collective deliberation and collective thinking to identify and form new shared objectives, envision new realities, and reach collective decisions (Boni et al. 2018, Ibrahim 2017, Murphy 2014). Hence, assessments of collective agency must go beyond the organisational capacities of the group and include information on what we may call people's opportunity to *imagine things together* to identify and devise *collective* goals.[10]

---

10   This does not mean, however, ignoring the many flaws and hindrances that this collective process may entail. For instance, to name a few, unequal power relations (Stewart 2005), social and economic inequalities (Dréze and Sen 2002), different levels of participation and voice (Boni et al. 2018), as well as different degrees of personal agreement, commitment, and involvement with the group (Hainz et al.

Bringing the three elements together means that a group of people acting as a collective agent must: validate a particular appraisal of the world, envision ways to modify it, organise together, and act to bring these changes about. In other words, a process of collective agency entails that the subject of action is a collectivity of people with 'joint intentions,' whose organising and subsequent activity require an element of coordination between the members and whose identity 'can survive changes of membership' (List and Pettit 2011, p. 31).

To illustrate how a collective assessment of agency differs from an individualist one, let's consider, on the one hand, the (collective) process of winning women's right to vote, and on the other hand, the multiple acts of (individual) agency taking place when women exercise their vote in national elections. Whereas both settings may involve a group of people, the former (acquiring rights to vote) differs from the notion of individual agency in a number of ways. First, the agent who performs the action is a group, rather than an individual. Second, there is a joint intention. Women who cast their vote individually do not necessarily have a common intention, as they might be voting for different social projects. In contrast, groups of women such as the suffragists who fought for the right to vote had a clear goal that members shared. Third, individual agency and collective agency also differ in whether the identity of a group of people depends on its members or not. In the example of individual women voting, the identity of a group of women changes as women enter and exit the polling place, whereas in the second case, the identity of the group remains even if membership changes.

Succinctly put, only the first scenario involved a group of people that *imagined* together and formed a joint intention, that *organised* their members and *acted together* to bring about change. If this reading seems acceptable, then we can interpret collective agency as an exercise of freedom composed of different practices of collective action: imagining things together (i.e., forming and identifying commons), organising around these shared objectives (i.e., developing rules and mechanisms to coordinate their actions), and achieving things together

---

2016, Rauschmayer et al. 2018), among others. Rather, than ignoring these issues, bringing this element to our conceptualisation implies that a useful measure of agency must be able to capture these deficiencies and make them visible.

(i.e., cooperating to bring about their objectives). An advantage of this interpretation is that, by disaggregating it into three different forms of collective action, we are in a better position to inform the development of indicators for each stage and to observe how a certain group of people fares in these distinct components of collective agency.

However, before briefly expanding in each of these dimensions, there is one more element to include in the conceptualisation of collective agency, namely, the socio-institutional context in which collective agency takes place—which may or may not facilitate these forms of collective abilities. This assertion follows on from a point discussed in the previous section, namely the profound influence of social structures on people's values, aspirations., and thus in the way they exercise their agency. But it also follows on from the recognition that the freedom we enjoy to exercise agency is both 'enabled and constrained' by the institutional framework (Claassen 2018, p. 58; Sen 1999a). In Crocker and Robeyns's (2009) words, '[...] social arrangements can also extend the reach of agency achievements and agency freedom.' In different social contexts, '[...] people have more or less freedom to decide, act, and make a difference in the world [...]' (p. 64; see also Biggeri et al. 2018, Cleaver 2007, Ibrahim 2006, 2008; Ibrahim and Alkire 2007, Pelenc et al. 2015).

Institutional arrangements structure people's actions and interactions through both formal and informal rules, which can include legal norms, institutionalised patterns of behaviour, social norms, cultural values (Claassen 2018). As such, this element works like an overarching component that cuts across collective action in all three of its forms. For instance, in addition to what people actually do to act collectively, the extent to which people are able to exercise this freedom depends on laws regarding freedom of speech and freedom of assembly, on whether people actually value this opportunity, on a community's level of social capital, on whether there are (non)governmental institutions that can provide them with support of one kind or another, and structural inequalities, among others. A measurement of collective agency freedom must also aim at capturing the extent to which the *structural and social processes* in a given population potentialise the shared freedom that people have at their disposal to collectively determine their own lives.

Therefore, flowing from the discussion presented so far, I propose the following conceptualisation to operationalise the concept of collective agency freedom for the common good: *the real opportunity of a group of people to exercise the shared freedom to define goals together, and to organise and act as a collectivity to reach such common goals (wellbeing or non-wellbeing related) in accordance with their common values and objectives.*

For practical purposes, this notion of collective agency freedom for the common good would call for empirical measures on the institutional background and the social dynamics within a community in the three dimensions identified above: the freedom to imagine things together, the freedom to organise around shared goals, and the freedom to achieve things together.[11] The actual selection and justification of indicators for each of these dimensions would involve different methodological decisions which are out of the scope of this conceptual chapter (see Chapter 3; see also Alkire 2009, Ibrahim and Alkire 2007). However, with the intention to motivate this discussion, here I briefly expand on what each of these dimensions could aspire to capture in practice and what sort of information might be included to do so.[12]

1. **People's freedom to imagine things together.** If collective agency is the source of a common good dynamic, then the real opportunity to imagine things together is the pre-condition of the freedom to act together. This dimension should aim to assess the ability of people 'to form collective intentions' (Davis 2015) or 'communal vision' (Ibrahim 2017). It is concerned with the extent to which people have the opportunity to talk to each other, listen to each other, reflect with each other, justify to each other their interests and, more importantly, co-construct common values, objectives, and ideas in public spaces. It serves also as a process of 'conscientisation' of their shared reality (Ibrahim 2017). As Pelenc et al. (2015) point out 'social

---

11   To a certain extent, this conceptualisation of collective agency freedom offers a collective understanding of Crocker's (2008) reconstruction of agency. He states, 'persons are agents to the extent that they are able to scrutinize critically their options, themselves decide (rather than have the decision made by someone else or some external or internal force), act to realize their purposes, and have [a positive] impact on the world' (pp. 219–220).

12   See Chapter 3 for the proposed indicators of collective agency freedom for the common good matrix presented in this book.

interactions, such as group discussions, community meetings, participatory workshops or informal conversations provide the opportunity for people to share their representation of the "common good" and wellbeing with others' (p. 228; emphasis in original). It accounts for the 'inventiveness and creativity' of associative life (Chapter 2). In practice, this dimension should assess to what extent people have a *real opportunity to participate* in the social and political life of the community through groups and organised collectivities. These groups can vary in their degree of formality and may include voluntary associations, neighbourhood meetings, NGOs and civil organisations, churches, schools, unions, village councils, etc. It should capture whether people in the community gather, whether they do it frequently, the extent to which these forms of organisation extend to the whole community, and the extent to which this freedom is valued in the community.

2. **People's freedom to organise around shared goals**. Aside from providing a space for the formulation of 'collective or joint intentions,' groups and collectivities provide the space to develop collective strategies 'and instruments for pursuing them, even in the face of powerful opposition' (Evans 2002, p. 56). Since it is not enough to want things together, this dimension aims at capturing the effectiveness of organising as a collectivity around a common desire, to procure a shared goal. This may involve coordinating the roles of group members (List and Pettit 2011), combining people's material and human resources (Pelenc et al. 2015), and establishing rules, sanctions, and mechanisms to solve conflicts (Ostrom 1990). As Bandura (2000) states, 'a group's attainments are the product not only of shared knowledge and skills of its different members, but also of the interactive, coordinative, and synergistic dynamics of their transactions'; this is a 'group level property' (pp. 75–76). In practice, this dimension should assess *the capacity and effectiveness of people to organise* themselves. An appraisal could include indicators of social capital, such as social and community networks, degree of solidarity, and norms of cooperation, reciprocity, and trust (Giraud and Renouard

2009, Ibrahim 2008, Pelenc et al. 2015, Rosignoli 2018). The group capacity to build consensus and synergies with other groups as well as with existing institutions in order to solve a common problem or reach a common goal (Ibrahim 2017).

3. **People's freedom to achieve things together.** Perhaps there is no better proof of the existence of collective agency than the actual dynamism of the community and its actual success in producing commons and social goods. This dimension makes reference to the actual actions taken by the group and its actual power to achieve their objectives. This is in fact what most scholars have in mind when they refer to the effectiveness of collective agency to promote people's freedoms or other social goods. We can relate this aspect to the notions of 'control' and 'effective power' mentioned by Alkire (2009) but from a collective perspective. *Control* would 'refer [...] to the [...] ability to make choices and to control procedures directly (whether or not [the group] is successful in achieving the desired goal).' *Effective power* 'is the [...] group's "power to achieve chosen results"' (Alkire 2009, p. 458; emphasis in original). According to Crocker (2008), this exercise of freedom by the people is a crucial aspect of the notion of collective agency, seeing them as the true masters and shapers of their common life. In practice, this dimension should measure *the capacity of the group to achieve its goals and shape their destiny.*

In short, these dimensions attempt to capture the real opportunity of a group of people to freely act together as agents of social change.[13] Such action refers to the processes through which people organise themselves to exercise their freedom in the three dimensions within an agency-enabling environment—hence the emphasis on freedoms in each dimension. By accounting for this freedom to act collectively, a people-centred approach to development can not only be a means to more efficient, sustainable results, but it can also promote a kind of development that better reflects our humanity and the process through which our societies, and our lives within them, develop (even if the

---

13 Even though here I present them as distinct components for analytical reasons, in practice, they interrelate and influence each other.

degree to which this freedom is valued and the forms it takes may vary greatly from one place to another).

Moreover, this collective development process represents not only an intrinsic aspect of development but also a common good in itself. That is because the process itself creates something of value: social dynamics that go beyond individual wellbeing and beyond the achievements of individual agency. Through collective action people establish rules in accordance with their social, cultural, and political environment to generate social benefits that improve their lives. In doing so, they also end up promoting a culture of political practice, a way of doing in the community, a way of conquering new spaces. These social practices develop through a constant process of social learning that goes beyond individuals; these processes originate within and gradually shape a culture that existed before and will remain even when those individuals of today are no longer there. Ultimately, the social institutions, the political culture, and people's ways of doing belong to the community as a whole and to its history; these things become an integrated part of the community and not the property of single individuals—even if institutions, culture, and ways of doing can later be modified by another group of people. In other words, collective agency represents both the embodiment of a common good and the source of causation of common goods.

Conclusion

Following the conceptual framework of this book and Sen's conceptual framework of development as freedom, I attempted to develop three points in this chapter. First, I argued that agency embodies the process aspect of freedom, which is in turn a central aspect of a process of development that is truly human. I also identified that agency can be interpreted either as 'an expansion of individual choice' or as 'the processes through which social change is generated,' and the primacy of the former in the literature comes at the expense of the latter. I showed that this bias in the literature has led to an over-individualisation of our understanding of agency, and consequently, to the indicators developed to measure agency. Instead, second, I identified that a notion of agency understood as the process aspect of freedom entails collective aspects. I argued that this collective interpretation of agency was the true engine of a common good approach that sees development as a dynamic process. Third, I developed a general notion of collective agency freedom in order to shed light on what it would entail to measure this collective aspect of the term.

Broadly speaking, I defined collective agency as the real freedom of a given population to self-organise in order to form goals, coordinate, and act together as a collectivity to achieve common goals. This definition tries to clarify that, while the opportunities of joining, forming, and belonging to groups or the exercise of political rights by a person are individual expressions of agency, the way in which these groups form, develop common objectives, organise, and achieve goals is a matter of collective agency. I argued that to properly understand and orient development dynamics, we must *also* aim to capture empirically a notion of collective agency, which accounts for the institutional framework and the processes through which people interact to produce their joint intentions.

While the conception offered in this chapter remains at an exploratory level, and several questions may remain open for a more complete understanding of collective agency in future work, I urge the reader to recognise that, by hyper-individualising our understanding of agency, we are missing an important aspect of a notion of development that is concerned with people living well *together* in society. Sen has long insisted that an 'adequate understanding of development' (p. 37) 'cannot be confined only to [its] outcomes', a freedom-based approach must also see freedom processes 'as constitutive parts of the ends of development in themselves' (p. 291; quotes are from Sen 1999a). To do so, I have argued, the theory and practice of development must leave conceptual and practical space for a notion of agency as a process freedom understood as something that we do together with others. Unless we do this, our ideas of development cannot be the true embodiment of a human-centred approach.

References

Alkire, S. 2005. Why the capability approach? *Journal of Human Development* 6/1, 115–135. https://doi.org/10.1080/146498805200034275

Alkire, S. 2007. Measuring Agency: Issues and Possibilities, *Indian Journal of Human Development 1/1*, 169–175. https://doi.org/10.1177/0973703020070110

Alkire, S. 2008. "Using the capability approach: prospective and evaluative analyses", in Comim, F., Qizilbash, M., and Alkire, S. (eds), *The Capability Approach: Concepts, Measures and Applications*, Cambridge: Cambridge University Pres. https://doi.org/10.1017/CBO9780511492587.002

Alkire, S. 2009. "Concepts and Measures of Agency", in Basu, K. and Kanbur, R. (eds), *Arguments for a Better World: Essays in Honor of Amartya Sen, Volume I*, New York: Oxford University Press, 455–475.

Alkire, S. 2010. *Human Development: Definitions, Critiques, and Related Concepts*, Human Development Research Paper 2010/01. New York: United Nations Development Programme (UNDP). https://papers.ssrn.com/sol3/papers.cfm?abstract_id=1815263

Alkire, S., and Deneulin, S. 2009. The Human Development and Capability Approach, in Deneulin, S. and Shahani, L. (eds), *An Introduction to the Human Development and Capability Approach: Freedom and Agency*. London; Sterling, VA; Ottawa, ON: Earthscan, 22–48.

Alsop, R., Bertelsen, M., and Holland, J. 2006. *Empowerment in Practice: From Analysis to Implementation*. Washington D.C.: World Bank. https://doi.org/10.1596/978-0-8213-6450-5

Ballet, J., Dubois, J. L., and Mahieu, F-R. 2007. Responsibility for Each Other's Freedom: Agency as the Source of Collective Capability, *Journal of Human Development 8/2*, 185–201, https://doi.org/10.1080/14649880701371000

Ballet, J., Bazin, D., Dubois, J.-L., and Mahieu, F.-R. 2014. *Freedom, Responsibility and Economics of the Person*, Abingdon: Routledge. https://doi.org/10.3917/cep.068.0219

Bandura, A. 2000. Exercise of human agency through collective efficacy, *Current Directions in Psychological Science 9*, 75–78. https://doi.org/10.1111/1467-8721.00064

Beretta, S. and Nebel, M. 2020. "Introduction", in Beretta, S. and Nebel, M. (eds), *A Special Issue on Common Good*, Rivista Internazionale di Scienze Sociali, 4, 367–381

Biggeri, M., Ferrannini, A., and Arciprete, C. 2018. Local Communities and Capability Evolution: The Core of Human Development Processes, *Journal of Human Development and Capabilities 19/2*, 126–146. https://doi.org/10.1080/19452829.2017.1411896

Boni, A., Millán Franco, G. F., and Millán Franco, M. A. 2018. When Collectivity Makes a Difference: Theoretical and Empirical Insights from Urban and Rural Communities in Colombia, *Journal of Human Development and Capabilities 19/2*, 216–231.

Chambers, R. 1995. Poverty and Livelihoods: whose reality counts? *Environment and Urbanization 7/1,* 173–204.

Claassen, R. 2017. An Agency-Based Capability Theory of Justice. *European Journal of Phylosophy 25/4,* 1279–1304 https://doi.org/10.1111/ejop.12195

Claassen, R. 2018. *Capabilities in a Just Society: A Theory of Navigational Agency,* Cambridge: Cambridge University Press. https://doi.org/10.1080/19452829 .2020.1741141

Cleaver, F. 2007. Understanding Agency in Collective Action, *Journal of Human Development 8/2,* 223–244. https://doi.org/10.1080/14649880701371067

Crocker, D. 2008. *Ethics of Global Development: Agency, Capability, and Deliberative Democracy,* Cambridge: Cambridge University Press. https://doi.org/10.1017/CBO9780511492594

Crocker, D. and Robeyns, I. 2009. "Capability and Agency", in Morris, C. (ed.), *Amartya Sen,* Cambrige: Cambridge University Press.

Cross Riddle, K. 2019. "Empowerment", in Drydyk, J. and Keleher, L. (eds), *Routledge Handbook of Development Ethics,* London and New York: Routledge, 171–182.

Davis, J. 2015. Agency and the Process Aspect of Capability Development: Individual Capabilities, Collective Capabilities, and Collective Intentions, *Filosofía de la Economía,* https://ssrn.com/abstract=2625673

D´Agata, A. 2017. Agency, socially contemplated, *Ethics and Economics 14/2,* 59–70. https://ethics-and-economics.com/wp-content/uploads/2021/10/ Agency-socially-contemplated.pdf

De Herdt, T. and Bastianensen, J. 2008. The circumstances of agency. A relational view of poverty, *International Development Planning Review 30/4,* 339–357. https://doi.org/10.3828/IDPR.30.4.2

Deneulin, S. 2008. "Beyond Individual Freedom and Agency: Structures of Living Together In Sen's Capability Approach to Development", in Comim, F., Qizilbash, M., and Alkire, S. (eds), *The Capability Approach: Concepts, Measures and Applications.* Cambridge: Cambridge University Press, 105–124. https://doi.org/10.1017/CBO9780511492587

Deneulin, S. 2011. Development and the limits of Amartya Sen's The Idea of Justice, *Third World Quarterly 32/4,* 787–797. https://doi.org/10.1080/01436 597.2011.567008

Deneulin, S. 2014. *Wellbeing, Justice and Development Ethics,* London: Routledge. https://doi.org/10.4324/9781315867090

Drèze, J. and Sen, A. 2002. Democratic practice and social inequality in India, *Journal of Asian and African Studies 37/2,* 6–37. https://doi. org/10.1177/002190960203700202

Drydyk, J. 2005. When is Development More Democratic? *Journal of Human Development 6/2*, 247–267. https://doi.org/10.1080/14649880500120566

Drydyk, J. 2013. Empowerment, agency, and power, *Journal of Global Ethics 9/3*, 249–262. https://doi.org/10.1080/17449626.2013.818374

Easterly, W. 2013. *The Tyranny of Experts: Economist, Dictators, and the Forgotten Rights of the Poor*, New York: Basic Books.

Evans, P. 2002. Collective Capabilities, Culture and Amartya Sen's Development as Freedom. *Studies in Comparative International Development 37/2*. https://doi.org/10.1007/BF02686261

Gammage, S., Kabeer, N., and Van der Meulen Rodgers, Y. 2016. Voice and Agency: Where are we now? *Feminist Economics 22/1*, 1–29. https://doi.org/10.1080/13545701.2015.1101308

Garza-Vázquez, O. and Deneulin, S. 2019. "The Capability Approach: Ethics and Socio-Economic Development" in Drydyk, J. and Keleher, L. (eds), *Routledge Handbook of Development Ethics*, London and New York: Routledge, 68–83.

Giraud, G. and Renouard, C. 2009. Relational Capability: An Indicator of Collective Empowerment. *ESSEC Working Paper*. https://core.ac.uk/download/pdf/52826806.pdf

Giraud, G., Renouard, C., L'Huillier, H., de la Martinière, R., and Sutter, C. 2013. Relational Capability: A Multidimensional Approach. *ESSEC Working Paper 1306*. https://papers.ssrn.com/sol3/papers.cfm?abstract_id=2333529

Gore, C. 1997. Irreducibly social goods and the informational basis of Amartya Sen's capability approach, *Journal of International Development, 9/2*, 235–250.

Hainz, T., Bossert, S., and Strech, D. 2016. Collective agency and the concept of 'public' in public involvement: A practice-oriented analysis, *BMC Medical Ethics, 17/1*. https://doi.org/10.1186/s12910-015-0083-z

Hamilton, L. 2019. *Amartya Sen*, Cambridge: Polity.

HDCA. 2013. Collectivity in the Capability Approach, *Special issue of Maitreyee, the E-Bulletin of the Human Development & Capability Association*, Number 22. https://hd-ca.org/publications/maitreyee-june-2013-collectivity-in-the-ca

Ibrahim, S. 2006. From individual to collective capabilities: The capability approach as a conceptual framework for self-help, *Journal of Human Development 7/3*, 397–416.

Ibrahim, S. 2008. "Collective Agency: Wider Freedoms and New Capabilities through Self-Help", in Dubois, J. L. et al. (eds), *Repenser L'Action Collective: une Approche par les Capabilitiés*, Paris: Réseau IMPACT Network.

Ibrahim, S. 2017. How to Build Collective Capabilities: The 3C-Model for Grassroots-Led Development, *Journal of Human Development and Capabilities 18/2*, 197–222. https://doi.org/10.1080/19452829.2016.1270918

Ibrahim, S. 2018. "Colectivivdades y Capacidades", in Deneulin, S., Valencia, A., and Clausen, J., (eds), *Introducción al Enfoque de las Capacidades: Aportes para el Desarrollo Humano en América Latina*, Buenos Aires: Ediciones Manantial.

Ibrahim, S. 2019. "Individualism and the Capability Approach. The Role of Collectivities in Expanding Human Capabilities", in Chiappero-Mratinetti, E., Osmani, S., and Qizilbash, M. (eds), *The Cambridge Handbook of the Capability Approach*, Cambridge, UK: Cambridge University Press, 206–226.

Ibrahim, S., and Alkire, S. 2007. Agency and Empowerment: A Proposal for Internationally Comparable Indicators, *Oxford Development Studies 35/4*, 379–403. https://doi.org/10.1080/13600810701701897

Kamruzzaman, P. and White, S. 2018. Empowerment and Community Participation, *The International Encyclopedia of Anthropology*, 1–10. https://doi.org/10.1002/9781118924396.wbiea2062

Kosko, S. J. 2013. Agency vulnerability, participation, and the self-determination of indigenous peoples, *Journal of Global Ethics 9/3*, 293–310. https://doi.org/10.1080/17449626.2013.818385

Kosko, S. J. 2019. "Cultural Freedom", in Drydyk, J. and Keleher, L. (eds), *Routledge Handbook of Development Ethics*, London and New York: Routledge, 299–309.

Leßmann, O. 2011. Freedom of Choice and Poverty Alleviation, *Review of Social Economy 69/4*, 439–463, https://doi.org/10.1080/00346764.2011.577349

List, C. and Pettit, P. 2011. *Group Agency: the Possibility, Design and Status of Corporate Agents*, Oxford: Oxford University Press. http://dx.doi.org/10.1093/acprof:oso/9780199591565.001.0001

Malavisi, A. 2109. "Epistemology", in Drydyk, J. and Keleher, L. (eds), *Routledge Handbook of Development Ethics*, London and New York: Routledge, 41–51.

Malhotra, A. and Schuler, S. R. 2002. "Measuring Women's Empowerment as a Variable in International Development", in Narayan, D. (ed.), *Measuring Empowerment: Cross-disciplinary Perspectives*, Washington, DC: World Bank, 219–246.

Mansuri, G. and Rao, V. 2013. *Localizing Development: Does Participation Work?* Washington DC: World Bank.

Mohan, G. 2014. "Participatory Development", in Desai, V. and Potter, R. B. (eds), *The Companion to Development Studies 3rd Ed* (2.10), London and New York: Routledge, 131–136.

Murphy, M. 2014. Self-determination as a Collective Capability: The Case of Indigenous Peoples, *Journal of Human Development and Capabilities 15/4*, 320–334. https://doi.org/10.1080/19452829.2013.878320

Nebel, M. and Herrera-Nebel, M. 2017. Midiendo la meta-capabilidad de agencia: base teórica para la creación de un indicador de responsabilidad. *Ethics and*

Economics 14/2, 4–24. https://papyrus.bib.umontreal.ca/xmlui/bitstream/handle/1866/18959/2017v14n2_Nebel%26Herrera-Nebel.pdf?sequence=1

Northover, P. 2014. "Development as Freedom", in Desai, V. and Potter, R. B. (eds), *The Companion to Development Studies 3ʳᵈ Ed.* (1.7), London and New York: Routledge, 33–38.

Ostrom, E. 1990. *Governing the Commons*, Cambridge, Cambridge University Press.

Ostrom, E., Burger, J., Field, C. B., Norgaard, R.B., and Policansky, D. 1999. Revisiting the commons: Local lessons, global challenges, *Science 284*, 278–282.

Otano, G. 2015. La libertad como relación social, *Revista Iberoamericana de Estudios de Desarrollo 4/1*, 98–127. https://doi.org/10.26754/ojs_ried/ijds.144

Pelenc, J., Bazile, D., and Ceruti, C. 2015. Collective capability and collective agency for sustainability: A case study, *Ecological Economics 118* (2015) 226–239. https://doi.org/10.1016/j.ecolecon.2015.07.001

Penz P., Drydyk J., and Bose P. 2011. *Displacement by Development: Ethics, Rights and Responsibilities*, Cambridge: Cambridge University Press.

Pham, T. 2018. The Capability Approach and Evaluation of Community-Driven Development Programs, *Journal of Human Development and Capabilities 19/2*, 166–180. https://doi.org/10.1080/19452829.2017.1412407

Rauschmayer, F., Polzin, C., Mock, M., and Omann, I. 2018. Examining Collective Action Through the Capability Approach: The Example of Community Currencies, *Journal of Human Development and Capabilities 19/3*, 345–364, https://doi.org/10.1080/19452829.2017.1415870

Robeyns, I. 2005. The Capability Approach: A theoretical survey, *Journal of Human Development 6/1*, 93–117, https://doi.org/10.1080/146498805200034266.

Robeyns, I. 2017. *Wellbeing, Freedom and Social Justice: The Capability Approach Re-Examined*, Cambridge: Open Book Publishers, https://dx.doi.org/10.11647/OBP.0130

Rosignoli, F. 2018. Categorizing Collective Capabilities, *Partecipazione e conflitto 11/3*, 813–837, https://doi.org/10.1285/i20356609v11i3p813

Ruiz-Bravo, P. 2018. *Análisis de las múltiples dimensiones y factores asociados al empoderamiento de las mujeres en el Perú a partir del uso de una aproximación de metodologías mixtas*. Perú: INEI.

Samman, E. and Santos, M. 2009. Agency and Empowerment: A review of concepts, indicators and empirical evidence, *OPHI Research in Progress Series*. https://www.ophi.org.uk/wp-content/uploads/OPHI-RP10a.pdf

Sen, A. 1985. Well-Being, Agency and Freedom: The Dewey Lectures 1984, *The Journal of Philosophy 82/4*, 169–221, https://doi.org/10.2307/2026184.

Sen, A. 1992. *Inequality Re-Examined*, Oxford: Clarendon Press.

Sen, A. 1999a. *Development as Freedom*, New York: Alfred A. Knopf, Inc.

Sen, A. 1999b. Democracy as a Universal Value, *Journal of Democracy 10/3*, 3–17.

Sen, A. 2002. Response to commentaries, *Studies in Comparative International Development 37/2*, 78–86, https://doi.org/10.1007/BF02686264

Sen, A. 2009. *The Idea of Justice*, London: Allen Lane. https://doi.org/10.1017/S095382081100046X

Sewell, W. 1992. A Theory of Structure: Duality, Agency, and Transformation, *American Journal of Sociology 98/1*, 1–29.

Stewart, F. 2005. Groups and Capabilities, *Journal of Human Development 6/2*, 185–204. https://doi.org/10.1080/14649880500120517

Stewart, F. 2013. *Capabilities and Human Development: Beyond the Individual—The Critical Role of Social Institutions and Social Competencies* (SSRN Scholarly Paper No. ID 2344469). Rochester, NY: UNDP.

Stewart, F., and Deneulin, S. 2002. Amartya Sen's Contribution to Development Thinking, *Studies in Comparative International Development 37/2*, 61–70. https://doi.org/10.1007/BF02686262

UNDP. 2002. *Human Development Report 2002: Deepening Democracy in a Fragmented World*, New York: Oxford University Press.

Volkert, J. 2015. Concepts of Agency, Sustainable Human Development (SHD) and Collective Abilities, *Collectivity in the Capability Approach, E-Bulletin of the Human Development & Capability*, Number 22, June 2013, 9–12.

5. The Systemic Outcome of Common Good Dynamics

Humanity

Clemens Sedmak

1. Being Human Together

We are human together or we are not human at all—this well-known idea, expressed in the influential concept of 'ubuntu', is a vivid illustration of the common good as the flourishing of a community in conversation with the flourishing of each of its members (Mnyaka and Motlhabi 2005, pp. 215–237). 'In conversation' should mean that there is a mutual dependence between the wellbeing of the community and the wellbeing of all the different members. This, then, would presuppose an idea of shared aspects of wellbeing and flourishing, in other words: a shared sense of humanity. It is for good reasons that the Truth and Reconciliation Commission in South Africa, chaired by Archbishop Desmond Tutu and committed to the common good of the country, embraced the concept of 'ubuntu' explicitly in its report as a guiding principle: 'The work of the Commission as a whole [...] underlined the need to restore the dignity of all South Africans. In the process, the sons and daughters of South Africa would begin to feel truly "at home".'[1] This commitment to 'all' and the idea of 'feeling at home' is a particular way to express dimensions of the common good, with its imperative of 'Do not leave anyone behind!'

---

[1] Truth and Reconciliation Commission of South Africa Report, Volume 1, p. 125 (https://www.justice.gov.za/trc/report/finalreport/Volume%201.pdf). An entire section of the first volume of the final report is dedicated to the concept of 'ubuntu' (pp. 125–131).

    https://doi.org/10.11647/OBP.0290.07

In this sense, a common good approach with its commitment to 'each person' and the entire community is, in the last analysis, incompatible with selective approaches of a utilitarian kind that are prepared to pursue the greatest good of the greatest number and thereby sacrifice the inclusion, wellbeing or flourishing of certain persons or groups. I do not want to deny that a common good approach is demanding and limited in its implementability, and that, practically speaking, there is a lot of overlap between a common good approach and utilitarian ways of proceeding, but there is a fundamental difference between the idea that each person counts and a more pragmatic outlook. The idea of humanity, expressed in a common good approach, includes the vision that 'it takes all,' the entire human family, to help us understand what it means to be human. There are many accounts of lessons learnt through people who have special needs and special gifts (e.g., Adam 2014, Beck 2011). We do not understand what it means to be human by looking at what Eleonor Rosch, founder of the 'prototype theory,' has called 'good examples,' culturally coded paradigms that we use to introduce a category (Rosch 1978, pp. 27–48). An able-bodied, adult, white male person is not a 'better example' for being human than a newborn diagnosed with Trisomy 18. It takes the entire community to teach us what it means to be human.

The common good can be seen as both the outcome and the condition of the possibility of 'living a fully human life,' a life truly in accordance with human dignity. The dimension of 'humanity' in the common good model explored in this volume is positioned as the result of the other dimensions. The humanity dimension in this model can be described as values of the nexus, specifically social goods, collective habits, and the transition towards the universal common good based on a sense of common humanity (see Chapter 2).

Two key dimensions have been identified in the model, namely 'basic common goods' (common goods needed by a person to gain access to her humanity, namely social goods such as life, family, work, health, education, political and associative life, cultural identity) and 'core habitus' leading towards human flourishing (approximated through the 'collective habits': freedom and responsibility, justice and solidarity, peace and concord, prudence and magnanimity, perseverance and courage, resilience and sustainability).

The fundamental understanding of the dimension of 'humanity' that I propose in this chapter is the ability to live a life in accordance with one's dignity and as a recognised member of the human family. The very idea of human rights expresses this point about 'belonging' to normative contexts beyond both individuals and states. Humanity is the intended 'end point' and ongoing point of reference for commitments to and efforts towards the common good. The realisation of the common good is a healthy, vibrant, and flourishing human community that allows each member to live a life in accordance with her and his human dignity and humanity.

This brings us to the question of what it means to be human. I will explore this question from different angles, reflect on the implications of these reflections for the understanding of (the social practices of) the common good, and provide four main indicators for 'humanity' as a key dimension of the common good-model discussed in this book.

2. On Reflections on Being Human

Before I dive into the exploration of what it means to be human one word about the 'methodology:' What are appropriate ways to reflect on this question of what it means to be human? There is a vast and multi-layered discourse; there are eye-opening debates on what it means to be human and negotiate the differences between human and non-human animals, between humans and machines (Kahn et al. 2007, pp. 363–390).[2] There are many interesting questions one could ask when one connects the discourse on 'being human' with the discourse on 'being a person:' What does it mean to become a person?[3] What do we know when we know a person?[4] How do we know that someone is a person?[5]

---

2   Peter Kahn and colleagues, for instance, have discussed the question of being human and exploring human-robot interaction by discussing possible benchmarks (autonomy, imitation, intrinsic moral value, moral accountability, privacy, reciprocity, conventionality, creativity, and authenticity of relation); in this way they arrive at relevant reference points for an understanding of humanness.

3   This is a question Carl Rogers (1961, pp. 107–124) asked in his attempt to get behind the mask and facade of the people he worked with and to encourage them to be themselves and discover themselves in and through their experiences.

4   Dan McAdams (1995, pp. 365–396) asked this question in his insightful text and distinguished between three levels: traits, personal concerns, and identity understood as an inner story of the self that integrates the reconstructed past, perceived present, and anticipated future to provide a life with unity, purpose, and meaning.

5   I will explore this question further below in conversation with Eva Feder Kittay.

These are questions that structure the landscape of reflections on what it means to be human. We are not neutral observers in and of this landscape, but participants on non-neutral ground. A philosophical reflection on what it means to be human will use a particular methodology, i.e., the tools of reflection and the reflective processing of experiences, and the tools of conceptual clarifications and distinctions. My contribution is not empirical, or evidence-based with an analysis of the biological foundations of the human species; for the sake of this brief text my text is also not 'reconstructive' by engaging in the vast philosophical literature on personhood and humanity. Rather, I will use a 'phenomenological method' that is based on philosophical reflections which are inevitably the result of a conversation with experiences and encounters. There is an undeniably subjective element in this approach which is presented as 'a conceptual and perceptual offer.' I have decided to first pursue a *via negativa* by learning about humanness and humanity from an extreme example of dehumanisation, and then to engage in a constructive suggestion on crucial elements of what it means to be human.

3. On Being Human

It is amazing and touching, horrifying and dreadful, what human beings are able to do and able to do to and with each other. Primo Levi's account of his experience of concentration camps, *Se questo è un uomo* (1947), talks about what it means to be human. On the evening before the deportation, all took leave, as he describes, from life in the manner which most suited them, praying, drinking, sleeping.

> The mothers stayed up to prepare the food for the journey with tender care, and washed their children and packed the luggage; and at dawn the barbed wire was full of children's washing hung out to dry. Nor did they forget the diapers, the toys, the cushions and the hundred other small things which mothers remember and which children always need. Would you not do the same? If you and your child were going to be killed tomorrow, would you not give him to eat today? (Levi 1959, p. 6)

Primo Levi talks about the systematic erosion of all the human and the humane in the concentration camp. Human beings, persons, people like you and me, are reduced to miserable and sordid puppets. We are transformed into [...] phantoms [...] Then for the first time we became aware that our language lacks words to express this offence, the demolition of a man. In a moment, with almost prophetic intuition, the reality was revealed to us: we had reached the bottom. It is not possible to sink lower than this; no human condition is more miserable than this, nor could it conceivably be so. Nothing belongs to us anymore; they have taken away our clothes, our shoes, even our hair [...] They will even take away our name. (p. 21)[6]

Levi describes the systemic attempt to create conditions that foster hatred among the prisoners, a 'homo homini lupus'-attitude, a loss of the meaning of life and will to live. But he also mentions the heroic attempts to uphold a sense of humanity in the midst of the cruel darkness. He refuses to believe 'in the most obvious and facile deduction: that man is fundamentally brutal, egoistic and stupid in his conduct once every civilized institution is taken away' (p. 100); he mentions the strength and pain drawn from the past and its memories, the hopes to reach the next day and maybe spring. He talks about a fellow human being, Lorenzo, who reminded him of his own humanity by being human:

I believe that it was really due to Lorenzo that I am alive today; and not so much for his material aid, as for his having constantly reminded me of his presence, by his natural and plain manner of being good, that there still existed a just world outside our own, something and someone still pure and whole, not corrupt, not savage, extraneous to hatred and terror; something difficult to define, a remote possibility of good, but for which it was worth surviving [...] The personages in these pages are not men. Their humanity is buried, or they themselves have buried it [...] Lorenzo was a man; his humanity was pure and uncontaminated, he was outside the world of negation. Thanks to Lorenzo, I managed not to forget that I myself was a man (Levi 1959, p. 142).

There can be light in the midst of utter darkness; but it is terrifying to understand that this darkness was created, inhumaneness human-made.

We can learn a lot from Primo Levi about what it means to be human— *ex negativo*; at the same time, the account of his experience teaches us

---

6   Levi talks about the 'satanic knowledge of human beings' (p. 102) and the annihilation of a sense of civilisation, citizenship, decency: 'The Kapo comes to us periodically and calls: "*Wer hat noch zu fressen?*" He does not say it from derision or to sneer, but because this way of eating on our feet, furiously, burning our mouths and throats, without time to breathe, really is "*fressen*," the way of eating of animals, and certainly not "*essen*," the human way of eating, seated in front of a table [...] "*Fressen*" is exactly the word and it is used currently among us' (Levi 1959, p. 85).

a lot about 'the common bad,' the opposite of the *bonum commune* we are looking for. We can see (i) how and that terror and unpredictability lead to toxic structures, (ii) how and that systematic disrespect for basic physical needs and elementary bodily functions lead into the destruction of a sense of Self, (iii) how a sense of a common good is undermined in the concentration camp through internal divisions and toxic hierarchies, (iv) how and that an almost complete loss of the possibility for intimacy and friendship can reduce the human person to a commitment-free shell, (v) how and that hell on earth is created to 'the loss of why,' the loss of justification and meaning making in the social world (the mistake of the Jewish person was not something she or he had done, but was on the level of being, an 'ontological defect,' as Vladimir Jankéléitch has named it). We can see that 'the common bad' can be systematically constructed. The concentration camps dehumanised the person by a detailed system of reducing a person to her biology whereby this very biological dimension was trampled upon (Wachsmann 2015).

So what does it mean to be human? If we were to teach a course on being human—what would we teach? If we were to tell aliens what it means to be human—what would we say?

In order to answer these questions, it could be fruitful and important to ask a simple question: reflecting on 'a human life'—which are features that are part of the human condition?

These thoughts are based on a philosophical commitment to the possibility of speaking about 'a human condition' in ways that transcend subjective and contextual differences. Martha Nussbaum's list of essential human capabilities has pursued a similar avenue. She has identified central human capabilities by analysing the human condition: Life, Bodily Health, Bodily Integrity, Senses, Imagination and Thought, Emotion, Practical Reason, Affiliation, Other Species, Play, Control Over One's Environment (Nussbaum 2003). Nussbaum presents this list as a normatively relevant list with an acceptance of universalism that Amartya Sen, co-creator of the capability approach, would not share. I do not intend to engage in a detailed discussion of Nussbaum's helpful list. I would like to offer more descriptive considerations, reflecting on the way human beings live their lives.

My considerations are based on the belief that there are aspects of life that we all share as human beings; I believe that there are certain characteristics of the human condition that are part of any human existence.

I want to offer a tentative 'list' of aspects that, each in its own way, co-constitute the human condition:

- 'being somewhere and unique': each person has a particularity in history and character, in 'place in time' and 'place in world'; there is uniqueness to a person so that she cannot be 'replaced' as the person she is.

- 'having a vulnerable body': each person has a body and this body is vulnerable, i.e., at risk of damage; the body shapes perspective and 'being-in-the-world.'

- 'depending on external circumstances': each person depends on a physical environment including natural resources, but also structures (to protect from the elements) and enable coexistence.

- 'having a history and a story that can be told': each person has a life with experiences that can be remembered and a life story that can be told as a unique story of a human life.

- 'seeking a "life place"': a life place is the analogy of a work place which is different from work—it is constituted by structures; the human person needs more than survival, she is yearning to have a place characterised (and constituted) by commitments, commitments she was offered, commitments she entered.

- 'living interdependently in special relationships': it is not the case that all relationships are on the same level and it is not the case that any person would be socially self-sufficient: the human person depends on other persons and each person has special relationships with special obligations based on closeness and attachment.

- 'knowing and creating darkness': the human person is able to create evil, to be cruel and destructive beyond description and imagination.

- 'being able to be moved and touched and hurt': the human person has the ability to host another person in her utmost inner, for her own good or for her own bad.

- 'showing an ability for the good': the human person is able to show amazing levels of moral and spiritual sainthood.

- 'having inner inexhaustible depth': the human person has inner complexity, a rich interior life, interiority with memories, beliefs, hopes, dreams...

- 'being finite and mortal and limited': the human life comes to an end, each person is limited by time, but also in terms of capability.

- 'desiring beyond the finiteness and mortality': the human person—in spite of her mortality—can cultivate imagination, desires, and hopes beyond these limits.

- 'learning and growing without losing the "before"': the human person changes, grows—but whatever has been part of her experience remains to be part of her life.

- 'seeking recognition': the human person seeks to have a 'face', seeks 'to be seen', seeks to be accepted as a person among persons.

- 'being open to the intangible': the human person is open to the immaterial and cannot be defined to what can be seen and cannot be reduced to what can be measured.

This is, of course, a tentative list, but it opens up the possibility for asking the kinds of questions that may be helpful to have a clearer idea of the 'humaneness' generated by common good-oriented policies.

This list gives me four main ideas about what it means to be human: (i) uniqueness and complexity; (ii) vulnerability and socialness; (iii) agency and the power to transform. And, with the claim that this list talks about characteristic aspects of the human condition, (iv) equality and existential closeness. We could connect these four elements with Primo Levi's account, which showed how uniqueness and complexity were trampled upon by the reduction and erasure of all personal traits, how vulnerability was exploited to create isolation, how agency was systematically taken away, and how equality was eroded by divisions and toxic hierarchies.

4. On Human Dignity

The list that I suggested—and the four reference points drawn from the list—may seem a bit arbitrary. Another way to think about 'being human' is a conversation with an influential normative tradition, the Universal Declaration of Human Rights. The first article of this declaration offers reference points for what it means to be human: 'All human beings are born free and equal in dignity and rights. They are endowed with reason and conscience' (UDHR, Art. 1).

Let me offer seven observations that reflect on implications of these two simple sentences of the first article of the declaration:

Observation 1: Vulnerability—the UDHR is based on the experience and the recognition of vulnerability which is also expressed in the Preamble ('disregard and contempt for human rights have resulted in barbarous acts which have outraged the conscience of mankind'); I would claim that there can be no discourse on human dignity without the experience of vulnerability.

Observation 2: The primacy of freedom (humans are born free—this can be interpreted to mean: restrictions have to be justified; the burden of proof lies with those restricting human freedoms; certain restrictions are incompatible with these freedoms).

Observation 3: Fundamental equality (the fundamental equality among human beings is so deep that hierarchies or stratifications cannot outweigh it).

Observation 4: 'Right to Reason/s' (reason is connected to dignity—this could mean that there is a 'right to use reason' and a 'right to be treated in a reasonable way').

Observation 5: Uniqueness ('conscience' is a category that expresses a deep personal sense of morality, where a person is to be treated on her own terms).

Observation 6: Respect (if we acknowledge that a person has dignity, we owe respect to this person).

Observation 7: Self-respect (if I acknowledge that I have dignity, I owe respect to myself).

These observations also offer some reference points for 'being human'. These observations can also be connected to the four main ideas about being human above: i) uniqueness and complexity can be connected to Observation 5, which comments on uniqueness, and to Observation 7, which talks about self-respect; (ii) vulnerability and socialness is strengthened by Observation 1 on vulnerability; (iii) agency and the power to transform is linked to the point about freedom in Observation 2, but is also connected to the 'right to reason', as expressed in Observation 4; (iv) equality and existential closeness express a similar concern to Observation 3 on equality, but can also be connected to the idea of respect (see Observation 6).

One could translate these points into the idea that living a life in accordance with one's human dignity means living a life that allows for (i) the expression of uniqueness, self-respect, the pursuit of complexity, (ii) the protection and cultivation of proper vulnerability, the entering of relationships, (iii) the experience of agency, respect for the right to reason and reasoning, the cultivation of the potential to transform the world into a better place, (iv) the experience of equality and respect.

This is rather sketchy, but it points to aspects of a dignified life where each person is on the search for 'her place' and needs the appropriate support structures to carve out the niche in the universe that is 'hers', 'inhabited', and 'owned' by the person.

Two excellent and also tragic example of this search would be Edward Said and Sally Morgan's journeys (Said 1999, Morgan 2012). Both accounts show tragic aspects of this search and exemplify *ex negativo* the need for appropriate support structures and access to sources of identity. Both accounts show that humanity is not only an individual feature, but also a relational good. If we think of humanity as an entelechy in an Aristotelian sense, it is a shared and common entelechy. We are only human together or not human at all. The human person is social by its very nature. We only achieve who we are by our interactions with others; the good of the human person is a relational good. We are only human if we work together to achieve this humanity in the practice that bounds us together as human beings.

Living a life according to one's dignity allows for robust identity, based on recognition. In accordance with Nebel and Medina (see Chapter 2), the 'humanity'-dimension of the common good can benefit from a translation of these aspects of the human person into social practices and collective habits. One such fundamental social practice is the practice of seeing a person in her uniqueness which is indispensable in pedagogical as well as professional contexts. Let me illustrate this point by making use of the idea of 'job crafting.' 'Job crafting' is the project of changing and creating relationships, shaping interactions, and (re)defining tasks and aspects of one's job (Wrzesniewski and Dutton 2001, pp. 179–201; Wrzesniewski et al. 2013, pp. 281–302). Job crafting is an important aspect of 'inhabiting a role.' A professional role is inhabited if it has been appropriated to fit the person of the job holder; the distinction between 'inhabited' and 'non-inhabited' has been inspired by Aleida Assman's (2011) distinction between 'inhabited memory' and 'non-inhabited memory' (pp. 19–135). The latter points to museums and archives and memory contents that do not stir emotions, that do not lead to conversations, that do not play a role in people's lives; the former ('inhabited memory') refers to cultures of remembering that shape communication and interactions, that show people's emotions. An inhabited role has been personalised and reflects the style and personality of the role's occupant. Honoring the uniqueness of a person allows the person to 'inhabit' her social space. French sociologist Alain Ehrenberg (2010) has shown that non-inhabited roles can lead to mental health challenges and an 'exhausted self', that cannot identify with or shape the role assigned to the individual. In other words, a life in accordance with the dignity of the person allows the person to identify and inhabit a place of her own.

5. A Caveat

I have offered a list of fifteen aspects of the human condition that can be folded into four main ideas which I have strengthened by seven observations on the first article of the Universal Declaration of Human Rights.

However, there are limits to lists like these: in her Presidential Address to the American Philosophical Association in 2017, Eva Feder Kittay tackles the question of being human and offers a reflection on the life of her daughter, 'a beautiful woman of forty-seven, with lively brown eyes and a winning smile,' and with 'very significant cognitive disabilities. She has no measurable IQ and can do nothing for herself by herself. She defies philosophical characterisations of what is human, namely, the possession of certain essential attributes assumed to be definitive of the human. She is often written out of our moral treatises, though human she surely is' (Kittay 2016, p. 24). Kittay is worried about abstract lists of essential attributes that amount to necessary conditions of being human. It is through interactions with her daughter, it is through being in the presence of her daughter, that anyone could sense her being human:

> she spends her weekends with us listening and thrilling to music ranging from Bach to Mahler and from Louis Armstrong to Bob Dylan. When favorite Schubert and Beethoven pieces play, she tries to catch my eye so I will hum along. And engaging her ability to choose between two options, she has indicated to me, as best as I can tell, that she prefers to be regarded as a young woman, not a child. Again, let me be clear, my daughter has no measurable IQ. (Kittay 2016, p. 24)

An approach outlining necessary conditions of humaneness in a list seems morally risky since it may exclude for abstract reasons persons who—in an encounter—will be accepted as 'human' without any doubt. There seem to be more appropriate ways of approaching the question of what it means to be human than through the construction of lists. Lists end each item with a full stop, a period. There is however space for the imagination to rethink the connections between the different items on the list and the imaginary space beyond the period. There is also the point of the limits of language and the phenomenon of touching a dimension that cannot be fully expressed. Humanity's mystery, humanity's life is left in between the different items of any list.

I teach a course on Integral Human Development; we dedicate a session or two to the explicit question of what it means to be human. We work with photographs and poems; we reflect, for example, on the Pulitzer Prize-winning photographs: the famous 1973 picture by Nick Ut capturing a naked nine-year-old girl (Phan Thị Kim Phúc) who is running toward the camera and away from a napalm strike; the terrible 1994 photograph by Kevin Carter for feature photography depicting a girl crawling to a feeding centre as a vulture waits nearby; the passionate 1997 photograph by Annie Wells showing a firefighter rescuing a teenage girl during a raging flood; and many more. We take our time to look at these 'signs of the times' and ask the question: what does this say about 'being human'? We talk about what a researcher from another planet would deduce about humanity looking at these photographs.

We reflect on poems, for example on poems written by Hilde Domin who had to flee from the Nazis, first to Italy, then to England, and finally to the Dominican Republic. Many of her poems express the 'longing for belonging', and the experience of loss. We reflect on sentences like 'A rose is a rose. But a home is not a home' or 'You eat remembrance with the spoon of forgetting' or 'we collect tears like marbles.' What does this language express that could not be expressed outside of poetry? What do poems say about humanity? What does Hilde Domin teach us about the human condition?

The very fact that due to its complexity the understanding of humanity is also elusive is an important aspect of the complexity and elusiveness of the common good that is never 'here' or 'there', but always in the making or in the breaking.

The fact that lists about humanity and being human are limited says a lot about the human condition. What does 'being human' mean, more practically speaking?

6. Indicators for Humanity

This book develops a specific model of the common good. Humanity has been identified as a central component of the model. Living in accordance with our dignity as human beings and building communities that reflect this understanding of universal dignity of the human person is the very point of the dimension of 'humanity'. The abovementioned list expressed important aspects of this project of a dignified life. I take the aspect of 'humanity' within the pentagram to mean: living a life according to the dignity of the human person; being able to live one's life as a member of the human family.

I have suggested four main ideas about living a human life in accordance with human dignity: uniqueness (and complexity and self-respect); vulnerability (and social dependence); agency (freedom and right to reason), equality (and existential closeness). These four ideas—uniqueness, vulnerability, freedom, and equality—shape the dimension of 'humanity', also with regard to the common good. We need to identify proper, dignity-sensitive ways to build social frameworks, cultures, communities, and institutions. If these dimensions are to be constitutive aspects of the realised common good, we will have to translate them into stable social practices and collective habits. Let me clarify terms first. I want to characterise social practices as follows:

Social practices are *expressions of coordinated human agency involving a significant number of people who incorporate these expressions of agency into their everyday life as members of a community in such a way that these patterns of agency build tradition and do not require explicit justification.*

Social practices are characteristic of a form of life and reflect a worldview that serves as the framework for further judgements, points we find well developed in Pierre Bourdieu's and Anthony Giddens' work. Social practices shape communal life as 'communal' and the identity of community members as community members. Examples of social practices include established celebrations like the 'Dia de los muertos' in Mexico, the culture of tipping as in the United States, and designs of interactions as ways of greeting another person. Social practices can be translated into collective habits: a habit is an established form of action; it is an acquired behavioural disposition, lives from repetition and is characterised by a certain effortlessness. The latter also makes habits so attractive—they make life easier, because I do not have to design new actions in every situation, but can resort to familiar patterns. This ease can become a pattern that makes it very tiring to act against the habit that, after a certain frequency of execution, is also 'automated', that is, behaviour that the actors do not think about. In 1799, the French Academy of Sciences announced an essay contest on 'Habits'. Pierre Maine de Biran, the subsequent winner, noted how difficult this task was, since habits, as familiar matters of course, are hidden from view. In short, they do not catch our eye. It is a paradox that the establishment of a habit leads to the evanescence of the habit, it loses 'perceptibility'. Some habits are the result of explicit decisions and efforts, other habits 'sneak in'. Some social practices have been intentionally established, others grow organically.

In line with the four aspects of humanity listed above I would like to suggest four indicators for humanity—in response to uniqueness and complexity: *practices of reconciled pluralism*; in response to vulnerability: *practices of deep inclusion*; in response to agency: *habits of well-reasoned integral ecology*; in response to equality: *patterns of permeability*.

(1) *Practices of reconciled pluralism* refer to the ability to deal with 'the different and the new'; the recognition of the uniqueness of the person requires proper respect for pluralism without destroying the idea of the common ground. Mechanisms of standardisation may increase social cohesion, but could undermine respect for the uniqueness of the person. Pluralism is a challenge to the concept of the common good that lends itself to a thicker reading of society (more in the line of 'community'). The litmus test for reconciled pluralism is a community's ability to accommodate newness.[7]

Questions to operationalise this aspect would be questions like: how does a community deal with newness that challenges established social practices? How does a community deal with the uniqueness of persons? How does a community deal with difference? With deviance? In other words: are there 'meta-social practices' that allow for the modification of existing, or establishment of new, social practices? Are there spaces for experiments? Are there provisions for non-standard approaches? How strict are the patterns of standardisation relating to different spheres of life within a community?

(2) *Practices of deep inclusion*: the common good is not a utilitarian approach, but is committed to 'leaving no one behind'. Each life matters and counts. The idea here is that the common good stands, to quote Stefano Zamagni,

> [in] contrast [...] with the notion of the total good. Whereas the latter can be rendered by the metaphor of an addition, in which the items to be added stand for the good of individuals (or the social groups that make up society), the common good is more like a multiplication, whose factors stand for the good of individuals (or groups) [...] Thus, if the goal is to maximize the total good (e.g., national GDP), anyone's good (or welfare) can actually be 'cancelled out' provided someone else's welfare increases by more than the other person loses. In a multiplication, on the other hand, cancelling out just one factor reduces the entire product to zero. In other words, the logic of the common good does not allow trade-offs: one

---

7   A fascinating case study on conflict culture and the challenge of negotiating pluralism has been provided by Adam Goguen and Catherine Bolten (2017, pp. 429–456) in their analysis of a conflict between two villages in Sierra Leone during the Ebola crisis, where the villages had to negotiate different conceptions of the common good and the relationship between 'the village good' and 'the national good'; the case study reconstructs a conflict that could not deal with 'reconciled pluralism', partly because of ideas of 'honour' and the limited range of reasons.

person's good cannot be sacrificed—whatever the person's life situation or social rank—in order to increase someone else's good, for the basic reason that the 'someone else' is still a human being. (Zamagni 2018, p. 86)

I accept this point to underline that my understanding of the dimension of humanity does not allow for 'a single person left behind'. This can be demanding since it may take a lot of effort to make sure that everybody can participate and contribute. Some people need higher levels of accompaniment than others. Some people have higher levels of vulnerability.[8] However, in light of an understanding of the common good as a 'multiplication', I want to propose to understand the 'humanity' dimension of the pentagram by way of the 'no one left behind' aspiration: is every member of the community invited into a life as a contributive agent, into a life in accordance with her dignity? Are there social practices that are committed to ensuring that no one is left behind, including especially those who need intensive and extensive levels of accompaniment? I want to call social practices that are committed to leaving no one behind even under adverse circumstances 'deep inclusion'. Such social practices are connected to 'going the extra mile', 'giving second chances', making a special effort to leave no one behind. like special assistance in schools for children with special needs, like special workplace provisions for people with special needs, like support structures for persons who cannot live a self-determined life. Social patterns of deep inclusion are social practices that resist exclusion.

(3) *Habits of integral ecology*: human agency in times of a fragile planet has to be based on sustainable reasons, i.e., ways of justifying individual and collective behaviour that take future generations and future communities into account. We have reached the point where the sustainable securing of agency cannot be separated from ecologically sensitive habits. I understand that this is a specific aspect of agency. However, the survival of 'humanity' depends on the realisation of 'integral ecology' that connects the ecological with the social and the cultural. Proper sustainability will include the poor. The prize for

---

8　An important aspect of this question of deep inclusion is the inclusion of children and youths—in discourses and practices of international development the challenge of recognising children and youths as contributing agents is real—see, for instance Fine and Lord (2015).

ecologically irresponsible living has to be paid, at least in the initial stage, by the poor. Hence, a life in accordance with human dignity cannot be separated from a life that respects the ecological aspect of human existence, the fact of non-human life. A third indicator, then, for humanity is the question of proper habits of integral ecology. The humanity dimension of the pentagram could suggest an 'inventory of habits' that contribute to integral ecology, especially insofar as they relate to social relations and ecological relations. This is based on the idea that 'habits' are crucial expressions of the dimension of humanity and that the connection between human dignity and the ecology is fundamental for a reading of the situation in which we find ourselves.

What are the defining habits of a community? How sustainable is the culture of agency in a particular context? What are the patterns of consumption in a particular community, the culture of using resources, the habits that form a lifestyle? A habit-inventory can look into the different areas of life (such as consumption, resource management, lifestyle) systematically.[9] Again, with social scientific sampling methods it is not too difficult to get a sense of where a community stands in terms of its consumption patterns, resource management, and lifestyle-habits. Socially and ecologically toxic habits can be identified and the contributions of policies to these habits can be tested.

(4) *Patterns of permeability*: the dimension of humanity requires the experience of a human dignity-based equality that takes priority over social stratification. That is why I would like to suggest as a fourth indicator for the dimension of humanity the aspect of social permeability: do the structures of public spaces and shared times allow for easy encounters across the social strata where human beings can interact as human beings? Any social structure is characterised by a hierarchy which is important for order and frameworks, but does make it more difficult to get a sense of equality that is crucial for an understanding of human dignity and an understanding of a dignity-based approach to the common good. Permeability is the feature of a social life that allows for transitions across the boundaries of social and cultural spheres, that

---

9   An illustrative case study was carried out years ago by British journalist Leo Hickman (2005), who systematically experimented with his life in the light of ecological challenges and was confronted with major challenges in four areas: transportation, consumption, waste, and the use of chemicals.

allows for interactions and encounters beyond the restrictions of class membership. Social practices that reveal patterns of permeability and facilitate cross-class encounters can be taken to be an indicator for a form of life shaped by an understanding of dignity.

An example would be widely accessible cultural events like village festivals that bring the entire population together. Religious celebrations or sports events can facilitate permeability, too. The key question is: are there non-stratified spaces and times for universal encounter and shared experiences of all? In other words: are there fora where class membership does not play a defining role, where class membership is not relevant for access conditions? These questions are connected to questions of public space: are there public spaces where encounters between different people can happen easily? Are there 'commons' that allow for permeability?

I have suggested four main ideas for being human: uniqueness, vulnerability, agency, and equality. I have suggested four tentative indicators for these four ideas respectively: practices of reconciled pluralism; practices of deep inclusion; habits of well-reasoned integral ecology; patterns of permeability.

Additionally, I would like to suggest one overarching indicator that is based on the idea of human dignity: in conversation with Avishai Margalit's *The Decent Society* (1998) I suggest non-humiliation as a minimum standard for honouring a person's dignity; this is clearly not 'deep inclusion', but a minimum threshold. This may not be full recognition of a person's uniqueness, but a non-negotiable bottom line. The dimension of humanity within the common good assessment of a community can also be approximated by mapping 'entry points for humiliation', with a special emphasis on institutions. Respect and self-respect have been identified as implications of the recognition of human dignity. I use Margalit's understanding of humiliation as 'any sort of behavior or condition that constitutes a sound reason for a person to consider his or her self-respect injured' (1996, p. 9). Self-respect is the kind of respect I owe myself on the basis of being human. Procedurally, this means accepting a subjective and an inter-subjective element—a community with its institution or an institution is well advised to ask its members whether and when they experience or perceive humiliation (the subjective element) and then enter into a discourse about the rationale behind this perception (the social element). I have experimented with 'mapping entry points of humiliation' within the institutional settings of a hospital and an educational institution. It has proved to be a worthwhile and feasible exercise. Patients in a hospital have identified bodily shame and nakedness, lack of privacy and loss of personhood in a hospital setting as possible entry points for humiliation; 'humiliation' is an important reference point in institutional and communal settings (Sedmak 2020, pp. 9–17). Humiliation dehumanises a person and undermines what has been identified as the 'humanity' dimension of the common good. Meaningful questions could be: where do communities and institutions create entry points for humiliation? Which entry points for humiliation are identified by individuals? Which are social practices that show a commitment to non-humiliation?

Reconciled pluralism, deep inclusion, integral ecology permeability, and non-humiliation could emerge as indicators for humanity in a community.

Conclusion

The dimension of 'humanity' is never a given, it is always a task and a responsibility. And this responsibility comes with a price tag that cannot be reduced to 'fun' or 'quality of life'. To live in accordance with one's dignity is not the project of having an easy life. The famous Polish pediatrician Janusz Korczak, who ran an orphanage in the Warsaw ghetto and was killed along with the children (whom he could have abandoned), once wrote a prayer: 'Dear God, I do not ask you for an easy life, I ask you for a difficult life, but useful, dignified, and beautiful.' His life was just like that: difficult, useful, dignified, beautiful—and cut short.

The dimension of 'humanity' in the common good or the concept of the common good is not to be reduced to aspects of quality of life; we need something more, a 'Magis', what I would call 'depth of life'. A sense of what counts and matters even at the cost of reduced quality of life. Ultimately, the indicator for humanity is: are we willing to uphold the sense of human dignity, each person's dignity, even under adverse conditions?

In Hilde Domin's beautiful words: 'Longing for a landscape this side of the border of tears doesn't work [...] What works is to ask please [...] that we, out of the flood, out of the lion's den and the fiery furnace will be released renewing ourselves even more wounded and even more healed.'

References

Adam, R. 2014. *Raising Henry. A Memoir of Motherhood, Disability, and Discovery.* New Haven, CT: Yale University Press.

Assmann, A. 2011. *Cultural Memory and Western Civilization: Functions, Media, Archives.* Cambridge University Press.

Beck, M. 2011. *Expecting Adam*, New York: Three Rivers Press.

Ehrenberg, A. 2010. *The Weariness of the Self: Diagnosing the History of Depression in the Contemporary Age*, Montreal: McGill-Queen's University Press.

Fine, P., and Lord, K. M. 2015. International Development's Awkward Stage, *Foreign Policy*, 13 March, https://foreignpolicy.com/2015/03/13/international-developments-awkward-stage-youth/.

Goguen, A. and Bolten, C. 2017. Ebola Through a Glass, Darkly: Ways of Knowing the State and Each Other, *Anthropological Quarterly 90/2*, 429–456. https://doi.org/10.1353/anq.2017.0025

Hickman, L. 2005. *A Life Stripped Bare. My Year Trying to Live Ethically*, London: Transworld.

Kahn, P. H., Ishiguro H., Friedman, B., Takayuki, K., Freier, N. G., Severson, R. L., and Miller, J. 2007. What is a human? Toward psychological benchmarks in the field of human–robot interaction, *Interaction Studies 8/3* (2007), 363–390. https://doi.org/10.1075/is.8.3.04kah

Kittay, E. F. 2017. The Moral Significance of Being Human, *Proceedings and Addresses of the American Philosophical Association 91*, 22–42.

Levi, P. 1959. *If This Is a Man*, New York: Orion Press.

Margalit, A. 1996. *The Decent Society*, Cambridge, Mass.: Harvard University Press.

McAdams, D. 1995. What Do We Know When We Know a Person? *Journal of Personality 63/3*, 365–396.

Mnyaka, M. and Motlhabi, M. 2005. The African Concept of Ubuntu/Botho and its Socio-Moral Significance, *Black Theology 3/2*, 215–237. https://doi.org/10.1558/blth.3.2.215.65725

Morgan, S. 2012. *My Place*, London: Virago Press.

Nussbaum, M. 2003. Capabilities as Fundamental Entitlements: Sen and Social Justice, *Feminist Economics 9/2–3*, 33–59. https://doi.org/10.1080/1354570022000077926

Said, E. 1999. *Out of Place: A Memoir*, New York: Alfred Knopf.

Sedmak, C. 2020. Dignity and Decency. Personal Integrity and Decent Institutions, *Journal of Hospital Ethics 7/1*, 9–17.

Rogers, C. 1961. *On Becoming a Person. A Therapist's View of Psychotherapy*, Boston: Houghton Mifflin.

Rosch, E. 1978. "Principles of Categorization", in Rosch, E. and Lloyd, B. (eds), *Cognition and Categorization*, Hillsdale, NJ: Lawrence Erlbaum.

Truth and Reconciliation Commission of South Africa Report, Volume 1. https://www.justice.gov.za/trc/report/finalreport/Volume%201.pdf.

Wachsmann, N. 2015. *KL: A History of the Nazi Concentration Camps*, New York: Farrar, Straus and Giroux. https://doi.org/10.1093/ahr/122.1.139

Wrzesniewski, A., and Dutton, J. E. 2001. Crafting a Job: Revisioning Employees as Active Crafters of Their Work, *Academy of Management Review 26/2*, 179–201. https://doi.org/10.2307/259118

Wrzesniewski, A., LoBuglio, N., Dutton, J. E., and Berg, J. M. 2013. "Job Crafting and Cultivating Positive Meaning and Identity in Work", in Bakker, A. B. (ed.), *Advances in Positive Organizational Psychology*, Volume 1, Bingley: Emerald Publishing Limited, 281–302.

Zamagni, S. 2018. "The Common Good and the Civil Economy", in Nebel, M. and Collaud, T. (eds), *Searching for the Common Good. Philosophical, Theological and Economic Approaches*, Baden-Baden: Nomos, 79–98. doi.org/10.5771/9783845283012-80

6. Governance, Commoning and the Unequal Terms of Recognition

Tom De Herdt and Denis Augustin Samnick[1]

'We define governance as the traditions and institutions by which authority in a country is exercised for the common good', wrote Daniel Kaufmann (2005, p. 82), then lead economist at the World Bank and one of the driving forces behind the World Bank's Worldwide Governance Indicators programme. Kaufmann's definition is focused entirely on governance by state authorities: how they function, how they manage the economy and how they are judged by their citizens. The governance indicators also draw on a particular understanding of what 'good' governance means—i.e., how these traditions and institutions need to function, to manage and to be perceived in order to realise the common good.

We do however not learn what 'common good' means. Kaufmann presumably thinks and writes within a liberal, if not utilitarian, tradition for whom 'the common good is simply a matter of satisfying consumer preferences' (Sandel 2020, p. 421). He also embraces, in a next step, what Amartya Sen (2009) would call transcendental institutionalism: equipped with a pre-established definition of the common good, Kaufmann allows himself to transcendentally identify the ideal set of institutions and rules—independently from context or history—to

---

1   The authors would like to express their thanks both to the editors of this volume and to two anonymous referees for their valuable comments and suggestions. Remaining errors are ours.

 https://doi.org/10.11647/OBP.0290.08

realise the common good and, further down the line, to design the 'worldwide governance indicators' as a measure to estimate the distance still to cover between a country's actual situation and this ideal.

In this chapter, we first take issue with such a liberal conception of the common good. Still within the confines of the transcendental institutionalism breathed by economics textbooks, we rehearse the claim, already made by others (e.g., Hardin 1968), that this conception falls short in trying to seek ways to produce common pool goods (or to avoid common bads). While some authors have, in response, delineated a third mode of governance (besides 'state' and 'market') as 'community', pointing to the need for recurrent interactions and face-to-face societies, in the rest of the paper we explore solutions that go beyond a rational, choice-based, institutionalist theory (e.g., Ostrom 1990). We argue that Michael Sandel's 'civic approach' to the common good as essentially a product of public deliberation, reflection and negotiation, may be quite helpful on this point. The focus of governance shifts, here, from Kaufmann's public authority to *commoning* (Fournier 2013), to the discursive encounters where we define, contest, and redefine who we are in relation to others, and how we engage with them in common ventures.

We argue our case by taking a closer look at the experimental literature on social dilemmas, which demonstrates well to what extent individuals ostensibly deviate from their self-interest in an attempt to do what we interpret as seeking social recognition.

In a final step, we argue about the importance of recognising commoning as a new field of public action—in line with what Vijayendra Rao called the *reflective paradigm for policy-making*, a family of policies that focuses on the institutional processes at work, rather than on the realised outcomes, in improving the quality of life. The complication is that, in situations of unequal terms of recognition, public action may be experienced as *in*action by marginalised groups, even if these actions ostensibly validate the common good.

1. Common Goods in Economics Textbooks

Economics textbooks generally start with the assumption that 'in the beginning there were markets'.[2] In other words, they consider all goods *by default* as goods that lend themselves to buying and selling by self-interested individuals through market transactions; others types of goods are then distinguished as special cases compared to this default. This is so because it can be proven that under a number of (quite stringent) conditions, transacting goods through the market leads to the most efficient allocation of resources, in the sense that, after all transactions have taken place, no party would be able to improve herself without any cost to another party. Such an optimal allocation first of all depends however on the conditions under which a market functions, and it depends on some particular characteristics of the goods themselves: What makes goods particularly apt for being marketed is that there is rivalry in consumption (the shoes I wear cannot be worn by you) and that they are excludable (it is relatively easy to exclude people refusing to pay for them from using them). The criteria of rivalry and excludability then lead to the definition of three other types of goods, besides market goods:

Table 1. Types of goods.

		Excludability of non-payers?	
		Yes	No
Rivalry in consumption?	Yes	Private goods	Common (pool) goods
	No	Club or toll goods	Public goods

Public goods, which are non-excludable and non-rivalrous: a national defence system for instance is non-rivalrous because the fact that I am protected does not necessarily imply that my neighbours cannot be

---

2   In actual fact, the expression was literally coined by Oliver Williamson (1975), who argued his theory of the firm in terms of a (new kind of) market failure. See also Gindis and Hodgson (2007, p. 378) for Williamson's justification of this.

protected from the same army. It is also non-excludable as there is no automatic exclusion of my neighbour from protection if he does not want to pay and freeride. Given this non-excludability, private providers would be reluctant to produce the goods. Indeed, non-excludability doesn't go well with market transactions. We would need a state to constrain people to pay taxes, which can then be invested in public goods.

Club goods or toll goods, which are non-rivalrous, but excludable: private providers would be able to provide them, given their excludability. Sports clubs, highways or trains do fulfil these criteria. Though, in practice, states can also organise such goods.

Common (pool) goods are perhaps the most intriguing category, being rivalrous goods, which are non-excludable: a fish stock in international waters is clearly rivalrous (my consumption of the fish would prevent you from consuming it) but also non-excludable. Beyond the domain of states, who would exclude people not wanting to pay for it?

This leads us to point to what we would call a missing mode of governance in the textbook economists' view of the world: self-interest can drive the allocation of market goods, government-backed constraint should come in to govern public goods, and club or toll goods can best be governed by either markets or states, but how could we possibly prevent common bads like over-fishing? The textbook answer is: we can't. This is exactly what the *tragedy of the commons* is all about: 'Freedom in a commons brings ruin to all' (Hardin 1968, p. 1244). To an extent, it is possible to deal with common goods by finding a way to solve the problem of excludability, e.g., by organising fishing licenses, but such solutions are far from perfect. In one way or another, the category of common goods (or bads) pushes us out of a worldview that tries to represent the world as populated by self-interested individuals and governed by either markets or states. Where would the necessary *self-restraint* come from if it cannot be explained by self-interest, nor by the external constraint provided by an institute embodying the 'legitimate monopoly on the use of violence', Max Weber's classic definition of the state?

2. There Is Such a Thing as Society

Before continuing, note that we constructed 'textbook economics' as a strawman here. Textbooks, notwithstanding some widely recognised deficiencies, may still retain a pedagogical value and our strawman can still keep up appearances as a textbook, even in a world that is markedly different from the way in which it is represented in a course of economics. The problem starts however whenever someone confuses the world and its representation. When Margaret Thatcher stated that 'there is no such thing as society'—in her eyes, there were just 'market' and 'state'—we think she did exactly commit this error.

Yujiro Hayami and Yoshihisa Godo (2005) call the missing mode of governance 'community', which they describe as repeated interactions between people who can monitor each other's actions. These are the conditions that (sometimes) can do the trick of aligning individual self-interest and collective interest through the enforcement of social norms: contrary to legal norms, social norms do not need to be backed up by professional norm-enforcers if all community members would be ready to punish free-riders. In these conditions, free-riding might be rewarding in the short run, though in the long run the prospect of being excluded from further transactions would tilt the balance towards the negative. Likewise, punishing free-riders may imply a short-term cost, but in light of the prospect of repeated interactions, such punishment may eventually become rewarding.

Hence, 'community' may in effect provide for a governance mechanism to solve a number of common (pool) goods problems, and it would do so without having to leave the textbook world of self-interested individuals. But we are far here from finding a solution to, for example, the problem of over-fishing in international waters: indeed, Hayami and Godo instead focus on collective action problems at the local level of say, a rural village, where both the conditions of repeated interactions and the ability to monitor each other are fulfilled. What about the more challenging common good problems that do not fall within the boundaries of local, face-to-face communities?[3]

---

3   Some have argued that 'community' has perhaps only reached macro-level proportions in Western Europe, due to a Christian heritage that promoted a generalised morality 'in which abstract principles or rules of conduct are considered equally applicable to a vast range of social relations beyond the narrow circle of personal acquaintances' (Platteau 1994, p. 770).

Well, empirically speaking, Hardin's prediction of a tragedy has in any case been refuted. In a review paper published twenty-two years after Hardin's publication, the authors conclude that 'a diversity of societies in the past and present have independently devised, maintained, or adapted communal arrangements to manage common-property resources. Their persistence is not an historical accident; these arrangements build on knowledge of the resource and cultural norms that have evolved and been tested over time' (Feeny et al. 1990, p. 13). In the same year, Elinor Ostrom publishes her 'governing the commons' book (Ostrom 1990), which tries to find some patterns in the multiplicity of working arrangements people have devised so as not to have to live the tragedy of the commons or worse, to depend on less efficient forms of governance such as the market or the state. As documented also in her later work, these arrangements can take different forms (varying from self-organised units, to government or private arrangements) and they can be situated at different levels and in different institutional ecologies (Ostrom 2007). What also transpires from this work is that '[e] vidence from field and experimental research thus challenges the basic underlying model of individual behavior used in neoclassical economics, public choice theory, and game theory. In some settings, individuals do contribute to public goods, do restrict their use of a resource, and do trust one another contrary to theoretical predictions' (2007, p. 255). It is not that this empirical work leads to an alternative theory, capable of predicting that common goods problems will invariably be solved, yet the evidence is sufficiently robust to reject the prediction of an invariable tragedy—also at levels and for cases very different from the local, face-to-face societies studied by Hayami and Godo.

3. Ultimatum Game Experiments

While Ostrom eloquently identifies this gap between empirically observed arrangements and the textbook assumption of individual self-interest, she also argues that the literature on game experiments may help us in exploring the unresolved puzzle of the micro foundations of common pool resources. Indeed, this literature allows us to build an argument that, at least on some occasions, at least some people's behaviour cannot fully be described by simply referring to self-interest

(Ostrom 2007, p. 255). In the Ultimatum Game, for example (Güth et al. 1982) one player (the Proposer, P) receives a fixed amount of money that s/he has to distribute between him- or herself and another player (the Respondent, R). R can accept or reject and when s/he rejects both players will not receive anything.

Experimental results, played among anonymous players, typically show that *average* offers are around 30–40% of the available amount and the *modal* offer by Ps is typically half of the available amount of money. At the same time, most offers of less than 20% are rejected by R (Camerer and Thaler 1995). These results are also valid when the amount of money to be distributed is increased, from $10 to $100 (Hoffman et al. 1996). Note that the Ps were able to *anticipate* the occurrence of punishment: perceiving that others would not hesitate to resort to 'punishment' (by refusing the offer), they already changed their behaviour before being punished. We can still understand Ps as rational actors, optimising their interests given what they believe, yet unlike in the world of textbook economics, they believe that many Rs will not behave rationally: they are ready to punish free-riders even at an individual cost to themselves.

But why wouldn't Rs indeed opt to get at least something out of the experimental setting, instead of refusing the proposal because it would be too inequitable? The experiments have in any case been set up in such a way that they do not have any material interest in punishing inequitable proposals. And neither does anyone oblige them to do this. Yet they do. And while this experimental game setting looks quite extraordinary, think of some everyday examples where people spontaneously engage in enforcement of a social norm, even at a cost to themselves. Doing this, they attempt (or propose) to reproduce a particular social ordering, not just at the micro-level but at the macro-level as well: in democracies, for example, people exert the effort to vote, at a known cost but with an unknown (and often insecure) benefit (Etzioni 2015).

Further refinements allow us to gain a better understanding of the 'inequity' that moves Rs to refuse a proposal: it is not really the unequal outcome as such that moves Rs to reject P's offer, since Rs do not systematically reject all unequal proposals. Indeed, Rs do readily accept highly unequal allocations when they know that P could not do otherwise (Falk et al. 2003) or when they play against a computer, for instance (Blount 1995). What seems to be at stake is something deeper than the material cost: it is not the matter that matters, but recognition, one's social position or one's relationship vis-a-vis others.[4] We are apparently much less reluctant to be dominated by 'chance and circumstances' (as Karl Marx argued), than to be dominated by others. Likewise, 'the nature of things does not madden us, only ill will does', said Rousseau (quoted in Berlin, 1958). Applied to the setting of an Ultimatum Game, purely self-interested action by P would crucially carry the implication that P would not fulfil his or her *relational obligation* towards R. We borrow this concept from Waheed Hussain's (2018) definition of the common good as 'those facilities—whether material, cultural, or institutional—that the members of a community provide to all members in order to fulfil a relational obligation they all have, to care for certain interests that they have in common'.

We go along however with Fournier's (2016) argument that those material, cultural or institutional facilities are themselves already the outcome of '*commoning* as organizing in common' (2016, p. 438). Likewise, for Michael Sandel (2020, p. 421) the common good 'requires deliberating with our fellow citizens about how to bring about a just and good society, one that cultivates civic virtue and enables us to reason together about the purposes worthy of our political community'.[5] While Hussain's definition focuses on the facilities, Sandel's definition focuses on the process or the activity of commoning on which these facilities are based.

Commoning would crucially hinge both on how different parties understand their relational obligations towards each other, and on what Mario Luis Small called *cognitive empathy*, 'the ability to understand another person's predicament as they understand it' (cited in Vijayendra Rao 2019, p. 187). Ultimatum Game situations appear to exemplify what exactly is at stake here: P's behaviour is crucially determined by cognitive empathy in figuring out what they stand to do to respect their relational obligation towards Rs. Lacking this empathy, they would offer a very unequal deal, which would subsequently risk being rejected by R. It is empathy that allows P to take into account the impact of his/her actions on 'the relationality of individuals; the political, social and cultural contexts within which they operate; and

---

4   For further discussion of this, see De Herdt and D'Exelle (2009).
5   See also Sen (2009) on rationality and public reasoning.

the impact of these processes on power differences, inequality and poverty' (Rao 2019, p. 186).

This mechanism apparently even works in a 'minimal institutional situation' (Ostrom 2007) where individuals don't know each other and where they can neither communicate with each other, nor influence each other in other ways.

To be sure, while empathy may make the difference in arriving at a settlement that can be agreed at by both players, and while this feature explains why *most* UG experiments do result in a cooperative outcome, the tragedy of the commons cannot always be ruled out. Contra Hardin, freedom in the commons doesn't bring ruin to all, but nor does it bring success to all. Perhaps the most important lesson to draw from these experiments is that what exactly a 'relational obligation' means in the (ultra-primitive) context of an Ultimatum Game is far from a universal given.

To begin with, Henrich et al. (2006) report on what they describe as cultural differences in playing UGs in different institutional contexts. In all 'cultures', one can observe the same dynamics, with proposers making a more equal proposal for distribution whenever responders have the possibility to reject, but at the same time, it can be observed that in some cultures, responders will be more lenient in tolerating inequality, or to the contrary adhere more strictly to the 50/50 distribution, and where proposers can follow suit in outguessing the reactions to their moves.

Even more intriguingly, small variations in Ultimatum Game experiments also show how easy it is to modify the experimental outcomes, just by changing the narrative introducing an experiment (Hoffman and Spitzer 1985, Larrick and Blount 1997). Even simply replacing the word 'opponent' with 'partner' in the experimental instructions can make a significant difference in increasing the cooperative outcome (Hoffman et al. 2000). Interestingly, in terms of the structure of incentives, the Ultimatum Game, with its focus on allocation between ego and alter, is also structurally equivalent to some versions of the 'social dilemma' experiments published in the field of social psychology. In the latter, the probability of an equal outcome is far higher as it focuses not on 'an amount of money' but on 'a common resource' or a 'joint product', the proceeds of which have to be distributed (Larrick and Blount 1997).

The high sensitivity of UG-outcomes to the precise way in which the game has been framed by a particular discourse informs us about 'how the mind works in real players' (Hoffman et al. 2000, p. 6). Incentive structures do undoubtedly co-determine the final outcome, but they do so only partly: the other part of the explanation is provided by how players see themselves in relation to each other while defining their entitlements and moving into action. However poorly defined the institutional context of Ultimatum Game experiments, real players' behaviour takes place in a discursive context that drives the results as much as the material stakes.

Of course, the 'minimal institutional context' in which most Ultimatum Game experiments have been carried out is also quite unrepresentative of the socio-economic world in which we are operating most of the time, even if they are increasingly carried out not in a lab but in concrete field settings, e.g., with Colombian peasants (Cardenas and Carpenter 2008) or Nicaraguan women's groups (D'Exelle and Holvoet 2011). But in everyday socio-economic interactions, people can, and do, talk and reflect together. It is a world of cooperative conflicts.

4. Entanglement in Cooperative Conflicts

Interestingly, the UG experiments show how difficult it is to 'extract' the role of self-interest as such as an explanation of human behaviour, independently from its discursive context, *and vice-versa*, even if the experimental variations of the UG succeed quite well in showing the role played by both. There is always such a thing as society, and in this sense, 'in the beginning was the market' is simply an economistic chimera. But at the same time, there is also always such a thing as an individual, articulating her self-interest in a particular social context.

The UG is perhaps the most primitive version of such situations of what Amartya Sen called 'cooperative conflict' (Sen 1987), where parties have partly conflicting interests, but also common interests in the sense that they have much to gain from cooperation. In his analysis of gender inequality, Sen argued for analysing household dynamics not just (i) in function of the ability parties have to opt out or exit from a particular relationship (an ability that is also captured by the bargaining models of (household) decision-making), but also (ii) in function of the perceptions they have about the interest they have in cooperating, and (iii) of their perception of the contributions they make to cooperation.

Elements (ii) and (iii) are evidently highly influenced by cultural practices and discourses.

Sen himself did not extend this analysis beyond the institution of the household, though Drèze and Sen (1989, p. 48) argued that 'There *are* many advantages to be gained by different people from cooperation and collaboration, and yet there are also elements of clash and divergence of interests. Such coexistence of cooperation and conflict is endemic in social relations'. Others, too, explored the pros and cons of such an extension more in detail (Gore 1993; Leach et al. 1999; Devereux 2001). Crucially, to the extent that people's entitlements are entangled in cooperative conflicts with others, these entitlements become as much a *source* of people's capabilities as a *function* of their doings and beings. What's more, they also become as much a source of *other* people's doings and beings, as other people's doings and beings are a source of theirs. Taking this observation seriously would inevitably tilt entitlement analysis out of the ordinary textbook economics world where individuals are stand-alone bearers of state-backed rights and where individuals' capabilities can be used as a basis to judge their quality of life, as if no such thing as society existed.

It is probably not a coincidence that Sen developed his 'extended entitlement analysis' at the level of the household only, it allowed him to keep on working with a methodological individualist framework right up to the doorstep of the household and to restrict the complexities of entangled entitlements at the household level. But if people's involvement in the arrangements that allow them to access particular resources and services is usually a deeply *collective* endeavour, and if their entitlements most often have a social dimension—either because of joint involvement in a productive venture or because of collective access to a valued resource—people's *individual* entitlements to the proceeds of such a productive venture or people's *individual* access to a valued resource will depend on the way in which these ventures or resources are regulated, and in this, *others'* agency plays a role at least as important as one's own. In this respect, it may be useful to compare Sen's conception of (different kinds of individual) freedom with the way in which the German sociologist Georg Simmel conceived of freedom:

> Freedom is not a solipsist being but a sociological doing, not a state in which an individual finds himself in but a relatedness, however freely

engaged in from the perspective of the individual [...] Within our relationships, freedom shows itself as a continuous process of liberation (Simmel 1908, p. 57).

Up to a point, the arguments of Sen and Simmel are not incompatible, in that the former focuses on the final result, whereas the latter concentrates on the process leading to this result. Even if, ultimately, it is individual freedom we care about, we need to trace this freedom back to the 'process of liberation' that produces it, since the interdependence intrinsic in this process also implies that much depends on how actors *perceive* themselves as entangled with others' predicaments.

5. A Discursive Layer of Inequality

One intriguing consequence of Drèze and Sen's view that cooperative conflicts are an endemic feature of social relations is that we need to evaluate relative or absolute advantage at two levels: one level is the 'deal one gets', the allocation of a resource or distributional outcome of a particular (partly joint) venture. The other level has to do with participation at the discursive level, with a more or less unequal 'ability to question, challenge, propose and ultimately usher in new ways of doing things' (Bebbington 1999, p. 2034).

Whereas there may be different arguments to justify unequal distribution in the first layer, one of the normative axes underlying the persistence of inequalities in commoning is a deficit concerning what Nancy Fraser calls 'the norm of parity of participation' (Fraser 2011, p. 50). Such an imbalance is inevitably accompanied by a lack of *intersubjective recognition of each person's particularity* (Honneth 2013, p. 31). When an *intersubjective obligation* (Honneth 2013, p. 85) is difficult to observe in the course of social interaction, consideration of the vulnerability of the other, of his or her existential difficulties and the public problems that result from them, is almost obliterated. We find ourselves here at the heart of social justice issues as formulated by Nancy Fraser.

But equality in participation at the discursive level is not only *intrinsically* important, it may also be *instrumentally* important to discuss and rethink arrangements that result in inequality in the first layer, the layer of resource distribution. The ability to use voice is of particular importance in ushering in a change in the way in which individuals gain access to resources or in the rules or arrangements they make in dividing the surplus of a joint venture among themselves, especially in circumstances where the structure of incentives points in a different direction.

This being said, 'exerting voice' is evidently a characteristic of a relationship; it cannot be attributed to an individual, as it supposes an ability to be heard by someone else. Voice is to be understood here as a necessary complement to *exit* and *loyalty*, two other ways of characterising an interaction between different subjects, as developed by Hirschman (1976). In a symmetrical relationship, A as well as B are as free to conform to (loyalty) or contest (voice) the other's expectations. They can also withdraw from the relationship (exit). Conversely, people in marginalised positions may *lack* 'voice to express their views and get results skewed to their own welfare in the political debates that surround wealth and welfare' (Appadurai 2004, p. 63). Appadurai suggests that, because poor people lack voice, the relations they entertain with others oscillate between loyalty and exit:

> Poor people have a deeply ambivalent relationship to the dominant norms of the societies in which they live. Even when they are not obviously hostile to these norms, they often show forms of irony, distance and cynicism about these norms. This sense of irony, which allows the poor to maintain some dignity in the worst conditions of oppression and inequality, is one side of their involvement in the dominant cultural norms. The other side is compliance, not mere surface compliance but fairly deep moral attachment to norms and beliefs that directly support their own degradation. Thus, many untouchables in India comply with the degrading exclusionary rules and practices of caste because they subscribe in some way to the larger order of norms and metaphysical propositions which dictate their compliance: these include ideas about fate, rebirth, caste duty and sacred social hierarchies. (Appadurai 2004, p. 65).

The upshot is that these two layers of inequality do not necessarily converge. It may be materially rewarding for poor people to go along with a downgrading discourse of the rich, a tactic Geoff Wood (2003, p. 468) has dubbed a *Faustian bargain*. Appadurai points in the same way to strategies of poor people to 'optimize the terms of trade between recognition and redistribution in their immediate, local lives. Their ideas about such optimization may not be perfect, but do we have better optima to offer to them?' (2004, p. 65). Asking the question is responding to it.

6. Commoning, Recognition and Public (In)Action

Thus, textbook economics generally propose an ideal architecture of market and state governance that ultimately builds on the assumption of individual self-interest, but such a framework cannot account for solutions to common goods or common bads. However, in the beginning, there were not markets, but social bonds: people relating to each other in a multiplicity of cooperative conflicts. Our ability to reason and organise collectively considerably enriches the institutional landscape, way beyond the textbook economics dichotomy of markets based on voluntary exchange and states based, ultimately, on the monopoly of violence. The way in which people can engage in 'commoning', i.e., jointly reflect on and conceive situations of cooperative conflict, can make an important difference, not only because such parity in participation is intrinsically important, but it is also instrumental in attaining more cooperative outcomes, even in situations where individual interests remain important. If commoning is the name for this third mode of governance, commoning is exactly what we need to seek solutions to common goods and bads.

By way of conclusion, we would like to discuss two other policy implications of our argument.

First, Drèze and Sen rightly point out that 'public action should not be confused with state action only. Various social and political organizations have typically played a part in actions that go beyond atomistic individual initiatives, and the domain of public action does include many non-state activities' (1989, pp. 18–19). This broad organisational set-up, sometimes also referred to as a policy network (Diemel and Cuvelier 2015, McConnell and 't Hart 2019), is often justified in terms of more efficient delivery of goods and services, but it may also carry the risk of hollowing out the public ability to exert effective voice, as argued by Rhodes (2007) for the case of the UK. Mbembe (1999) likewise coins the concept of indirect private government to describe the privatisation of public policy, such as security and public administration. Indirect private government may not only highlight the capacity of networks and lobbies to appropriate the state, it is also accompanied by *a gradual dismantling of public power* (Mbembe 1999, p. 103) and, by extension, of its capacity for social regulation. To the extent that a state does not necessarily guarantee parity in participation, however, this argument lacks a foundation. To be sure, however more efficient such arrangements might be for particular groups of citizens, this efficiency may also be partly paid by delimiting the space for commoning, the ability 'to reason together about the purposes worthy of our political community' (Sandel 2020, p. 428). Everything depends on who defines what 'efficiency' means in particular contexts.

Second, the governance of public action is confronted with a double problem when it does not get around the problem of unequal recognition and social justice. Indeed, in settings where people or groups of people face widely adverse terms of recognition, public action at the same time risks becoming a source of discriminatory public governance and public *in*action with respect to the most disadvantaged. Since the latter are given little consideration in group interactions, a discrepancy is often observed between their lived experiences and the frameworks that sustain the definition of public problems and the organisation of public action (Lavigne Delville 2017, p. 51). This is all the more the case for common goods, whose successful provision hinges on the delineation of boundary rules 'which determine who and what is in and out of a provision organization' (Ostrom 2007, p. 248).

To illustrate (Samnick 2020), the Cameroonian police officer (or, for that matter, the American police officers targeted by the BLM movement) who captures an innocent street-child for a crime he or she did not commit, knows very well that such an arrest will be welcomed both by his or her hierarchy and by society, due to a judgment that is a priori in vogue, according to which most street-children are first and foremost criminals. The capture or imprisonment of such a child will be perceived by society as a repressive public action against crime, while the policeman will only know in his soul and conscience that the child is just a scapegoat that allows him to hide his public inaction in relation to real criminals. Even the street-child themself may go along with the police officer's judgment in a Faustian bargain, hoping that, at a later point in time, and out of the public eye, they will eventually be able to negotiate a quicker way out. Public action is ostensibly complete, but only at the price of public inaction from the perspective of those groups facing adverse terms of recognition.

References

Appadurai, A. 2004. "The capacity to aspire: Culture and the Terms of Recognition", in Rao, V. and Walton, M., *Culture and Public Action*, Stanford: Stanford Social Sciences, 59–84.

Berlin, I. 1958. *Two Concepts of Liberty* Oxford: Clarendon Press.

Bebbington, A. 1999. Capitals and capabilities: a framework for analyzing peasant viability, rural livelihoods and poverty, *World Development*, 27/12, 2021–2044.

Blount, S. 1995. When social outcomes aren't fair: The effect of causal attributions on preferences, *Organizational Behavior and Human Decision Processes 63*, 131–144.

Camerer, C. and Thaler, R. H. 1995. Anomalies: Ultimatums, Dictators and Manners, *Journal of Economic Perspectives 9/2*, 209–219.

Cardenas, J. C. and Carpenter, J. 2008. Lessons from field labs in the developing world, *Journal of Development Studies 44/3*, 311–338. https://doi.org/10.1080/00220380701848327

Devereux, S. 2001. Sen's entitlement approach: critiques and counter-critiques, *Oxford Development Studies 29/3*, 245–263. https://doi.org/10.1080/13600810120088859

De Herdt, T. and D'Exelle, B. 2009. "Fairness", in Peil, J. and van Staveren, I. (eds), *Handbook of Economics and Ethics*, Cheltenham: Edward Elgar Publishers.

D'Exelle, B. and Holvoet, N. 2011. Gender and network formation in rural Nicaragua: a village case study, *Feminist Economics 17/2*, 31–61. https://doi.org/10.1080/13545701.2011.573488

Diemel, J. A., and Cuvelier, J. 2015. Explaining the uneven distribution of conflict-mineral policy implementation in the Democratic Republic of the Congo: The role of the Katanga policy network (2009–2011), *Resources Policy 46*, 151–160.

Falk, A., Fehr, E., and Fischbacher, U. 2003. On the nature of fair behavior, *Economic Inquiry 41*(1), 20–26. https://doi.org/10.2139/ssrn.203289

Feeny, D., Berkes, F., McCay, B. J., and Acheson, J. M. 1990. The tragedy of the commons: twenty-two years later, *Human Ecology 18/1*, 1–19.

Fraser, N. 2020. *Qu'est-ce que la justice sociale? Reconnaissance et redistribution*. Paris: Gallimard. https://doi.org/10.4000/lectures.5207

Etzioni, A. 2014. "Common Good", in Gibbons, M. T. (ed.), *The Encyclopedia of Political Thought*, Oxford: John Wiley & Sons, 603–609.

Fournier, V. 2013. "Commoning: on the social organization of the commons", in: *M@n@gement 16/4*, 433–453.

Gindis, D. and Hodgson, G. 2007. An interview with Oliver Williamson, *Journal of Institutional Economics 3/3*, 373–386. https://doi.org/10.1017/S1744137407000768

Gore, C. 1993. Entitlement relations and 'unruly' social practices: a comment on the work of Amartya Sen, *The Journal of Development Studies 29/3*, 429–460.

Güth W., Schmittberger, R., and Schwarze, B. 1982. An experimental analysis of ultimatum bargaining, *Journal of Economic Behavior and Organization 3*, 367–388.

Hayami, Y. and Godo, Y. 2005. *Development Economics: From The Poverty to the Wealth of Nations*, Oxford: Oxford University Press. https://doi.org/10.1093/0199272700.001.0001

Hardin, G. 1968. The tragedy of the commons, *Science 162*, 1243–1248.

Henrich, J., McElreath, R., Barr, A., Ensminger, J., Barrett, C., Bolyanatz, A., Cardenas, J. C., Gurven, M., Gwako, E., Henrich, N., and Lesorogol, C. 2006. Costly punishment across human societies. *Science 312/5781*, 1767–1770. https://doi.org/10.1126/science.1127333

Hirschman, A. O. 1970. *Exit, Voice, and Loyalty: Responses to Decline in Firms, Organizations, and States* (Vol. 25), Cambridge, Mass.: Harvard University Press.

Hoffman, E. and Spitzer, M. L. 1985. Entitlements, Rights and Fairness: An Experimental Examination of Subjects' Concepts of Distributive Justice, *Journal of Legal Studies 14/2*, 259–297.

Hoffman, E., McCabe, K., and Smith, V. 1996. On Expectations and Monetary Stakes in Ultimatum Games, *International Journal of Game Theory 25/3*, 289–301.

Hoffman, E., McKabe, K., and Smith, V. 2000. The Impact of Exchange Context on the Activation of Equity in Ultimatum Games, *Experimental Economics 3*, 5–9. https://doi.org/10.1023/A:1009925123187

Hussain, W. 2018. "The Common Good", in Zalta, E. N. (ed.), *The Stanford Encyclopedia of Philosophy* (Spring 2018 Edition), https://plato.stanford.edu/entries/common-good

Honneth, A. 2013. *La lutte pour la reconnaissance*, Paris: Gallimard.

Kaufmann, D. 2005. *Myths and Realities of Governance and Corruption*. MPRA paper n° 8089, https://mpra.ub.uni-muenchen.de/.

Larrick, R. and Blount, S. 1997. The claiming effect: Why players are more generous in social dilemmas than ultimatum games, *Journal of Personality and Social Psychology 72*, 810–825.

Lavigne Delville, P. 2017. Pour une socio-anthropologie de l'action publique dans les pays 'sous régime d'aide', *Anthropologie & Développement 45*, 33–64, https://doi.org/10.4000/anthropodev.542

Leach, M., Mearns, R., and Scoones, I. 1999. Environmental entitlements: dynamics and institutions in community-based natural resource management, *World Development 27/2*, 225–247.

Mbembe, A. 1999. Du gouvernement privé indirect, *Politique Africaine*, 73, 103–121.

McConnell, A. and 'T Hart, P. 2019. Inaction and public policy: understanding why policymakers 'do nothing', *Policy Sci 52*, 645–661, https://doi.org/10.1007/s11077-019-09362-2.

Ostrom, E. 1990. *Governing the Commons; The Evolution of Institutions for Collective Action.* Cambridge: Cambridge University Press.

Ostrom, E. 2007. Challenges and growth: the development of the interdisciplinary field of institutional analysis, *Journal of Institutional Economics 3/3*, 239–264. https://doi.org/10.1017/S1744137407000719

Rhodes, R. A. 2007. Understanding governance: Ten years on, *Organization Studies 28/8*, 1243–1264. https://doi.org/10.1177/0170840607076586

Samnick, D. A. 2020. Empirical and Epistemological Perspectives of Public (in) Action in Central Africa: An analysis of the Struggle against Urban Banditry in Cameroon. Mimeographed.

Sandel, M. J. 2020. *The Tyranny of Merit: What's Become of the Common Good?* New York: Farrar, Straus & Giroux.

Sen, A. 2009. *The Idea of Justice.* London: Allen Lane, and Cambridge, MA: Harvard University Press. https://doi.org/10.1017/S095382081100046X

Sen, A. 2010. Adam Smith and the contemporary world, *Erasmus Journal for Philosophy and Economics 3/1*, 50–67. https://doi.org/10.23941/ejpe.v3i1.39

Rao, V. 2019. Process-Policy and Outcome-Policy: Rethinking How to Address Poverty and Inequality, *Daedalus 148/3*, 181–190. https://doi.org/10.1162/daed_a_01756

Stern, N. 2006. *The Economics of Climate Change: The Stern Review*, Cambridge: Cambridge University Press. https://doi.org/10.1111/j.1728-4457.2006.00153.x

Williamson, O. E. 1975. *Markets and Hierarchies: Analysis and Anti-Trust Implications: A Study in the Economics of Internal Organization*, New York: Free Press.

7. Organising Common Good Dynamics

Justice

Rodolfo De la Torre[1]

Introduction

The common good refers to those social conditions that members of a community provide to everyone in order to fulfil a relational obligation they all have to care for certain interests that they share. In very general terms, justice is what we owe to each other, and underlies the will to render to each his or her due. So, justice is part of a relational obligation necessary to promote common interests and requires the provision of particular social conditions to be fulfilled.

The 'nexus of the common good' is a collection of interrelationships between various specific common goods in a given society. As a nexus, the Common Good, capitalised to distinguish it from specific common goods, is a set of social relationships to fulfil voluntarily shared commitments. Justice is one of these communal links for the accomplishment of reciprocal duties.

The relationship between justice and the Common Good is a key element for a meaningful measurement of the Common Good itself. In this link, there is a difference between a *shared meaning* of justice, which is abstract and general, and the implied share of the *common benefits* created by a common good, with concrete rules to operationalise the

---

1   Centro de Estudios Espinosa Yglesias.

    https://doi.org/10.11647/OBP.0290.09

concept of justice. The former is the practical reason to accomplish an equitable distribution of the latter. Both could be examined in terms of moral values, either consequential (i.e., having utility) or not.

The *social meaning* of what is just, intangible as it is, has to be translated into a concrete and measurable way to decide individual conflicts about what is exclusive and competitive. Several questions arise: what is understood by justice at the level of concepts and procedures? What role should be given to an appraisal of their outcomes? Considered as ways and/or consequences, justice is one of the normative dimensions of any model of the Common Good. It is one of the social functions that regulate the nexus's organisation.

The goal of this chapter is to explore possible metrics for the justice component of the nexus of the common good concept, building on Nebel and Medina (Chapter 2). The proposed metric should be focused on the nexus's procedural or distributional relationships, and it should be simple and unambiguous. As a nexus, the Common Good should be conceived as social cohesion stemming from shared meaning in a specific society and providing unity, identity, stability, and resilience to the community.

Justice should include a shared perception of goals, a shared procedure for achieving them, and a shared way to distribute benefits or results. Justice implements acceptable interactions (procedural justice) and what is fair (distributional justice) in the nexus. Justice watches to make sure the nexus does not disintegrate, and it seeks to promote a dignified and flourishing life for each and every person in the nexus, which in turn promotes justice.

The present document is divided into four sections. The first revises the concepts of the common good and the nexus of the common good, and the normative dimensions proposed to measure the quality of the nexus. This section discusses the link between the common good and two economic concepts related to both the idea and mechanisms of justice: social welfare and public goods. The second section analyses the meaning of the concept of justice as a normative dimension of the common good. Finally, the last two sections explore alternative ways to measure 'justice', including justice as equality of opportunity.

The chapter proposes the following:

1. Justice cannot be reduced to a separate dimension on its own, isolated from the agency (see Chapter 4), humanity (see Chapter 5), governance (see Chapter 6), and stability (see Chapter 8) components of the Common Good. However, it makes sense to distinguish this dimension for analytical and measurement purposes. This means that the measurement exercises are unavoidably quite static and limited in scope.

2. It is convenient to conceptualise the justice component of the Common Good as dealing with the fair generation of social goods and the possibility of shared benefits according to individuals' contributions to the production process of the Common Good, but in a context of social solidarity. For this to happen, individual agency must be protected, which implies that the procedural aspect of justice be measured.

3. One way to translate the concept of distributive justice to a measurable index that goes beyond equality of results is through the idea of equality of opportunity. Solidarity requires that circumstances beyond the control of individuals— circumstances that put them at a disadvantage with respect to others—be compensated for, so results are determined only by effort, which is under each person's control. The inequality of results explained by circumstances is an indirect measure of 'unfairness' or distributive injustice.

The chapter concludes by describing actual measurements of inequality of opportunity for several countries, including how the concept relates to the idea of social mobility. The chapter presents measures of inequality of opportunity at the state level in México, and suggests ways to obtain such indices at the municipal level. Finally, several limitations and warnings about the inequality of opportunity approach are presented.

1. The Common Good

Embodied in institutions, goods, and practices, a common good is a set of shared values and interests within a group of autonomous individuals who relate in a certain way with respect to each other (e.g., as members of a family, as part of an organisation, or as citizens in a society). A common good is a set of conditions that enable the members of a group to attain for themselves reasonable objectives, for the sake of which they have reason to collaborate with each other in a community (Finnis 2011). A common good approach focuses on groups or communities while concentrating on the process through which they achieve and maintain social goods (see Introduction, Chapter 1 and Chapter 2).

The common good is a concept that can be used to assess the moral goodness of social states in which the explicit position and the relationships of each participant with respect to others is important. It does not entail that individuals have the same values; it implies only that there be some set of conditions that needs to be present if each person is to attain their own objectives. Unlike the economic notions of 'efficiency' or 'social welfare,' or even transcendental institutionalism's views of justice (Sen 2009), the common good goes beyond the anonymity of individuals or just the consideration of end results.

The common good is a notion of what is good within the boundaries of a social relationship. It consists of the conditions and interests that members have a special obligation to care about due to the specific relationship they have with other members of a group. In a neighbourhood, for instance, public goods, like street lamps that work, or clean sidewalks, are part of the common good because the bond of sharing the same public spaces requires members to take care of them in order to ensure safety and sanitary conditions for all.

I. Social Welfare and the Common Good

Economic values that are intended to be universal, such as efficiency or maximum social welfare, transcend the relationships in a specific community. Unlike the common good, these concepts set out fully independent standards for the goodness of social states with no fundamental reference to the requirements of a social relationship. According to economic efficiency defined by the Pareto criterion, for example, opportunities to improve some members of a society should be judged impartially without worrying about who benefits, as long as at least one individual improves without making others worse. But in a relationship that defines how individuals should act towards one another—e.g., neighbours should prefer to improve their neighbourhood if this does not harm others—the neutrality of efficient allocations does not satisfy the requirements of the relationship.

Social welfare notions that incorporate efficiency and distributive elements—e.g., inequality aversion—closely relate to the idea of distributive justice and could be useful within the boundaries of a relationship. For example, giving priority to the worst-off member of the neighbourhood, implied by a maximin Social Welfare Function, is closely related to the Rawlsian idea of transcendental justice, and makes sense when solidarity has been established in a community. But even equality-sensitive notions of the good retain other features that make it difficult to see how these notions could be internal to a relationship (Sen 1993a). One example is agent neutrality, which implies that the correct course of action does not change with the relationships that the agent happens to have (Williams 1973). Understood in this way, the common good requires an agent to perform an action in a non-neutral way, from the standpoint of her relationship with her group, instead of doing what is optimal for the world's welfare in the abstract.

Because it is a non-neutral notion, the common good requires, for example, neighbours to prioritise their own circumstances such that doing so would bring about the best result for the welfare of the group. A neighbour might be required to act this way, even when increasing the welfare of her neighbourhood would lead to a suboptimal level of welfare in the world as a whole. These implications clearly take into account the ordinary understanding of the agent-relative character of relational requirements.

Social welfare criteria used to evaluate situations present in a society (social states) are not based on conceptions of the common good. Even the economic value of social relationships, based on concepts like social capital, is concerned with non-positional concepts of what is socially preferred: notions of the good or value that are independent of any particular social relationship. Nonetheless, an economic account of individual preferences for behaviour with a social benefit may incorporate a conception of the common good as part of agents' motivation to contribute to aggregate welfare.

II. Public Goods and the Common Good

As a concept, social welfare is related to the idea of common good, since welfare is affected by changes in social behaviour guided by common good criteria and vice versa. Although they are not the same, the understanding of one concept enriches the other. Another important relationship to draw is between the common good and a public good. In economic theory, a public good is a particular type of good that all members of a community can enjoy (*non-exclusion*) without the consumption of one individual interfering with the consumption of any other (*non-rivalry*) (see Chapter 6).

A public good is hard to achieve by market mechanisms, where each agent is motivated only by their own self-interest. For example, imagine that the residents in a town could enjoy clean common areas if every resident followed the simple rule of not littering and paying their taxes, which in turn pay for cleaning. Cleanliness costs time and money, but every resident would be better off taking the time to put the trash where it belongs and paying their taxes in order to enjoy life in sanitary conditions. If most residents follow the rules, everyone in the town will enjoy the benefit, even those residents who do not comply. But there is no feasible way to exclude those who do not respect the rules from enjoying the benefit.

The optimal provision of a public good requires a non-egoistic course of action from each individual (see Roemer 2020). Take any resident in the town described. From the standpoint of their own self-interest, they should not follow the rules, but let others adhere to them. However, if they overcome their own self-interest, by a strong common conviction or internalising other people's welfare, for example, they will produce the good of clean surroundings for all. In this way, shared values that define a common good due a particular social relationship can be confused with a public good or a set of public goods. But it is important to keep the two ideas distinct.

The facilities make up the common good look like public goods because they are open to everyone (e.g., the administration of justice). This means that it is not possible to exclude those who do not contribute from enjoying the benefits, and as long as the facilities are not congested to the point of not allowing more cases, the administration of justice for one does not preclude the same treatment for the rest. The facilities that make up the common good serve a special class of interests that all citizens have in common, i.e., the civic relationship of justice, but each citizen will have private interests that could be in conflict with these common interests. From the standpoint of a citizen's egoistic rationality, such a facility may not be a net benefit to all and thus not a public good.

Despite the differences, some public goods are closely related to some common goods: specifically, collectively produced public goods that involve social capital (see Table 1). That kind of good (X) requires the participation (effort time T) of at least a certain number of individuals ($i = 1,2,3...n$) in a community; a single agent cannot produce them. X is a public good since it provides satisfaction when consumed at the same time by several individuals (X_i is the simultaneous consumption of individual i). The perceived consumption depends on the empathy level toward other individuals (a_i, represents how much X benefits i, taking into account other people's welfare; more empathy increases a_i), and all individuals' perceptions make the good public (the sum of all a_i is one in the case of private goods and more than one of a public one). Social capital here is conceived as empathy; for each individual the welfare of others is part of their own welfare (Robison and Ritchie 2019). This is very similar to a common good defined by shared empathy values that demands collective action for its production.

Table 1 Collectively produced public goods that involve social capital.

Concept	Formally	Implications
The public good is produced collectively	$X = X(T_{1x}, T_{2x}, T_{3x}, ..., T_{nx})$	Production of the public good takes time T_{ix}
My share of the public good depends on social values	$X_i = a_i X$ (ai is an empathy coefficient)	ai is a measure of shared values (empathy)
Individuals purchase and consume private goods	$Y_i = w T_{iy}$ (w is the real wage)	There is a market for labour and private goods
Individuals value the public and the private goods	$V_i = V_i(X_i, Y_i; T_i)$ $T_i = T_{ix} + T_{iy}$	Individuals maximise V_i subject to a time constraint

Concept	Formally	Implications
Social welfare depends on individual values	$W=W\,(V_1, V_2, V_3,...,V_n)$	Social welfare depends on the public good

Individuals can purchase a private good (Y_i) with labour income $(w\,T_{iy})$, but not the public good, which they have to generate with others. So they allocate time for private consumption and time to produce the public good (T_{ix}), maximising the value of the joint consumption, subject to a time constraint (T_i). The production of the public good demands coordination, which is not provided by market forces as in a private good, but both goods contribute to social welfare (W) throughout the individual value obtained by each individual (V_i).

In this schematic model some public goods and common goods are excluded. For example, a single agent contracting labour and inputs in the private market can provide a park or a library, which produce fresh air and a repository of knowledge, even in a sub-optimal way. But other public goods, like the rule of law in a state or public policies against discrimination, cannot be offered by a single agent but require the involvement of at least a certain majority of individuals. In this case the public good is closer to the nexus of the Common Good, and it is to that relationship that the collectively produced public goods involving social capital are relevant.

III. The Nexus of the Common Good

What human beings living in society hold in common are relationships and interactions. Community is, among other things, a unifying link between persons. As conscious and intelligent beings, individuals share connections in the physical and biological world, in the context of a culture and with similar objectives. Common interests are required to assemble conditions that are beneficial to achieving similar objectives, and those conditions can be said to be a good common for a group of people, a common good. A set of common goods requires a set of relationships, a network of them; this persistent network of common goods is its nexus. It enables human beings to reach their potential to do and be what they have reason to value. A stable, sustainable and resilient nexus is valuable beyond the production of specific goods. It has an intrinsic value, conferring a sense of belonging and identity on its members, for example, and an instrumental value (see Chapter 2).

In summary, as introduced in Chapter 2, there are five key characteristics of the nexus of the common good:

1. It considers **agents'** shared concerns that arise from explicit relationships;

2. It promotes and helps to fulfil the potential of **human lives**;

3. Its **stability** has intrinsic and instrumental value;

4. The quality of its **governance** enables effective collective action;

5. It has a component of procedural and distributional **justice**.

These five dimensions of the nexus—agency, humanity, stability, governance, and justice—should be conceptualised and measured (see Figure 1).

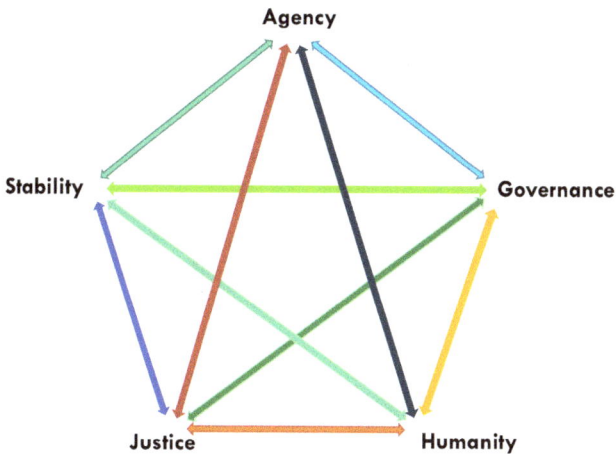

Figure 1. The common good pentagram. Source: Nebel and Medina (Chapter 2)

Clearly, a complete measurement should take into account the twenty links between various dimensions of the nexus.

2. Justice and the Common Good

The Common Good, as a set of conditions that allow the members of a community to collaborate to achieve or carry out objectives or values for themselves, implies justice as the practical will to favour and promote the common goods of the communities themselves. Thus, the nexus of the common good needs practical guidance in order to reach collective decisions that a purely private society would not be able to make. Collective decision-making must unfold in public life to transcend the limitations of individual concerns (e.g., market failures) and promote shared benefits (e.g., public goods), and governance must facilitate such decision-making if it is to be successful. Governance must include at least some restraints against interference in any individual life-plan and any form of association, that is, some form of 'negative rights.' Upholding such rights is a form of 'justice,' albeit an incomplete one (Berlin 1969).

The nexus of the common good has a component of social justice (e.g., respect for basic rights, freedoms, and distributional principles) but goes beyond that because it must maintain patterns of conduct that serve common interests. Members of a community share concerns that limit competing private claims about total resources through a distributive principle that determines how the group should respond to such particular interests.

Justice encompasses several elements (Finnis 2011): one's relations and dealings with other individuals; what is owed to another and, consequently, what that other person is entitled to, and; a type of equality, in the sense of balancing different characteristics, processes or results in the same way for all individuals, which could be called equity.

The realisation of the common good faces two problems. First, the distribution of resources, opportunities, results and responsibilities; in general, everything that serves the common good until it is appropriated by particular individuals (distributive justice). Second, the admissible dealings between individuals and/or groups, where what can be distributed is not directly in question (commutative justice).

Distributive justice implies a reasonable solution to the problem of assigning something that contributes to the Common Good but which must be appropriated by individuals. Commutative justice deals with criteria for determining what relationships, in the sense of interactions, are appropriate between individuals, including groups. This distinction between distributive and commutative justice will be useful to distinguish approaches on the way of considering the community to which one belongs, the obligations towards it, and a certain sense of equity.

In the following sections, a general conception of justice and specific ways of understanding different aspects of the concept will be developed, for which it is convenient to remember the distinction between distributive and commutative justice.

3. Justice

Justice refers to how persons are treated when they have conflicting claims in entering into specific relationships; justice always concerns interpersonal relationships, and something is a matter of justice only where there is a plurality of individuals dealing with one another. As free agents in a particular community, individuals have shared concerns that define a common good, and justice is part of that. Justice requires an agent or group of agents willing to alter the circumstances surrounding the conflicting claims.

Conflicting claims can involve freedoms, opportunities, resources, or any other entitlement that has value for the individual or her community. Justice implies rights, that which can be claimed from others, and duties, that which is owed to someone else. This means that there are some limits that have to be respected in social interactions (do not harm others) and there are some claims that involve changing boundaries in social interactions (expand opportunities). Justice thus has consequences for both the potential and the fulfilment of human lives.

Justice is related to equality in a broad sense. To treat two individuals 'equally' under equal circumstances is a form of justice, but to treat them equally when they are not equal is not. This begs the Aristotelian question: equality of what? Whatever the answer, a crucial aspect of justice is a sort of proportionality. This is the basis for distributive justice of resources or entitlements in a community. In turn, the level and distribution of entitlements influences the possibility of dispensing justice in some other sense.

As for the 'equality of what?' question, Sen (1980) has forcefully defended the idea that capabilities, the set of possible beings and doings open to individual choice, should be of capital importance for an appraisal of well-being, but also for a theory of justice (Sen 2009). Any substantive theory of justice has to choose which informational space is pertinent to assess what is just or unjust. The concept of capability is of particular value because it is linked closely with the opportunity aspect of freedom, although the process of choice itself is important. Allowing, for example, a person not to be obliged to accept some state because of constraints imposed by others (see Chapter 4).

Capabilities define effective freedom, the opportunity to pursue people's objectives—those things that a person values. They focus on human life, on the actual possibilities of living, not on the means to do so or the subjective valuation of what is accomplished. This informational basis is consistent with diverse individual theories of the good. Sen (1993b) explicitly asserts that 'quite different specific theories of value may be consistent with the capability approach' and that 'the capability approach is consistent and combinable with several different substantive theories.' So, the idea of justice for the common good, and the concept of the common good itself, would benefit from the adoption of the capability approach to effectively enhance individuals' living conditions.

A way to further explore effective freedoms is the theory of justice as equality of opportunity (Roemer 1996). In this theory there is a boundary between what people are responsible for and what they are not. It recognises a particular conception of responsibility, denoting a situation in which a person has the control. Separating responsibility situations from circumstances that are out of individuals' control means that egalitarianism has the specific purpose of leveling opportunity. Equality of opportunity for welfare is equalised if transferable resources have been redistributed so that the observed inequality is only due to different preferences and choices (and some residual luck). So, equality of opportunity is just in the sense that it recognises individual responsibility and inequality that is beyond the individual's control.

Whether dealing with plurality, conflicting claims, or equality, the requirement of justice is to favour and foster the common good of the relevant community and the basic aspects of human flourishing. This means conforming to a standard (procedural justice) and taking no more than one's share (distributional justice). In realising the common good, there are two issues to resolve: first, what is required for individual wellbeing, which arises in relationships and dealings between individuals and/or groups in a community; and second, how to distribute resources, opportunities, and advantages. But there is also a perception problem.

The perception of justice has an impact on the stability of human interactions. To suffer from an unjust social structure implicitly entails the recognition that something 'legitimate' has not been granted. We are deprived of some social good that should exist. To ignore the identity, ability, or contributions of individuals to their community is unjust. Justice is then measured according to a society's ability to ensure conditions of mutual recognition, where identity formation and individual self-realisation can develop (Honneth 2004).

A sense of injustice undermines the basis for a cohesive and resilient group. Similarly, a sustainable and balanced set of social relationships could favour social justice. Involvement in the community is key for justice. In some theories, the basic supreme principle is equality of participation (Fraser 2010), which requires equality in the distribution of material resources, regardless of differences of sex, age, race, or any other characteristic of the participants. In this view, redistribution has priority over recognition and representation.

Democratic equality integrates the principles of distribution with demands for equal respect, reconciling equality of participation and recognition (Anderson 1999). It guarantees citizens who follow the law equal access to the social conditions for their effective freedom. It justifies the required redistribution by appealing to the obligations of citizens in a democratic state. Since the fundamental objective of citizens in the construction of a state is to ensure the effective freedom of all, the distributive principles of democratic equality are not intended to tell people how to use their opportunities (for which they have a legitimate claim), nor do they seek to judge how responsible a person is for the choices that may lead them to unfortunate results.

Justice as recognition, participation, or democratic equality can be rightfully claimed against the agent imparting it, which in turn has the obligation of dispensing justice. The state has that role, since the administration of justice is a public good practically impossible to provide privately. And the state has the duty to do so, since it is the social mechanism that amalgamates individual values into social choices.

Three kinds of actions are required from the state in matters of justice: to govern the relationship of subjects to the state, to be in charge of the state's relationship with its citizens, and to regulate the relationship of one private person or entity to another. To effectively impart justice in these matters, it has to be enforceable in society, which requires some kind of collective action. The governance of the nexus of the common good is closely connected to the ability to dispense justice, which in turn can enhance the potential for good governance.

4. Measuring Justice

As can be seen from the previous discussion, to measure justice directly or indirectly is a multidimensional and complex exercise. It involves taking into account plurality, rights and duties, and equality. It can be procedural or distributional. The materials of justice can be resources, capabilities, opportunities, recognition, participation, or equal respect. Justice involves the willingness of agents to acknowledge and/or modify the circumstances of possible injustices, the resources and authority granted to attend injustices, the perception that conflicts are solved, and the quality of institutions and rules to administer justice.

To complicate matters more, strictly speaking, justice cannot be reduced to a separate dimension on its own, isolated from the agency, humanity, stability, and governance components of the nexus of the common good. To do so means ignoring justice's full scope (see Chapter 2), and implies that a modest measurement should concentrate on the most salient elements of a particular idea of justice, sacrificing many of its components, since the whole complexity of the concept is beyond the scope of a specific measure.

Another constraint is the availability of relevant information. To obtain a proxy for the relevant concepts, many compromises have to be made in terms of the definition of variables and their interpretation. Even then, space and time comparability are not possible sometimes, so it is necessary to work with more limited information. But the measurement exercise demands us not to stop there. For practical diagnosis and public policy, the measures should be simple, transparent, and replicable.

In what follows the focus is on the distinction between justice as a procedure and distributive justice. The first emphasises the violation of rights and freedoms, while the other requires that available resources and entitlements be shared according to relevant criteria. In the second case, the key emphasis is on the difference between end results and opportunities. The basis for measurement is the set of available indices that can be explored at the local level.

I. Justice as Freedom

Perhaps the most basic idea of justice is its protections for individual freedom, conceived as the absence of obstacles, barriers, or constraints, in such a way that an individual is able to take control of her own life and realise her fundamental purpose (negative liberty). In the words of John Locke (1689), freedom implies that an individual should not 'be subject to the arbitrary will of another, but freely follow his own.' Thus, justice poses stringent limits on coercion and state intervention, even beyond protecting the right not to be subjected to the action of another person or group (negative rights).

A way to measure this conception of justice is through negative liberty indices. There is a plethora of composite indices covering the subject (see the inventories by Bandura 2011, and Yang 2014), but the most salient are the Human Freedom Index (Cato Institute, Fraser Institute, Friedrich Naumann Foundation), the Economic Freedom of the World Index (Fraser Institute), the Index of Economic Freedom (Heritage Foundation), Freedom in the World (Freedom House), and the Democracy Index (Economist Intelligence Unit).

In their simplest terms, these indices measure noninterference by others. They are focused on procedural justice, in which the right means justify any and all results. Respect for human integrity, private property, and voluntary contracts is the basis of justice. But not all indices are restricted to this concept, and sometimes they include the removal of constraints that impede the fulfilment of potential, as the individual understands it. Typically, following Hayek (1960), the first three indices listed above ignore a broader concept of freedom.

For example, the Human Freedom Index (HFI) focuses on the absence of coercive constraint to human agency in the world, based on a broad measure that encompasses personal, civil, and economic freedom. It uses objective and perception data obtained by experts; its sub-dimensions include the rule of law, security and safety, movement, religion, association, assembly, civil society, expression and information, identity and relationships, size of government, legal system and property rights, access to sound money, freedom to trade internationally, and regulation of credit, labour, and business.

An example is the HFI for six different countries (see Table 2). Mexico is second to last in the selected group.

Table 2. Human Freedom Index for selected countries.

Country	Human Freedom Index Value	Human Freedom Index Ranking (159 countries)
United Kingdom	8.49	14
United States of America	8.46	15
Spain	8.12	29
Chile	8.15	28
Mexico	6.65	92
Brazil	6.48	109

Source: Vásquez and Porcnik (2019).

There are at least ten other indices similar in conception to the HFI, but focusing on particular sub-dimensions of the index, mostly on economic and political freedoms. Another group of indices emphasises the rule of law and access to effective and impartial institutions of justice.

It should be noted that measures similar to the HFI are sometimes complex and demanding in terms of data and information, and sometimes not relevant for subnational political units since many negative freedoms are a matter of national institutions or public policies. However, at least a number of the components of the HFI have been disaggregated at the subnational level.

Mexico's HFI, like that of other countries, is composed of two indices: a personal freedom index and an economic freedom index (see Table 3). The first considers basic civil rights, the second economic liberties, such as a smaller government, a solid system of property rights, sound monetary institutions, freedom to trade, and few regulations.

Table 3. Components of Mexico's Human Freedom Index.

Country	Index Value	Ranking (162 countries)
Personal Freedom	6.38	106
Economic Freedom	6.93	76
Human Index Freedom	6.65	92

Source: Vasquez and Porcnik (2019).

Stansel, Torra and McMahon (2019) have calculated an index for the Mexican states as part of their analysis of North America for the Economic Freedom of the World Index; see Figure 2 for their classification of the Mexican states according to economic freedom. However, many national indicators had to be dropped since they are not features of subnational units. This problem increases with the level of disaggregation to the point that it is extremely difficult to measure negative rights at the municipal level.

II. Justice as Equality of Results

An alternative conception of justice goes beyond negative liberties and rights, requiring a substantially equal distribution of advantages. In this distributive justice approach, resource and welfare egalitarianism are two central notions. Fundamental to justice from this perspective is the principle of equal concern and respect for persons, meaning that equal resources or welfare should be guaranteed to each member of society. People are morally equal, and equality in resources or welfare is the best way to further this moral ideal.

A more elaborate account of the argument in favour of resource egalitarianism asks, if one is an egalitarian, should one try to equalise resources available to agents, or try to equalise their welfare? With a suitably general conception of what resources are, equality of resources cannot be distinguished from equality of welfare (Roemer 1986). A practical implication of this result is that every person should have the same level of alienable resources and, if possible, be compensated for those inalienable ones.

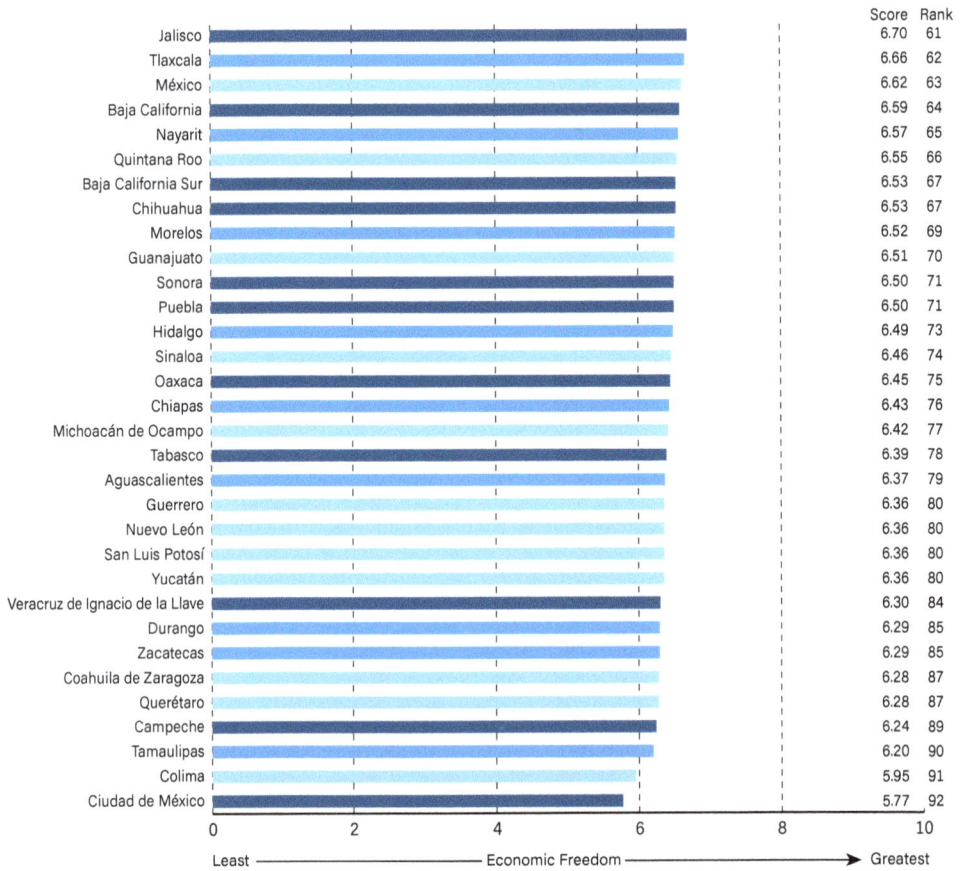

	Score	Rank
Jalisco	6.70	61
Tlaxcala	6.66	62
México	6.62	63
Baja California	6.59	64
Nayarit	6.57	65
Quintana Roo	6.55	66
Baja California Sur	6.53	67
Chihuahua	6.53	67
Morelos	6.52	69
Guanajuato	6.51	70
Sonora	6.50	71
Puebla	6.50	71
Hidalgo	6.49	73
Sinaloa	6.46	74
Oaxaca	6.45	75
Chiapas	6.43	76
Michoacán de Ocampo	6.42	77
Tabasco	6.39	78
Aguascalientes	6.37	79
Guerrero	6.36	80
Nuevo León	6.36	80
San Luis Potosí	6.36	80
Yucatán	6.36	80
Veracruz de Ignacio de la Llave	6.30	84
Durango	6.29	85
Zacatecas	6.29	85
Coahuila de Zaragoza	6.28	87
Querétaro	6.28	87
Campeche	6.24	89
Tamaulipas	6.20	90
Colima	5.95	91
Ciudad de México	5.77	92

Least ——————— Economic Freedom ——————→ Greatest

Figure 2. Economic Freedom Index of Mexican states by quartiles. Source: Stansel, Torrea and MacMahon (2019).

In resource egalitarianism, there is the problem of the construction of appropriate indices, because it is necessary to measure the aggregate level of goods if they are to be distributed efficiently, that is beyond an egalitarian distribution of each and every good. Money is an imperfect index for the value of material goods and services. Nevertheless, using a monetary value, either for income or wealth, is the most common response to the index problem.

An additional difficulty is the choice of an inequality index, since each measure embodies different properties and value judgments (Sen 1973). Because inequality indices aggregate all income differences with different weights, they implicitly embody value judgments about which gaps matter most. Atkinson (1970) argued that such judgments should be explicit about the social welfare function underpinning each index and should avoid the indiscriminate use of any index, understand the welfare implications of their weights, and try to make explicit the associated 'inequality-aversion.'

The most common index for measuring income inequality is the Gini coefficient. If income is distributed equally, the Gini is zero; if all income is concentrated in one person, the Gini has a value of one. As a result, the Gini coefficient can be interpreted as the percentage of the maximum inequality present in the current distribution of resources. The Gini coefficient—along with other commonly used measures—is a consistent measure that satisfies several principles (e.g., if a poorer person makes a transfer to a richer person, the measure should record a rise in inequality, regardless of where they are in the distribution).

Here is an example of the Gini coefficient as a measure of distributive injustice (see Table 4). With a different ranking than the HFI, Mexico is now in fourth place.

Table 4. Income Gini coefficients for selected countries.

Country	Gini coefficient Value	Gini coefficient Ranking (138 countries)
Spain	0.35	97
United Kingdom	0.36	88
United States of America	0.41	56
México	0.47	33
Chile	0.52	18
Brazil	0.55	13

Source: UNDP (2020).

The information necessary to calculate Gini coefficients at the subnational level is increasingly available, at least for income, and income distribution is relevant for identifying local conditions that impact the wellbeing of households and individuals in small political units. Mexico's National Council for the Evaluation of Social Development Policy (CONEVAL) releases such information at the state level every two years (see Figure 3) and at the municipal level every five years (see the example of the state of Puebla in Figure 4) (Coneval 2020).

Inequality of results, as measured by the Gini for household or individual income, however easy to calculate, is not a convincing way to illustrate a lack of justice, since inequality not only ignores the process leading to outcomes but also oversimplifies the connection between resources and welfare. Also, as discussed in Section 2 above, inequality does not consider effective freedom, and there is no place for individual responsibility.

III. Justice as Equality of Opportunity

One problem with the concept of justice as protection of negative rights is that it ignores the different sets of possible beings or doings open to individuals. In other words, equality of treatment does not imply equality of effective freedoms. On the other hand, pursuing justice as an equality of final resources ignores, among other things, the role of individual choice in economic outcomes. That is, even if equality of

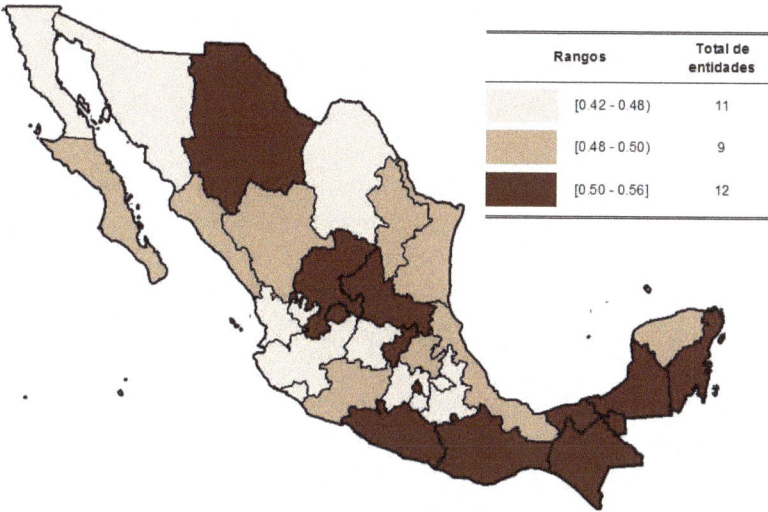

Figure 3. Income inequality of Mexican states by Gini ranges. Source: Coneval (2020).

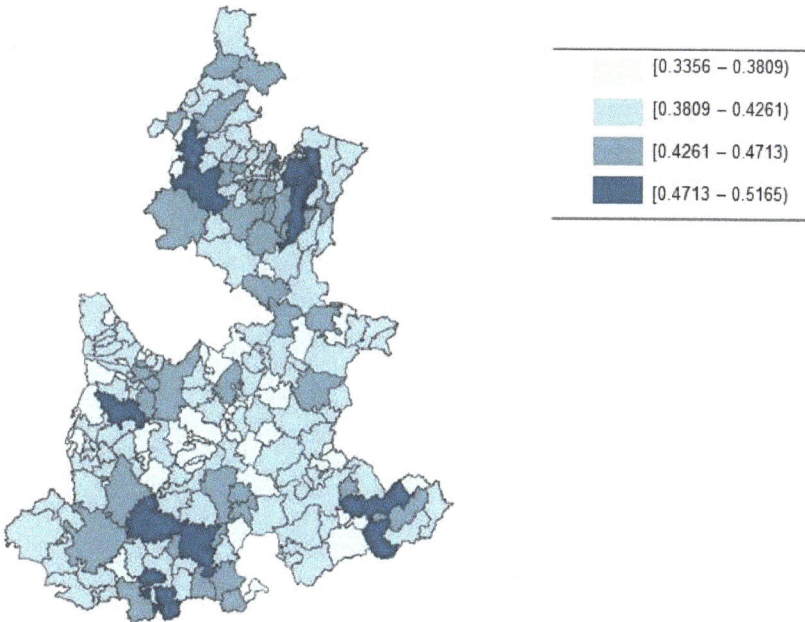

Figure 4. Income inequality of Puebla municipalities by Gini ranges. Source: Coneval (2020).

results means equality of effective freedoms (which is not necessarily implied), it can undermine individual responsibility.

A central question of distributive justice might be formulated in this way: under what conditions are the protection of liberties and the distribution of final resources just or morally fair? One reasonable answer is that justice requires equality of opportunity, which means that non-chosen inequalities should be eliminated to give equal initial conditions and a fair framework for interaction to all individuals (Roemer 1998). The idea is that justice requires a degree of protection of negative rights and a level playing field so that individual choices play out and dictate the final results.

The conception of equality of opportunity is a component of a theory of justice, but not the only component, even if it is the central core. Justice requires at least leveling the playing field by rendering everyone's opportunities equal (Anderson 1999). When fully elaborated, this view specifies both to what extent it is not morally acceptable that some people are better off and the level of inequality that is implied (Brunori, Peragine and Ferreira 2013).

One example of this approach to measuring justice is the EU and OECD Social Justice Index (SJI) (Hellman, Schmidt and Heller 2019). The Social Justice Index is informed by the paradigm that, within the scope of his or her own personal freedom, every individual should be empowered to pursue a self-determined life course, and that specific unequal starting points should not be allowed to negatively affect self-realisation. By focusing on opportunities for personal development, such a concept of social justice avoids the blind spots of formal procedural justice on the one hand and equality-of-results distributional justice on the other. The SJI takes into account the following:

> Instead of an 'equalizing' distributive justice or a simply formal equality of life chances in which the rules of the game and codes of procedure are applied equally, [... the] concept of justice is concerned with guaranteeing each individual genuinely equal opportunities for self-realization through the targeted investment in the development of individual 'capabilities.'[...] Thus, within the scope of his or her own personal freedom, every individual should be empowered to pursue a self-determined course of life, and to engage in broad social participation. (Hellman, Schmidt and Heller 2019).

Following Merkel and Giebler (2009), the SJI is concerned with six dimensions: poverty prevention, access to education, labour market inclusion, social cohesion and non-discrimination, health, and intergenerational justice. The index comprises twenty-one quantitative and eight qualitative indicators. The data for the indicators is derived from OECD databases and from evaluations by experts responding to a survey on various policy areas. In order to ensure compatibility between the quantitative and qualitative indicators, all indicators are collected or undergo a linear transformation to give them a range of 1 to 10. More weight is given to the first three dimensions of the SJI (poverty, education, and labour). Figure 5 summarises the components of the index.

An example of the values and the rankings provided by the SJI can be seen in Table 5. Again, the ranking differs from the previous tables, and Mexico is in sixth place. (The Brazil information is not available, so for this table it is replaced by Turkey because of the similarities in economic development between Mexico and Brazil).

Table 5. Social Justice Index for selected countries.

Country	Social Justice IndexValue	Social Justice Index Ranking (41 countries)
United Kingdom	6.64	11
Spain	5.53	28
United States of America	5.05	36
Chile	4-92	37
Turkey	4.86	40
Mexico	4.76	41

Source: (Hellman, Schmidt and Heller 2019).

The shortcomings of the SJI are similar to those of the HFI: the information needed to calculate the index at the subnational level is demanding, and many of the indicators depend on national policies rather than on local conditions. However, it is possible to propose a more rigorous version of the inequality of opportunities approach that is simplified and requires less information.

Social Justice Index

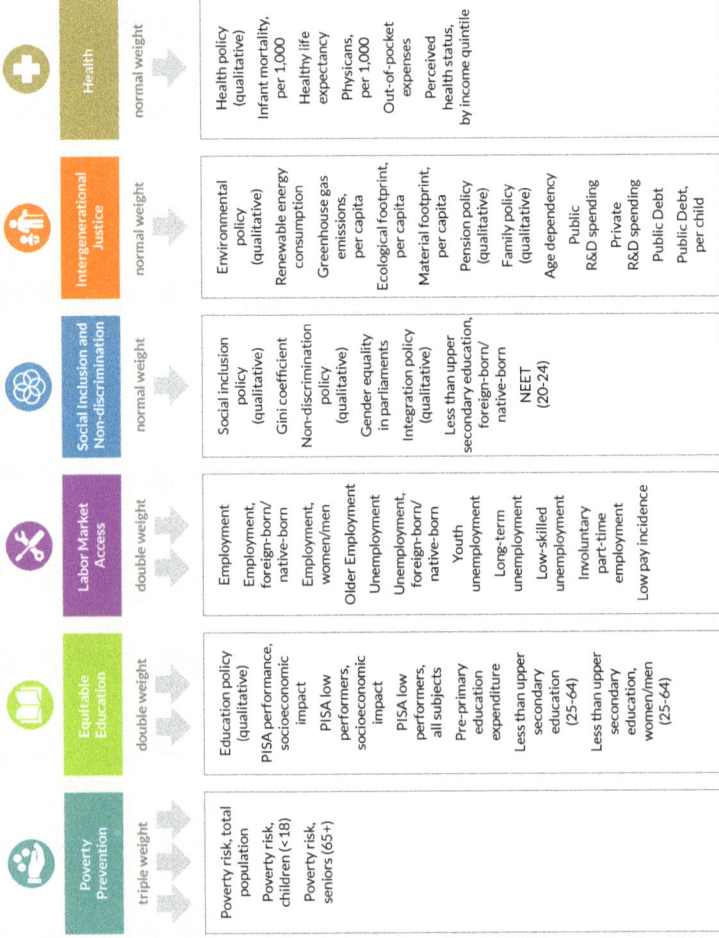

Poverty Prevention	Equitable Education	Labor Market Access	Social Inclusion and Non-discrimination	Intergenerational Justice	Health
triple weight	double weight	double weight	normal weight	normal weight	normal weight
Poverty risk, total population	Education policy (qualitative)	Employment	Social inclusion policy (qualitative)	Environmental policy (qualitative)	Health policy (qualitative)
Poverty risk, children (<18)	PISA performance, socioeconomic impact	Employment, foreign-born/ native-born	Gini coefficient	Renewable energy consumption	Infant mortality, per 1,000
Poverty risk, seniors (65+)	PISA low performers, socioeconomic impact	Employment, women/men	Non-discrimination policy	Greenhouse gas emissions, per capita	Healthy life expectancy
	PISA low performers, all subjects	Older Employment	Gender equality in parliaments	Ecological footprint, per capita	Physicians, per 1,000
	Pre-primary education expenditure	Unemployment	Integration policy (qualitative)	Material footprint, per capita	Out-of-pocket expenses
	Less than upper secondary education (25-64)	Unemployment, foreign-born/ native-born	Less than upper secondary education, foreign-born/ native-born	Pension policy (qualitative)	Perceived health status, by income quintile
	Less than upper secondary education, women/men (25-64)	Youth unemployment	NEET (20-24)	Family policy (qualitative)	
		Long-term unemployment		Age dependency	
		Low-skilled unemployment		Public R&D spending	
		Involuntary part-time employment		Private R&D spending	
		Low pay incidence		Public Debt	
				Public Debt, per child	

Figure 5. Social Justice Index dimensions and variables. Source: (Hellman, Schmidt and Heller 2019).

The existing literature has two main approaches to measure inequality of opportunity, the non-parametric and the parametric. The first defines types of individuals according to their circumstances (e.g., parents' years of schooling) and calculates the inequality between types to obtain an index of inequality of opportunity (e.g., educational inequality of the present generation). The second finds the correlation between relevant variables from the two generations and uses this parameter as an index of inequality of opportunity (in fact, the square of the correlation coefficient; see Ferreira and Gignoux 2011).

Each method has advantages and limitations, but the second is convenient because of its simplicity, since it has a built-in partition of individuals and a selection of inequality measures. Thus, a very simple indicator of inequality of opportunities corresponds to the percentage of the inequality of results transmitted from one generation to another. This indicator is directly related to the correlation between the results of one generation and the next (e.g., between parents' education and that of their children).

Table 6 shows an example of the values and the rankings provided by the Intergenerational Correlation of Educational level (ICE) as an index of inequality of opportunity. This time, in this new ranking, Mexico improves its position with respect to Brazil and Chile.

Table 6. Intergenerational correlation coefficient in education for selected countries.

Country	ICE Value	ICE Ranking (44 countries)
United Kingdom	0.31	39
Spain	0.45	19
United States of America	0.46	16
México	0.47	14
Brazil	0.59	5
Chile	0.60	4

Source: Velez, Campos and Huerta (2013).

One advantage of the ICE is that it can be calculated at the subnational level. In the case of Mexico, it is already available for several regions (see Figure 6) and a proxy can be calculated at the state level with data from the Household Income and Expenditure Survey provided by the National Institute of Statistics and Geography.

Obtaining information at the municipal level would require conducting an ad-hoc survey that asks the respondents for retrospective information about their parents' schooling because no current source has the necessary data. Another route would be to use imputation techniques to obtain proxies for the relevant inequalities (Elbers et.al. 2002).

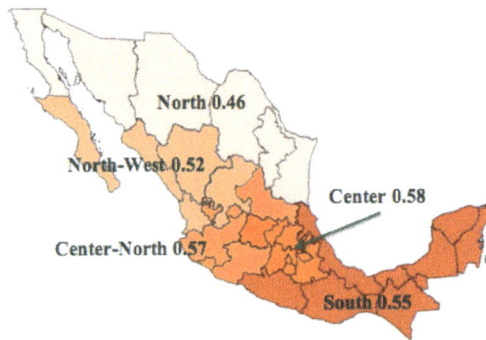

Figure 6. Intergenerational correlation of education by regions. Source: Own calculations with ESRU-EMOVI (2017).

5. Towards a Local Survey to Measure Justice of the Common Good

The dimension of justice should capture the local-level collective processes and institutions through which people share common goods (in their valuation, production, and transmission). The common good metric for justice should seek to understand this dimension in a broad sense, paying attention to both the formal presence of institutions (procedural justice) and the final distribution of goods and opportunities (distributional justice).

From this perspective, the dimension of justice should capture citizens' perspectives on institutions, current distributive results, and intergenerational inequality of opportunities. Justice in these three forms could be measured in relation to three common basic goods: rule of law; inequality of basic opportunities (health, education, and employment); and intergenerational transmission of inequality of opportunity.

The dimensions of justice should be measured in terms of rights, distribution of current opportunities, and intergenerational transmission of inequality of opportunity, according to the survey questions laid out in Table 7.

This basic set of questions could be extended to the necessary means to preserve freedoms and rights (i.e., police resources, absence of corruption, the way the judicial system works), to the distribution of other basic resources (i.e., wealth, income, consumption), or to other ways to measure the transmission of opportunities (i.e., persistence of socioeconomic status, social mobility, coefficient of determination in multiple regressions). However, the questions in the table define the indispensable information needed to measure the dimension of justice for the common good.

Conclusion

There are several implications of the analysis previously laid out in this chapter:

1. To measure the basic aspects of justice, the metric should capture justice's procedural and distributional dimensions. A measure of those dimensions should focus on institutions' effectiveness in protecting freedoms and rights in a narrow sense, on current distributive results, and on intergenerational inequality of opportunities. Justice in these three forms could be measured in relation to the rule of law, inequality in health, education, and employment opportunities, and the intergenerational transmission of inequalities.

2. Justice conceived as limitations on what people can do to others to avoid coercion or the unacceptable loss of autonomy seems to be more a matter of agency than of opportunities to be free. However, procedural justice demands only particular ways to establish social relationships within the nexus of the common good.

Table 7. Basic questionnaire for the measurement of justice at the local level.

Questions	Justification	Related quantitative data
Basic common good: 'Rule of Law' 1. In my locality, the rights, freedoms, and contracts of each person are respected.	- The rule of law understood as the basic protection of negative rights, liberty, and voluntary agreements	1. Data on criminality.
Basic common good: 'Equal distribution of present opportunities' 2. In my locality, people have access to public health services. 3. In my community it is important that everyone is able to go to school. 4. In my locality, people have the opportunity to obtain decent work.	- Health understood as a basic common good, needed for functioning in a community. Education understood as a basic common good for sharing knowledge. - Work understood as a basic common good to transform individual and social surroundings.	2. Data on access to health services through formal work or other means. 3. Data on years of schooling. 4. Data on employment.
Basic common good: 'Intergenerational transmission of opportunities' 5. Years of schooling. 6. Parents' years of schooling.	- These questions link the results between generations to measure non-chosen inequalities.	5. Intergenerational correlation of education.

3. The conception of justice as protection of negative rights has a limited scope but is a key ingredient to defend the agency aspect of freedom. It is unsuitable as a measure of distributive justice, not only because it ignores effective freedoms, but also because it is insensitive to the effect of end results on social welfare.

4. If the objective is to measure the basic aspects of distributive justice at the municipal level, the equal opportunities approach has conceptual advantages, although it requires making geographical imputations of the simplest correlation index or surveys representative of municipalities. Both exercises are technically feasible, but represent very different strategies in terms of the research involved and its costs.

5. The equal opportunities approach can be elaborated to include multiple dimensions (correlations between the achievements of parents and children can involve, for example, health, occupational position, and income) and even address public policy interventions, such as the EU and OECD Social Justice Index. The greater the number of dimensions and components in the selected index, the lower its viability or relevance in the calculations for a particular municipality.

6. While income inequality indices are relatively easy to calculate, it is difficult to justify them as indicators of distributive justice. Equality of resources, although it has its advocates, generally implies ignoring the agency of individuals or their differences to transform resources into effective freedoms.

7. The complexity of the concept of justice makes any of its measurements a pale reflection of what we are trying to measure. In particular, any indicator of justice must not be isolated from other elements, such as the notions of agency, governance, stability, and humanity.

8. The concept of the common good, designed to evaluate the good of a situation, involves not only the positions but also the relationships between the individuals, with the solidarity between them particularly important. Solidarity among the members of a group implies concern for those who are in a

disadvantaged position, which translates into providing equal opportunities to progress on their own. Hence, equality of opportunity is also a relevant concept to measure this aspect of the common good.

The formalisation of the concept of the common good as 'social conditions that individuals provide as relational obligations to shared interests' has a long way to go in providing better grounds for the measurement of its components. Justice as what we owe each other is not completely captured by the current measures. But sometimes an imperfect measure is the only thing we need to avoid patent injustice.

References

Anderson, S. E. 1999. What Is the Point of Equality?, *Ethics 109*, 287–337.

Bandura, R. 2011. "Composite indicators and rankings: Inventory 2011". Technical report, Office of Development Studies, United Nations Development Programme (UNDP), New York.

Berlin, I. 1969. "Two Concepts of Liberty", in Berlin, I., *Four Essays on Liberty*, Oxford: Oxford University Press.

Brunori, P., Peragine, V., and Ferreira, F. 2013. *Inequality of Opportunity, Income Inequality and Economic Mobility: Some International Comparisons*, IZA Discussion Paper No. 1755. https://doi.org/10.2139/ssrn.2210795

CONEVAL. 2020. *Cohesión social*, https://www.coneval.org.mx/Medicion/Paginas/Cohesion_Social.aspx.

Elbers, C., Lanjouw, P., Mistiaen, J., Özler, B., and Simler, K. 2002. *Are Neighbors Equal? Estimating Local Inequality in Three Developing Countries*, Washington, DC: World Bank. https://www.wider.unu.edu/publication/are-neighbours-equal-estimating-local-inequality-three-developing-countries

ESRU — EMOVI. 2017. Encuesta ESRU de Movilidad Social en México (ESRU — EMOVI). https://ceey.org.mx/contenido/que-hacemos/emovi/

Ferreira, H. G. F. and Gignoux, J. 2008. "The Measurement of Inequality of Opportunity: Theory and an Application to Latin America. Policy Research Working Paper No. 4659, Washington, DC: World Bank,https://openknowledge.worldbank.org/handle/10986/6859.

Finnis, J. 2011. *Natural Law and Natural Rights*, New York: Oxford University Press.

Fraser, N. 2010. *Scales of Justice. Reimagining Political Space in a Globalizing World*, New York: Columbia University Press.

Hayek, A. F. 1960. *The Constitution of Liberty*, Chicago: University of Chicago Press.

Hellmann, T., Schmidt, P., and Matthias Heller, S. 2019. *Social Justice in the EU and OECD, Index Report 2019*, BertelsmannStiftung. https://www.politico.eu/wp-content/uploads/2019/12/Social-Justice-Index-2019.pdf.

Honneth, A. 2004. Recognition and Justice: Outline of a Plural Theory of Justice, *Acta Sociologica 47/4*, 351–364, https://doi.org/10.1177/0001699304048668.

Hussain, W. 2018. "The Common Good", in Zalta, E. N. (ed.), *The Stanford Encyclopedia of Philosophy (Spring 2018 Edition)*, https://plato.stanford.edu/archives/spr2018/entries/common-good/.

Locke, J. and Hollis, T. (ed.) 1764 (1689). *The Two Treatises of Civil Government*, London: A. Millar et al., 1764, Liberty Fund, at Online Library of Liberty, https://files.libertyfund.org/pll/titles/222.html.

Merkel, W. and Giebler, H. 2009. "Measuring Social Justice and Sustainable Governance in the OECD", in Bertelsmann Stiftung (ed.), *Sustainable Governance Indicators 2009. Policy Performance and Executive Capacity in the OECD*,Gütersloh: Bertelsmann Stiftung, 187–215.

Roemer, E. J. 1986. "Equality of Resources Implies Equality of Welfare", *The Quarterly Journal of Economics 101*, 751–784, https://doi.org/10.2307/1884177.

Roemer, E. J. 1996. *Theories of Distributive Justice*, Cambridge, Mass.: Harvard University Press.

Roemer, E. J. 1998. *Equality of Opportunity*, Cambridge, Mass.: Harvard University Press.

Roemer, E. J. 2010. Kantian Equilibrium, *Scandinavian Journal of Economics 112/1*, 1–24. https://doi.org/10.1111/j.1467-9442.2009.01592.x

Sen, A. 1973. *On Economic Inequality*, Oxford: Clarendon Press.

Sen, A. 1980. "Equality of what?", in McMurrin, S. M. (ed.), *Tanner Lectures on Human Values*, Cambridge: Cambridge University Press.

Sen, A. 1985. *Commodities and Capabilities*, Amsterdam: North-Holland.

Sen, A. 1987. *On Ethics and Economics*, Oxford: Basil Blackwell.

Sen, A. 1993a (2002). Positional Objectivity, *Philosophy & Public Affairs 22/2*, 126–145. Reprinted in Sen, A. 2004. *Rationality and Freedom*, Cambridge, Mass.: Harvard University Press.

Sen, A. 1993b. "Capability and Well-Being", in *The Quality of Life*, edited by Amartya Sen and Martha Nussbaum, Oxford: Clarendon Press, 30–53.

Sen, A. 2009. *The Idea of Justice*, Cambridge, Mass: Belknap/Harvard University Press. https://doi.org/10.1017/S095382081100046X

Stansel, D., Torra, J., and McMahon, F. 2019. *Economic Freedom of North America 2019*, Fraser Institute.

UNDP. 2020. *Income Gini coefficient*, https://hdr.undp.org/en/content/income-gini-coefficient.

Vasquez, I. and Porcnik, T. 2019. *Human Freedom Index 2019*, Cato Institute, the Fraser Institute, and the Friedrich Naumann Foundation for Freedom. https://www.cato.org/human-freedom-index/2019

Williams, B. 1973. "A Critique of Utilitarianism", in Smart, J. J. C. and Williams, B., *Utilitarianism: For and Against*, Cambridge: Cambridge University Press, 82–118. Reprinted as "Consequentialism and Integrity", in Scheffler, S. (ed.) 1988. *Consequentialism and its Critics*, Oxford: Oxford University Press, 20–50.

Yang, L. 2014. *An Inventory of Composite Measures of Human Progress*, Occasional Papers, UNDP Human Development Report Office. https://hdr.undp.org/en/content/inventory-composite-measures-human-progress

8. Development and Stability

Flavio Comim

Introduction

Stability is one of the most neglected aspects in conceptualising the common good nexus. This happens for several reasons: stability is less tangible, it comprises overlaps with other normative dimensions, such as governance, and unlike other elements of the common good, it can be normatively ambiguous. Thus, more agency freedom is better than less, more governance is better than less, more justice is better than less, and more humanity is obviously better than less (this does not mean that they cannot have negative unintended consequences). But is more stability better than less? And if so, how can we measure the stability dimension of the common good?

Within this context, this chapter starts with a conceptual discussion about the stability dimension of the common good, exploring its links with similar constructs such as sustainability, and resilience (WCED 1987). Then, it examines the normative character of stability, echoing Anand and Sen's (2003) critique of the use of the sustainability concept. The main point is examining positive and negative aspects of stability. Thirdly, it delves into technical issues related to the measurement of this dimension, such as the issue of intertemporal rates of discount (Stern 2007) and the use of RBM to link common objectives to a single framework. Finally, it puts forward a very tentative classification of stability common good indicators according to their usefulness in empirical common good nexus models.

There are several normative and technical challenges that need to be tackled in order to assess and operationalise the stability dimension

    https://doi.org/10.11647/OBP.0290.10

of the common good. Thus, it seems *prima facie* natural to suggest that whereas the normative challenges should be solved by stakeholders, there are technical issues, involving handling attribution problems, counterfactual inferences and the use of econometrics, that are better left to technical analyses. This chapter explores however the complexities necessary in this kind of articulation for taking stability as a key element of the common good.

1. The Stability Dimension

In the context of the 'nexus of the common good' project led by Nebel, Garza-Vázquez, Sedmak, and colleagues, there is a methodological decision to focus not on a specific list of common goods but on how specific common goods build up. So, the choice of common good metrics should not reflect a simple assessment about the supply or availability of key common goods (as important as they might be) but rather about how they can be used to characterise the processes that takes place in the production of these goods, or in other words, how different interactions can create common goods. This is not a trivial point because often common good analyses are structured around the provision of common or public goods such as health, education, and infrastructure (Etzioni 2015; Kaul et al. 1999).

Stability is an equivocal term. As such, it can be used to designate different processes. In order to avoid misunderstandings, it is useful to distinguish between four different senses in which the concept of sustainability could be used, namely:

1. The dictionary sense of stability: in common parlance, stability means a state of continuity without change or with very minor changes. It could also refer to the absence of its opposite, namely, the absence of instability, such as excessive fluctuations in a variable of interest. Quite often, this sense of stability refers to outcome variables. From this ordinary language interpretation, stability of the nexus of the common good would mean simply the continuity or permanence over time of the outcomes that it generates. This is indisputably a valuable property but it does not provide a sufficient criterion depending on its normative quality. Two issues are relevant

here. First, in the dictionary sense of stability, the stability of the nexus of the common good would be the constancy of its outcomes and not necessarily the constancy of the nexus *per se*. Secondly, we should suspend judgment for a while about the normative nature of these results (this topic is further discussed below);

2. The process sense of stability: some aspects of stability are related to governance and the underlying processes that it can control and generate. This criterion focuses on processes rather than on outputs or outcomes. They might even include them, for instance in situations that could be characterised not as culmination outcomes (only final results matter), but as comprehensive outcomes (including processes and their final outcomes), as argued by Sen (2009). In other words, stability means the continuity or permanence of certain processes that might or might not give rise to certain outcomes. In this sense stable processes can produce unstable results and there is nothing unexpected or unnatural with this sense of stability when we see traditional economic systems (very stable in this sense) producing the deterioration of environmental conditions and further instability at the level of outcomes. This seems to provide an interpretation of stability much closer to the concept of the nexus of the common good;

3. The fairness sense of stability: in social terms, stability is not simply about good outcomes or good processes. It can also refer to political or social consensus, to agreement, to harmony. Rawls (2001) employs this sense of stability to argue for the importance of agreement on his principles of justice. Thus, stability becomes an important element for effectiveness, for a public basis of justification, for criteria that might prove relevant for discussing political questions. For this reason, stability is considered a sufficient criterion for supporting a sense of justice. In other words, the common good nexus can be stable because people agree with it and therefore there is no other force of disagreement that will push for its change;

4. The sustainable sense of stability: mostly in environmental terms, stability refers to conservation of ecosystems without undermining people's ability in using them in the future or without unbalancing other social and economic priorities (WDR 2003). Here, stability is not simply about continuity or the absence of changes but about keeping a balance among competing social claims. This is not about processes, nor about governance. It is still about results and about how they should be normatively balanced, but with a clear focus on environmental issues. From this perspective, it is possible to be sustainable, protecting the environment without protecting or even caring about human beings.

Thus, stability is not simply about continuity of outcomes and processes but about their political and normative significance. From this perspective, the issue of stability can be understood in relation to other constituents of the nexus of the common good. Unfortunately, this has not been the rule in sustainability debates. For instance, in the Brundtland Report, *Our Common Future* (1987), the notion of stability, beneath the concern for sustainability, contains a negative moral evaluation of current generations for future ones. The report is careful in specifying that sustainability does not depend on the same level of resources but on the nexus that would allow different generations to maintain their common good. Its view is that this nexus is at risk by practices that do not take into account the nexus of the common good for future generations.

The Earth Charter (1992) highlights an important characteristic of sustainability that can influence future stability prospects, namely, people's acknowledgement of their interdependence and fragility. This point cannot be ignored, because it provides a simple, but essential, link between stability and the common good, mediated by the use of natural resources. Instability comes as a result of our lack of acknowledgement of our interdependence and common destiny. Stability is thus an outcome of a common good based on respect for nature, universal human rights, economic justice and a culture of peace. There is clearly a mix of different conceptual perspectives here but it should not detract us from the main point about stability being a feature of societies in which people assume responsibility to one another, including the challenge of taking into account future generations.

Having said that, it should be noted that both paradigms (Brundtland and the Earth Charter) are based on a well-established diagnostic of instability regarding not simply the dominant patterns of production and consumption, their negative environmental impacts with consequent depletion of resources, but also their unequal impacts on poverty, education and the wellbeing of the world population. These reports argue for a 'shared vision of basic values' that could provide an ethical foundation for the nexus of the common good that they are proposing. However, they articulate this vision based on a set of principles that gave rise to an approach to tackle these issues consolidated by the Millennium Development Goals (MDGs) and further extended to the current Sustainable Development Goals (SDGs). Within these frameworks the issue of stability disappears and sustainability becomes the achievement of particular goals within very specific timeframes. The dictionary sense of stability seems to become prominent in these frameworks given that their main emphasis is on outcomes. It is true that some of them might refer to processes that generate these outcomes but issues of fairness among goals are very difficult to tackle within this perspective.

The concept of resilience, understood as a capacity to manage negative shocks without suffering long-term losses, is also relevant to this discussion because it addresses underlying conditions that can explain stability over time. It has been applied to a wide range of disciplines, such as environment studies, education, psychology, medicine and sociology (Southwick et al. 2014). We can talk about resilient individuals, resilient ecosystems, resilient families, resilient organisations, and resilient societies. When societies are not resilient, they suffer long-term, irreversible losses. When they are resilient, they can recover and return to their previous (one would assume 'stable') trajectory. Often, resilient societies might learn in the face of adverse social experiences or events.

Resilience is then the capacity to maintain a stable trajectory despite adverse shocks. This does not mean that stability cannot be affected by a brief period of instability (or disequilibrium) but that, overall, its underlying structures have this potential to recover, bouncing back to stability. When we apply this concept to the nexus of the common good, we can appreciate how some unstable outcomes can temporarily coexist with a stable nexus or how even some elements of the nexus can be transitorily unstable as part of a resilient nexus. This is an important acknowledgement because we should not expect a stable nexus to always appear stable. This is not a necessity.

If stability shares similar properties as the concept of resilience, it might entail a demand for actually moving forward, namely, that as a result of adverse shocks there is a learning from the experiences that potentialise future gains (rather than losses). In fact, the more a system is exposed to adverse situations and recovers from them, the stronger its capacity for resilience will be.

Overall, it is important to acknowledge that there are different senses in which the stability of the common good nexus can be interpreted. Thus, we should not restrict it to mere notions of continuity. Rather, it entails aspects of interdependence, fragility, shared values, and counterfactual notions of how the nexus can manage adverse shocks (and might suffer or benefit from them). Therefore, stability cannot be simply assessed by what we can empirically see from the nexus. It has to refer to normative features of the nexus—the point that is examined in the sequence.

2. Stability: The Good, the Bad and the Ugly

Stability and sustainability are different concepts. But they are intrinsically related because stability involves certain things to be sustained. This is not however a trivial relationship. As Anand and Sen (2000, p. 2036) note, 'The approach of sustainable development presupposes some basic agreement on what is to be sustained'. This opens a range of normative issues related to the processes, or the nexus, behind the social choice of these 'certain things to be sustained'. For instance, these things to be sustained can be *underspecified* in such a way that nothing concrete can be preserved for future generations. As such, they can become an article of political speeches, rather than concrete goals for policy-making. Alternatively, they can be *overspecified*, making it harder to actually achieve those specific things to be preserved. This overspecification can also be conducive to a generalisation of targets, leading to a homogenisation of results. In both cases they are not operational in a policy sense. Be that as it may, the real complexity behind the notion of sustainability and stability is their normative status. As Anand and Sen (2000, p. 2038) put it:

> There would, however, be something distinctly odd if we were deeply concerned for the well-being of the future—and as yet unborn—generations while ignoring the plight of the poor today. The moral obligation underlying sustainability is an injunction to preserve the capacity for future people to be as well off as we are. This has a terribly hollow ring if it is not accompanied by a moral obligation to protect and enhance the well-being of present people who are poor and deprived. [...] It would be a gross violation of the universalist principle if we were to be obsessed about *inter*generational equity without at the same time seizing the problem of *intra*generational equity: the ethic of universalism certainly demands such impartiality.

This argument challenges any conception of stability and sustainability that would claim to be normatively neutral. There is a *good side* of stability when the ethical principles that it stands for and the universalist principles of intra- and intergenerational equity are respected. On the other hand, there is a *bad side* of stability when it entails contradictory principles that might perpetuate situations of injustice or (unfair) inequality. When applied to the nexus of the common good this means that the normative aspect of stability needs to be added to this concept. For instance, stability of institutions might lead to a lack of adaptation to new environmental challenges and can actually act as a conservative force against the common good. In addition, stability of discrimination or prejudices can undermine the common good of societies. So, unlike the other pillars of the common good nexus, namely, agency freedom, governance, justice and humanity, the dimension of stability can be normatively ambiguous and therefore needs a normative anchor to make sense in the nexus. Thus, the *ugly side* of this discussion is to ignore this important aspect of the stability dimension.

Indeed, the stability dimension projects the nexus into the future and embraces issues related to its dynamics (see Chapter 2). But what does it mean? It means that stability involves a comparison of elements of the common good nexus at different moments in time. This means that intertemporal issues cannot be ignored. But neither can intratemporal issues, as Anand and Sen (2000) argued. A good example of issues that combine inter- and intratemporal equity concerns would be for instance the current trends of inequality in the world. According to the World Inequality Report (2018) there is a rising inequality (within our generation) from 1980 to 2016 of the top 10% share income across the world, which is today achieving levels of 37% in Europe, 47% in the US, and 61% in the Middle-East. From a historical perspective, this increase in inequality marks the end of the postwar egalitarian era in the world. From a conceptual perspective, this increase undermines the stability of the common good nexus. But this is only the case because these very high levels of inequality can be considered normatively negative. Otherwise, we would have to investigate whether particular levels of inequality would not be positive, in the sense of conducive to higher incentives and higher prosperity. So, the selection of what are positive and what are negative aspects of stability will depend on the normative anchor that we attach to them. The good and the bad, as we call them here, depend on the values about what is to be sustained.

Common bads, such as bad institutions, bad public schools or bad democracy, can be very stable and this does not make them any better, quite the opposite. This is not simply a conceptual issue but a practical one affecting how different dimensions and scales are to be harmonised when part of a composite index. It is important to note that behind any index there are conceptual links establishing their dimensions. In the case of the nexus of the common good there are five key normative dimensions (stability is one of them) that contain among themselves potential good and bad features of stability, as described by Table 1 below.

If agency freedom depends on individual and collective capacity for action and interaction (see Chapter 4), it is to be expected that a minimum of predictability and stability are necessary for them to happen. A society where individuals randomly change their views is a society with immense difficulties for coordination and interaction. Indeed, collective agency freedom would be extremely difficult to achieve under these conditions. At the same time, stability could not be supreme such that the freedom (understood here as opportunities or possibilities) could not be characterised. Indeed, Buchanan (1954) argued that what makes democracy an ideal political regime is the possibility of revising its agreements. If the outcomes of collective choice processes were cast in stone, this would undermine the possibility of revision that for Buchanan is the core of democracy. This means that the optimum level of stability of the common good nexus, as far as agency freedom is concerned, should be defined at an intermediate level. Too little stability cannot support individual and collective agency, but too much stability can undermine the foundations of freedom and agency.

Humanity (see Chapter 5), as recently argued by Nussbaum (2019), should count on a material basis for its flourishing. The original Ciceronian-Stoic ideas of respect for humanity need duties of material aid that are enjoyed by everyone in a given society. Within this perspective, social goods are essential for defining people's conditions of life. In their turn, these conditions affect not only people's values, habits and collective processes of choice, but the imbalance of power between people from different walks of life. So, part of the stability of humanity can be achieved by external social goods, not simply for their influence on individual practical reason and moral choice but for their impact on the values relevant for collective processes. Rawls's (2001) concern, for instance, with primary goods was related to fairness and impartiality in defining constitutional principles. Nussbaum's argument is more about the moral psychology necessary for motivating humanity in the promotion of common good. Here, stability depends on a constant provision of fundamental social goods, not because of the goods *per se* but because of their implications for common good processes.

Table 1 Good and bad features of the stability of the common good nexus.

Normative dimensions	Stability: good features	Stability: bad features
Agency freedom	Consolidation and coherence of social views, stability, predictability and revisable goals	Uncertainty and irregularity of social views, unpredictability and non-revisable goals
Humanity	Social goods as guarantees of stability; collective values crystallised into habits and harmony towards the universal common good	Humanity not materialised into a shared basis of social goods; random collective values

Normative dimensions	Stability: good features	Stability: bad features
Governance	Existence of a management capability is important to guarantee the integration and stability of the nexus; capacity of efficient management and provision of common goods; stability as expansion of the nexus	Lack of governance undermines the stability of the nexus; the nonexistence of an efficient provision of common goods challenges its stability; the nexus can be impoverished and shrink
Justice	Stability of shared arrangements and implementation in the generation and distribution of social goods	Absence of shared arrangements and instability in the processes that are behind the implementation of generation and distribution of social goods

Nebel and Medina (Chapter 2) observe how the dynamic nature of the nexus is inherently fragile. What gives materiality to it is its governance that adapts new demands towards a common future and consolidates past achievements (see Chapter 6). But governance cannot exist without stability. Governance needs structures, with institutions and organisations and their corresponding norms, protocols, etc., that do not come out of nothing and that cannot be changed all the time. In fact, many instruments of governance might be defined constitutionally, thereby meaning that a qualified parliamentary majority is required to change them. When stability promotes a deeper and broader integration of the nexus, it fosters governance. When conflicts and new situations do not allow a minimum of stability for governance, it cannot fulfil its basic functions. So, stability is a key ingredient of management capability, helping not simply with the functionality of governance but its ability to tackle new issues. In its turn, governance can also impact negatively on the stability of the nexus, characterising their interdependence. One interesting case is when governance is not stable but it is resilience, that is, it is able to adapt to shocks without losing its functionality. The concept of stability can also be understood as a form of resilience.

Finally, stability seems a critical element for the promotion of justice, in particular distributive justice. In the common good nexus, justice is not simply about how people participate in the generation of social goods and how these goods are shared among them, but how the nexus itself incorporates processes of interaction, cooperation, and collaboration necessary for these results (see Chapter 7). Of course, these processes need to be stable somehow, because otherwise they cannot take place. As such, they demand stability in the way that different individuals recognise each other at a societal level and that the state consolidates in rights and laws the results of these processes of interaction, cooperation, and collaboration. For many, justice can only be achieved when these more consolidated, stable elements are in place. This is as much the case of philosophers in the liberal tradition such as Rawls, Sen, and Nussbaum as it is the case of philosophers in the critical tradition such as Honneth. Therefore, the common good nexus demands stability in the establishment of shared meanings of justice and implementation of socially just arrangements.

In order to achieve the social function of justice a minimum stability is also required, otherwise we would see much volatility in the processes necessary for certain basic arrangements of justice. One cannot develop a certain relation with others and then suddenly change it in a random way. The element of 'togetherness' of justice needs some minimum stability for its evolution.

Stability is neither good nor bad *per se*. It depends on how it complements other dimensions of the common good nexus. As much as it is true that it seems important for the characterisation of other dimensions of the nexus, it needs to be further clarified in relation to its normative quality. We can have good stability and bad stability and probably only participatory and communicative processes, similar to what Rawls named public reason or overlapping consensus, can establish this normative quality in democratic states. At the bottom, there is an element of collective choice in defining the normative quality of stability. We cannot forget however that different social groups have different powers and voices and that somehow these processes will always be imperfect. There is an aspect of ugliness in considering this imbalance in power and voice as shaping the normative guidelines of the common good nexus. But it is a reality that needs to be faced.

Sometimes, the common good nexus defined by societies might reflect the power and prestige of a select few.

3. Measuring the Stability of the Common Good Nexus

Assuming however that the normative aspects of the common good nexus work in a democratic and stable environment, it remains a challenge to operationalise these measures of stability of the nexus. Indeed, there are several technical issues involved in the measurement of this dimension. Let's start with the most evident: given that stability involves different moments in time, how do we compare them? This would be a trivial question if not for the fact that people (and societies) normally have a time preference. That is, enjoying the benefits of the common good nexus today is better than enjoying the same benefits tomorrow. Or, alternatively, enjoying the common good nexus today is better than enjoying the common good nexus tomorrow. But if we prefer to have it today, how much are we willing to pay to have it today, rather than tomorrow? This will depend on our time preference. The result will define our intertemporal rate of discount.

This is a traditional common problem that has not been fully addressed by well-known sustainability definitions such as the one from the Brundtland Report (1987), according to which sustainability involves a kind of development that satisfies the needs of the current generations without compromising the ability of future generations to meet their own needs. But why should current generations bother about future generations, if quite often they will live longer, and be more educated and richer? Thus, the issue of discounting is not a trivial one. More importantly, behind this technical issue there is a serious debate about the notion of intergenerational equity. The same thing applies to the common good nexus. Why should we bother about the common good nexus today and not about the common good nexus tomorrow? But if we do, should we discount the future common good nexus in relation to our current one or not? If we discount it, we are actually favouring our generation over the future generation.

We can proceed with the current generation discounting the common good of all future generations, and each successive generation doing the same for their successors. But should we allow discounting on a regular basis? As Solow (1993, p. 165) has argued,

You may wonder why I allow discounting at all. I wonder, too: no generation 'should' be favored over any other. The usual scholarly excuse—which relies on the idea that there is a small fixed probability that civilization will end during any little interval of time—sounds far-fetched. We can think of intergenerational discounting as a concession to human weakness or as a technical assumption of convenience (which it is).

However, not everyone would be happy with this alternative. In analysing the issue of climate change, which comprises very long timeframes (such as 50–100 years), Stern (2007) advocated for a zero-discount rate on the ethical basis that every person should count equally in this problem. There is also a practical issue. Because the timeframe is very long, even a very small rate of discount will produce net present values of their flows (of wellbeing, for instance) that will be close to zero.

This raises a key issue when we talk about the stability of the common good nexus, namely, what is its temporary? Is the nexus something that lasts four to five years, as part of a political cycle, or is it something that might last a generation? Or even longer, if we consider that it can reflect the political history of a country? In this last case, one can approach the issue following Stern's advice of discounting less and less the outcomes of the common nexus that will flow to future generations. But if we are talking about arrangements (in terms of agency freedom or governance) that might have a more immediate impact, then perhaps we should discount the outcomes for future generations. How much this discount would be is an important policy issue to be discussed depending on the particular configuration of a certain common good nexus.

This will have another important implication concerning the use of strategic planning behind the promotion of a particular common good nexus: the choice of outputs (what one does) and outcomes (the results of what one does) within different timeframes. This is different from the theoretical frame that establishes the logical relations between the different dimensions. When stability and time are the essence of the matter, as is the case in strategic plans, one should move towards implementation issues and distribute outputs and outcomes in time. Because all different dimensions of the common good nexus have different time horizons, concern with stability might suggest different arrangements between the dimensions of the common good nexus. By doing so, the pure conceptual model can be translated into a diversity of 'impure' empirical models, such as one that tackles the empirical links between governance and agency freedom towards a particular justice issue (Figure 1):

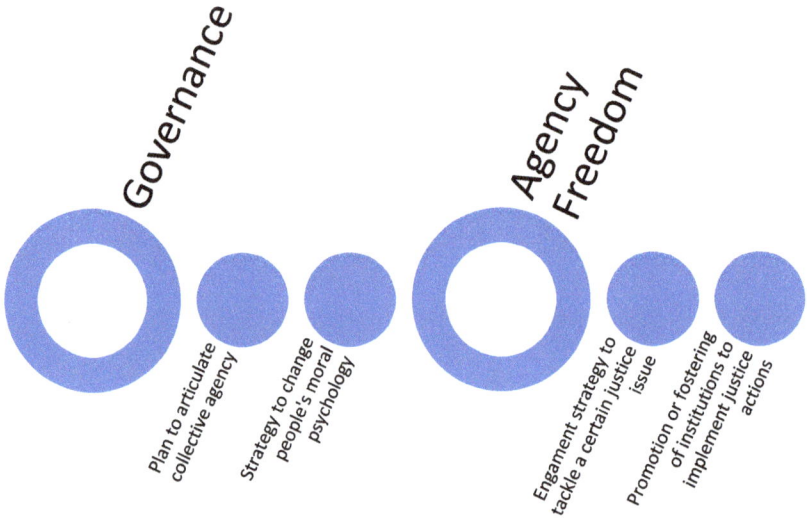

Figure 1. Illustration of a possible empirical model of common good nexus.

Stability in these dimensions would imply different timeframes for each of these outputs and their corresponding activities. In fact, the methodology of RBM (Results Based Management) would be most convenient here, allowing an analysis of the degree of coherence of the stability of different dimensions of the common good nexus. This analysis is relevant depending on the implementation model of the nexus (for instance, bottom-up vs top-down). Quite often, bottom-up models would take more time to be implemented and would add more demand on the stability component whereas top-down models tend to be accompanied by stronger governance elements and might, at least for the short-term, be more stable.

There is an additional complication that might arise in terms of stability: if the common good nexus can be employed to achieve different policy objectives, it is natural that the nexus can be affected by the temporality of these objectives. Not to mention that some of these objectives, following Cunha and Heckman (2007), might be subject to *sensitive* and *critical* periods. For instance, if the common good nexus is applied to the promotion of child education, the dimensions of humanity, governance and justice should be considered altogether for a period of at least eight to nine years for primary school and twelve years for primary plus secondary school for many countries in the world, allowing the nexus to finish a cycle of human flourishing. The situation might be different if the common good nexus is to be used to tackle for instance a pandemic, such as the one resulting from COVID-19. The nexus necessary for fostering short- to middle-term agency freedom should be built (empirically) on well-grounded forms of governance that need strong stability to cope with an emergency situation. So, different timeframes for different policies or institutions can be translated into distinct policy commitments with specific stability requirements. We should expect a multi-stability requirement because there are diverse durations that will produce or enable multidimensional human flourishing.

Different dimensions can also show different sensitivity to change. Altogether, this makes the measurement of the stability dimension of the common good nexus very complex and to a large extent dependent on the aims for its use. For this reason, it is important to make a distinction between the common good nexus theoretical model presented in this book and its several different empirical manifestations. One should expect, as Sen (2009, 2017) warns us, that empirical counterparts of the common good nexus (as other justice artefacts) would at their best be incomplete, partial, and limited in their outreach. We should expand further on this discussion in the next section, but for the moment it is important to acknowledge that several technical issues involved in seriously taking the stability issue into account would comprise an extended concern with intertemporal rates of discount, empirical models of the common good nexus, different timeframes, and attention to different policy objectives.

4. Stability Indicators: A Tentative Taxonomy

Whereas most indicators focus on outputs and outcomes, stability indicators are more concerned with processes and as such seem suitable for use in analyses about the common good nexus. They are part of what Sen named 'comprehensive indicators', tackling not only culmination outcomes but also their processes. This means that they should not be seen as a list or a checklist about the provision of common goods. Rather, they should focus on the normative aspects involved in the stability of the common good nexus, such as fairness and equality. This is not a minor point. The normative or ethical aspects of stability indicators should not be ignored, because unlike other dimensions there is no clear scale in the stability dimension. One can perpetuate unequal and unfair arrangements and therefore a simple notion of continuity is not enough to assess the common good nexus in this situation.

Stability indicators can be classified according to the influence that they have on particular dimensions that we are talking about. We should however keep in mind that these dimensions interact, either logically or empirically, and as such they might provide a much more complex picture resulting from their integration. This is normally the case when the nexus is part of policy planning. Stability indicators should also respect some technical issues that cannot be ignored once we employ the common good nexus for social policy objectives. Similarly, they should adapt to particular empirical models that do not by necessity have to comprise all dimensions of the common good nexus. Table 2 below offers a tentative and simplified picture of this taxonomy (with some examples as illustrations).

One important point to remark on is that not all indicators need to be quantitative. In the absence of quantitative information, qualitative indicators can be used, where ratios can be compared, trends can be analysed, different assessments and scenarios can be considered, etc. The key issue is that indicators should contain a threshold or any other indication about the normative status of the situation that one is analysing. That is, one should know whether the situation is good or bad, as simple as that. When this is not possible, an alternative, as suggested by Sen (2017) could be the use of partial rankings or complementation strategies with the use of other informational spaces (subjective views, resources, etc.).

Another key point is that this table offers a series of examples of stability within selected common good dimensions taken in isolation. This is often not the case both conceptually and empirically. In fact, the common good nexus is precisely about the interaction of these dimensions. However, it is very difficult to assume or to guess what

Table 2 A taxonomy for stability indicators.

	Agency freedom	Humanity	Governance	Justice
Normative anchor	Indicators of the degree of consolidation and coherence of social views. Example: difference of time trend between what governments want vs what opinion polls suggest Indicators of revisability of values. Example: number of times collective agency freedom changed during a certain timeframe (this can be seen here as a positive aspect)	Indicators of stability of moral psychology and collective values. Example: evolution of values measured by a well-known scale Indicators of coherence of collective choice. Example: existence of incoherent claims and inconsistencies over time (this can be a qualitative indicator)	Indicators of quality of stability of management. Example: qualitative trend suggesting evolution of management on similar or different governance nexus Indicators of expansion of the common good nexus. Example: number of times that governance changed to favour common good policies	Indicators of the degree of generation and distribution of social goods. Example: proportion of the top 20% poorest and top 20% richest appropriators of a country's social goods
Characteristics of processes	Indicators of aggregation of individual agency freedom. Example: qualitative availability of referendums or compilation of initiatives of popular participation	Indicators of provision of social goods. Example: degree of decentralisation (or other process characteristic) of provision of basic social goods	Indicators of stability of governance. Example: progressive vs radical changes in the constitution of the governance apparatus	Here, it depends on how we consider justice. For instance: if injustice is understood as a lack of legislation necessary to achieve a certain end, a compilation of this legislation could be a good process indicator of the nexus.

	Agency freedom	Humanity	Governance	Justice
				Alternatively, if justice is a question of income distribution one can assess the processes that are conducive to unequal income distributions, as part of the nexus. The key element is to see how these processes evolve over time in relation to these fair or unfair outcomes
Policy objectives	Indicators of discount rate in cases where the policy in question is long-term. Example: assessment of the use of discount rates for different groups of people in society (and their respective agency freedom)	Indicators of representativeness of humanity. Example: degree of stability in the collective values inbuilt in certain policy objectives (this depends on the policies in question)	Indicators of implementation power. Example: degree of coherence between policy objectives and the power constituted for a governance nexus structure	Indicators of alleviation or mitigation of injustices over time. This will clearly depend on specific policy objectives. Example: with the objective of managing a pandemic, the stability of the common good nexus in relation to objectives and justice can be given by the proportional share of sacrifice demanded from different sectors of society and how this evolves over time.

	Agency freedom	Humanity	Governance	Justice
Empirical model	Empirical indicators of stability of individual or collective agency freedom. Example: indicators of stability of municipal agency or indicators of stability of community agency, measured by a series of questions focusing on a particular link between a partial form of agency freedom and certain outcomes (one of the features of an empirical model would be its partiality)	Indicators of sensitivity to change (should change be necessary). Example: subjective indicators about how people feel affected by a certain category of interventions	Indicators of implementation timeframe. Example: indicator of density of governance during a certain period of time, related to a particular activity or to a particular timeframe	Indicators of sustainable achievable outputs and outcomes. Example: indicators of constancy of provision of certain common goods
Timeframes	Indicators of duration of agency freedom (individual and collective). The point is that the duration might not be compatible with expected timeframe. Example: time of mobilisation of certain collective agency freedom	Indicators of transmission of culture. Example: assessment of intra- and intergenerational transmission of certain cultural values Indicators of projection of human community. Example: subjective indicators of aspirations and expectations	Indicators of duration of governance within a certain policy frame. Examples are context dependent	Synchronicity indicators. Within the context of RBM one should find certain synchronicity and coherence among timeframes. It is not possible that an input to a certain process takes more time to be achieved and is not available when needed

the appropriate stability indicators would be without knowing the particular problem at hand. This does not mean however that we have no guideline in this task. Instead, the table above can provide a starting point, with some suggestions. But these should be complemented with indicators that will register the stability of interactions between all of the other dimensions. This would be tantamount to a 3D picture (given that the table above already crossed the stability dimension with other dimensions, as if we had a 2D picture, to use the same metaphor).

One additional complication is that all of the five vertices in the common good nexus are bi-directional, suggesting that some indicators might not be symmetrical when we add time, which is precisely the case with the issue of stability. Perhaps when we use the political (Rawlsian) notion of stability, the temporal dimension might be less pronounced, but for those of governance, humanity, and agency this seems to be less the case.

Of course, there will be trade-offs to sort out and normative issues to be settled before the nexus is established. In certain cases, where the nexus depends on overcoming certain violations of human rights and key hurdles, such as gender discrimination, these should be tackled before a nexus can be established. This is what Sen (2009) suggests when he argues that justice should not be seen as a perfect concept. Instead, common good can be promoted by tackling several senses of injustice on a realisation-focused basis. The common good nexus does not need to be all encompassing when applied to the messy real world. In addition, the stability of basic institutions of society should be viewed critically as evidence (or not) of agents' disposition to construct the common good in the short and long term. We cannot take for granted that stability is a desired property of the common good nexus and attention to its appraisal should be constant.

Conclusion

The stability dimension is one of the most complex and intricate dimensions in the common good nexus. This happens because there is not as much reflection about it as we find for other dimensions such as agency, humanity, governance, and justice. But this does not mean that stability is less important, only that we know less about it and how it interacts with the other dimensions.

Perhaps one of the reasons why it is not as popular as the other dimensions is that it does not have a clear normative scale behind it. One can achieve stability from within a very bad state of affairs. Therefore, there is not a clear line separating good and bad, as there is in the case of other dimensions where we can see the lines between agency and anomy, good and bad governance, good and bad moral sentiment, and just and unjust arrangements. This means that we should first clarify what the normative sense behind certain kinds of stability within the nexus is. Only after this has been sorted should we face operationalisation issues.

These technical challenges are far from trivial, and quite often they can only be addressed within empirical counterparts of the common good nexus. This reflects a clear distinction between the design and implementation of social policies. But here, because the focus is on the nexus, on the processes that generate the common good, we have to factor in the additional complexity of the interaction between different dimensions. The suggestions offered here are just the beginning of an agenda that should entail attribution problems, counterfactual inferences and the use of econometrics, that are better left to empirical analyses.

References

Anand, S. and Sen, A. 2000. Human Development and Economic Sustainability, *World Development 28*/12, 2029–2049. https://doi.org/10.1016/S0305-750X(00)00071-1

Brundtland Report. 1987. https://en.wikisource.org/wiki/Brundtland_Report.

Buchanan, J. 1954. Social Choice, Democracy, and Free Markets, *Journal of Political Economy 62*, 114–123.

Cunha, F. and Heckman, J. 2007. The Technology of Skill Formation, *American Economic Review 97*/2, 31–47. https://doi.org/10.1257/aer.97.2.31

Earth Charter. 1992. https://earthcharter.org/discover/the-earth-charter/.

Etzioni, A. 2015. "Common Good", in Gibbons, M. (ed.), *The Encyclopedia of Political Thought*, London: John Wiley and Sons.

Kaul, I., Grunberg, I. and Stern, M. (eds) 1999. *Global Public Goods: International Cooperation in the 21st Century*, New York: Oxford University Press.

Nussbaum, M. 2019. *The Cosmopolitan Tradition: A Noble but Flawed Ideal*, Cambridge, MA: Belknap Press. ISBN: 9781541434318

Rawls, J. 2001. *Justice as Fairness: A Restatement*. Cambridge, MA: Belknap Press. ISBN: 9780674005112

Sen, A. 2017. *Collective Choice and Social Welfare, Expanded edition*. London: Penguin Books. ISBN: 0241244609, 9780241244609

Sen, A. 2009. *The Idea of Justice*. London: Penguin Books. https://doi.org/10.1017/S095382081100046X

Solow, R. 1993. "An almost practical step toward sustainability", *Resources Policy*, 162–172, https://web.stanford.edu/class/econ155/coursework/CourseMaterials/Readings/Solow-Sustainability.pdf.

Southwick, S., Bonanno, G., Masten, A., Panter-Brick, C., and Yehuda, R. 2014. Resilience definitions, theory and challenges: interdisciplinary perspectives, *European Journal of Psychotraumatology 5/1*, 1–14. https://doi.org/10.3402/ejpt.v5.25338

Stern, N. 2007. *The Economics of Climate Change*. Cambridge: Cambridge University Press. ISBN: 9780521700801

WCED. 1997. *Our Common Future*. Oxford: Oxford University Press.

World Development Report. 2003. *Sustainable Development in a Dynamic World*. Washington, DC: World Bank. ISBN: 0821351508

World Inequality Report. 2018. *World Inequality Lab*. https://wir2018.wid.world.

PART III
CASE STUDIES AND APPLICATIONS

Introduction to Part III

Aim of Part III

This third part introduces some applications of a common good approach to development, either as a framework to analyse a situation, or as a metric. The different chapters highlight the different possibilities opened by a matrix of common good dynamics. Helen Alford's chapter gives a general introduction into the prospects of the approach and shows how they can be applied to good business practice. Then Patrick Riordan uses the model to analyse the peace process in Mindanao, while Valente Tallabs and Mathias Nebel analyse common good dynamics in the rural town of Atlixco (Mexico), identifying proxies for the five key drivers. Finally, Simona Beretta shows how a common good approach may help understand the dynamic of prison programmes aiming to reinsert inmates into society. These 'case studies' are not meant to be a rigorous application of the approach, but rather to illustrate how it may apply to a highly diverse set of realities, proving to be as much an analytical tool as a potential metric.

To Whom Is It of Interest?

This third part will mainly be of interest to politicians and development planners. To the first group it may appeal as a source of a different kind of politics, one based on promoting common good dynamics. To the second, it will open up new ways to draft policies and plan interventions. Both may find that the approach procures a new way of seeing reality. To focus on basic commons and the network existing between them; to pay attention to the way these common goods interacts and how they are built into a dynamic system of commons highlights aspects of social processes

 https://doi.org/10.11647/OBP.0290.11

seldom seen otherwise. Indeed, our approach helps individuals to grasp the complexity of social interactions through a united and flexible framework, making sense of a complex social process. It associates the ethical dimension of development with a framework which is sensitive to the complexity and specificities of practical situations. As such, this part shows the many potentialities of our approach.

Why Does It Matter?

Many development practices lack a sound theoretical background. Duflo, Banerjee and Kremer famously argued that the complexity of reality was irreducible to theories and that we should ground development practice mainly in experience. We do not share this view. It is ultimately a fantasy about 'pure' experience where 'facts' talk for themselves and somehow add up to form a body of knowledge 'untainted' by presuppositions. Rather, we think that public policies as well as development programmes are dependent on the theoretical background that they explicitly or implicitly assume. This is normal and good. To make sense out of reality you need some sort of theoretical framework. But, then, theoretical frameworks are futile if they do not translate into action. By addressing both theory and practice, by bridging the two, this book avoids this trap. Part I, the theoretical part, lays the ground for Part III, dedicated to practice, while the case studies illustrate and enrich the theoretical framework.

9. Do We Need a Common Good Approach to Development?

Helen Alford

1. Let's Start with Two Stories

Over thirty years ago now, I became acquainted with a professor of English in a university in the US. Teaching English did not pay very well so he earned his real income from teaching courses in marketing communication. In one lecture, he showed his students an advertisement with a picture of a woman wearing a pair of jeans. The implication of the picture, reinforced by the text that went with it, was that young women wearing these jeans become more attractive to the opposite sex. He pointed out that nothing was said about the kind of material from which the jeans was made, nor was any other information given about the nature of the product. He then said something which stunned his students: "this message is clearly a species of lying". As he continued to explain why, the atmosphere in the classroom became colder and colder, until finally one of the students in the class raised her hand and asked "what's wrong with selling dreams?"[1]

And then there is the story of Ian Goldin (2018), the author of the *Very Short Introduction* on development, which he recounts in his talk at Google. In both, he synthesises the current state of play on development in a way that only someone who has dedicated his life to it could manage,

---

[1] Indeed, a quick check of the search term 'selling dreams' in any search engine on the Internet will bring up videos aimed at sales people with titles like 'Sell dreams not products', and articles with titles like 'Selling Dreams is the Secret to Customer Loyalty'.

      https://doi.org/10.11647/OBP.0290.12

someone who was exiled from South Africa during apartheid and who never thought he would see his country change—until it did. Yet, despite all that he has seen and done, the most emphatic statement in his talk is: "ideas are the driving force of history". The way we think about the world and about ourselves within it creates the framework within which we can imagine something new and better (a 'more developed' state).

Why open with these stories? Well, stories can impress us with a truth that can elude us in reading purely academic texts. In the first story, we can see the power of selling dreams. The students were shocked that the professor should 'unmask' this process; they did not feel gratitude to him for having opened their eyes to how they were being sold illusions. Indeed, they *wanted* to be taken in by the advertisement, so that they could aspire to the dream it promised. At the same time, aspiring to a dream seems good. The young people could be forgiven for finding their professor's criticism unhelpful. Even though the professor's contention seems right, it still doesn't seem easy to side with him against the students. Insofar as development is about aspiring to a dream—a world that could be, but which is not yet—this story raises a crucial point for us here. What development dreams are 'true' (not lies)? And why does a dream that, on one level, we can see as a lie, still seem to inspire us? We will come back to this intriguing and vexing problem towards the end of this chapter.

Goldin's comment—"ideas are the driving force of history"—leads us to the main issue we will discuss here: the way we think about development will be a driving force behind that development itself. Changing our ideas, or what I would like to call our 'mindset', that is, an integrated set of ideas for understanding what we need to do—can change our history. Real improvement in our mindset may thus bring about real change for the better in our history.

My main argument in this chapter is that we face development today within a mindset that was largely defined during the Enlightenment of the 1700s, and which is no longer fit for purpose. The mindset that was synthesised during the Enlightenment became a powerful driving force, changing history and driving many improvements.[2] We only have to look at many parts of the world that have not been through the processes

---

2   Among the many texts that could be mentioned here, Larry Siedentop's (2014) is particularly enlightening.

generated by the Enlightenment to see the difficulties with which they must often contend today, including nepotism, a lack of meritocracy and difficulty in maintaining the rule of law. The Enlightenment mindset has a lot going for it. However, like all other syntheses of this kind, it was at least in part a product of its time and of the problems that needed resolving then, so it was focused on resolving some issues and not others. Its key issue was individual freedom: for all sorts of good normative and historical reasons, defending the freedom of the individual had become a central problem by the time we arrived at the eighteenth century. Let's look briefly at two consequences of this mindset. Firstly, if individual freedom is central, the social systems of which individuals are a part become problematic. Such systems become a real, or at least a potential, threat to the exercise of that freedom, and ways have to be found to keep that threat at bay. Secondly, protecting individual freedom means protecting the possibility for each individual to define for themselves what the goals or purposes of their life should be. Social problems then become reduced to economic and procedural questions, because we can only share with each other *how* we achieve the goals of our lives, not what those goals are. This mindset also did other things which both allowed us to make progress and created collateral problems for us. Focusing on these key elements, however, can help us identify some of the strengths of this mindset, as well as its limitations, in the face of the problems we must face today.

In the 1700s, we still had very powerful systems of social control, which operated through the local communities of which people were a part and involved the religious traditions to which those communities belonged. The industrial revolution had not yet begun; the mass of poor people in every country far outnumbered the small number of aristocrats and the new, rising 'middle' classes. It was quite reasonable to see the need for more individual freedom as crucial, and to reduce social problems to economic ones, with the creation of wealth as the key 'development' issue.

Nowadays, we face problems that are very different. We might even go so far as to say that our problems are the mirror image of those of the eighteenth century. We face pressing social problems like inequality and systemic existential crises like climate change. Our difficulty today is to find shared solutions to these problems, harmonising the exercise of our individual freedom with a common goal—a good life lived together, and a life-giving relationship with our environment. We cannot avoid these problems anymore, but our inherited mindset was not designed to deal with them. Just as the Enlightenment thinkers recognised that what they had inherited was not fit for purpose in their day, and developed a new mindset to confront their problems, so now we need to recognise that what they bequeathed to us is not able to give us the basic vision we need to confront our problems.

If we look at development questions, we can see reflections of these issues in the literature.

We are in a context where development is seen primarily through the lens of the 2030 Agenda and the seventeen Sustainable Development Goals. On the one hand, this agenda is the result of a long process of negotiation, and in many ways is a really remarkable achievement. Yet we can see problems with it that changing the mindset we are talking about here could help us resolve, such as thinking about human development as a final goal, and the integration of the sustainable development goals.

Human development emerged in a powerful way within the development discourse with the launch of the Human Development Reports in 1990. The new 'Human Development Index' was a symbolic triumph; the report's initiator, Mahbub ul-Haq, correctly understood that an alternative indicator was needed to rival GDP, in order to have any chance of drawing attention to a human development agenda. It consisted of a combination of measures dealing with income, education and health. However, the text of the 1990 report did not have a clear definition of human development, and did not always refer to it in the same terms as the index measured it. Near the beginning of the 'Overview' of the report, we read: 'Human development is a process of enlarging people's choices. The most critical of these wide-ranging choices are to live a long and healthy life, to be educated and to have access to resources needed for a decent standard of living. Additional choices include political freedom, guaranteed human rights and personal self-respect' (UNDP 1990). This last phrase shows that the idea of human development was not resolved between two positions: one focused on freedom of choice (building on the Enlightenment mindset we have been discussing), and the other focused on the substantive or normative issues of life expectancy, health, education, and a decent standard of living. The tension between these two positions is captured in the last phrase just cited: 'Additional choices include political freedom, guaranteed human rights and personal self-respect'. Can 'guaranteed human rights' really be called an 'additional choice'? The text tries to hold together the idea of human development as the widest possible choice with the idea that it consists in certain forms of substantive change (what Sen would call improved 'capabilities'). The contradictions between these two are not easy to resolve. It is not a surprise, therefore, that subsequent HDRs did not try to do so. Similarly, while the 2030 Agenda aims to create an overarching approach to sustainable development, in practice the various sustainable development goals were not negotiated as an integrated set and are the results of various negotiation processes (e.g., see Dodds et al. 2017). Each goal has its own logic and its own targets which have been affected by the jockeying between interests in arriving at them. At least potential contradictions exist within them, such as between the goal for decent work and economic growth (Goal 8) and climate action (Goal 13); the hope is, of course, that these tensions will be resolved *in via*. There are the five transversal dimensions (people, planet, prosperity, peace, partnership), and Goal 17 does focus attention on partnership towards the achievement of the goals, so there is attention to some kind of practical integration, on the operational level. At the same time, this is not the same as being able to explain the unity between the goals as part of an integral vision and mindset.

These are very complex issues that cannot be resolved only by a change in mindset. Nevertheless, as Goldin suggests, our mindset influences our capacity to act and to imagine how we could change and develop. We can introduce new techniques for measuring development progress or progress towards a common good, but if we do not link those measures to a changed mindset or frame of mind, supported by a community of living that carries these ideas forward, we are doing what we have often seen before—we change the name of something, we change *how* we do things in some way, we may change the measurement tools and indicators, but we do not address the ultimate, underlying, fundamental question on which the name, the way of doing things and the measurement system depend—the question of *what* we want to do and *why* we want to do it.

The mindset we need now should not throw out all that has been achieved using the individualistic mindset adopted during the

Enlightenment. Much has been achieved within that philosophical approach, even if it always had limitations, limitations which have now become untenable and which are leading to an unsustainable way of life. Instead, we need to build on it, keeping what is good in it, but opening it up in two main ways. Firstly, we need to recognise a 'bigger' view of the human being. Our individuality is real, but so is our intrinsic relationality. Much empirical research in the field of happiness shows that we can only really achieve our goals in communion with others, not just because others provide us with economic or other goods that allow us to achieve our individual goals, but because our relationships in themselves are important.[3] Loneliness and its related mental health problems are becoming some of the key problems blocking our development, particularly in more wealthy countries (McDaid et al. 2017). Our competition with each other for our individual needs demonstrates our individuality, while the happiness research demonstrates our relationality. GDP and other measures of wealth can increase, but our happiness and sense of wellbeing may not. By recognising that we have both individual (material) and relational (non-material, spiritual) dimensions—by bringing the relational/spiritual dimension back into the picture—we can begin to imagine development in social and systemic ways, allowing us to give individual freedom its proper place within a bigger, more sustainable picture of human flourishing.

Secondly, we need to bring back a sense of working towards a common goal, and creating a common good together, on the basis of which all of us can achieve our individual goals. With a shared goal or purpose, we have the chance to unite our fragmented sustainable development goals into a unified picture, each one of them being achieved as part of an overall development goal. The drive to re-introduce thinking about our overall goal or purpose is most clearly displayed today in business, where the idea that businesses need a 'purpose' that inspires them beyond making money and which can guide them in aligning themselves to a genuine development agenda (many of them try to show how their strategies are aligned to the sustainable development goals) is now widely discussed

---

3   See the series of World Happiness Reports starting in 2012, available at https://worldhappiness.report/. See also the results taken over a lifetime from the Harvard Study of Adult Development https://www.adultdevelopmentstudy.org/.

and adopted.[4] Achieving social and environmental goals is no longer a side activity or an optional extra for socially-aware business managers—it has become core to achieving the good of the business as a whole, as a part of the wider society. 'Business cannot succeed in societies that have failed' is a phrase that circulates widely in the business world today.

The practical relevance of this synthesis between a renewed view of the human being, seen as a 'duality' of individual and relational, and of the common good, providing us with a goal towards which to work and on the basis of which individual goods can be achieved, can be demonstrated in the success of a movement known as the 'Blueprint for Better Business'. Founded in the UK in 2012, Blueprint works with some of the leading FTSE 100 companies, helping them to define and operationalise a purpose that builds on the dignity and duality of the human person and promotes the common good.[5] Focusing on mindset change—the 'why' and 'what for' of purpose—it does not aim at producing new tools for being a purposeful business—the 'how' of purpose—which is what many consultants and coaches do. Instead, Blueprint draws together key elements to help businesses change their mindset from two fundamental sources: firstly, key ideas from the millenarial 'wisdom traditions' represented by the great world religions and the great philosophical systems, like Aristotelianism and Confucianism, which have stood the test of time and which were often sidelined at the time of the Enlightenment, and secondly, modern scientific results that challenge the Enlightenment mindset but which converge in the direction of the ideas proposed by these ancient traditions of thought.[6] Although Blueprint has focused on businesses, its mindset has wider significance, and could be applied in the public and non-profit sectors, and to development as a whole. In applying this mindset, Blueprint has seen leading financial businesses ask themselves 'what is the right level of profit for our business?', and commit themselves to gaining economic returns from creating social value.[7] It has seen others

---

4   See, for instance, the results of 'The Future of the Corporation' programme of the British Academy, https://www.thebritishacademy.ac.uk/programmes/future-of-the-corporation/.

5   https://www.blueprintforbusiness.org/.

6   The idea of the 'wisdom traditions' was taken from the book by R. J. Blomme and B. van Hoof (2014).

7   In an interesting parallel, see the comment on finding 'how much profit is enough' for a financial institution from the CEO of Nationwide Building Society in the 2020

identify various options for how they could become more responsible, ranging from 'being a follower', to 'being a leader', to 'using our position to create a coalition to change the game, to raise the standard for the whole of our sector', and committing to being either the second or the third. In the context of the pandemic, it has seen major companies that had previously committed to paying all their workforce a living wage maintain that commitment, despite the economic shock experienced, by cutting the salaries of those higher paid in the business. Given the ever-widening impact of Blueprint, and given that the mindset change it wants to bring about focuses on resolving the social and systemic problems we face today, we will present the Blueprint mindset as an example of the direction in which we need to go, and then comment on it with regard to the problematic issues in the field of development that we highlighted above.

A Changed Mindset[8]

Our first issue is to discuss how a human being can be both an individual and intrinsically relational at the same time, with two integral yet distinct aspects of being human. In a theory known as 'personalism', which is a twentieth-century development within a tradition of thought that dates back over two thousand years and is often called 'Aristotelian-Thomistic', we find the human being presented as two-dimensional: one dimension is 'individual' and the other is 'personal' or 'relational'. In philosophical thought, and even in general conversation, we are used to talking about two dimensions of the human being, but we usually use terms like 'body and soul' or 'matter and spirit', distinguishing between a material and an immaterial aspect. In the personalist view, the way of thinking about the 'soul' or 'spirit' is slightly developed, for it is this dimension which is 'intrinsically relational', that is, it is the dimension through which we relate to others as part of who we are, not only as useful to us in obtaining what we need as individuals.

---

publication of the UK's Financial Conduct Authority, *Driving Purposeful Cultures*, https://www.fca.org.uk/publication/discussion/dp20-1.pdf.

8   The mindset used in Blueprint draws on many resources, but two in particular are worth mentioning here: Maritain and Jacques (1947), and Alford and Naughton (2001).

As physical individuals, we are needy and fragile. Other individuals, needy and fragile like we are, will be in competition with us for the scarce goods that we need to satisfy our individual needs. These are not only material goods—money, a place to live, adequate food and healthcare—but also positions in hierarchies, giving us status and social approval. If we feel that we are threatened in any of these ways—a threat to our wealth, or to our position in a social system that is important to us—we can become defensive or even aggressive. All of this is part of who we are, and is well-attested to in the scientific literature. At the same time, much scientific literature also tells us that we are relational. One of the most striking sets of scientific results on this point comes from the happiness literature, as we already mentioned. This shows us that it is in our relationships with others that we find the deepest fulfilment and satisfaction. Our relational dimension, which is the spiritual or non-material aspect, is almost the opposite of our individual dimension—instead of being fragile and needy, it has a kind of interior energy and super-abundance; instead of being threatened by others, it looks to relationships with others as gifts, as forms of enrichment; it moves outwards, constantly transcending itself, looking outside itself for relationships with others simply because they are good in themselves.

It seems like these two dimensions are contradictory, especially when we think about how we relate to others. How can we be fragile and needy, in competition with others and potentially threatened by them, while, at the same time, being strong and overflowing with energy, cooperating with each other in building relationships that bring us long-lasting fulfilment? Well, the first thing to say is that the scientific results tend to show that we are like this, that we do relate to others in these two ways *at the same time*. The results of the games that game theorists get people to play, for instance, show that we can put more or less emphasis on our capacity to compete or to cooperate, depending on the circumstances that we are put in. For instance, if we feel that our counterpart, our player, is not trustworthy, we will tend to start protecting ourselves. If, however, we receive a gift, something that we do not feel that we deserved, we are inclined to share it with others, to pass on our good fortune, not to hoard it for ourselves.[9] Secondly,

---

9   See an interesting discussion about the result of games in relation to our mindset in Ghoshal (2005, pp. 75–91).

we can note that there are also examples of other theories that seem to rely on contradictory elements. Perhaps the most famous is the theory of the wave-particle duality of light. There are some experiments that physicists have done with light that they can only explain if they think of light as a particle, while there are others (such as when light bends) that they can only explain if they think of light as a wave. We cannot get to a simpler explanation of what light is: we can only say that it displays the characteristics both of a particle (or quantum) and of a wave. In his writings, Maritain uses other analogies. For instance, he uses the example of a work of art, which is at one and the same time a material object that is made up of various chemical substrates and a source of inspiration and enlightenment to us. Games are full of competition, but only work if the players cooperate with each other by keeping the rules, and the whole idea of 'sportsmanship' goes beyond adherence to rules. In all these examples, things that are contrary, or at least completely different, are found at one and the same time in the same object or activity.

With the idea of the human being in two dimensions, individual and intrinsically relational, we are able to think differently about the common good too. We can create goods between us, as part of our intrinsically relational side, which are held in common between us. Since relationships can be intrinsically important to us, part of who we are, we can work towards genuinely shared objectives (as friends do) from which we both gain something individually, but, more fundamentally, we both gain together. Friendships either exist between friends or they do not exist at all, and only on the basis of their shared friendship do friends gain individually from their bond. This happens in the wider society too, when we are working towards a common, shared objective. When different groups cooperate together in different ways in a local community, for instance—politicians, local government officials, working people, local investors, suppliers, customers and so on—it is only on the basis of what they achieve together (the success of the life of the community itself) that they can each get something out of it individually (perhaps career advancement, or return on investment, or more secure custom, or better service, or whatever). When we are dealing with each other in a local community, therefore, we are creating a common good together, on the basis of which we can each gain some individual benefit too (which usually includes some financial reward, but is not limited to that). Wherever people are acting or working or cooperating together, they are producing common goods, and all these shared goods, in a wonderfully varied and articulated way, build up into the wider common good of societies as a whole (see Chapter1).

It is helpful to look at what we produce when we work towards shared objectives in three ways. Firstly, as we have been saying, we can recognise that shared goods, created between us as we try to achieve an objective together, create the basis for distributing the individual goods that we all need. A reasonable level of literacy, created through the shared good of education, allows a community to be able to create more business activity, and thereby more wealth that can then be distributed to individuals. We participate in the good of education. A 'participated' good like this is interesting because it can be shared with others without anyone losing by that sharing, and, indeed, the more people are educated, the more we all benefit from that. In the case of education, we can have 'gatekeepers' who can control access to education, but we can also find ways of sharing knowledge that circumvent the gatekeeper, as, for instance, various uses of the Internet have demonstrated. Participated goods create the framework within which each one of us can benefit individually, that is, each of us can receive goods that can only be shared by allocation (like a pie can only be shared by cutting it up and giving a piece to all those around the table). If we are members of a business and we all work hard together, towards our shared purpose, we will create products and services that serve society and an economic return as a result of that—our pie—which can then be allocated to all of us individually (the basis of the allocation also needs to be a participated good—a sense of fairness or justice—if it is not to create tension and to damage our motivation to work together for our common good). Businesses can only be successful within societies that are flourishing; local communities can flourish within regions and nations to which they are contributing, in whose good they participate, and from which they draw benefit.

Secondly, we can recognise that achieving any shared goal requires what we can call 'foundational goods'—which lay the foundations for a good life and which include things like enough economic wealth, infrastructure and capital equipment, policies, norms and legal systems—and 'excellent' goods, which are what constitute the good life itself, or what we could call human development in community, or a deeper and wider set of capabilities (see Chapter 2). Without enough foundational goods, our life together is threatened, just as weak foundations threaten the house which is built upon them. But spending all our time on creating foundational goods and not on what the foundational goods are for—the 'house' made up of excellent goods—leads us to a lack of fulfilment and unhappiness. Doing this as a community is like the avaricious man who only lives to make more money. We can see the problem with this relatively clearly on the individual level, but our Enlightenment mindset tells us that we should focus only on foundational goods at a community level, and this limits our capacity to imagine what a good life in community could be like.

If ideas are the driving force of history and allow us to imagine our future, very basic ideas such as these can provide a mindset that could undergird, gradually, a new way of thinking about development. These mindsets act slowly over time; we could say that the Enlightenment mindset gradually had its influence over the last 300 years. Perhaps the most emblematic example of how a basic mindset can change the way we think about things is that of the Benedictine monks and their attitude to manual labour. As we know, classical civilisation thought of manual work as only for slaves, but over hundreds of years, the positive view of work to be found in the Rule of St Benedict gradually had its impact, allowing many later developments and much economic growth. If we can get some simple ideas right and clear, they can be of fundamental importance for development prospects.

If we were to adopt a mindset like this one in regard to development, we would start to expand our development focus. For instance, the relational aspects of development would be much more important to us. We would be interested in the goods held in relationships, alongside the individual goods with which we are more familiar (the latter being what Blueprint would call 'foundational' and 'allocated' goods). The IPBC project already demonstrates this kind of mindset change by focusing on the nexus of goods, their integration, the density and quality of relationships, and the coherence of normative elements within the nexus (see Chapters 1 and 2). We could imagine a post-2030 Development Agenda in which goals are developed in a relational way, with indicators and measures like the IPBC's nexus to track them. The more this mindset with its recognition of the fundamental importance of our relational dimension for our wellbeing, can drive our imagination, the more we will see it driving our history, that is, the way we develop.

We would also begin to be able to talk about shared final goals, held in the relationships between us, but which also allow for individual human freedom to express itself in the realisation of these goals. Both will be needed to allow different communities and cultures to develop in a way that is meaningful and shared, as well as in a way that recognises individual and historical diversity. The IPBC metric captures this (see Chapter 3), too, by, on the one hand, measuring certain key variables while, at the same time, allowing a partial re-ordering of priorities among the normative dimensions (as an expression of local agency and local knowledge).

We said that there are three ways of looking at the common good. The third and last way brings us back to the story of selling dreams. For if we are promoting the common good, we need to ask ourselves: is the good that we are working towards really good, or is it just apparently good? This is the most difficult question for us to ask ourselves, not least because it goes against one of the basic elements of the Enlightenment mindset that we have been talking about (it makes us discuss our final goals, rather than leaving everyone open to decide that for themselves). 'Selling a dream' isn't bad, but is it really good? The idea of something being 'apparently good' is useful here, since it recognises that we are all trying to do something good—the marketers 'selling the dream' are trying to do that for their customers—but do they actually end up doing that? We could say, for instance, that this type of advertising plays on the kind of vulnerabilities that women often have—of feeling bad about their self-image—and thereby it ends up perpetuating this vulnerability, even if the women themselves want to buy these products. Is that good? The answer in a case like this is not clear—but we can all see that there is a question here that is worth exploring. Maybe we will end up still selling dreams, but the dream we sell could be a better one, one that does not thrive on the weaknesses of our customers.[10] In other words,

---

10   We can see something like this in the 'Campaign for Real Beauty' promoted by the Dove brand of beauty products, owned by Unilever, see https://www.dove.com/uk/stories/campaigns.html.

we could start to move our activities from the arena of apparent good to true good. The relevance for development should be obvious. We need to ask ourselves the question: is what we are doing really for our human, social, and ecological good? We need to listen to many voices and to hear their answers, and allow ourselves to be inspired by great artistic and religious voices too. We can also come to learn over time that something we once thought was good turns out not to be so. No one who was behind the carbon-based industrial revolution set out to threaten the very ecosystem that supports life itself, but we can now see that this will result from our industrial production system unless we change it. So, we cannot always know in advance if what we are doing is only an apparent rather than a real good, but if we had always been asking ourselves: 'is what we are doing truly good?', we might have started to realise the problem and to change earlier, instead of facing a crisis of truly existential proportions as we do now.

Development is about life, and needs practical action. A discussion of our fundamental mindset may seem a luxury in the face of the critical social and systemic problems we need to resolve. Nevertheless, witnesses like Ian Goldin and the Benedictine monks tell us that foundational ideas really change practical outcomes. Let us close with words from John Maynard Keynes on this point: 'The ideas of economists and political philosophers, both when they are right and when they are wrong, are more powerful than is commonly understood. Indeed, the world is run by little else. Practical men, who believe themselves to be quite exempt from any intellectual influences are usually the slaves of some defunct economist [...] It is ideas, not vested interests, which are dangerous for good or evil' (Keynes 1953, p. 306).

References

Alford, H. and Naughton, M. 2001. *Managing as if Faith Mattered: Christian Social Principles in the Modern Organization*, South Bend: UNDP.

Blomme, R. J. and Van Hoof, B. 2014. *Another State of Mind: Perspectives from Wisdom Traditions on Management and Business*, Basingstoke: Palgrave.

British Academy. 2017. *The Future of the Corporation*. https://www.thebritishacademy.ac.uk/programmes/future-of-the-corporation/.

Dodds, F., Donoghue, D., and Roesch, J. L. 2017. *Negotiating the Sustainable Development Goals: A Transformational Agenda for and Insecure World*, Abingdon: Earthscan/Routledge.

Ghoshal, S. 2005. Bad Management Theories Are Destroying Good Management Practices, *Academy of Management Learning and Education* 4/1, 75–91. https://doi.org/10.5465/amle.2005.16132558

Goldin, I. 2018. *Development: A Very Short Introduction*, Oxford: Oxford University Press, https://www.youtube.com/watch?v=YJ7pnQ_MkPA.

Harvard Study of Adult Development. https://www.adultdevelopmentstudy.org/.

Keynes, J. M. 1953. *The General Theory of Employment, Interest and Money*, New York: Harcourt Brace Jovanovich.

Maritain, J. 1947. *La personne et le bien commun*, Paris: Desclée de Brouwer. [Fitzgerald, J. J. (trans.) 1947. *The Person and the Common Good*, New York: Charles Scribner's Sons.]

McDaid, D., Bauer, A., and Park, A. 2017. *Making the Case for Investing in Actions to Prevent and/or Tackle Loneliness: A Systematic Review*, briefing paper, https://www.lse.ac.uk/business-and-consultancy/consulting/assets/documents/making-the-economic-case-for-investing-in-actions-to-prevent-and-or-tackle-loneliness-a-systematic-review.pdf.

Siedentop, L. 2014. *Inventing the Individual: The Origins of Western Liberalism*, Cambridge, MA: Belknap.

UNDP. 1990. *Human Development Report 1990: Concept and Measurement of Human Development*. New York, https://www.hdr.undp.org/en/reports/global/hdr1990.

10. Bangsamoro: A Case Study in Governing for the Common Good

Patrick Riordan S.J.

This chapter provides a case study of a newly inaugurated autonomous region in the southern Philippines, in terms of its common goods. The common good is invoked in the Preamble of the Constitution of the Republic of the Philippines, and it is mentioned in Article XII dealing with national economy and patrimony, and in Article XIII dealing with social justice and human rights. Following the overthrow of the Marcos regime of martial law in 1986, the newly elected President Cory Aquino convoked a commission to draft a new constitution. The country saw itself at that time as recently liberated from an oppressive regime that many qualified as a dictatorship, in which the rule of law and the respect for human rights had been disregarded. The adoption of a new constitution expressed the desire for self-government as appropriate to a republic, in the pursuit of freedom, equality and prosperity.

> We, the sovereign Filipino people, imploring the aid of Almighty God, in order to build a just and humane society and establish a Government that shall embody our ideals and aspirations, promote the common good, conserve and develop our patrimony, and secure to ourselves and our posterity the blessings of independence and democracy under the rule of law and a regime of truth, justice, freedom, love, equality, and peace, do ordain and promulgate this Constitution.

Constitution of the Republic of the Philippines, Preamble

Typical of a republican constitution is the affirmation of the sovereignty of the people that provides for itself a constitution. It acknowledges

   https://doi.org/10.11647/OBP.0290.13

the twin dimensions of the social and the political. These are distinguishable but not separable. Building 'a just and humane society' is done in tandem with establishing and maintaining a government of a state. The purpose of government is to promote the common good. This is not further explained in the text, but its meaning embraces the various other values listed, values that the people wish to secure for themselves and their posterity. Together they act to pursue the good they hold in common. Law professor Joaquin G. Bernas, a member of the Constitutional Commission, commented on the text of the Preamble in a publication issued in advance of the Constitution's ratification. He noted the preference for the term 'common good':

> The change from 'general welfare' to 'common good' was intended to project the idea of a social order that enables every citizen to attain his or her fullest development economically, politically, culturally and spiritually. The rejection of 'general welfare' of the old version was based on the fear that the phrase could be interpreted as meaning 'the greatest good of the greatest number' even if what the greater number wants does violence to human dignity [...] It was thought that the phrase 'common good' would guarantee that mob rule would not prevail and that the majority would not persecute the minority. (1987, p. 2 n. 8)

The various occurrences of the term and cognates in the body of the Constitution reinforce the basic line formulated in the Preamble that people are attempting to secure a social and legal order and thereby assure a certain quality of life for themselves. The management of property and its use, the creation of business corporations, and the responsibility of government in relation to these, warrant the invocation of common good as the overarching value. Similarly, in the article on social justice and human rights, common good is invoked as a guiding value in relation to the equitable distribution of wealth and political power, and regarding the urgent need to provide housing for the urban poor. Subsequent attempts to legislate these matters have been controversial, with the general criticism voiced that the common good was not strong enough to prevail over established and socially integrated interests, such as those of the more powerful oligarchic families who provided the political leadership in the country, the Aquino family itself included.

Article X of the 1987 Constitution, on local government, provided for the creation of two autonomous regions, in Muslim Mindanao in the south, and in the Cordilleras, the mountainous area in Luzon in the north. As Bernas notes in his commentary, the Constitution provides for only two such regions, that have a claim to special treatment because they exhibit 'common and distinctive historical and cultural heritage, economic and social structures, and other relevant characteristics.' The distinctiveness warranting this autonomy is differentiation from the 'characteristics of the dominant national communities.' He notes also that the constitutional recognition and provision replaces measures of autonomy created 'merely by presidential decree' (Bernas 1987, p. 71 nn. 23–14). It should be borne in mind that while there is a recognition of the goods in common that are to be protected and promoted within the region, this is in the context of a vision of a shared national common good.

1. History and Context of the Bangsamoro Autonomous Region in Muslim Mindanao

The Philippines is an archipelago of islands, large and small. The large northern island, Luzon, is where the largest city and capital, metro Manila, including the seat of government for the country, Quezon City, is located. Between Luzon and the southern island, Mindanao, with its satellite islands, is a group of islands named the Visayas. The archipelago has had a fraught and varied history, which is not uniform across the islands (Gloria 2014). For various reasons, Mindanao, the southernmost large island of the archipelago, is different. One reason is that it is home to the large Muslim population (c. 4.2 million) that is a minority within the predominantly Catholic population of the country as a whole (c. 100 million). Another reason for its distinctiveness is that neither of the colonial powers, the Spaniards up to 1898 and the Americans subsequently until 1946, ever completely succeeded in pacifying Mindanao and incorporating the native populations into the national community. When the United States of America replaced Spain as the colonial power at the end of the Spanish American War in 1898, the Americans believed they were taking over an already pacified country, but that was far from the case. As well as having to suppress an insurgency in Luzon, the Americans also had to establish their rule as the first colonisers in Mindanao (Gloria 2014). A third element in the distinctiveness of Mindanao within the Philippines is that it was uniquely targeted as a territory to be colonised, not by foreigners, but by other Filipino peoples. To deal with the problems of overpopulation and the associated peasant disquiet in the northern islands, and with the problem of unrest in the south, both American and subsequently Filipino governments pursued policies of settlement, inviting people from Luzon and the Visayas to settle in Mindanao. These settlement policies including those pursued by Ferdinand Marcos as President, resulted in grave injustices to the native populations. A fourth factor in explaining the uniqueness of Mindanao concerns the internal structure of the population. While the general labels of indigenous peoples (IPs) or Muslims might give the impression of a coherent homogenous culture, the reality is very different. While there had been traditional forms of government with ruling elites, such as the Sultanates of Maguindanao and Sulu, these were not unified, and many tribes retained their independence and separate traditions. One author reports a total of thirteen different groups among the Muslim population, and in addition eighteen indigenous tribes with their own animist religious culture (Yusingco 2013, pp. 17–21). Another source identifies 179 ethnic groups in BARMM, understanding an ethnic group as sharing distinctive cultural identity. Many of these are very small in size. Three major groupings make up over 70% of the population, and a further 25% is comprised of seven groups.[1] The interests of some indigenous peoples are in tension with the political agenda of the Muslim insurgency leadership, and are in danger of being neglected, possibly because their advocates have not resorted to armed violence (Alejo 2014, pp. 65–70).

These four factors provide the context for both the turbulent history of the island and the attempts to provide solutions. First, a relatively large Muslim population, but not organised in a coherent unity for political effectiveness, alongside many indigenous groups who are pagan, neither Christian nor Muslim. Second, a history of independence, resistance and insurgency against colonial powers. Third, a history also of incursion with government backing by mostly Christian settlers from the north. Finally, the economic deprivation arising from the marginalisation of the area is paired with the growing exploitation of natural resources, whether through illegal or quasi-legal logging of the

---

1   Access Bangsamoro: Ethnic Groups in BARMM.

native forests, or mining activities encroaching on ancestral domains. Multinational economic agents, abetted by legislators in Manila, pursue their own interests in the island, often relying on private security firms both to protect and enforce their interests.

The Bangsamoro Organic Law (henceforth BOL) was signed into force by President Duterte in August 2018. It is the latest in a series of attempts to provide a form of autonomy to the Muslims of Mindanao. The previous structure, the Autonomous Region of Muslim Mindanao (ARMM), was instituted following the adoption of the 1987 Constitution under President Cory Aquino. It was subsequently deemed to have been a failure. Its failure is seen in the years of violence perpetrated by various Muslim organisations, harnessing the frustration of young men who found themselves without educational or employment opportunities, despite the growing affluence of the country as a whole. The MNLF (Moro National Liberation Front) and the MILF (Moro Islamic Liberation Front) conducted campaigns of armed insurgency over recent decades. Peace agreements between the Government of the Philippines and the MNLF were signed in 1976 (Tripoli) and 1996. But it is from the framework peace agreement achieved between the Government of the Philippines and the MILF (October 2012) that the demand for and commitment to the creation of the Bangsamoro Autonomous Region arose.

It has taken much longer than expected to produce the legislation and to have it signed into law, which finally happened in July 2018. Further steps of implementation included the plebiscite in January 2019 and the inauguration of the Bangsamoro Autonomous Region in Muslim Mindanao (henceforth BARMM) in March 2019. The commitment of both parties to this peace process and to the implementation of the Bangsamoro has remained resolute, despite serious threats arising from the violence of dissident groups (Lau 2014, pp. 260–273).

At the heart of the grievances of the Muslim population leading to armed insurgency was the destruction of their traditional villages and way of life by the confiscation of their lands and the imposition of forms of rule alien to their customs (Yusingco 2013, p. 31). An initial documentation of these grievances has been achieved by the 'Transitional Justice and Reconciliation Commission,' whose report in 2016 illustrated in painful detail the typical injustices suffered by the peoples of

Mindanao. Far from being an ideologically driven international Islamic conspiracy, as the world media sometimes like to characterise it, the insurgency has always been a response to experienced injustices at the hands of government, whether native or colonial.

The challenge faced by the BARMM as a new structure of autonomous regional government is enormous. There is no unified society, given the distinction between Muslim and other indigenous tribes, and even the Muslims are divided among themselves, belonging to groups traditionally in competition with one another. The creation of this regional form of government will require shaping the shared meanings of the population with a view to fostering agreement on the worthwhileness of the project. However, despite the enormity of the challenge, the lack of a single unified society need not be a fatal flaw for the project, as some commentators have feared (Yusingco 2013, p. 26). In response, I have argued elsewhere that in terms of Aristotle's claim that a political community presupposes a shared vision of the good, agreement on the need for such a structure to put an end to war, and to remove the causes of frustration leading to violence, can be sufficient as shared meaning to establish the Bangsamoro (Riordan 2014, pp. 35–56). This presupposes a lot of imaginative work in fostering understanding and building agreement, and that work remains to be done. The outcome of the initiative to establish the BARMM is not a foregone conclusion.

The creation of the BARMM establishes an autonomous region within the Republic of the Philippines and not a separate state. Furthermore, the possibility of secession is blocked by ensuring the continuing integration of the region within the state, subject to the Constitution of 1987. National government will continue to have jurisdiction in matters of defense, external security, immigration, and international relations and treaties. However, the distinctiveness of the region as expressed in the phrase 'asymmetrical relationship' allows for a special position within the state, not on the same terms as other regions, but acknowledging the special characteristics that warrant the creation of an autonomous region. As noted, these include the peculiar history and composition of the region's population. A significant feature is the incorporation of Islamic *Shari'ah* Law applicable to Muslims only, along with the traditional tribal justice systems of the indigenous peoples. These traditional forms of justice may not be so applied that fundamental human rights are jeopardised.

Accordingly, the Bangsamoro Organic Law attempts an integration of international human rights law, national legislation, and the local forms of justice. Anticipation of tensions between the jurisdictions leads to a mapping of norms of precedence. The attempt is to devolve as much responsibility from national government as possible, allowing for local responsibility regarding policing, protection of the environment, exploitation of national resources, and commerce. Worries have already been expressed concerning the position of women in the BARMM (Risonar-Bello 2014, pp. 87–102), the ancestral domain of indigenous peoples and their associated rights (Alejo 2014, pp. 65–70), and the position of some Muslim groups not aligned with the MILF (Arpa 2014, pp. 83–86).

Viewed from the outside, the initiative of the BOL in response to the Peace Agreement is an attempt to realise the common good in the broadest sense in this region. The BOL itself does not use the language of common goods, and that is not surprising, since this language is more at home in the political discourse of concerned citizens and representatives of affected groups. While lawyers refine formulations and anticipate legal issues, the articulation of political, cultural and religious concerns in terms of the common goods at stake should be of service to the actors charged with implementing the legislation and the newly created processes and structures. However, the Preamble to the Bangsamoro Organic Law has resonances with that of the National Constitution, cited above, in which the term 'common good' is explicitly invoked.

> Imploring the aid of Almighty God, in recognition of the aspirations of the Bangsamoro people and other inhabitants in the autonomous region in Muslim Mindanao to establish an enduring peace on the basis of justice, balanced society and asserting their right to conserve and develop their patrimony, reflective of their system of life as prescribed by their faith, in harmony with their customary laws, cultures and traditions, within the framework of the Constitution and the national sovereignty as well as territorial integrity of the Republic of the Philippines, and the accepted principles of human rights, liberty, justice, democracy, and the norms and standards of international law, and affirming their distinct historical identity and birthright to their ancestral homeland and their right to chart their political future through a democratic process that will secure their identity and posterity, and allow genuine and meaningful self-governance, the Filipino people, by the act of the Congress of the

Philippines, do hereby ordain and promulgate this Organic Law for the Bangsamoro Autonomous Region in Muslim Mindanao. (20180727-RA-11054, Preamble.)

The values enumerated here resonate with those of the 1987 Constitution but in the context of acknowledging the special circumstances of the Muslim region in Mindanao. While adverting to the legitimacy of the special claims of this region, the BOL is deliberately stated as a law enacted by the Congress of the country as a whole. Accordingly, it is possible to read in this undertaking several levels of goods in common. There is the common good of the country as a whole, in ending the violence, insecurity and drain on scarce resources linked to the instability in Mindanao. There is the common good of Mindanao, a larger entity than the BARMM, which needs a resolution of the Muslim insurgency for peace, stability and future development. There are common goods of the peoples of Bangsamoro, both the institutions now being created, and the wellbeing, prosperity, peace and stability that is their purpose. Finally, there are the goods of humanity, both those rooted in the solidarity with suffering people, and the potential to learn from the Bangsamoro experiment lessons that can be applied in other contexts of violent conflict.

2. Operationalising the Common Good: The Pentagram

The language of common goods is ancient but does not always appear relevant to modern political issues. The development of an appropriate set of tools for the application of common good to contemporary concerns, undertaken by a team of experts led by Professor Mathias Nebel of the IPBC, is documented in this volume (see Chapters 1, 2, and 3). It offers a map to sketch the nexus of the principal dimensions of the common goods of local government. This project is outlined more extensively elsewhere in this book, so it suffices here to note the key elements. Five core values of the common goods are identified (referred to as the pentagram; see Chapter 2, Figure 4), and these outline the scope of what is to be realised by local government. These values are stability, agency, governance, justice and humanity (see Chapter 2). Important social norms such as those of democracy, the rule of law, good governance, subsidiarity, participation, empowerment and human flourishing can be read from the matrix of the combinations of the five core values. The matrix provides a total of twenty headings, with each combination of values providing a pair, one for each direction. For instance, the combination of agency and governance delivers participation, while in the opposite direction, governance and agency delivers empowerment. In what follows I apply the pentagram to the Bangsamoro Organic Law (BOL) with a view to generating a metric for evaluating the success (or failure) of the BARMM. The BOL does not use the language of common goods, although the project is evidently an attempt to achieve and solidify goods in common. The opportunity to bring these two conversations together may prove to be mutually enriching. On the one hand, it could provide those charged with implementing the BOL with a map or outline to sketch the range of tasks involved and to evaluate performance. On the other hand, the opportunity to test the usefulness of the pentagram in the implementation of one significant project of revision of regional government may help confirm, consolidate and refine the pentagram.

3. Common Goods of the BARMM

I. Justice

There is no order of precedence in the five core values—they are all equally essential. But in the application of the pentagram to the situation in Mindanao, it would seem appropriate to begin with justice, given the historical context, and the element of transitional justice involved. The injustice suffered by the peoples of Mindanao in the past century belongs among the motivations for creating the autonomous region. Section 3 of Article I of the Organic Law establishing Bangsamoro declares the purpose of the law as follows:

> The purpose of this Organic Law is to establish a political entity, provide for its basic structure of government in recognition of the justness and legitimacy of the cause of the Bangsamoro people and the aspiration of Muslim Filipinos and all indigenous cultural communities in the autonomous region in Muslim Mindanao to secure their identity and posterity, allowing for meaningful self-governance within the framework of the Constitution and the national sovereignty as well as territorial integrity of the Republic of the Philippines.(20180727-RA-11054, I. Sec. 3.)

This situation of the BARMM marks it out as distinctive. The affirmation in this cited section as also in the Preamble of the legitimacy of the Muslim population's claim to secure their distinctive identity and to exercise self-government is an expression of the BOL's attempt to do justice.

The actual historical background provides a context in which the rectification of injustice is as important as the facilitation of justice for the future. The Bangsamoro Parliament is tasked to make laws and create processes to achieve the desired ends of rectification and restoration (20180727-RA-11054, IX. Secs. 1 & 2.). The task is enormous and may prove impossible to fulfil. The issue of land is particularly problematic. The link to the land is central to the sense of identity for traditional tribes. The memory of the injustice of the manner in which they were removed from their lands motivates a demand for rectification. Historically, tribal land holdings, ancestral domains, did not rely on any form of land registration, but on the customary practices of the indigenous peoples. The introduction of a land registration system to cultures that did not understand the concept, and the requirement to submit claims within a very narrow window, meant that the settlers brought in from the north could implement claims against which the traditional occupants had no legal redress. On the one hand, the law signals the desire to right these historical wrongs, and that is an important acknowledgement of the injustice of dispossession and relocation. On the other hand, the law burdens the new regime and its government with a task that, no matter how well it is performed, inevitably will leave some people feeling badly done by. They may be indigenous people whose claims are not recognised, or they may be settlers who, in all they (or their ancestors) did, believed themselves to be acting legally with the approval and encouragement of the national government.

The tragedy of Mindanao, like so many other areas of conflict, is that the past is very much present to peoples' consciousness as it shapes their everyday experience. It seems as if the formulation of the law has tied the new regime to its past by requiring these measures of transitional justice; on the other hand, the law could not have remained silent on the historical injustices and complaints of the population in seeking their commitment to a new form of government. On this fundamental point we find the core value of justice at the heart of the BARMM.

Among indigenous peoples there are some tribes that have been converted to Islam, some have been Christianised, and others retain their ancient animist religion. From the point of view of the BARMM, there is particular concern that the non-Islamic tribes within the Bangsamoro territory do not suffer any discrimination (20180727-RA-11054, IV. Secs. 7 & 9; VII. Sec. 5). The rights of indigenous peoples are enumerated in the Organic Law, echoing earlier national legislation (Indigenous Peoples' Rights Act, IPRA) designed to protect the traditional lands and cultures of indigenous peoples, ensuring that their free, prior, informed consent is obtained before any exploration or exploitation of natural resources within their ancestral domains (I 20180727-RA-11054, XIII. Sec. 8). That law had not been completely effective, since the designation of who exactly is entitled to give the consent is unclear. In many cases, it seems, self-appointed leaders provided the consent against remuneration, but this was without formal structures of representation. The new arrangements will have to ensure there is no such abuse if the willing compliance of the tribal peoples in the Bangsamoro is to be evoked.

Article IX on basic rights specifies obligations of the BARMM government to provide many elements that contribute to overall wellbeing. It is not a matter of merely ensuring that systems are in place and functioning, but the Organic Law seems to require that the Bangsamoro government actually create and operate such systems, to provide healthcare, housing, employment, education, and to support arts and culture. Time is a factor in the realisation of such aspirations, and it may be idealistic to include these in articles under the heading of justice. It is at least evidence of the Organic Law's comprehension of the double lists of thin and thick factors concerning justice, the former outlining the basic needs and the latter identifying elements of flourishing. Nebel and Delgadillo might be thought to have the Bangsamoro situation in mind when they suggest that the enactment of law is the first creative step towards providing justice within a very complex social context: 'To proclaim a constitution is but a very easy task compared to making these rights and freedoms real for each and everyone in the country. For formal rights to become real they need to be implemented' (see Chapter 2, § 'Justice as a Normative Driver of Common Good Dynamics').

The variety of customs, norms and practices among the peoples of the Bangsamoro pose a challenge for the creation of a unified system of government that respects rights and freedoms across the whole population, and at the same time fosters the flourishing of each community according to its own values.

II. Stability

Given the history of injustice, exclusion, and the resorting to armed conflict that has characterised this region over several decades, the stability of the BARMM will depend on the establishment and maintenance of peace. History has seen many armed groups, MNLF, MILF, Abu Sayyaf, and BIFF, among others, who have resorted to violence, but this in turn has provoked the defensive and aggressive action of settlers' militias, and the Armed Forces of the Philippines. In addition, mining companies, politicians, and prominent families with traditional ruling authority, have also maintained private armies, for self-protection as well as for status in a very volatile atmosphere. Banditry, relying on kidnapping, robbery and extortion, has been a way of making a living in the absence of legitimate economic possibilities.

The BARMM attempts to bring this violence to an end. It will only succeed if it is supported by the various armed groups. The MILF is preeminent in the BARMM government, having participated in the peace talks leading to the Framework Agreement on Bangsamoro in October 2012, and the Comprehensive Agreement in 2014. The principal demand of the insurgents is met in the provision of self-government with the recognition of distinctive identity. However, further steps are required to ensure stability. One such measure envisaged in the BOL is to offer the members of these organisations the possibility of joining the police service of the autonomous region. This has the obvious advantage of permitting formerly armed men and women to find respectable roles in the new regime (20180727-RA-11054, XI. Sec. 2; XIV. Sec. 1). On the other hand, it has the disadvantage of giving people who have lived from banditry access to new avenues of extortion and corruption. The success of this move will be an indicator of the success of the BARMM as a whole.

The stability of BARMM depends on securing peace. Among the measures envisaged to sustain peace, the BOL commits the government of the autonomous region to implement widespread peace education.

While it must be among the basic motivations of supporters of the BARMM to bring an end to violence and establish peace, there is acknowledgement that the motivation is fragile and vulnerable to disappointment and setbacks. Hence the commitment in the article on basic human rights to peace education (20180727-RA-11054, IX. Sec. 16).

Stability has another urgent aspect in the diverse population of Bangsamoro. The challenge facing everyone is to build a political entity relying on the commitment of diverse groups who traditionally have been competitors if not enemies. Stability with the assurance of continuity and sustainability into the future will not be achieved without the construction of genuine practices of collaboration between the different groups. The indigenous peoples (IPs) of Mindanao are not all Muslim; many are animist in their religious orientation; and in addition, there are communities of settlers in among the indigenous peoples. The Organic Law reflects awareness of this issue in Article X on the planned system of justice. Government must deliver justice, which is understood as a fair balance in the collaborative production and distribution of collective goods. Considering the dangers of imbalance or even exclusion, the law anticipates the need to ensure participation and inclusion so that all affected persons can perceive themselves as participants in the BARMM. This is considered critical for the sustainability of a stable regime of self-government (20180727-RA-11054, X. Sec. 17).

Widespread acceptance that the autonomous authority has the resources and competence to deliver peace and harmony and that these in turn will foster prosperity will be essential to stability. Accordingly, stability is among the values targeted in the article considering patrimony and the economy, in which the objective of sustainable development is determined (20180727-RA-11054, XII. Sec. 2).

III. Governance

Good governance presupposes both a vibrant civil society and a responsible but also effective government. The BARMM inherits forms of government and civil society that need reform, adaptation, and development. Goods of cooperation can only emerge if there are social practices that engage local tribes and their members in deliberation and decision-making about what is worthwhile, and such practices must be rooted in the values and ideals of the relevant communities. Governance presupposes that the communities look with confidence to the institutions of government for the achievement of their deliberated goals. For institutions of government, responsiveness to society will ensure accountability and transparency regarding processes of decision-making and implementation. This requires a high level of virtue throughout the administrative framework, and an absence of corruption. There will be no privileging of favoured persons or groups, and no possibility of buying favours.

In a formal sense the initiative for Bangsamoro comes from above, from national government enacting the peace agreement with the MILF, leading to the Bangsamoro Organic Law enacted by Congress, and signed into force by the president in August 2018, with the BARMM inaugurated in March 2019. The value of governance requires movement in both directions, but it is understandable if the BOL concentrates on the responsibilities of government, including the responsibility to effect empowerment of citizens and groups. The bottom-up dynamic of initiatives arising from the people of Mindanao themselves will be considered under the heading of the value of agency.

The BARMM is designed in the BOL with a sense of the importance of the values of good governance, especially transparency, accountability, and the absence of corruption. The powers of government are laid out in a distinct article (20180727-RA-11054, V. Sec. 2). The revenue of the BARMM will be secured with a block grant from central government, but the specifications for budget and appropriations are provided in another article (20180727-RA-11054, VII. Sec. 27–28). The related values of good governance, of accountability, full disclosure, and publication of proposals and records are reflected in the requirements imposed on the regional government (20180727-RA-11054, XII. Sec. 2; 24 &40). As is to be expected in such a law as the Organic Law, the specification of the powers and responsibilities of government includes an article outlining the rights of citizens. With each of the rights listed there is a commitment of government to deliver and to ensure protection. One section in particular might be taken to represent this value of governance on behalf of all the other sections, namely, the assurance of equal and open access of all persons to basic services, thereby ensuring social justice (20180727-RA-11054, IX. Sec. 8).

IV. Agency

Agency is both a precondition and a consequence. On the one hand, the pursuit of goods in common presupposes agency and freedom from constraint to engage in the relevant deliberation and activity. On the other hand, to facilitate the agency of all participants is a common good of collaboration, a common purpose. The creation of the BARMM is a political project designed to enable and enhance the agency of a population which has been excluded from a share in the exercise of power. The IPBC research document says that agency 'describes how a given population gathers around common issues, drafts some solutions and achieves them. It is first and foremost a positive freedom' (Nebel and Delgadillo, Chapter 2 of this volume). The common issues for BARMM are rooted in their history, being largely linked to the marginal status of Muslim and tribal communities in the political, cultural, and economic life of the country. The design of the Bangsamoro governmental structure is intended, in the language of the research document, to 'give them the possibilities to organize around common issues.' Details of that design can be reconstructed in terms of facilitating agency.

For any collaboration, agency must be presupposed as already present to some significant extent, so that the new structures can be adopted and fruitfully operated. The agency exercised to date in the armed struggle has had its counterpart in the political campaign that has borne fruit in the achievement of the peace agreement and the creation of the BARMM. But that agency may have been exercised by a limited number of individuals in the upper echelons of the relevant organisations, predominantly the MILF and the Philippine Government. The new structures require participation at all levels, so that the aspects of agency must be found among members and followers and not only among the leaders. The agency of individuals cannot be separated from that of the collective, the agency of the governed is inseparable from the agency of the government.

The value of agency is at the heart of the BARMM as outlined in the BOL. The key objective is to restore self-government to people excluded from power (20180727-RA-11054, IV. Sec. 2). Measures are planned that will expand the opportunities for participation and that require the Bangsamoro government to consult widely (20180727-RA-11054, VII.

Sec. 5 & 7), including in matters of planning for development (20180727-RA-11054, XIII. Sec. 5–6). Those most likely to be marginalised in the processes of participation and consultation have their rights affirmed in the article on basic rights. In particular, the government is to ensure the participation of women and members of the indigenous peoples in government (20180727-RA-11054, IX. Secs. 11 & 12). This is in addition to the specifications for representation of all communities and interests in the parliament. Among the envisaged eighty members of the parliament there are to be a minimum of eight seats reserved for representatives of sectoral interests such as women, youth, traditional leaders, and the Ulama (20180727-RA-11054, VII. Sec. 7c). The indigenous peoples are charged with selecting their representatives according to their own traditions and customary laws (20180727-RA-11054, VII, Secs. 7 & 8). Customary rights and traditions are also explicitly secured and protected in the article on basic rights, so that government is obliged to facilitate the agency of people from the margins (20180727-RA-11054, IX, Sec. 4).

V. Humanity

The IPBC discussion of humanity as the fifth dimension of common good in a local community parallels the outline of justice, in identifying both a minimalist and a maximalist account (see Chapter 2, § 'A List of Basic Common Goods and Core Habitus'). As justice was discussed both as satisfying the demands of a thin theory of the good, and as addressing the aspirational goods of human flourishing, as described in a thick theory of the good, so too the dimensions of humanity are sketched in two lists. One list corresponds to basic needs, while the other identifies values to be striven for in the collaborative and institutional life of a society. They are contrasted in terms of human needs and human aspirations, survival as distinct from flourishing.

The first list (A) suggests as basic goods corresponding to human needs the following: Work, Education, Culture, Solidarity, Rule of Law. The second list (B) maps areas of wellbeing corresponding to flourishing or aspirations for the good life. Freedom and responsibility; justice and solidarity; peace and concord; prudence and magnanimity; perseverance and courage; resilience and sustainability. As both values and virtues, they are immanent in the pursuit of common goods.

Surveying the Bangsamoro Organic Law we find a comprehensive embrace of both dimensions of this value of humanity. The BOL signals the desire to recognise the humanity of each of the constituent tribes and cultures and to acknowledge their entitlement to pursue their fulfilment as stipulated by their own cultures and traditional values. Constraints such as compliance with international human rights law, and national legislation, may reveal challenges requiring astute and careful accommodation so that all may be satisfied. Concern for the basic needs of all its peoples is expressed in the many references to general welfare. These are to be found in the articles on the powers of government and on the structure of government in the Bangsamoro (20180727-RA-11054, V.; VII. Sec. 5). The theme recurs in the article on basic rights (Ibid., IX. Secs. 9 & 22) and in the sections of that article dealing with special cases such as the welfare of the indigenous peoples, people with special needs, and seniors (Ibid., IX. Secs. 3 & 23). Of course, welfare need not be reduced to satisfaction of basic needs but could include also the aspirations for wellbeing and flourishing in a full sense. We find resonances of this second list in the Preamble and other statements of purpose and vision. Furthermore, several sections of the fourth article on general principles and policies reflect this spectrum, from securing the minimum to pursuit of the maximum. The former is reflected in the commitment to social justice: *'The Bangsamoro Government shall ensure that every Filipino citizen in its territorial jurisdiction is provided the basic necessities and equal opportunities in life. Social justice shall be promoted in all aspects of life and phases of development in the Bangsamoro Autonomous Region.'* (Ibid., IV. Sec. 7). The aspiration to full development in all dimensions is expressed in an earlier passage: *'In the exercise of its right to self-governance, the Bangsamoro Autonomous Region is free to pursue its political, economic, social, and cultural development as provided for in this Organic Law.'* (Ibid., IV. Sec. 2). This latter formulation refers to the flourishing of the community, but this is not to be understood as in tension with or at the cost of individual fulfilment, given the assurance of respect for individual human rights.

4. Indicators

The ambition of the IPBC's international research project is to generate some instrument to enable municipal and regional governments to assess their performance in relation to their common goods. Beyond the enumeration of the pentagram, the five core values, and the twenty associated relations, it should become possible to generate sets of indicators that could be applied in an evaluation. The determination of the relevant indicators should ideally be the responsibility of the political leaders themselves, based on what they find useful in the pentagram. In the following I do not wish to usurp this role, but merely to suggest how indicators might be formulated for the evaluation of the implementation of the BARMM in terms of its espoused common goods. The preceding discussion has shown that the five core values are indeed reflected in the commitments and aspirations of the Bangsamoro Organic Law. Taking these values in the order in which I have considered them—justice, stability, governance, agency and humanity—what kinds of indicators might be suggested?

We begin with the value of justice. Given the emphasis on transitional justice in the BOL, it would appear unwise to make transitional justice in the sense of rectification of historical wrongs a significant indicator of the success of the BARMM. The danger with a backward looking and legally weighted approach is that a forward-looking political approach is neglected. There are enormous difficulties in resolving historical grievances particularly concerning land disputes in which there is no accepted common basis of establishing claims. If resolutions must be according to law, court cases are likely to require a lot of time and resources (Murphy 2017, Nagy 2008). Rather than risking diverting resources into legal disputes I suggest that the construction of the new political and legal structures should be given priority. The BOL sets the tasks of creating structures of government and adjudication, and these rather than historical grievances can be the basis for review. Progress in assembling the parliament and evidence of laws made and implemented can be easily reviewed. Similarly, undertakings to avoid discrimination, and to uphold basic rights, can be reviewed with evidence of the operation of the relevant structures, and timely response to accusations of violation of these high standards. Given the sensitivity concerning the Indigenous Peoples and claims to ancestral domain, this will be a particularly important indicator for the performance of the BARMM.

The common good of peace is absolutely necessary for the stability of the Bangsamoro project. Hence, an indicator of success or failure in relation to the value of stability will be the absence or occurrence of outbreaks of violence. While every society must deal with crime, including armed assault and/or robbery, such events in a fragile setting like Mindanao can reverberate and signal either a lack of acceptance or a lack of competence of the governing authority (Murphy 2017). It would be unrealistic to expect that peace and the rule of law will become established immediately—there will have to be a period of adaptation, and this is reflected in the planned transition period. Through this time, and beyond, key indicators will be the measures of violent crime. Success in dealing with private security and other armed actors will be critical for the acceptance of the BARMM Government's authority.

Commitments made in the BOL suggest other indicators. For instance, that former members of insurgent groups could be normalised and incorporated in the police force.

Essential for the stability of the BARMM is that practices of collaboration between the various tribes and participant bodies should emerge and develop from the grassroots. Widespread effective engagement should lead to the growing stability of institutions and practices. It should not be difficult to find measurements for this growing density of interaction.

The third value, governance, is strongly linked to stability. Local and tribal communities exhibit strong cohesiveness and fidelity to traditional values and to espoused religious worldviews. But how well are those cultural forms and practices adapted to democratic forms of deliberation and decision-making in collaboration with groups and tribes with different traditions and priorities? The necessary adaptation will be a challenge, because it can be expected to undermine traditional forms of authority and expectations of compliance. Where the cultures involved are traditionally autocratic, the practices of social authority include on the one side the expectation of being obeyed, and on the other side the expectation that obedience to strong command will be rewarded with the benefits of social cohesion. The wider Filipino experience has seen the survival of structures of patronage and sectional loyalty within the forms of democratic government. Similar carry-over in the BARMM is likely to undermine the whole project, since the new formal structures may simply provide new avenues for the traditional practices of domination and submission. Accordingly, the capacities of administrators and politicians to implement the new structures will be critical. The creation of the BARMM is not in a vacuum, but in a milieu that has seen an earlier attempt to create an autonomous region, ARMM, as formulated in the 1987 Constitution. However, that attempt foundered for various reasons, including corruption, failure of governance and oversight, and lack of popular participation.

There is a wisdom in the IPBC prognosis about governance as an aspect of common goods:

> Whenever public decisions, public policies are decided elsewhere and without consultation with the people they affect, then the authority of the decision or the policy will decay in the long run. People do not obey a policy only because it brings about a utility or because they fear punishment, but because it makes sense, generating a common good we value. Hence a governance for the common good is but a federation of institutions that governs in common. Its ordinary functioning is an organic subsidiarity which brings about stability and efficiency only in the long run. (see Chapter 2, § 'And What about Governance?')

This challenge is addressed primarily to those affected by the structures of government: their engagement at grassroots level is the precondition for the success of the structures in achieving stability and efficiency in the long run. It is not an immediate effect but will require time and patience to embed the new practices and forms of collaboration. Indicators for the success of the implementation of BARMM will measure the vibrancy of civil society as well as the transparency and accountability of local government. The key test for the institutions is whether they succeed in facilitating participation at all levels, and whether local initiatives can emerge and be sustained through the various levels of administration. Evaluators will look for evidence of practices, joint undertakings, equality of treatment and operation of measures of transparency and accountability.

Governance and agency are linked in the relations of empowerment (GA) and participation (AG). While the aspiration of the BOL to allow access and to empower each of the groups and their members is unrestricted, it remains an enormous challenge to accomplish the enabling of agency on this scale. Inevitably some groups will be better placed to succeed than others, granted the inherited skills associated with the practices of trading, for instance, in comparison with the more self-sufficient and self-contained tribes, far from the main trading routes. It will not be a surprise, therefore, if the agenda of empowerment suffers setbacks in some cases. It would therefore be useful to identify key indicators for participation. Some will be easy to identify, such as voter turnout in relevant elections, but voting alone is insufficient to indicate the degree of engagement needed for the success of the BARMM.

Anticipation of the groups least likely to participate could be useful, especially where a baseline can be established, to measure progress in acceptance of and identification with the BARMM. Similar indicators might be developed for the value of humanity, especially considering the list-pair suggesting the span between the minimum satisfaction of needs and the maximum realisation of fulfilment. The literature on social development can be a source for relevant indicators (Nussbaum 2000)

As noted above, the exploration of possible indicators is offered here as a suggestion of what might be useful. The determination of actual criteria for evaluation of the success of the Bangsamoro project must be the responsibility of the political community and its leaders. They set the agenda for the BARMM and they undertake to deliver it in the spirit of transparency and accountability.

5. Testing the Pentagram

The BARMM is a courageous initiative to make it possible that peoples of Mindanao who historically have been excluded and denied their proper place in the national story can participate in and contribute to the building of a modern, viable state. It attempts this by creating an autonomous regional administration, seeking to include *Shari'ah* law and tribal traditions within the procedures of the state. This venture is attempted in full consciousness of the legitimate complaints of injustices in the past. The focus is on building for the future, and in this it is appropriate to use the language of the common good. The four subjects with common goods have been identified above: the country as a whole;

Mindanao, which is more than the Bangsamoro region; the peoples of Bangsamoro; and humanity. The Bangsamoro Organic Law does not explicitly mention the term 'common good,' but that does not preclude a commentary which identifies this dimension. The availability of the rhetoric of common goods can strengthen the project, as it adds a layer of meaning to what is being attempted.

The IPBC analyses the common good in terms of the pentagram, the five aspects of the common goods of political communities, namely stability, governance, agency, justice, and humanity (see Chapter 2). In the review of the BOL we have seen the relevance of these aspects to what is ambitioned. The pentagram is shown to be a valuable instrument to map the values at stake in the BARMM since all five values are found to be central in the attempt to create an autonomous region. The language of common goods is valuable for expressing what is at stake, both in the instruments created and the purposes for which they are applied. The formulation of indicators to establish the achievements of the BARMM is enabled by the model. Suggested indicators are merely examples for how the participants themselves might determine the criteria they wish to apply to their efforts.

While acknowledging the usefulness of the model, the particularities of the situation in Mindanao provoke reflections on possible limitations of the pentagram as articulated to date. The circumstances of the BARMM, with its historical context and the measures undertaken to generate solutions, suggest that the pentagram must be capable of adaptation to accommodate the features of different political situations. Three aspects appear on an initial review. First, religion is critical in the situation of Mindanao, but not well accommodated in the model. Second, the timeframe for implementation of new structures should be factored in and the danger of premature assessment identified. Third, the several levels involved in the realisation of common goods suggest that problems of integration of micro-mezzo-macro levels should be anticipated and points of possible tension and conflict identified. A brief comment on each of these three is offered.

I. Religion

Religion is a major factor in the Philippine context, because of the difficulties associated with the presence of several religions, Christianity, Islam, and forms of animism, each of which has its own legal and political perspectives. The history of Mindanao and its islands and of the country is a history of violence, in which Islamic insurgency and Christian repression have shaped the memories and expectations of people with regard to justice and the rectification of injustice. The pentagram does not thematise religion. It may include religion under the heading of 'cultural identity' in list B of 'humanity' that may be broadly enough construed to cover religion, religious practices and religious affiliation. In BARMM that would not suffice for the exploration of common goods. Because the historical experiences of oppression have been very explicitly linked to religious discrimination it was necessary to foreground religion in the Organic Law. As might be expected in any liberal constitution, religious liberty, the freedom of expression and worship, the freedom of association, and public participation in religious practices are guaranteed (20180727-RA-11054, IX. Sec. 5). But that is not sufficient to restore self-government to the Bangsamoro peoples. The structure and governance of the BARMM provides for the location of religion at the heart of government with the affirmation of the religious identity of the Muslim population and its entitlement to self-government according to its own religious beliefs. As observed by colleagues at the Ateneo de Davao (2014) University when commenting on the draft law: '*Congress must not forget that in the Bangsamoro, religion is the basis of everything. From religion, all others (governance, justice, culture, relationships, family, etc.) come to life. What is religious is political and conversely, what is political is religious because the two are so intertwined in the life of Muslims.*' The inclusion of religion in the law goes beyond the purely negative rights in the guarantees of non-interference. The BOL includes *Shari'ah* law as permeating all of social life, to the extent it is compatible with international human rights law, and national legislation. The situation in Mindanao and the BARMM would require a more expansive consideration of religion, and this need might be replicated in other parts of the world, for which the pentagram might also prove useful.

This comment is not intended to identify religion as a component of the problem. Religion is so integral to the cultures of Mindanao that it must also be a significant resource for construction of the solution. Shared meaning is crucial for any political project and the construction of BARMM is no exception. For people to be able to buy into the new structures of government they must be able to find roots in their own deeply held convictions and recognise there a confluence of values. A possible resource for Christians and Muslims to find common ground in faith commitments is the joint statement issued by Pope Francis and the Grand Imam of Al-Azhar Ahmad Al-Tayyeb in Abu Dhabi in February 2019, *A Document on Human Fraternity for World Peace and Living Together*. These two leaders find in their respective traditions perspectives that are shared and that can support peaceful life together. This may indicate one way for the religious beliefs of the constituent peoples of the Bangsamoro to ground the core values of the pentagram and to articulate the links between their beliefs and their common goods. Of course, this articulation must be done by the people themselves, and by the relevant civil society organisations and bodies such as churches and the Ulama (Association of Islamic Scholars) and peace-building NGOs, and it would be a misplaced charge to expect the outline research discussion paper of the IPBC to provide this. However, there may be a possibility of strengthening the acknowledgement of the possible critical role of religion in the pentagram. This might be done in the set of relations, as for instance between humanity and justice, where in one direction a shared rationality can be explored, one rooted in a worldview that embraces a relationship with the Creator, and in the other direction, justice and humanity, identified as flourishing, the comprehension of fulfilment will include friendship with the divine. This is intended as a suggestion to be explored, but with the qualification that the dimension of religion cannot be confined to only one value or one pair of relations.

II. Timeframe

The second remark for the improvement of the pentagram concerns time. In the creation of new structures, and embedding them in the culture, it is important to factor in a timescale for the measurement of performance and evaluation of effectiveness. The pentagram might be expanded with inclusion of a timescale factor, commensurate with how 'new' or 'mature' the relevant social arrangements are. In creating new structures there is a danger of unrealistic expectations that downplay the necessity of their adoption by the populace. Adoption and integration might take considerable time, even a generation, when fears and suspicions must be allayed, and trust must be fostered. Premature evaluation may well be counterproductive in undermining confidence due to the slow pace of change and may strain peoples' patience and their willingness to endure the discomforts of the transition period. Hence, the model might consider when it is meaningful to evaluate achievements in the domains of stability, justice, agency, governance and humanity. Given human experience in implementing peace agreements, a matter of generations in some cases, it is critical to allow time for the new practices to become established. Some indication of a scale for sufficient time might also be included in the model. This would be helpful also for managing the expectations of citizens who will look for the peace dividend and the fruits of their patience.

III. Integration of levels

A third learning point arising from this case study concerns the integration of different levels of government. The pentagram mentions the micro, mezzo and macro levels, and that is helpful. The BARMM exemplifies a mezzo level organisation and poses significant questions as to how it might be integrated with the very local, and with the macro levels of national government. The relations with micro level government will pose particular challenges for the BARMM given the commitment to respecting traditional tribal practices. The BOL addresses issues of intergovernmental relations in a separate article, which provides structures for organising and monitoring relations between the mezzo and macro levels (20180727-RA-11054, VI.). This is wise, based on the expectation that there will be tensions that will have to be managed. Already some such tensions are emerging, as members of the National Congress call for review of the implementation of the BARMM. This connects with the previous point about timescale, which arises in a particular way in the different responsibilities of government at various levels. The integration of levels will arise also in the domain of adjudication as well as government. The commitment of the BOL to ensure adherence to international human rights law along with national legislation while incorporating *Shari'ah* law will lead to issues of jurisdiction in disputed cases. The points of integration and the expected difficulties arising there need to be identified. The pentagram might be expanded to provide resources for such tasks.

Acknowledgement of different levels is appropriate, and the associated interconnections reveal vulnerabilities. However, it is not simply that the mezzo level is vulnerable to the macro level, and by these we understand the relations between regional and national government. National government in turn is vulnerable to global dynamics, and events beyond national control can have a devastating impact on a country. Climate change and associated environmental impact can directly constrain the freedom of action of a state, and consequently, its regions. Similarly, events affecting global commons, such as epidemics, global economic recession, and world peace (or war), condition the scope of action of national and hence regional government. Such global commons, that are public goods or bads, can also be common goods or bads, and for the sake of completeness any mapping of common goods should include them (Riordan 2015). An awareness of the great scale of the undertaking that is the BARMM and its implications for good for so many people includes an awareness of its vulnerability. The particular situation of the Philippines and Mindanao at this juncture of their history reveals their vulnerability to global events in all the categories just mentioned. China's role in the Asia-Pacific Region, its aggression towards its island neighbours, and the risks of a trade war, may undermine any pursuit of common goods.

References

Access Bangsamoro. *Ethnic Groups in BARMM*. https://accessbangsamoro.ph/2019/08/23/ethnic-groups-in-barmm/.

Alejo, A. 2014. "IPRA in the BBL", in Tiu, M. D. (ed.), *Draft Bangsamoro Basic Law: Reviews, Commentaries, Recommendations*, Davao: Ateneo de Davao University Publication Office, 65–70.

Arpa, D. H. J. and Hussayin A. 2014. "Position Paper on the Bangsamoro Basic Law", in Tiu, M. D. (ed.), *Draft Bangsamoro Basic Law: Reviews, Commentaries,*

Recommendations, Davao: Ateneo de Davao University Publication Office, 83–86.

Ateneo de Davao. 2014. "Recommendations", in Tiu, M. D. (ed.), *Draft Bangsamoro Basic Law: Reviews, Commentaries, Recommendations*, Davao: Ateneo de Davao University Publication Office.

Bernas, J. G. 1987. *The Constitution of the Republic of the Philippines: An Annotated Text*. Manila: Rex Book Store.

Castro Guevara, M. C. (ed.) 2016. *Report of the Transitional Justice and Reconciliation Commission*. Makati City, https://asiapacific.unwomen.org/sites/default/files/Field%20Office%20ESEAsia/Docs/Publications/2016/10/TJRC%20Report.pdf.

Gloria, H. K. 2014. *History from Below: A View from the Philippine South*. Davao: Ateneo de Davao University Publication Office.

Lau, B. 2014. The Southern Philippines in 2013: One Step Forward, One Step Back, *Southeast Asian Affairs 2014*, 260–273. https://doi.org/10.1355/9789814517966-018

Murphy, C. 2017. *The Conceptual Foundations of Transitional Justice*. Cambridge: Cambridge University Press. https://doi.org/10.1017/9781316084229

Nagy, R. 2008. Transitional Justice as Global Project: Critical Reflections, *Third World Quarterly 29/2*, 275–289. https://doi.org/10.1080/01436590701806848

Nebel, M. and Medina Delgadillo, J. "From Theory to Practice. A Matrix of Common Good Dynamics", in

Nussbaum, M. 2000. *Women and Human Development. The Capabilities Approach*. Cambridge: Cambridge University Press. https://doi.org/10.1017/S0892679400007541

Nussbaum, M. and Sen, A. (eds) 1993. *The Quality of Life*. Oxford: Oxford University Press.

Pope Francis and Al-Tayyeb, A. 2019. *A Document on Human Fraternity for World Peace and Living Together*, 4 February Abu Dhabi: shttps://w2.vatican.va/content/francesco/en/travels/2019/outside/documents/papa-francesco_20190204_documento-fratellanza-umana.html.

Reinert, K. A. 2018. *No Small Hope: Towards the Universal Provision of Basic Goods*. Oxford, Oxford University Press. https://doi.org/10.1111/padr.12260

Republic Act No. 11054. 2018. *An Act Providing For The Organic Law For The Bangsamoro Autonomous Region In Muslim Mindanao*, https://www.officialgazette.gov.ph/2018/07/27/republic-act-no-11054/.

Riordan, P. 2015. *Global Ethics and Global Common Goods*. London: Bloomsbury.

Riordan, P. 2014. "The Bangsamoro Basic Law, Aristotle, and the Common Good", in Tiu, M. D. (ed.), *Draft Bangsamoro Basic Law: Reviews, Commentaries,*

Recommendations, Davao: Ateneo de Davao University Publication Office, 35–56.

Risonar-Bello, J. F. 2014. "Basic Human Rights, Women's Rights, and the BBL", in Tiu, M. D. (ed.), *Draft Bangsamoro Basic Law: Reviews, Commentaries, Recommendations*, Davao: Ateneo de Davao University Publication Office, 87–102.

Yusingco, M. H. 2013. *Rethinking the Bangsamoro Perspective*. Davao: Ateneo de Davao University Publication Office.

11. Assessing the Nexus of the Common Good

The Case of the Municipality of Atlixco, Mexico

Valente Tallabs and Mathias Nebel

Introduction

This chapter studies a preliminary application of the 'pentagram of the common good' (PCG) model in the municipality of Atlixco, in the State of Puebla (Mexico), seeking to analyse the dynamics of the nexus of common goods in this particular locality. The community of Atlixco displays interesting characteristics for analysing the common good dynamics, such as its size and sociodemographic composition, historical legacy, cultural wealth, and productive activity, as well as its proximity to the state capital.

The matrix of common good dynamics presented in Chapters 2 and 3 is the result of the work of a multidisciplinary research team convened by the Instituto Promotor del Bien Común (IPBC). The model is a novel and alternative methodology to the metrics of governance; one that does not focus exclusively on the effectiveness of governmental performance.

What is interesting in the proposed matrix is its systemic understanding of a municipality as a nexus of common goods; that is, it does not focus solely on the functions of democratic and legal authorities, but on the total sum of social institutions that govern common life.

https://doi.org/10.11647/OBP.0290.14

The matrix addresses the gaps or contradictions existing between the mostly rhetorical use of the common good language in political discourse or public policies, claiming to work for the common good, and the *real provision of commons* in a community. This inconsistency is largely due to a superficial understanding of the notion of the common good. There is indeed a practical difficulty to pinpointing and capturing what the common good requires in terms of public policies and governmental actions, as well as a lack of assessment capabilities in terms of their impacts on the common good. In this sense, public policies claiming to work for the common good are usually ambiguous, not only by design but also because of a lack of assessment tools that capture their impact on the common good. Most of the time public policies claiming to act for the common good, act, at best, on intuitions or subjective interpretations.

Nonetheless, if the concept could be specified and brought back to the level of policies, it may help us to overcome some of the known limits and contradictions of development policies, as Alford argues in Chapter 9. The matrix of common good dynamics provides such a clarification and this chapter tries to show how it may be applied to a municipality.

Revising Existing Governance Indicators

While there is a vast literature on the relationship between government, politics and the common good, a specific and practical discussion on the relationship between governance and the common good is actually scarce in political sciences.[1] And the few texts that address the topic adopt a normative stance, hardly ever analysing empirical data or offering practical recommendations.

On the other hand, many authors have proposed some kind of metric of 'good governance' at the local level.[2] But these indicators usually avoid

---

1   To mention just a few works: *The Art of Public Strategy: Mobilizing Power and Knowledge for the Common Good* (2008) by Geoff Mulgan; *Advancing the Common Good: Strategies for Businesses, Governments, and Nonprofits* (2019) by Philip Kotler; *Dismantling Democracy: The forty-year attack on government and the long game for the common good* (2018) by Cohen; *In the Search for the Common Good: Manual of Public Policies* (2012) by Emilio Graglia, etc.

2   In the wake of the good governance agenda lauched by the World Bank in the 1990s, measuring governance became fashionable and this brought a lot of attention to the question. However, the expectations that governance indicators may improve development practice were not met with results and the World Bank brought the experiment to a close in 2020. See https://info.worldbank.org/governance/wgi/.

the concept of the common good and cannot be considered similar to our common good approach to development (see Table 1). As mentioned by Nebel and Garza-Vázquez, these governance indicators heavily rely 'on individual-level data [...], leaving out the *structural dimension of development'* (see Introduction). Adopting a provider approach of the state, these indicators capture how citizens perceive the quality of public administration and services. Even if they include participation as one of their features, they usually do not capture governance as a collective capability and a shared achievement of the local community.

Table 1. Governmental performance indicators in Mexican municipalities.

INDICATOR	MAIN MEASUREMENT VARIABLES
ICMA (*International City Management Association*)	Strengthens the institutional capacities of governments and professionalises their operation: planning, result-based budgeting, e-government, public finances, ethics, and public services.
SEDEM (*Municipal Performance Evaluation System*)	1,140 indicators that consider all municipal management institutions.
CIMTRA (*Citizens for Transparent Municipalities*)	Government's transparency regarding budget expenditure, public works, provision of services, administration, urbanisation, councils, and spaces for the participation of citizens.

Source: Own elaboration.

None of the indicators mentioned above manage to capture what Nebel and Medina (Chapter 2) understand as a 'common good approach to development', which they propose should be based on information from groups or communities rather than individuals, focusing on the quality of *social processes* whereby basic common goods are produced in the community.

Other governance indicators/municipal indicators adopt a social responsibility approach of the public sector. They might at first sight seem more coherent with our purpose. However, a closer look reveals that they focus on the legitimacy of political authority and institutional outputs, eschewing again the social processes through which basic common goods are achieved in a community (Table 2).

Table 2. Indicators of the responsibilities of the municipal public sector.

INDICATOR	MAIN MEASUREMENT VARIABLES
Social responsibility indicators applied to public administration (those with a "glocal"[3] approach such as International Labor Organization, OECD, Green Books, Global Reporting Initiatives, ISO 26000)	• public value creation • competitiveness • social cohesion • transparency • sustainability • human rights
UNE 66182:2015 (smart cities)	• institutional development for good governance • sustainable economic development • inclusive social development • sustainable environmental development
ISO 18091:2014	• efficiency and effectiveness of local governments and their policies to improve the management and relationship of citizens with their municipalities

Source: Own elaboration.

Finally, there are indicators that do propose a common good approach, such as Felber's 'Economy of the Common Good' (Felber 2011) or La Moneda's 'Government of the Common Good Index' (La Moneda 2013). Although these two are novel (see Table 3), they lack a solid theoretical framework that supports their general conceptualisation. Their claim to be a 'radical alternatives' form of organisation or even a 'revolutionary model' of society is greatly overdone.[4]

---

3   "Glocal" is a combination of globalisation and locality. For the purposes of this work, it refers to the idea of 'thinking globally to act locally.' The concept comes from the Japanese term *'dochakuka'* (derived from *dochaku*, 'he who lives in his own land'), although many references credit Ulrich Beck as the creator and diffuser of the term.

4   For example, the German-based Association 'Economy for the Common Good' (ECG) developed a matrix and an indicator that attempts to measure the contributions of economic and public actors to the local common good. It assumes

Table 3. Government and common good indicators in the municipality.

INDICATOR	APPROACHES	MAIN MEASUREMENT VARIABLES
Common Good Economy (Felber)	**Methodology** • matrix, balance, and common good • creation of 'energy fields' (local networks) • municipalities of common good • systematising good municipal practices • citizen participation as a key element of municipal management	• human dignity • equality • social justice • solidarity • democracy • transparency • trust • ecological sustainability

that the economy must serve a community and rejects utility as the main driver of economic behaviours. By focusing primarily on community participation in the creation and redistribution of wealth, the ECG sees itself as attempting to revolutionise economics. However, the movement borrows most of its intuitions from the ubiquitous model of 'social economy', hardly a 'revolutionary' position in the German context. The proposed matrix of the ECG common good is limited in scope. It considers the stakeholders of economic activity, namely a) Suppliers, b) Owners, c) Employees, d) Customers and business partners, e) Social environment—and assesses the impact of economic activity on: a) human dignity, b) solidarity and social justice, c) environmental sustainability, and d) transparency and co-determination. This is definitely a rather narrow approach to the common good that reduces its scope to the impact of economic activity. The notion of the common good is broader and deeper than that. It includes a wide range of social actors and considers all types of social interaction through which common goods are generated. Similarly, the four dimensions proposed—while interesting—lack the coherence and specificity that would distinguish this from other development approaches (UNDP, World Bank, OECD, UN Development Goals). Cf. Felber (2015).

INDICATOR	APPROACHES	MAIN MEASUREMENT VARIABLES
Government of the Common Good (La Moneda)	**Fundamental Principles** • participation and democracy • cooperation • transparency and ethics in all government actions	• human dignity • equality • social justice • solidarity • democracy • transparency • trust • ecological sustainability

Source: Own elaboration with information on each indicator from Felber (2011) and La Moneda (2013).

We will thus develop in the following sections a concrete proposal to approach and measure the common good dynamics in a municipality. It goes beyond management and public administration of a city or town hall and looks at the way citizens and political actors together generate and resolve public issues regarding the basic commons of the municipality. How they understand each other, so that on the one hand, politicians and administrators learn to include citizens in their decision-making process and, on the other hand, citizens are committed to politics in a broad sense.

To do so, we will follow the matrix of common good dynamics proposed in the PCG and seek, for its five dimensions, the sort of data and indicators that could be relevant to capture the local common good dynamic. This proposal, we will argue, can be an important contribution to the construction of a responsive government and a participative community.

The Common Good Pentagram (PCG) and the Subdimension Proposed to Measure Each of Its Five Key Normative Drivers

The matrix of common good dynamics presented in Chapter 2 is an analytical tool that helps us visualise the interactions between the five key normative drivers the IPBC team theorises are necessary for a common good dynamic to exist in a local community. Crucially, it allows us to consider the social interactions structuring the community as the key element of analysis. The model suggests that the density and quality of the relationships between its five key normative drivers form a matrix whereby it is possible to measure the quality of the common good reached by a specific local community. The common good pentagram allows us therefore to read a dimension through its relation to others, as can be seen in Figure 1 (see also Chapter 2). Agency, for example, can be understood and captured through its relations to humanity, stability, justice and governance.

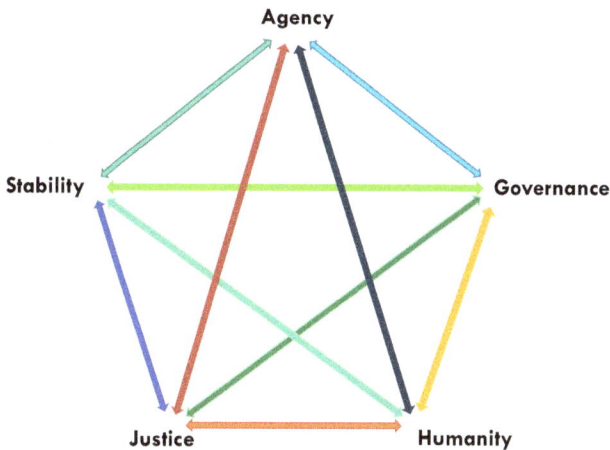

Figure 1. The common good pentagram.

We will not repeat here an explanation of the five dimensions proposed in the model that can be found in Chapter 2. Let us just add that while the model provides an analysis of the current conditions of the nexus in a locality, it is also a powerful tool for decision-makers. It allows them to identify opportunities and challenges, defining short- and long-term strategies, as well as designing public policies aimed at triggering or strengthening the common good dynamics in the municipality.

In Tables 4–8 below, we try to identify for each of the five normative drivers of the PCG a set of subdimensions considered relevant to capture them, according to the following criteria:

1. Each subdimension should comply with conceptual aspects addressed by the literature for each normative dimension (see Chapter 2).

2. Each subdimension should capture one relationship of this specific normative dimension with those of others (describing, for example, how Governance is related to Justice or Stability).

3. That although many of these variables or subdimensions can be used interchangeably between dimensions because they capture them in various ways, for the convenience of the indicators, each one will be used in just one dimension, the one it best interprets.

Table 4. Governance Nexus.

Normative Dimension	Subdimensions	Relationship to Other Normative Dimensions (Nexus)
Governance	1. Transparency	Governance => *Stability*
	2. Co-governance	Governance => *Stability* Governance => *Agency*
	3. Participation	Governance => *Agency* Governance => *Stability*
	4. Governance	Governance => *Justice*
	5. Sustainability	Governance => *Stability*
	6. Expectations	Governance => *Humanity*

Table 5. Humanity Nexus.

Normative Dimension	Subdimensions	Relationship to Other Normative Dimensions (Nexus)
Humanity	7. Human Rights	Humanity => *Agency* Humanity => *Governance*
	8. Rights of the person in community (Political rights)	Humanity => *Justice* Humanity => *Stability*
	9. Rights in community (Group rights)	Humanity => *Agency* Humanity => *Stability*

Table 6. Stability Nexus.

Normative Dimension	Subdimensions	Relationship to Other Normative Dimensions (Nexus)
Stability	10. Right to Life	Stability => *Humanity* Stability => *Justice* Stability => *Governance*
	11. Life and Family Planning	Stability => *Agency*
	12. Collective Planning	Stability => *Agency*
	13. Policy	Stability => *Governance*
	14. Identity	Stability => *Humanity*

Table 7. Agency Nexus.

Normative Dimension	Subdimensions	Relationship to Other Normative Dimensions (Nexus)
Agency	15. Use of free/spare time	Agency => *Stability* Agency => *Justice*
	16. Freedom of association	Agency => *Humanity* Agency => *Stability*
	17. Freedom of expression and information	Agency => *Stability* Agency => *Governance*

Table 8. Justice Nexus

Normative Dimension	Subdimensions	Relationship to other normative dimensions (nexus)
Justice	18. Equality	Justice => *Humanity* Justice => *Governance*
	19. Effectiveness (availability/ accessibility)	Justice => *Stability*
	20. Social Mobility	Justice => *Agency*

Methodology and Objectives

As can be seen, the model consists of the five normative dimensions of the pentagram interpreted through twenty subdimensions. The calculation of where they intersect with one another can be translated into fifty indicators that will allow us to measure the dynamics of the nexus of the common good in a municipality.

The relevant indicators for each subdimension were chosen as a tradeoff between the existence and availability of data on the one hand, and the capacity of the indicator to capture the core of each subdimension. In organising the information, we took for each indicator the most recent data available. For example, one of the subdimensions measuring the dimension of Governance is 'Participation', which in turn is explained by means of three indicators: (1) number of social networks or groups in the municipality, (2) number of civil associations, and (3) number of governmental activities designed to bolster civic participation.

Before presenting the mapping of the dimensions and their indicators in the test case of Atlixco, it must be made clear that this exercise does not intend to incorporate any complex statistical methodology, since its objectives, as outlined above, are merely descriptive and exploratory for what may become an instrument for policy planning. Thus, for this first exercise, a basic 'traffic-light' criterion— green/adequate; yellow/ partial; red/inadequate—will be used to indicate whether the conditions of the variable being analysed are met based on its respective indicators and sub-indicators. The criteria for assigning a degree of compliance include the following:

1. The comparison is with respect to the average data of municipalities in the State of Puebla or in Mexico, depending on the availability of information.

2. When there is no data for comparison at the municipal level in Mexico, we will follow the recommendations of a recognised body specialising in such variables.

3. When there is no statistical data available, we will use first-hand information through consultations with municipal officials or community reference persons (priest, civil officers, etc.).

The following graph is used to represent the results of the traffic light methodology:

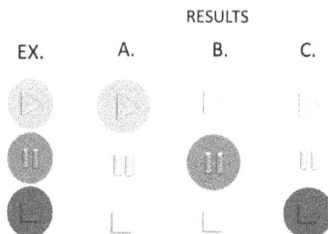

Figure 2. Traffic light indicator. Source: Own elaboration.

The light grey scale in A equals green and indicates *adequate* status, with the metric being on-target or better; the grey scale for B equals yellow and indicates *partial* status, with the metric being off-target and in need of improvement; and the grey C scale is equivalent to red, an *inadequate or poor* status, with the metric being off-target and unacceptable. Black indicates no information available. The criterion for assigning the conditions for this exercise are determined by comparing the local indicator to the average that the State of Puebla and/or Mexico has for that indicator.

In addition to the main objective of this exercise, we can consider that a second purpose, with a view to future exercises, is to determine whether the application of the PCG is sufficient or insufficient for municipalities with the characteristics of Atlixco (i.e., semi-urban and of average population for a Mexican city); whether there is enough information for generating meaningful analyses; and how difficult is it to obtain it when it is available.

Finally, a third purpose is to test the relevance and utility of such a mapping for public governance and decision-making process, as well as to inform citizens of the strength and fragility of the municipality.

In the description below of the Mexican municipality of Atlixco, the application of the PCG model is the central objective, finding advantages and disadvantages in the selection of the interpretive variables proposed to illustrate the nexus of the common good.

Description of the Municipality of Atlixco
(State of Puebla, Mexico)

Atlixco is located in the central-western area of the State of Puebla, thirty-one kilometres from the city of Puebla de Zaragoza, the capital (see Figure 3). According to the last national census (INEGI 2015), the municipality has 134,364 inhabitants, of whom 63,603 are men and 70,761 are women, with an average age of twenty-five years. Its area, 291.9 square kilometres, makes it a relatively small municipality, representing only 0.9% of the area of the State of Puebla.

Atlixco has a strategic location, due to its proximity to the capital and to some of the most important and populated municipalities of the state, such as Cholula and Izúcar de Matamoros. Even Mexico City is fairly close (158 km by road). This location has given it outstanding highway connectivity, linking it with large urban centres, a characteristic which favours the development of various economic activities.

The rapidly developing urban part of the municipality has an area of approximately 64 km², which is equivalent to 22% of its total area. This urbanised growth has occurred both in its central area and in the area near the Popocatépetl Volcano in the western part of the municipality. The new growth is somewhat dispersed, partly responding to the location of two of its main productive activities: flower greenhouses and the textile industry.

According to Mexico's National Council for the Evaluation of Social Development Policy (CONEVAL) between 56% and 59% of Atlixco's population lives in poverty, putting the municipality at a high level of poverty (CONEVAL 2017). Although Atlixco has a diversified economy, it also has a high degree of migratory flow to the United States (CONAPO 2010). It should be noted that although Atlixco has an indigenous population of only 7.3% (INEGI 2010), about 33% of the population self-identifies as indigenous (CDI 2015), and 4.6% speak some indigenous language (INEGI 2015).

Atlixco means 'water in the valley or on the surface of the soil' in Nahuatl, the local indigenous language. Since the beginning of Spanish colonisation, Atlixco was a privileged and coveted place. Its fertility and abundance of water and labour led to a great agricultural wealth, based on the growing of wheat, which led to the area being considered the first granary of New Spain. The city also stands out for its good climate, with an average annual temperature of 20ºC; it is popularly known as 'the place with the best climate in the world' (Atlixco City Council 2018).

Likewise, due to its location, landscape, and physical and economic characteristics, in 2015 the municipal seat was incorporated into the 'Programa de Pueblos Mágicos' (Magical Towns Programme) (SECTUR 2016).

Interpretation of PGC Dimensions in Atlixco

Governance Dimension

This dimension considers six subdimensions that in turn translate into eleven indicators. Using the values obtained for each subdimension and indicator, Table 9 (available at https://hdl.handle. net/20.500.12434/2f7d12se) shows the traffic light status according to the determining factors regarding the governance of the common good in the municipality of Atlixco.

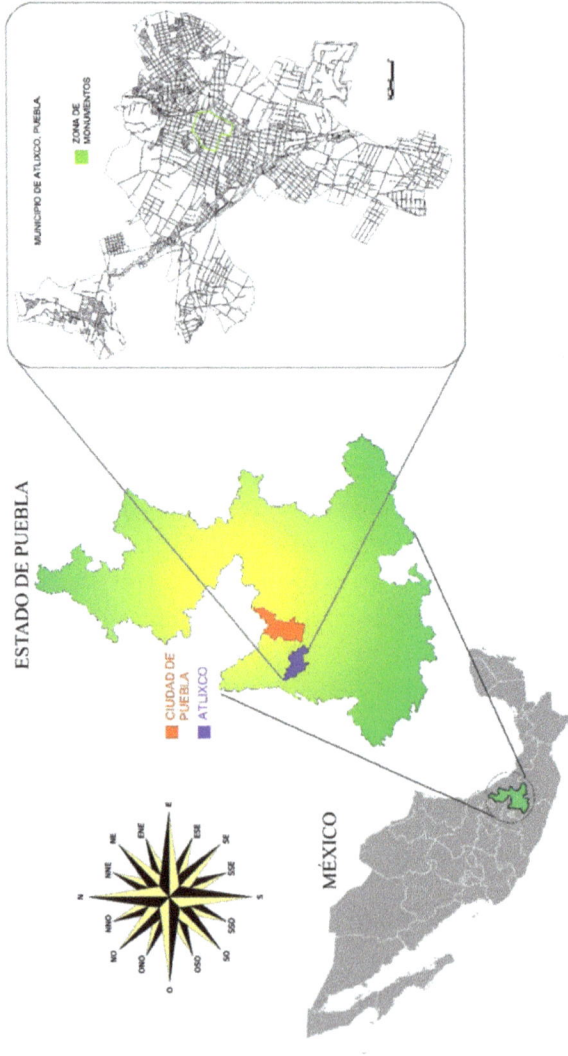

Figure 3. Map and location of Atlixco. Source: Francisco Ruiz Herrera (2017).

Regarding the transparency variable, the Institute of Transparency, Access to Public Information, and Protection of Personal Data of the State of Puebla has fulfilment data regarding the queries requested from the municipality of Atlixco, including time taken to respond and the form of response. The institute estimates, however, that for the size and conditions of the municipality, the number of consultations should be higher, and that the public information available on the city hall webpage as of 2018 is sufficient and clear. Thus, we are not facing a problem or an issue of efficiency or management effectiveness, but rather a matter of transparency and an accountability culture that ideally would permeate even more in the citizenry as something desirable and of real public utility. This seems to be a pending issue of public policy.

Regarding co-government in Atlixco, we find that there are both instances of and possibilities for citizen participation in the exercise of shared power and civic participation. However, there could be more initiatives, given the possibilities, but such initiatives do not exist, according to the information provided by the municipal government. Note that the 'Illuminated Villa' project, which takes place during the December holidays, does have a policy character, but we did not have information to confirm the specific policy outcomes of this event.

Regarding the government activities variable, there is a clear problem regarding homicide rates and perceived insecurity. The number of homicides recorded by the Public Prosecutor's Office for Atlixco is high, even for Mexico, and has been sharply increasing over the past ten years. Furthermore, the data only captures the 'officially recorded homicides', a figure which is known to be substantially lower than the real rate. We must therefore assume that the degree of homicides in the municipality is likely to be greater and that the worsening trend is growing.

Regarding the sustainability of governance, planning times from Atlixco's political authority are strictly what the law requires (municipal policy planning presented in the first three months of the new administration must span three or four years). However, in recent years, there have been no efforts to plan a long-term project (of ten or fifteen years). Moreover, there is no continuity in government programmes beyond a given administration (whether or not they are successful). The fact is that each new municipal administration traditionally proceeds to change almost all the administrative positions of the municipalities (clientelism). In other words, there is neither institutional memory, nor support for efficient governmental actions between successive administrations, even when the same political party wins the municipality. Municipal authorities openly admit to this difficulty—the phenomenon is fairly common in Mexico—but do not seem willing to seek continuity.

Finally, in the area of expectations, we find that there is no information on institutional trust and degree of happiness for the municipality of Atlixco, although these data do exist for other municipalities in Mexico, including the state capital of Puebla.

Agency Dimension

The agency dimension considers three subdimensions and six indicators. Using the value obtained for each subdimension and indicator, Table 10 (available here) shows the determining factors of the agency dimension of the common good in the municipality of Atlixco.

Our data indicate that the level of agency is good, with metrics being on-target in Atlixco. However, some specific aspects must be taken with a grain of salt.

First, even if the level of employment in the labour market is good or at least proportionately similar to those for the State of Puebla, it also includes in that number people working in the informal economy, whose employment is not submitted to the minimum legal standards.

As for Internet use and family life, no such information was available for this municipality (although it exists for others). As noted previously, it would require the gathering of specific information to capture how people occupy themselves in their free time.

Similarly, we would need a specific qualitative study to capture association life, mechanisms of social participation, and social activities in Atlixco. However, the perception of officials and civil society leaders is that 'participation in public life' in Atlixco is good, considering the range and diversity of activities enabling the participation of the citizenry.

Finally, it also seems that for the size of the municipality's population and its geographic area, there is a convenient variety of local media, in addition to the other state and national media available in Atlixco.

Justice Dimension

For this dimension, four subdimensions and fourteen indicators were considered. Using the values obtained for each indicator, Table 11 (available here) shows the determining factors for justice in the municipality's common good nexus.

Regarding common good dynamics in Atlixco, justice is clearly one of the two dimensions creating an imbalance in the system of common goods and hindering the possibility of development. The several deep negative scores in this dimension highlight various aspects of justice that demand both more detailed analysis and urgent attention. According to our model, these shocking levels of poverty and opportunities must have an adverse impact on the whole nexus of common goods in Atlixco, because the five normative dimensions are relational. Thus, a negative reading for justice also undermines stability, governance, agency and humanity, even if some of these are positive.

Without question, the most serious problem in Atlixco is poverty, with more than half of its population considered as poor. Poverty is linked to inequality and to the possibility of accessing social services such as health, education, social security, etc. The proportion of the population living with less than USD 1.25 per day is very high, indicating that, despite an acceptable employment rate, workers' wages are low—i.e., insufficient to buy basic foods for their families—and people's working conditions do not allow them access to better life opportunities. This situation is in turn corroborated by the municipality's large, informal economy.

As for the effectiveness of justice in the municipality, the 'availability of' and 'access to' basic public services is usually bad, with some noteworthy exceptions. On the one hand, it has a fair coverage of electric light and the percentage of homes with access to drinking water is very high; on the other hand, the quality and distribution of these services is not sufficient, which in turn may affect the inhabitants' health. Something similar occurs with educational coverage which is quite good (most are able to attend school), nevertheless the percentage of educational backwardness is high, revealing the poor quality of the system that 'leaves many behind'. However, the most negative aspects have to do with *public health coverage* (>50% population does not have access to the public health system); with the lack of an *effective public transport*; and with *Internet access* in the municipality (the technological gap, which currently puts people at a disadvantage in terms of information and education, work, and communication activities offered online).

Humanity Dimension

The humanity dimension considers three subdimensions and six indicators and is the most complex dimension to capture in our approach, as it deals with 'standard expectation of behaviours' created by the institutional framework of the municipality. However, for the exploratory and analytical purposes of this first exercise, we thought that various forms of human rights could be proxies for a minimum standard of human behaviour in the municipality. Thus, according to the values obtained for each selected variable, Table 12 (available here) shows determining factors in the municipality of Atlixco for the humanity dimension.

As far as respect for human rights is concerned, we find that Atlixco does not rank high in reports of complaints of human rights violations in Puebla's municipalities; however, the mere existence of such complaints in the municipality cannot be considered a good indicator.

Regarding the rights of the person in the community, the negative relationship of economic factors that comes to light in other dimensions also appears here. A high percentage of the population lacks social security, which has to do with the percentage of people working in the informal economy, which in turn impacts the public health of the population. Although there is not a high degree of people suffering from malnutrition or addictions compared to other municipalities, these conditions are elements to keep in mind and upon which to improve. The amount of green spaces per inhabitant exceeds the international optimum level of 15m² / hab. However, this fact sharply contrasts with the accessibility to open public spaces such as parks, plazas, gardens, sports facilities, etc., which are concentrated in the urban part of the municipality, meaning that people who live far away do not have easy access to them. Therefore, we deem the distribution of these spaces in the municipality inadequate.

Finally, the municipal government's provision of collective rights is positive, noting that the municipality does have a protected nature reserve (Sierra del Tentzo) and a diversity of museums for the municipality's size, public art, and cultural free events.

Stability Dimension

This dimension is made up of five subdimensions and fourteen indicators. Using the values obtained for each of these, Table 13 (available here) shows the determining factors for the stability dimension.

There is a good deal of variation in the stability dimension, as detailed below. On the one hand, in the 'lifetime' variable, the data indicate that with respect to the local and national average, child mortality is an aspect to improve in Atlixco. On the other hand, the life expectancy of the municipal population is similar to the national average, seventy-six years.

In the 'family life' variable, two indicators stand out negatively: marriage and maximum level of schooling. In the first, we clearly see a growing crisis in life planning by couples who decide not to marry, which indicates that conjugal union, either religious or civil, is no longer considered an option. As family in Mexico functions as the most important social security network, this phenomenon already has and will have more negative consequences in terms of vulnerability and poverty. Of special concern is the increase in unregistered children (i.e., children without birth certificate), which in turn hinders schooling or inheritance.[5]

---

5   This is an extremely complex problem in predominantly rural and very traditional municipalities. In particular, in Puebla the civil registry was until a couple of years ago a municipal responsibility. Given the diversity and complexity of some communities, determining the specific procedures for, say, registering a newborn, sometimes left some children unregistered (e.g., when the civil registry denied registration of a baby born out of wedlock). This has, in turn, created the problem of unregistered kids, which in turn creates complex situations when these kids want to actualise their right to attend school.

Few in the population plan out their work lives. The majority of the population does not expect or plan to have a professional career. Empirical evidence indicates that the lower this indicator is, the lower the economic returns by its citizens and the lower the chances of reducing poverty (Psacharopolous and Patrinos 2004), discouraging social mobility.

With regard to politics, in the last two local elections Atlixco's electoral participation was good, and similar to national and state levels. Through the political alternation that the municipality has experienced in recent years, we can see a clear willingness of the population to participate in political decisions and to either endorse or punish efforts that do not meet citizens' expectations. However, data regarding confidence in democracy, while not available for Atlixco, are low at the state and national levels. The population doesn't have a positive perception of democracy, but values it as an important tool of public influence; proof of this are the positive electoral participation and the frequent alternation of political parties in power.

Finally, as far as identity is concerned, the municipality has deep-rooted traditions and values. There is remarkable pride and interest in its main festival, the Hueyatlixcayotl, which not only seeks to preserve tradition, but is the community's main cultural reference. Religious holidays are nourished and also represent a living legacy, involving a large portion of a population that identifies as predominantly Catholic.

Conclusions: Assessing Our Results

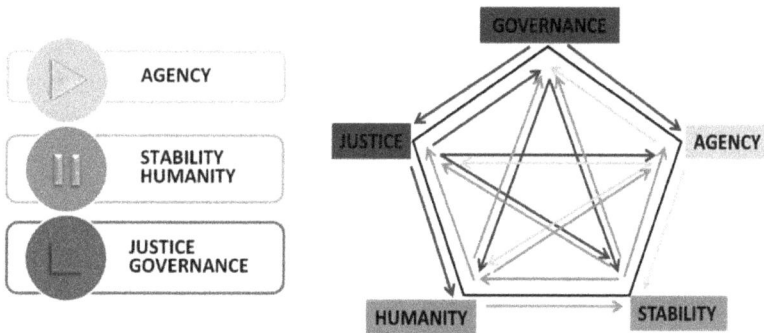

Figure 4. Results matrix for Atlixco.

The graphic expression of the results matrix of the pentagram of Atlixco's links of the common good gives us an interesting picture of the nexus of the common good in this municipality. The overall balance is not positive for the municipality as only 'Agency' turns out to be positive. As the model is relational, when one of the dimensions comprising the pentagram is negative, it will drag the other four dimensions back, generating structural dysfunctions that are hard to overcome. Now in Atlixco, two dimensions are negative and two others fragile. Development policies in these circumstances will most certainly fail if they do not explicitly address this systemic dimension.

More specifically, the negative readings for the 'Governance' and 'Justice' dimensions signal issues that must be urgently addressed if we want to trigger a development process in Atlixco. And of these two, the priority is 'Governance'. According to the model's conceptual definition of these dimensions, we can assume that there is a strong component of direct responsibility by the municipal government for the indicators being so critical. Take, for example, the high level of crime in the municipality. One of the basic tasks of government is security. The high levels of criminality in Atlixco are a failure of the government, past and present, to mitigate the phenomenon by implementing strategies to contain and prevent crime. Moreover, by letting the social context deteriorate over time (see Justice Dimension above), the municipal government created the level of marginalisation prevailing nowadays in Atlixco, which is a constant breeding ground for criminality (people without a future, without decent work, without access to healthcare or social security).

Proposals for public policies regarding 'Justice' and 'Governance' could be grounded in those indicators whose scores are negative. It would, for example, undoubtedly help to have a long-term planning process that considers the needs and demands of the citizens beyond the three years required by law. Long-term objectives (of ten to twenty-five years) set by the community itself could serve as guidelines to the successive governments, framing their policies toward achieving these communal goals. It would also be pertinent for the elected authorities to have the political maturity to respect the institutional memory of good actions and government practices that people value, regardless of their partisan origin. In addition, it would be helpful to have an adequate public policy framework generated on the basis of reliable data collected in time series extending beyond the three-year mandate. Finally, strengthening professionalisation and creating new mechanisms for conflict resolution would be desirable, although it would be useful to have more accurate analysis and evaluation regarding this indicator.

The dimensions of the common good with intermediate results in their assessments are 'Stability' and 'Humanity'. Two elements draw our attention regarding the 'Stability' dimension: (a) the erosion of the family as the institution that traditionally provided social security and stability to individuals; (b) the average schooling years in Atlixco and their effect on social mobility.

There is a clear and growing crisis of the family institution. Couples no longer value getting married (either civil or religious unions) and many people enter and exit multiple relationships in their lifetime leaving them without rights, duties or protection. The children of these unions are frequently the worse off (they are abandoned or unrecognised, which hinders their schooling and access to work). Thanks to the crisis of marriage, the valuable stability and social certainty provided to a community by the institution of marriage is lost. Undoubtedly, there is an urgent need for a public policy supporting the family; policy that has nothing to do with mass marriage programmes, reduction or remission of civil marriage expenses, etc. What is needed is an integral policy recognising the role of families in providing stability to society, especially as the first and most important primary network of solidarity and help that individuals can access. As a pillar of stability and solidarity in a poor country, the family deserves the support of the state (transmission of communal experience, structuring of human values, culture of peace, basic support, etc.).

The low average schooling years of Atlixco is another challenging aspect of 'Stability'.[6] Most people in Atlixco only achieve the secondary school diploma and do not seek or cannot access the higher education system. This, added to the lack of professional training, means that members of the local population enter the labour market in a position of fragility, which becomes visible in the low rate of upward social mobility for Atlixco. There is an urgent need for a public policy providing professional education locally, and facilitating access to the higher education system in Atlixco. Equally important is an assessment of the labour market in Atlixco and the creation of incentives to diversify employment opportunities in the municipality. Indeed, the people who do access higher education usually do not return to Atlixco once they graduate.

The dimension of 'Humanity' has one strength that should be highlighted: the environmental calling of the municipality. Atlixco is recognised as the regional reference point in terms of the cultivation of flowers and vegetables and as a centre for both cultural tourism, for the variety and quality of its festivals, for recreational tourism, and for its climate, spas, gastronomy, etc. Atlixco's inhabitants benefit directly from this reputation, which they pride, care for, and seek to enhance.

Finally, we find that 'Agency' is the highest-valued dimension in this exercise. While there is much to improve in terms of its labour and economic indicators, the social strength and capacity of the Atlixco community, in terms of organisation, expression and participation, stands out. These elements positively influence the other dimensions, somehow mitigating the other, more worrisome aspect highlighted previously. As society's backbone, the government must rely on the strength of these social conditions to generate desirable dynamics in government actions, whether through authentic public policies or participatory planning schemes that last beyond a single administration.

---

6   Stability doesn't describe the conservation of social order, but its constant reinvention in order to create a future for all.

It should be borne in mind that since municipal governments have a decisive role in the implementation of public policy, analyses such as this one contribute to publicising trends and to defining strategic lines for local development in their present and future perspectives. The common good approach helps us to conduct a collective analysis beyond the simple dimension of the user or individuals, because the common good considers not only the welfare but also the general good of the municipality. In this way, this approach is a tool that serves to guide the dynamics of the much-desired common good.

References

Ayuntamiento del Municipio de Atlixco. 2014. *Plan de Desarrollo Municipal de Atlixco*, Puebla 2014–2018, https://ojp.puebla.gob.mx/.

Centro Estudios Espinosa e Yglesias (CEEY). 2018. *La movilidad social y el desarrollo de México*, https://ceey.org.mx/.

Comisión Nacional del Agua (CONAGUA). 2016. *Situación del Subsector Agua Potable, Drenaje y Saneamiento*. México: CENAPRED, CEPAL y SEGOB.

Comisión Nacional para el Desarrollo de los Pueblos Indígenas (CDI). 2015. *Indicadores socioeconómicos de los pueblos indígenas de México*, 2015,https://www.gob.mx/cdi/articulos/indicadores-socioeconomicos-de-los-pueblosindigenas-de-mexico-2015-116128?idiom=es.

Comité Estatal de Información Estadística y Geográfica del Estado de Puebla (CEIGEP). 2018. http://ceigep.puebla.gob.mx/informacion_basica_municipio.php.

Consejo Nacional de Evaluación de la Política de Desarrollo Social (CONEVAL). 2015. *Medición de la pobreza, Estados Unidos Mexicanos, 2010–2015. Indicadores de pobreza por municipio*, https://www.coneval.org.mx/.

Consejo Nacional de Población (CONAPO). 2012. *Sistema Urbano Nacional, CENAPRED, CEPAL y SEGOB*, https://www.conapo.gob.mx/.

Felber, C. 2012. *La economía del bien común*. Barcelona: Deusto Editorial.

Instituto Estatal Electoral del Estado de Puebla. 2018. *Histórico de Resultados Electorales.* https://www.ieepuebla.org.mx/categorias.php?Categoria=Resultados_Elec

Instituto Nacional de Estadística y Geografía (INEGI). 2010. *Censo de Población y Vivienda. Resultados definitivos.* https://www.inegi.org.mx/programas/ccpv/2010/.

Instituto Nacional de Estadística y Geografía (INEGI). 2014. *Censos Económicos.* https://www.inegi.org.mx/programas/ce/2014/.

Instituto Nacional de Estadística y Geografía (INEGI). 2017. *Anuario estadístico y geográfico de Puebla.* https://www.datatur.sectur.gob.mx/ITxEF_Docs/PUE_ANUARIO_PDF.pdf.

Instituto Nacional de Estadística y Geografía (INEGI). 2017. *Encuesta Nacional de Victimización y Percepción sobre Seguridad Pública (ENVIPE).* https://www.inegi.org.mx/programas/envipe/2017/.

Instituto Nacional de Estadística y Geografía (INEGI). 2017. *Encuesta Nacional de Empleo y Ocupación. Resultados definitivos (ENOE).* https://www.inegi.org.mx/programas/enoe/15ymas/.

Instituto Nacional de Estadística y Geografía (INEGI). 2018. *Esperanza de vida al nacimiento por entidad federativa según sexo de 2010 a 2017.* https://www.inegi.org.mx/app/indicadores/?ind=3106002001&tm=8.

Instituto Nacional de Estadística y Geografía (INEGI). 2018. *Estadísticas de Museos.* https://www.inegi.org.mx/programas/museos/.

Instituto Nacional de Estadística y Geografía (INEGI). 2015. *Panorama sociodemográfico de Puebla, 2015.* https://www.inegi.org.mx/contenido/productos/prod_serv/contenidos/espanol/bvinegi/productos/nueva_estruc/inter_censal/panorama/702825082314.pdf.

Instituto Nacional de Estadística y Geografía (INEGI). 2012. *Registros administrativos de mortalidad, 2012. Consulta interactiva de datos por entidad y municipio de registro y edad.* https://www.inegi.org.mx/programas/mortalidad/.

Instituto Nacional de Estadística y Geografía (INEGI). 2015. *Tabulados de la Encuesta Intercensal, 2015. Estimadores de la población ocupada y su distribución porcentual según posición en el trabajo por municipio.* https://www.inegi.org.mx/programas/intercensal/2015/.

Instituto Nacional de Estadística y Geografía (INEGI). 2015. *Tabulados de la Encuesta Intercensal, 2015. Estimadores de las viviendas particulares habitadas y su distribución porcentual según disponibilidad de agua entubada y acceso al agua por municipio.* https://www.inegi.org.mx/programas/intercensal/2015/.

Instituto de Transparencia. 2018. *Acceso a la Información Pública y Protección de Datos Personales del Estado de Puebla (ITAIPUE).* https://itaipue.org.mx/portal2020/

ISO. 2014. *Sistemas de gestión de la calidad de Gobierno Locales Confiables.* A https://www.iso.org/.

La Moneda, D. I. 2013. *Yo soy tú*, Madrid: Octaedro.

Nebel, M. 2018. Operacionalizar el bien común. Teoría, vocabulario y medición, *Metafísica y Persona 10/20*, 27–66. https://doi.org/10.24310/Metyper.2018.v0i20.4830

Nebel, M. and Medina-Delgadillo, J. 2018. "Measuring the Nexus of the Common Good", Discussion paper prepared for the IPBC research seminar, Barcelona, IQS, May 23–24, https://upaep.mx/biencomun/templates/biencomun/IPBCDiscussionpaperIIMay2018.pdf.

Norma UNE. 2015. https://www.une.org/.

Ostrom, E. 2011 (1990). *El gobierno de los bienes comunes. La evolución de las instituciones de acción colectiva*, México: Fondo de Cultura Económica.

Psacharopoulos, G. and Patrinos, H. A. 2002. *Returns to Investment in Education: A Further Update, Policy Research Working Paper; No. 2881*. Washington, DC: World Bank, https://openknowledge.worldbank.org/handle/10986/19231.

Riordan, P. 2008. *A Grammar of the Common Good: Speaking of Globalization.* London: Bloomsbury.

Ruiz, F. 2014. *Atlixco ciudad con perfiles coloniales. La homogeneidad de la época Colonial.* Puebla: BUAP. https://doi.org/10.5821/siiu.9076

Secretaría de Turismo (SECTUR). 2016. *Pueblos Mágicos: Atlixco*, https://www.sectur.gob.mx/.

Secretaría de Gobernación (SEGOB). 2018. *Secretariado Ejecutivo del Sistema Nacional de Seguridad. Incidencia delictiva del fuero común, municipal 2011–2017.* https://drive.google.com/file/d/17Ptg6_zOPPLoOCpeRoRVgFtWYcH0EHQr/view

UDLAP. 2017. *Índice Global de Impunidad (IGI)*, https://www.udlap.mx/igimex/assets/files/2018/igimex2018_ESP.pdf.

United Nations Office on Drugs and Crime (UNODC). 2013. *International Homicide Statistics (IHS). Metadata and Methodological Text*, https://www.unodc.org/documents/data-andanalysis/IHS%20methodology.pdf.

United Nations-Habitat. 2015. *Cálculos con base en la cartografía SCINCE 2010 del Instituto Nacional de Estadística y Geografía (INEGI)*. http://gaia.inegi.org.mx/scince2/viewer.html

12. Assessing the Transformative Impact of Love-Based Microsocial Communities

From Existential Peripheries into the Nexus of the Common Good

Simona Beretta

This chapter draws a parallel between the macro-social dynamics of the nexus of the common good and the dynamics of personal agency within micro-social communities, where peripheral, vulnerable people experience stable relationships of personalised care. This parallel is plausible: authentic human and social development are both rooted in having experienced, at least embryonically, a possible answer to one's innermost aspirations—love, truth, beauty, justice...—and freely walk along that path.

This paper summarises our research on micro-social relations, discussing how they can contribute to understanding and measuring the nexus of the common good. Do transformative micro-social relations also generate a dynamic of the common good, and how? What can we learn about the inner dynamics of the common good at the macro level, by looking at the micro-dynamics of personalised relations of care involving vulnerable people? These are reasonable questions: one can argue that the good of peripheral people is also good for society (we find echoes of this idea in different visions—from Rawls to Christian social teaching); or even that peripheries are a privileged viewpoint for observing reality.

    https://doi.org/10.11647/OBP.0290.15

1. The Transformative Impact of Micro-Social Relationships

Care, human development and the common good are closely related. Human babies develop into creative youngsters and adults through personalised care. Accompanying marginalised or excluded persons along their path, with personalised care and support, can immediately better their human conditions, but can also empower them to become protagonists of their own lives, 'dignified agents of their own development' (Pope Francis 2015), and eventually active agents for the common good. The analogy may seem incautious, yet even caring for a baby is ultimately about enhancing, in due time and with due manners, the baby's own agency. Over time, the initially one-directional care evolves into a well-rounded relationship, that promotes the common good of all involved.[1]

The transformation of vulnerable people from passive dependence to dignified agency can be so deep, that we incontrovertibly speak of 'success stories'. Here is one story: two young, Italian, formerly substance-addicted persons complete their rehab at Casa Famiglia Rosetta, a faith-based rehab community in Sicily, Italia. They get married, wishing their family to become a Casa for other people in need. They agree to move to Brazil, heeding a call for help from a local bishop, to serve as a 'family-community', and welcoming vulnerable people into their home. Another success story: an orphan child from Burundi, included in a schoolchildren's sponsorship programme run by AVSI, successfully completes schooling in his country, and goes on to receive support from the Italian sponsoring family, until he completes a master's degree at *Università Cattolica del Sacro Cuore*.

Success stories can powerfully convey awareness of the potential transformative impact of human development initiatives that are based on relations of love and care; and narratives have a transformational power of their own.[2] Some questions, however, remain: can we provide

---

1   « *Demandez à ce père si le meilleur moment /N'est pas quand ses fils commencent à l'aimer comme des hommes, / Lui-même comme un homme, / Librement, / Gratuitement.* [...] *Demandez à ce père s'il ne sait pas que rien ne vaut / Un regard d'homme qui se croise avec un regard d'homme.* » Péguy 1911, p. 107.

2   Powerful narratives of transformative experiences are widely used in the humanities and social sciences; narratives indeed have a power of their own to affect behaviour (Collier 2016).

empirical evidence on the ordinary transformative power of care and accompaniment, beyond narratives of extraordinary success stories? Can we reach a deeper understanding of the inner dynamism of micro-social relations triggering human development? And can this knowledge provide new insights on what drives societal change, and even lessons for improving policymaking?[3]

We started tackling these questions, that in some sense mirror the questions behind the research on the nexus of the common good, in 2012.[4] We built our methodology out of elemental anthropological premises: we feel good when we are loved, and bad when we are mistreated, or lied to; we basically learn to love by being loved and taken care of; to trust, by being trusted. Hence, our overarching hypothesis is that the tangible experience of receiving love and care can transform both material and non-material dimensions of life. We studied different experiences of accompaniment and care, performing longitudinal studies (time matters!) on how being exposed to stable relations of love and care within a community (relations matter!) can transform the lives of vulnerable people, both in material and non-material outcomes (Beretta and Maggioni 2017). We studied decision and choices of real persons, not 'brains in a vat'; people acting 'here and now', whose decisions encompass emotions and passions, beliefs and narratives, aspirations and hopes; real persons, in other words, embedded in relations.[5]

As we developed our results, we found interesting connections with recent strands of behavioural economics literature, that explore

---

3   These research questions underline a number of connected research projects at *Università Cattolica del Sacro Cuore* that were developed in the last few years, including a number of ongoing research projects (for example, the one titled *Working Out of Poverty. Accompanying the poor to became dignified agents of their own development*, in collaboration with UPAEP).

4   This research line was initiated in 2012, a risky and unusual endeavour for economists, by Mario A. Maggioni and myself. Our enthusiasm benefitted from generous financial support by the Fetzer Institute, Kalamazoo, directed at the time by Larry Sullivan, Professor Emeritus of Theology and Anthropology, University of Notre Dame, Indiana. The relationship with him was surely transformative for us, so it is only appropriate to name him here.

5   We are indeed rational, but in a sense that largely exceeds typical economic models, often implying a procedural rationality so narrow that 'even rats can do it', and 'robots can do it better': Beretta Maggioni, libro e special issue. Even when we need to decide in conditions of dismal ignorance, our choices need to be reasonable in some sense, well beyond narrow procedural rationality. The typical reasonable background we resort to is embedded in relations, as important advances in decision theory highlight as in Schmeidler and Gilboa 2001, 2011.

various channels through which social groups shape individual preferences, influence individual choices, and change social group dynamics.[6] Particularly interesting was Hoff and Stiglitz's (2016) distinction between two paradigms that depart from standard models of maximising individuals: quasi-rational individuals, as in traditional behavioural economics; and what they call 'enculturated' actors, whose preferences, perceptions and cognitions are not given—as normally assumed in economics—but shaped within society: 'exposure to a given social context shape who people are' (2016, p. 26).

Sound anthropology recognises that we are persons-in-relation: with ourselves, with others, and with reality—which always hints at realities beyond itself. Each person can tell who she is by referring to the narrative of her personal history of contingent, multifaceted encounters: from birth (her genealogy) through all subsequent encounters (with things and people), up to the 'here and now'. I owe to Angelo Scola (Scola and Rusconi 2006) my introduction to the dialogue between Christian anthropology and the social sciences, with the powerful suggestion of defining the acting person as an I-in-relation, building upon Romano Guardini's reflection on polar oppositions (Guardini 2019; Ghia 2019) as constitutive of one's inner self (Scola 2006; Borhesi 2017). No aggregation of details can fully account for the 'incandescent nucleus' of a person's inner self.

Two polar oppositions are clearly in action in transformative experiences: body/spirit, and I/we.

Body/spirit: we are inseparably bodily and spiritual beings, a duality that does not contradict our uniqueness; we experience living in a body which is subject to the laws of nature, and yet we experience spirit transcending the cosmos. We realise and appreciate the symbolic value of material exchanges; we know the power of non-material drivers of material actions. We know that shame, dependency, and humiliation are particularly negative features of being poor, so that poor people 'rarely speak of income, but focus instead on managing assets—physical,

---

6   This line of research about individual/community interplay portrays economic behaviour as a 'reflexive interplay between economics and social forces' (Snower 2016, p. 1, presenting JEBO 2016 special issue), where identities, norms, and narratives influence individual beliefs and, consequently, choices. Narratives, in particular, seem to represent the crucial link connecting individual decisions to social influences (Akerlof and Snower 2016).

human, social, and environmental — as a way to cope with their vulnerability' (Narayan et al. 2000, pp. 4–5).

The I/we polarity refers to the constitutive tension between individual and community, which is especially relevant for the nexus of common good: as individuals, we are distinctly unique, yet we recognise our belonging to the human family. Personal good and common good matter to us: the two polarities, I and we, are in dynamic opposition, not in static contradiction. While evil and good contradict each other (evil is not opposed to good: it negates good) the I/we polar opposition is such that each polarity does not exclude but rather presupposes the other; each cannot exist without the other. The two are inextricably connected, in a tension which offers no static conciliation, but keeps the concrete dynamics of human life going.

Living in a community means finding a dynamic path where the I-we polar opposition is neither resolved by annihilating the person in the community, nor by affirming the individual against the community. The two opposing polarities are not enemies, but opportunities for a process of comparison and dialogue; the polarities are the concrete path people have to walk in life; they are the practical form of living together that does not cancel differences, and does not eliminate conflict.

Another tradition I owe something to, in this regard, comes from Oriental cultures (Kasulis 2008), where relations (among persons, including relations enabling the possibility to know all forms of reality) are not represented as external connections between two entities (two persons, or a person and an object), like an arrow connecting two autonomous, self-contained, 'integral' realities. In the Oriental perspective (*kokoro*), relations imply 'intimacy', that can be represented as an overlapping of two entities.

A simple graph can help. Figure 1 represents the relation between two entities as the arrow connecting them, along an 'integrity' perspective; Figure 2 shows the 'intimacy' perspective, typical of *kokoro*.

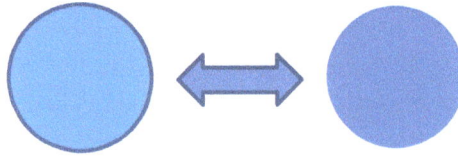

Figure 1. Relations: 'integrity' perspective as defined by Kasulis 2008.

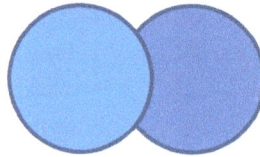

Figure 2. Relations: Kasulis 2008's 'intimacy' perspective.

When a relationship breaks up, the two entities are actually reshaped in the *kokoro* perspective, as in Figure 3.

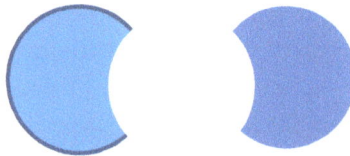

Figure 3. End of a relationship in the 'intimacy' perspective.

Not so in a 'Western technocratic' mentality, according to Kasulis. When a relationship is interrupted, only the arrow disappears from Figure 1, leaving the two entities apparently unscathed in their integrity. Thus, interpersonal relations tend to be conceived as if they can be built and dismantled at will, while relations with objects are a matter of control and instrumental use.

The Christian and the Oriental visions, where relations are constitutive for the human person, have curiously convergent implications for the process of knowledge, including scientific research. Both visions expose in different ways the limitations of the dominant (Western) technocratic paradigm, where knowledge is assumed to result from dispassionate (distant) observation of the object, which often needs to be fragmented (dissected) to achieve a deeper knowledge (compare Western and Oriental medicine, as an example).

With some simplification, the dominant Western paradigm tends to be very effective in mastering details, and thus very efficient in solving particular problems (within the *ceteris paribus* assumption, as is normal in economics). But by methodologically and practically neglecting our interdependence, unexpected feedback is likely to end up spoiling even the smartest technocratic solutions—which happens all too often.[7] The intrinsic limitations of a technocratic paradigm are especially applicable to human and social science, where overcoming individualistic perspectives is mandatory, as interdependence is the factual experience of everyday life.

A final caution: the distinction between an 'integrity' and 'intimacy' perspective is intriguing, but should not be taken as a matter of either/ or, that is, as an exclusive choice. They *both* describe the relational dimension of humans, and will thus be more or less appropriate for understanding different situations. All relations are deeply ambivalent and a matter either for good or for bad; in particular, 'intimacy' relations can either accompany or frustrate human development; the closer relations are, the stronger the effects (think of care *versus* mobbing). In a sense, I would maintain that intimacy and integrity can be best approached as a polarity's dynamic opposition.

2. Assessing Microsocial Transformative Experiences: Three Case-Studies

Our research on the transformative impact of care relationships on vulnerable individuals' material and non-material outcomes is an ongoing, imperfect process of implementing a relational perspective.

---

7   Francis, *Laudato si'*, pp. 106–107 speaks of the globalisation of the technocratic paradigm: '… [H]umanity has taken up technology and its development *according to an undifferentiated and one-dimensional paradigm*. This paradigm exalts the concept of a subject who, using logical and rational procedures, progressively approaches and gains control over an external object. This subject makes every effort to establish the scientific and experimental method, which in itself is already a technique of possession, mastery and transformation. […] [M]any problems of today's world stem from the tendency, at times unconscious, to make the method and aims of science and technology an epistemological paradigm which shapes the lives of individuals and the workings of society.'

Studying experience and exposure of peripheral people experiencing community life requires actors to be observed in real life situations (lab-in-the-field approach), and in real time (longitudinal study). Which means that we could provide appropriate control groups only in some cases, and that randomisation was simply not a practical option. We especially aimed at capturing relevant non-material dimensions of personal experience; hence, besides collecting data on material situations and outcomes, we also collected behavioural economic choices, psychological data, and textual data. As observable behaviours (*a fortiori* experimentally observed behaviours) are only a proxy for real human actions, providing a very rudimental tool for assessing subjective traits, attitudes, and motivations, we also asked people involved in experimental games to speak or write about their choices, providing comment and their motivations so that we could learn something about the *meaning* they give to their decisions.

The three case studies presented below appear, at first sight, to have very little in common. They refer to three continents (Europe, North America, Africa), three different forms of marginalisation (suffering from substance addiction, being in prison, being an orphan or vulnerable child), and consider three different forms of community support (small rehab communities for addicts in Italy, the GRIP offender accountability programme in Californian prisons, and the AVSI schoolchildren sponsorship programme in the Democratic Republic of Congo). All of these experiences, however, represent forms of community-based treatment; they are built on, and are aimed at fostering, personalised relations of love and care, where each person is so valuable as to be invaluable. Thus, they naturally resonate with the person-in-relation paradigm, where human flourishing and development occurs within personalised care relations, and where one feels the privilege of being uniquely loved. In each case, we applied modified versions of our multi-instrument, longitudinal methodology; our results, some preliminary and some already published, some very robust and some still tentative, support the relevance of the person-in-relation framework for understanding personal development.

Casa-Famiglia Rosetta and Community Rehab for Addicted Persons

Our encounter with the late Fr. Vincenzo Sorce was especially important in launching this line of research. A person of profound faith and culture and passionate humanity; a social innovator in the heart of Sicily, Fr. Sorce was immediately sympathetic to our project and trusted us to perform our pilot studies within two rehab communities belonging to the *Association Casa Famiglia Rosetta* (CFR), which he founded in the early 1980s.

CFR is both a powerful experience of love-based rehab,[8] and a think-tank engaged in self-reflection, scientific research and dissemination concerning rehabilitation strategies and social policies[9]—which explains Fr. Sorce's support for our project. CFR is but a small network of rehab communities (a drop in the ocean of rehab needs). In the heart of Sicily, a story of micro-relations (Rosetta was the first guest to die in the home that Fr. Sorce opened for welcoming people with severe illnesses that lived alone) evolved into a socially and economically relevant network, a centre of innovative caring practices with an international reputation, and the first non-state employer in the Caltanissetta province—a Sicilian area with a stagnating economy and deep-seated mafia organisation. This is why CFR seems to me the perfect example to start with, in a chapter that aims at bridging micro-relations for human development and social innovation for the common good.

After completing the pilot study on CFR, we extended the study to other Italian love-based rehab communities; the full-fledged research project currently enrolls about thirty communities (Beretta and

---

8   We named as 'love-based rehab' those initiatives where personalised interaction in a small community is key, and where common rules are mainly meant to serve the purpose of living together. This is quite a different approach with respect to other rehab initiatives, which are centred on either individual treatment (typically pharmaceutical and psychological), or close peer control under strict rules ('rule-based' rehab).

9   See https://www.casarosetta.it/. The CFR network offers reception, care, rehabilitation and social inclusion programmes to people with physical and/or mental disabilities, people with alcohol, drug abuse and gambling dependence issues, at-risk minors or minors living in dysfunctional families, elderly people, people affected by AIDS, and women in need (housing, outpatient, home, extramural and daytime services). Since 2009 it is recognised as an Organization with Consultative Status with the United Nations ECOSOC.

Maggioni 2017). Treatment in love-based communities is quite simple. It consists in: (a) sharing daily life with other people in rehab, with the constant presence of community workers (both paid and voluntary workers); (b) following basic common rules (wake up time, common meals, time for rest) that provide an orderly space where relations can develop. Month after month, people in rehab learn back how to take care of relationships: first of all relationships with themselves (self-consciousness, self-forgiveness, self-esteem); then relations with the material reality (typically, agricultural work allows guests to see fruits, vegetables, and flowers grow as a result of their care).[10] Later in the process, people in rehab learn to build relations outside the community, normally by providing service work and support to persons in need (for example, children with physical and mental disabilities). They also develop other social relations, especially through artistic expression or craftmanship, and refine their previous job skills or acquire new ones in order to be able to reintegrate the society.

Persons in rehab can however always quit the community—and they frequently do so, because the rehab process is very hard work. Remaining in the community is in and of itself a factual indicator that something humanly convincing and attractive can be found there; strong enough to create stability and overcome the inevitable hardships of community life. The Italy-wide average rate of dropouts from rehab communities is over 70%; in our research, out of a batch of 195 valid questionnaires collected at the monument of entering rehab, only 73 valid questionnaires were collected in the second wave of interviews, nine months later. That is, 122 community members out of 195 interrupted their rehabilitation programme, with an attrition rate of 62.6% in nine months, which is lower than the national average but still very significant. Attrition is indeed a problem: despite clear qualitative evidence of rehab producing personal change in community members that remain in rehab, the statistical significance of our quantitative results is insufficient to support strong claims. For example, by longitudinally comparing the scores reported in the Dictator Game[11] (a proxy for generosity/altruism or for fairness/

---

10   *'Everything that receives love, grows'*, reads a stone set among the branches of a magnificent olive tree, in the orchard of Eremo del Falco, the community where Fr. Sorce lived.

11   In the Dictator Game, each agent is endowed with a given amount of a good (usually money; in our research concerning people in rehab, the good is cigarettes, as

inequity aversion), we see that the score increases over time, implying on average the emergence of a more generous attitude after treatment. The direction of change confirms our expectations (that rehab positively affects altruistic behaviours), but the coefficient attached to this variable is not statistically significant. We observe similar patterns (expected direction, non-significant parameters) in other behavioural indicators (trust, inequality aversion, gratitude, impulsivity) and psychological tests (self-esteem, self-forgiveness); but we need more robust empirical evidence. This is why the interview process is still ongoing.

What is the relevance of this case study in light of the nexus of the common good? After all, we do not get strong statistics, and there is no obvious control group. First, the case seems to me a paradigmatic example of how a common good dynamic can flourish: a personal *élan of freedom* (*agency freedom*) starts and continues building *durable relations* (*stability*); this produces social innovation (*governance*), which becomes a durable reality only out of systematic critical reflection on the *how* and the *why* of everyday actions[12] (*justice; humanity*). Second, because it provides clear evidence that all dynamics of the common begin and rest upon the collective *élan* of freedom of a 'we', including the free decisions of addicts to remain, to do their part, and to reach the point at which they can reenter society as I-in-relation, as 'dignified agents of their own development'. This confirms the importance given to agency freedom in the normative model provided by the IPBC (see Chapter 2).

---

community members are not allowed to use money). The agent (Dictator) is asked to freely decide whether, and how much of, the endowed good is to be sent to the anonymous partner, who is known to have received none. Standard self-interested behaviour would be to give nothing; the Dictator Game investigates whether this occurs in real choices.

12   Open-questions interviews with directors, staff members, and people who have completed rehab in different communities allowed us to better understand their treatment. The variety of non-trivial words used in answering simple descriptive questions (about practical organisation, daily activities, and so on) signals the powerful emotional experience of community life, and offers nuanced descriptions of each community's identity. The remarkable prevalence of words such as 'love (*amore*), 'respect' (*rispetto*), 'forgiveness' (*perdono*), 'communion' (*comunione*), in answering very practical descriptive questions highlights the key role of non-material dimensions in the rehab communities under study.

II. 'Leaving the Prison before You Get Out': The GRIP Program

The Guiding Rage Into Power (GRIP) Program is an offender accountability programme run by the NGO *Insight-Out*, active in San Quentin for two decades and currently operating in different Californian prisons. GRIP works as a peer education model, providing prisoners with tools that enable them to learn how to stop violence, to become emotionally intelligent, to cultivate mindfulness, and to come to understand victim impact. In the words of the NGO founder Jacques Verduin, GRIP enables prisoners to 'turn the stigma of being a violent offender into a badge of being a non-violent peacekeeper', 'becoming agents of change', that is, 'people with skills to defuse conflicts around them', thus 'leaving the prison before you get out.'[13] The programme originates from the founder's vision that violence and unlawful behaviour are often connected to a previous lack of close relationships, or experience of violent ones. The core idea is to address each prisoner as a person, rather than merely as a problem; and to make them feel loved and respected within a community, without neglecting the gravity of the offence. Experience and anecdotal evidence about reduction in recidivism reveals that the GRIP programme has a considerable effect in helping prisoners to get a second chance in life, and to build sound and long-lasting relationships.

The programme usually spans an 'academic year,' and develops through fortnightly lessons, focused on specific topics, with four macro-objectives: stopping violent behaviour; cultivating mindfulness; activating emotional intelligence; understanding victim impact. Classes include formal lessons, group work, and participation of external guests. The key point of classwork is creating friendly relationships and a strong group identification: classmates, of different ethnicities and backgrounds, work together as a 'tribe'—the positive version of a gang. New interpersonal bonds within the (multi-ethnic) 'tribe' create a common culture of accountability and peace—a radical alternative to normal prison culture. The GRIP programme, by helping prisoners reflect on their lives, enables them to effectively experience the possibility of a different daily life in their externally unchanged, and quite hard,

---

13   See the webstite or the NGO: https://grip-traininginstitute.org/.

prison environment. Personal narratives and evidence available on the *Insight-Out* website provide impressive evidence of the transformative impact of the programme. GRIP 'graduates' *have* so much in common because they have deep experience of *being* in common (see the impressive videos of their meetings on the GRIP website). Moreover, informal and self-reported evidence suggests that GRIP graduates who return to society on parole (a small number, as most GRIP graduates are life-sentenced) tend not to come back to prison—or they come back as GRIP tutors. Reducing recidivism is quite an accomplishment from a 'common good' perspective, but we found it virtually impossible to access formal data on recidivism in order to provide hard empirical evidence, including for privacy reasons.

For our research, we interviewed both GRIP participants and a control group of inmates not attending GRIP, using a simplified, paper version of our questionnaire (Beretta and Maggioni 2017). Individual responses collected in two waves of interviews were analysed with a Difference-in-Differences technique, a statistical method which measures the effects of a treatment over a variable by comparing the average change over time in that variable for GRIP participants and for the control group. In particular, with a Trust game[14] payed using dehydrated soups[15] as payoff, we showed that generalised trust significantly increased in GRIP participants, compared to the control group: unexpectedly, we found 'trust behind bars' (Maggioni et al. 2018). The results are robust for alternative estimation techniques, and for the inclusion of an endogenous behavioural measure of altruism (Dictator Game). Thus, in addition to its primary aim, exposure to an offender accountability programme build on strong community bonds also enhances inmates' prosocial preferences: this result underlines the importance of community relationships.

---

14   We use a version of the Trust Game, also known as the Investment Game (Berg et al. 1995, Camerer and Weigelt 1988). A Proponent is provided with an exogenous endowment, and he/she is matched with an anonymous partner who has received no endowment. The Proponent's decision concerns whether and how much of his/her endowment to send to the anonymous partner, knowing that the experimenter will multiply (triple) any amount sent. The Respondent, once they have received the amount sent by the Proponent, duly multiplied, will choose whether, and how much of the total amount received, to send back to the Proponent. The final payoff of the Proponent will thus be equal to the initial endowment, less the amount sent to the Respondent, plus the amount the Respondent sends back.

15   Dehydrated soups are both a consumption good and a sort of 'currency' in Californian prisons, where money cannot be used.

We also asked inmates to provide written comments on their behavioural choices. The linguistic profile of the answers is quite simple but highly informative, providing vividly different interpretations of inmates' behavioural choices. For example, inmates faced with a Dictator Game provide comments on their decision, clearly showing that the same observable behavioural choice may accompany very different narratives, such as fairness, generosity, reciprocity, and 'me-first' motivations.[16] The longitudinal comparison of keyword incidence across GRIP and non-GRIP inmates shows different (at times, opposed) trends, once their comments are grouped according to their content: we observe equality and generosity increasing among GRIP participants, but decreasing for members of the control group; *vice versa*, reciprocity and me-first attitudes decline among GRIP participants and increase for members of the control group.

One can reasonably ask: do actions speak louder that words? This is an intriguing question, especially relevant when empirical studies collect self-declared information on behaviours and attitudes. On the one side, we know that talk can be cheap; but this is no reason to believe that quantitative behavioural parameters are the solution. The texts we collected severely warn us against assuming that behavioural choice can be mechanically interpreted, and tell us the full story about the dynamism of action.

---

16   Here are some examples: "I personally brought four soups, popcorn and a cookie for lunch today. I have plenty for myself and to share with others. I don't need the soup. So, without knowing the other person's situation I feel he can have these, and hopefully share them with others" (inmate AV006, who decided to give all ten soups). "I feel I am generous so I gave half" (inmate MC010, giving 5 soups). "Fifty-fifty seem the fairest" (inmate MC036, giving 5 soups).
"Since I have ten soup for myself giving half to the other person would help him, would be fair plus I still have five for myself. Just how I would treat a celly or friend without anything to eat" (inmate MC011, giving 5 soups).
"I really don't know the person. That is why I gave him four soup. If I knew him, I would maybe give him half of the soup or more" (inmate AV044, giving four soups).
"Ten percent of everything I own I give to the Father. Ten percent of everything I own go to savings and eighty percent of everything I own is to splurge spend" (MC013, giving two soups)

Distance Support for African Schoolchildren: Does 'Feeling' Supported Improve Learning Outcomes?

The third case study focuses on sponsorship of international schoolchildren, which represents a widely used form of durable, personalised support from a donor (a person, a family, a school-class), to a child (and indirectly to his/her family) living in a low-income country and facing special challenges in attending school. While very little studied, this form of international support involves a significant number of donors and schoolchildren (9.14 million sponsored children in the world in 2017) (Wydick et al. 2017, pp. 434–458); tentative estimations suggest private financial flows to internationally sponsored children exceeding US$3 billion annually (Wydick et al. 2013, pp. 393–436).

We decided to study schoolchildren sponsorship programmes activated by AVSI Foundation, an international NGO founded in Italy in 1972. We implemented a research project on the longitudinal outcomes and the possible transformative impacts of the AVSI Distance Support Program (DSP), which sponsors vulnerable schoolchildren worldwide (over 23,000 children have been sponsored through this initiative so far).[17] DSP provides predictable money flows and allows for personalised relations between one specific child or adolescent, and one specific donor who can exchange mail and photos, and receives regular information about the child. Local AVSI officers in the destination countries design individualised intervention plans for the sponsored child, their family and community, and provide material support and accompaniment within a stable network of relations that are easily accessible to local families and communities.

During the 2015–2016 schoolyear, AVSI-DRC activated their DSP for the first time in Goma (Democratic Republic of Congo, in the Kivu region). This involved a significant group of new children, all of whom entered DSP at the same time, and attended school in a number of local educational institutions. This event posed a very favourable opportunity for our research: in Goma, we were able to collect longitudinal data for a sample of 309 children, 121 treated and 188 control, all attending ten local

---

17   AVSI's mission is to promote the dignity of the person through development cooperation activities, with special attention to education, in accordance with the social teachings of the Catholic Church. https://www.avsi.org/en/.

schools. More recently, starting in the 2017–2018 schoolyear, a similar 'mass' activation of DSP was applied in Rwanda, so we could replicate the longitudinal research in two schools (Munyinya and Nyinawimana) in the Kigali district. At present, the results for Goma have been both collected and thoroughly elaborated; we are still working on those for Rwanda.

In both Goma and Kigali, we formed control groups of schoolmates not accessing DSP on a 'matching-pairs' basis (matching in terms of school, class, sex, and age). In practice, for each schoolchild accessing DSP, we identified two other children as members of the control group. The longitudinal study collects individual surveys and personal information from the children (both DSP and control group) at the very beginning of the DSP 'treatment'; we then collect them again after the completion of two schoolyears. School staff in both research situations agreed on providing (coded) information on school attendance and school performance, with the approval of children's parents or legal guardians.

We used the same survey in the two studies, with minor adjustments in translating from French into the locally spoken language. The behavioural situations and games included in the survey are the Dictator Game, the Sincerity Test,[18] and other simple experimental situations meant to assess the prosocial attitudes and preferences of children. Payoffs were delivered to children in the form of locally available packets of cookies. We also collected textual information, i.e., children's own explanations of the reasons for their decisions to give (or not to give) packets of cookies to the other (anonymous) child in the Dictator Game. At the end of individual surveys, we also administered a 'cookie' version

---

18   The Dice Rolling Game measures sincerity/truthfulness in self-reporting. The agent is asked to report the results of a series of single die-throwing tasks. Before every throw, the agent is asked to choose, in his/her mind, either the up or down side of the die, and to memorise this decision without revealing it. With African schoolchildren, we opted for using two dice, one red and one blue, to make the test more straightforward to understand. After completing the throw, the agent gains the points corresponding to the side he/she declares. That is, the agent can gain by cheating in reporting the outcome, strategically declaring his/her non-observable choice after the throw in order to maximise the value of his/her rewards. Observing the average reported scores provides (stochastic) information about the attitudes of a given group or population to truthfully reporting a series of favourable/unfavourable events. The results are thoroughly analysed in Mario A. Maggioni, Domenico Rossignoli (2020).

of the so-called Marshmallow Test,[19] observing children's behaviour with respect to self-control and delayed gratification. School principals were very collaborative: they introduced the group of external interviewers to the children, reassured the children that the interviewers were adults that could be trusted, and that the cookies were tasty, healthy, and safe. The bilingual (French and Swahili) interviewers were familiar with the environment of the children, and were thus well-suited to interact with them. They showed the children the alternative choices in a clear, visual manner, and transcribed the children's choices and verbal expressions in Swahili with French translation on a coded individual questionnaire.[20]

Using microdata for the sample of 309 children in Goma, we applied Difference-in-Differences techniques to measure if, and how, schoolchildren sponsorship (DSP) impacts the children in question's learning outcomes, behaviours, and narratives over time. Thanks to the active support of school officers and local AVSI staff, we succeeded in collecting a broad set of alternative educational outcomes: performance scores (grand total, and four different subjects); failure rates; and school drop-out rates. The most striking comparison between the DSP children and the control group concerned learning outcomes: we found that sponsored children reported significantly lower drop-out rates,[21] and

---

19 This test allows us to observe children's behaviour with respect to self-control and delayed gratification. Basically, children are provided with a packet of cookies; they will receive two if they do not open it while the interviewer goes away for a while (ten minutes). The 'Cookie' Test is a variant of the more famous Marshmallow Test, as described in https://www.newyorker.com/magazine/2009/05/18/dont-2.

20 The comments children provided for explaining their decisions for the Dictator Game are, as in the case of Californian inmates, quite illuminating. Children received five packets of cookies, and explained their decision, clearly pointing to the concreteness of relationships for them. The anonymous partner allocated in the behavioural game tended to make little sense to them. In some cases, they justified keeping the cookies in order to give them to other people than the anonymous partner: « *Je lui donne deux parce que je vais donner le reste à mes petits-frères* »; « *je donne un paquet pour que je puisse partager avec les autres enfants chez nous à la maison* » ; « *Je lui donne un paquet parce que je ne peux pas priver mes petits frères et ces quatre paquets nous suffisent* »; « *je veux donner un paquet de biscuits parce que les autres enfants* [schoolchildren that were not interviewed] *me demanderont et je veux leurs donner* »). In other cases they clearly stated : « *je lui donne un paquet parce qu'on ne se connaît pas* » ; « *je lui donne deux paquets de biscuits parce que je ne le connais pas* ». In other cases, they identified with the anonymous partner, who became a real person in their mind: « *je lui donne deux paquets parce que je l'aime, il est élève comme moi* »; « *Parce que l'autre aussi a faim* ».

21 Out of the initial 134 DSP children interviewed in the first wave (2015/16), only 8 dropped out from the sample in the second wave of data collection (corresponding

lower failure rates,[22] with respect to their peers. As to grades, while lagging behind in terms of grades at the moment in which they entered the sponsorship programme, DSP children managed to catch up with their peers in all subjects over the two-year period that we monitored. These results are robust to the introduction of control variables,[23] as well as alternative forms of robustness check.[24]

The differential improvement in performance of DSP schoolchildren deserves some discussion. What can we infer from this information about the relational dimension of children's experiences, and about the dynamic of the common good? By removing *external* constraints, in particular by guaranteeing paid school fees, school sponsorship after all simply provides 'equal' access to schooling; yet, despite attending the same school, with the same teachers, in the same environment, and for the same number of days (all of these variables were controlled), we observed a remarkable catch-up by AVSI DSP children. This evidence was indeed observed across all grades and subjects; it can be explained in terms of the alleviation of the socio-economic and sanitary constraints faced before sponsorship, but also in terms of the reduced uncertainty for DSP children about how they perceive their future ability to regularly attend school. Convergence in learning outcomes corroborates the idea that being supported (in material terms) and perhaps also 'feeling' supported (in non-material terms) makes the difference for them.

Our findings are in fact compatible with the suggestion that personalised sponsorship programmes (each child having a one-to-one

---

to 6%), due to their families' moving to other places, as we confirmed with AVSI. Once we looked at the drop-out rate in the control group, we found an impressively higher value, of 76 out of 264 children (about 29%). Even excluding the 22 control group children that are known to have moved to another school (and can potentially complete their primary education elsewhere), the drop-out rate for the control group children remains significant, at 21%. See Rossignoli et al. (2019).

22 The failure rate of the control group remains constant across the two observed schoolyears, whereas DSP children experience a notable decrease in their failure rate during the same period. While the share of children failing in 2015–2016 was significantly larger for the DSP children than for the control group, this difference becomes statistically insignificant by the end of the 2016–17 schoolyear.

23 DSP children and the control group are substantially balanced in terms of pre-treatment background features, with only the exceptions of likelihood of being orphaned, and of housing precariousness or inadequacy. For this reason, we included the corresponding controls in the analysis.

24 The results are robust after implementing a sound matching technique (Coarsened Exact Matching) that exploits the structure of the data to produce unbiased estimates and perfect ex-post balancing.

relationship with the sponsor, and stable relations with the local AVSI staff) may also alleviate *internal* constraints to learning, such as the lack of aspirations/hope that can be associated with the experience of uncertainty. Without the DSP, children may attend school at some point in time, but are uncertain about their future ability to continue attending, and can thus become demotivated. School sponsorship, then, can be seen as a way to support children's emotional development and agency, through the reasonable hope that they are not abandoned, and that they also have a future. 'Feeling' supported may play for children a sustaining role that is as significant as the material fact of 'being' sponsored: a less hostile anticipated future can reinforce self-esteem, aspirations, and self-expectations. The success story of the Burundi child (now adult) who I mentioned in the early pages of this chapter is an example of this process; tour study shows that a similar dynamism can be observed as a statistically significant feature of DSP, and that this is observable even over the short timespan of two years.

In sum, I am suggesting that the combined effect of DSP (a stable relationship, encompassing monetary transfers and actual interaction) consisting in the removal of *external* as well as *internal* constraints,[25] can be a driver of differential impact on even short-term school performance, as we found over two years in our comparison of DSP children with their peers. Aspirations and hopes are indeed receiving increased attention as important drivers of personal development, and of development *tout court*. That is, non-material drivers of actual observable outcomes are key elements in the dynamic of human flourishing, possibly contributing to the common good of families, local communities, and society at large.

---

25 Our results resonate with one of the few research studies on school sponsorship (Wydick and Glewwe 2013; 2017), which finds large, statistically significant impacts of school sponsorship on life outcomes in terms of years of schooling; primary, secondary, and tertiary school completion; and the probability and quality of employment. This study also maintains that evidence suggests that these impacts are due, in part, to increases in children's aspirations.

3. Micro-Social Relations:
The Incandescent Nucleus of Human Experience and
the Nexus of the Common Good

The relational, dynamic perspective of our research on the transformational impact of microsocial accompaniment experiences quite naturally resonates with the perspective of this volume on the common good. In this section I would like to reconsider the methodological framework and the empirical results of the three micro-social case studies in light of the macro-social, more exquisitely political perspective of the research on the common good.

Here, I will highlight similarities and complementarities between the two research streams. They have been independently developed and pursue different aims; in many ways, however, they converge in contributing to a practical, dynamic, relation-based understanding of human and social development. As in the research on the nexus of the common good, we try to go beyond individualised, static measures, in order to appraise the dynamic process through which personal development occurs. In one case, we find compelling evidence of changes in personal traits and attitudes (GRIP); in another, we observe different trends in learning outcomes (DSP schoolchildren); in the third case, we are still in the learning process. In all cases, however, we seek to understand, within a relational perspective, *how* and *why* transformational outcomes are generated.[26] We are also interested in exploring the micro-social relational processes that are likely to produce *persistent* effects, rather than the one-off effects that are typical of top-down aid. The perspective of the nexus of the common good focuses on the *quality of interconnections*, and we also highlight the transformative potential of interconnections in order to understand human development dynamics.

Actions (rather than accomplishments) are indeed our focus: we are interested in the transformation processes that occur within factual constraints, uncertainties, and ambivalences, and are embedded in a

---

26   Take the evidence of improving school performance (dropout rate, failure rates, school grades): this improvement could potentially occur for a number of different reasons—including exasperated competitive pressure and individualistic incentives. Same outcome, quite different driver!

story of relationships—with things, with others, and with the ultimate inner drivers of human decisions: the needs, evidence, aspirations, and motivations that encompass and yet transcend material conditions. I think that learning about human actions with reference to the micro-social, practical experience of vulnerable, peripheral people permits simplicity as opposed to complexity;[27] this can also be useful for tracing process in a common good perspective. Sure, the tools we have at our disposal for capturing the person-in-action (behavioural parameters, textual materials, psychological tests) are far from perfect; but even learning about how they connect, and about their shortcomings, is a worthwhile effort.

I found the normative dimensions of the pentagram very helpful in revisiting the micro-social processes we studied. At the core of both micro-social transformation and common good dynamics, there is indeed *agency freedom*—not in any abstract sense, but in the concreteness of life. The freedom of people in the nexus, or more precisely their personal and collective freedom to act, is set as one of the five normative dimensions of the matrix, and is described as the engine of the common good dynamic. From the micro-social perspective, the incandescent nucleus of the human heart drives human actions towards a 'more' human life, contributing to the inner dynamism of the nexus of the common good. In the love-based communities we consider, agency freedom (on the side of care-givers, as well as on the side of the people being cared for) is indeed the engine of both personal and social change; durability and *stability* of community relationships is key in the care itself; and *humanity* is a very appropriate name for what protagonists (again, both care-givers and the people being cared for) achieve by living their story together. Each of the five elements of the pentagram is discussed below.

---

27 'The complexity of the experience of man is dominated by this intrinsic simplicity. [...] The whole experience, and consequently the cognition of man, is composed of both the experience that everyone has concerning himself and the experience of other men [...] All this tends to compose a whole in cognition rather than to cause complexity.' Wojtyła 1979, p. 8.

I. Agency Freedom, and the I-We Dynamism

There is a very interesting passage in the foundational paper, identifying agency freedom in the nexus as a collective achievement and duty (See Chapter 2). That is, in the nexus, we are free together because we all value that freedom (this is a powerful vision, quite different from social contract theories, where the collective dimension amounts to the aggregation of individual freedoms—which may, or may not, converge into common agency). As a consequence, 'individual and collective agency freedom are considered as concomitant, it is pointless to disentangle the two... we are born in social relationships that shape the acquisition of our own personal freedom' (Nebel and Medina in Chapter 2; see also Chapter 4).

We are indeed social beings; however, some disentanglment and discussion of how personal and collective freedoms relate to each other may be appropriate. In fact, harmony between individual and collective dimensions is a possibility, not a necessity; and relationships are ambivalent—they are desired, but also feared, the more so the closer they are. In my view, the I-we polarity can usefully complement, clarify and dynamise the relation between personal good and social good: the two are not contradictory, but they do remain in dynamic tension with each other, as long as our life in common is preserved.

I also have some comments on the observation that external constraints, including those connected with social and political institutions, can condition or even coerce human actions. In a society of slaves, no dynamic of the common good can exist (see Chapter 4). This remark about slavery is obviously more than justified, at a time where human trafficking, child labour and forced labour are booming once again. Slavery is taking new forms, but produces the same devastating impact on agency and human rights as the slave-ships of old.

The expression 'slavery', however, brings to my mind other forms of (inner) slavery that may exist with no externally apparent constraints to one's agency—indeed, they may resemble free choices. For example, slavery of addictive behaviours, old and new, is in seeming expansion today. The same can be said for slavery born out of different forms of idolatry: pursuing one limited goal, say money, at whatever cost.[28] In

---

28   See the opening images of Salgado's movie, *The Salt of the Earth*: are those persons slaves? Are they 'free' slaves, living in self-imposed slavery?

the Western world, we often worship exasperated individualism and freedom of choice (the kind of static freedom that applies better to supermarket choices, than to interpersonal relations). As with all idolatries, individualism also risks falling into its own trap, albeit at different stages: initial euphoria at being master of one's life; freely choosing to experience short-lived, instrumental relations with others; at some point, incapacity to admit to one's need for help; finally, utter loneliness. 'Single, not sorry' is indeed a widely popular, but very short-run slogan.[29] Static freedom of choice, nevertheless, is not the only kind of freedom we can experience. When we recognise the fact that structurally we are persons-in-relation (with our innermost being, with nature, with others, with ultimate meanings), self-determined forms of slavery may not be the ultimate word. Dynamic freedom, the kind of freedom that does not fear living the I-we polar tension, can always regenerate the possibility of human agency. After all, we have ascertained that this regeneration is possible, as people can sustainably exit addiction, and 'leave prison before getting out'.

What about situations where people experience external conditions that severely limit personal and collective agency? Freedom of choice and expression might be brutally restricted; yet, external slavery cannot quench the incandescent nucleus of the persons-in-relation. We know, for example, that the Gulag and Auschwitz did witness extreme forms of cruelty and suffering, but also luminous experiences of humanity. One may recall some of Solzhenitsyn's characters in action; or Maximillian Kolbe's free decision to give up his life for saving a neighbour: this is the kind of freedom that is borne out of love. In addition, we can observe that sparks of humanity tend to be contagious: in recent years, Vietnamese prison authorities were forced to frequently change Card Van Thuận's custody agents, because his hope and serenity—amidst cruel treatment—kept transforming custody agents' attitudes, from harshness into kindness.

Using the words of a self-declared non-believer, Vaclav Havel, all that is needed for the incandescent nucleus to change reality is 'living

---

29 In the UK, the Minister for Loneliness Tracey Crouch speaks of loneliness as a generational challenge, affecting people of all ages and backgrounds. See the 2020 report at https://www.gov.uk/government/publications/loneliness-annual-report-the-first-year/loneliness-annual-report-january-2020--2.

in truth' (1989). In his essay 'The Power of the Powerless', Vaclav
Havel (1985) tells the tale of a greengrocer—a fictional character, quite
impressive in his realism—to explain what it is to resist a totalitarian
power: as totalitarianism and post-totalitarianism thrive by manipulating
all expressions of life, any free expression of life can indirectly threaten
the system. Here is the greengrocer's story:[30] the manager of a fruit-and-
vegetable shop routinely places in his window, among the onions and
carrots, the slogan: '*Workers of the world, unite!*' He has been doing this
for years, as one of the thousand details that guarantee him a relatively
tranquil life 'in harmony with society'. Then, one day something in our
greengrocer snaps. He rejects the ritual and breaks the rules of the game.
He discovers once more his suppressed identity and dignity. He gives his
freedom a concrete significance. His revolt is an attempt to live within
the truth. Now, the greengrocer has not committed a simple, individual
offense, isolated in its own uniqueness; but something incomparably
more serious. By breaking the rules of the game, he has exposed it as
a mere game. Havel concludes the essay with a quite serious political
statement: 'One thing, however, seems clear: the attempt at political
reform was not the cause of society's reawakening, but rather the final
outcome of that reawakening' (Havel 1985, p. 43).

   This story has a powerful message: the greengrocer's incandescent
nucleus, rooted in the elemental sense of one's true self within a
community, can be stronger than totalitarianism—especially the sneaky
version of it, which leads people to be content with passive conformism.
There is indeed an ultimate point of reawakening of humanity that
we can call upon, at the micro and macro levels, in any circumstance,
even in the soft kind of conformism masked as freedom of choice
that we live in, especially in Western countries. Individual creativity
(the person-in-action) embedded in a story of meaningful relations
(the person-in-relation) can transform reality. Lasting relationships
are especially important: individual persons choosing to act as a 'we'
(creative minorities, community agencies, development partnerships,
cooperatives, etc.) can generate sustained social innovation from the
local to the global level. As they create communities of care, they can
also engage in conflict management and peacebuilding; as they care

---

30   What follows is a summary that tries to use Havel's own expression as much as
     possible.

for their immediate environment, they can also contribute to global sustainability.

II. Justice and Love

Chapter 2 recalls that justice as participation, solidarity, and inclusion cannot be proclaimed by law: rather, collective habits of justice and solidarity are the true books where justice is safeguarded. Books and habits, law and love, however, are not simple opposites of each other: they are also polarities in dynamic tension. The reawakening of society, participation, solidarity, and inclusion may require a vital process of learning in order to become collective habits, and to eventually find their way into books. Each generation must do its part in building just and inclusive institutions, in learning from the wisdom, and the failures, of previous generations; however, when habits are not transmitted (Bellamy 2014), books (formal rules) may even come handy.

In the case of rehab communities, we register the (successful) existence of both rule-based, and love-based communities. Now, both caring attitudes and rules are necessary in any form of coexistence, be it a family or a rehab community. On the one hand, rehab can work by trusting formerly addicted persons to act appropriately, persuading them by loving oversight to respect the basic rules of the community, including their daily schedule (when they wake up, work and eat); prohibited activities (drugs); limited activities (maximum number of cigarettes per day), and so on. On the other hand, rehab can also work when participants have to obey the strict rules of the community, with zero tolerance; rules that may include wearing uniforms, having no personal belongings, spending the closely structured day within a predetermined group of peers (that share a common room, common work, and must agree on common use of their free time). We have discovered that both of these paths can lead to personal rehabilitiation.

When we initially thought to assess the transformative impact of experiencing love-based treatment, we imagined that real rehab communities could be located, along a hypothetical line, on a continuum from rule-based to love-based communities; for our empirical work, we would have liked to compare the transformative impact of the two kinds. Rethinking our research today in light of common good dynamics, I see that both love-based care and respect for rules (the former resembling a collective habit, the latter being more similar to 'justice by the book') are indeed polarities in the dynamism of rehab practices, and not simple alternatives. Love and rules are and remain in reciprocal tension: they are both necessary, and neither side can be overcome by the other.[31] Their tension, as polar oppositions, can only be solved at a higher level (one might name this higher level 'gratuitousness', or 'generative attitudes').

In the case of Californian prisons, the link with the issue of justice is very evident. A prison is indeed a community, and its own common good has unique features. Rules are very strict—both legal rules and deep-seated informal rules, especially those concerning inter-ethnic and peer relations. What we learnt about the GRIP experience can exemplify what a broad notion of justice in prison, based on upholding the dignity of each person, implies. A 'just' prison should not be about society's revenge, and punishment; it should stand for offenders' rehabilitation: self-awareness, and awareness of victim impact; and for restoration, including re-entry into society. Restorative justice has been gaining growing attention in peace-building, post-conflict and post-dictatorial situations—thus, it is key for thinking about the common good in society. Restorative justice belongs to both traditional reflection—including notable illuminists such as Cesare Beccaria—and ideal practice—for example, *'Vigilando redimere'* is the motto of Italian custody agents (despite the well-known lamentable state of many Italian prisons). Safeguarding restorative justice, and similarly safeguarding justice as participation, solidarity and inclusion, requires us to address the micro-social foundations (education, accompaniment) that can practically regenerate institutions from within.

III. Forgiveness: Regenerating Social Bonds

Dysfunctional individuals, dysfunctional families, and dysfunctional communities exist. Even more dramatically, their existence tends to exhibit self-reinforcing features, leading to vicious cycles. Addiction is an all too obvious example. Think of corrupt or violent communities:

---

31 Being a parent provides a very vivid representation of what it means for love and rules to be in a generative tension with each other in practical daily life, and shows that no 'middle of the road' can provide a theoretical, perfect solution to that tension.

their inner dynamics are equally likely to perpetuate corruption and violence. It is very difficult to break with common habits and distance oneself from behaviours that are so widespread as to be perceived as 'normal'; and it is very easy for a member of a corrupt community to slip back into common habits, even when trying to change.

What about the common good in these situations? For these persons and communities, only a complete change of path, a full U-turn, will work. How can vicious spirals that perpetuate violence, corruption, and addiction be interrupted and reversed?

In studying community accompaniment for addicts and for inmates, we soon learnt about the key role of forgiveness: forgiving and being forgiven. When we initially spoke with founders of rehab communities, they underlined the importance that, first of all, people in rehab could forgive themselves; and also, forgive those they felt had had a role in their fall into addiction.

We later learnt that self-forgiveness, and asking for forgiveness, is also key in GRIP. Mindfulness in GRIP starts in fact with measuring time, and answering two questions: how much time it took me to commit the violent crime for which I am in prison (a few minutes, maybe?); and how much time I have already spent in prison (years, or decades). Each GRIP 'tribe' is named after a number, equal to the total number of years (often hundreds!) that its members have spent in prison. Through this exercise, the tribe members recognise, as individuals and as a community, that 'they are not their crime'. Concretely experiencing that this does happen in the 'tribe' is quite a U-turn for inmates.

We also learnt that the word 'forgiveness' cannot be taken lightly. We cannot expect acts of forgiveness to happen just because we rationally 'see' that they are necessary. In Italian, the word '*per-dono*' means the highest form of gift (*dono*). One can even can say that forgiveness is the single act that can only happen in the most incandescent part of our inner nucleus—where our heart most deeply yearns for infinite love, truth and beauty. We also learnt that forgiveness does indeed have the power to transform, and to heal, both the forgiven and the forgiver. This transformation is especially necessary when we encounter dysfunctional persons, families, and communities.

The metric of the common good, as developed in the pentagram, is about measuring, but also supporting, functional local communities in their collective discernment, and their common action. Should it be applied to dysfunctional communities, I think that the role of forgiveness could be made more explicit in the metric.

IV. Stability, Resilience and Care

The foundational chapter s (Chapter 1 and 2), very appropriately, underline the need for relational stability, referring to those relations that bring about human flourishing. Our research quite naturally resonates with this point, and with the repeated emphasis on the need to transmit a common narrative about what it is to be human. As mentioned above, we need the living transmission of community culture. Here, the key word seems to me to be the adjective 'living': transmission of a living memory is in fact an act that changes both those who hand down the memory, and those who receive it. Once again, the I-we polar tension is at work.

Living transmission of memory can favour innovation in continuity, and this is very important. However, individual people and communities that are trapped in addiction, violence, vulnerability, marginalisation, or exclusion, definitely need to experience discontinuity in their life, so as to move from abandonment into care and accompaniment. They need to encounter once again someone who can vividly communicate what it is to be human. In less extreme situations, the transmission of a community culture about the sense of humanity may be fading because words keep being repeated, but their inner fire is too pale: once again, some sort of discontinuity is once again necessary. A living minority that simply upholds what it is to be human can become an agent of regeneration through discontinuity, like Havel's greengrocer.

Offenders in Californian prisons tend to be the product of gang violence, and gangs are known to develop their own culture, which is often trapped in an 'us-them' confrontation. People in Italian rehab communities are often former inmates, with different national and religious backgrounds. Yet, we observe that encounters with and experiences of durable care in love-based communities can be transformative for them. How can this happen? What common narrative about being human can be transmitted? Especially for dysfunctional individuals, and possibly for dysfunctional communities, we need to turn to the deepest layer we have in common, to the inner, incandescent nucleus of humanity. The fundamental common *enracinement* is the elemental experience of being human—an experience that is both totally singular, and truly universal, common to all.

Transmitting the common memory of what it is to be human within living experience of personalised care can be both the source and the fulfilment of transformative experiences. Speaking of care, what we learn at the micro-social level may also be relevant at macro-social levels. We can draw a parallel between caring for each other, and caring for the nexus of the common good. We know that the nexus of the common good of a given community can be disrupted, for instance by carelessness in preserving a living memory of its origin (I cannot help but think of the European Union). Politics is indeed about care: citizens need to both avail themselves of the existing nexus of the common good, and take care of it.[32] Once again, let me use the example of Charta 77: caring that the existing Helsinki Declaration be respected in Czechoslovakia, and making it possible for people to avail themselves of the declaration's provisions, can bring about an epochal, and bloodless, revolution.

V. Humanity and Listing the Goods that Provide the Common Good

In Chapter 4, humanity is defined as the overarching good resulting from the common good dynamics, the good that is immanent to the interactions within the nexus. Movement towards the universal common good, such as an achievement, is also a return to the original common good we share by being members of the human family: the elemental experience of humanity. The living experience of our own incandescent nucleus is the most precious 'given' reality that the all-of-us has in common. This given common provides the basis for the I-we polar opposition that drives agency freedom.

In discussing humanity, Chapter 2 also provides a list of the core set of common goods that structure personal rationality and freedom, and a list of basic common goods conducive to a good life, which

---

32 'To take a stand for the common good is on the one hand to be solicitous for, and on the other hand to avail oneself of, that complex of institutions that give structure to the life of society, juridically, civilly, politically and culturally, making it the *polis*.' Benedict XVI, *Caritas in veritate*, 2009, n. 7.

captures human values and expresses human aspirations whose concrete practice signals the humanising features of the nexus. Lists are obviously necessary, but they deserve careful drafting; they need to be well-thought-out, and at the same time considered with sound humility: no list can truly encompass all that we need to experience the fullness of humanity.

In the current consensus on goals and targets for the international community, and in view of sustainable development (a very ambitious overarching aim, yet not as much as a 'global common good'), I see the practical risk of short-circuiting, where pursuing any of the 169 targets is by definition good enough for building the global common good. It is true that refined theoretical discourses about sustainable development specify that the SDGs should not be understood as a list, because sustainable development should be pursued from a holistic perspective, since individual targets are clearly disparate from one another. Yet, a realistic description of operational steps, based on decisive processes as they practically unfold, leads us back to the short-circuit: any policymaker—just like any non-state actor—will select actions out of the list of SGDs.[33] Thus, some targets will inevitably be more likely to be pursued: because they are more politically attractive, either domestically or internationally; or easier to fund; or for other reasons entirely. Obviously, it's better to build actions upon an agreed list than to openly disagree. But a list, at the end of the day, remains a list—not a nexus.

Conclusion

The common good of a micro-social community and of society at large cannot be captured in a set of external conditions to be met, as if the *how* and the *why* did not matter. It is the process of pursuing the actual good of the all-of-us living together in families, neighbourhoods, associations, political communities, from small to large, to the family of nations. It is a good generated by concrete human interactions (which are always imperfect), and embedded in the most elemental common good we all share to start with: our existence as human beings.

---

33   Even the outcomes of academic research tend to be classified with reference to one or more SDGs—meaning that the seventeen SDGs are indeed a list!

Human and common development are indeed in reciprocal dynamism, and they both share in the same paradox, in the same polar opposition: already, and not yet. We have not yet reached, and we strive to reach in fullness, that with which we have already been endowed: the incandescent nucleus of our own humanity.

References

Bellamy, F. X. 2014. *Les déshérites ou l'urgence de transmettre*, Paris: Editions Plon.

Beretta, S. and Maggioni, M. A. 2017. *Time, relations and behaviors: Measuring the transformative power of love-based community life*. Helen Kellogg Institute for International Studies Working Papers 421, 1–52. https://kellogg.nd.edu/sites/default/files/working_papers/421.pdf.

Borghesi, M. 2017. *Jorge Mario Bergoglio. Una biografia intellettuale*, Milano: Jaca Book.

Collier, K., Coyne S., Rasmussen, E., et al. 2016. Does parental mediation of media influence child outcomes? A meta-analysis on media time, aggression, substance use, and sexual behavior, *Developmental Psychology 52/5*, 798–812. https://doi.org/10.1037/dev0000108

Ghia, G. 2019. La verità è polifonica: rapsodia dell'opposizione polare e dottrina del metodo in Romano Guardini, *Humanitas: rivista bimestrale di cultura LXXIV 2/3*, 215–226.

Guardini, R. 2019 (1925). *Der Gegensatz: Versuche zu Einer Philosophie des Lebendig-Konkreten*, Freiburg: Matthias Grunewald Verlag.

Havel, V. 1985 (1978). *The Power of the Powerless*, London: Routledge.

Hoff, K. and Stiglitz J. E. 2016. Striving for balance in economics: Towards a theory of the social determination of behavior, *Journal of Economic Behavior & Organization 126/B*, 25–57. https://doi.org/10.3386/w21823

Kasulis, T. P. 2008 (2002). *Intimacy or Integrity: Philosophy and Cultural Difference*, Honululu: University of Hawai'i Press.

Maggioni, M. A., Rossignoli, D., Beretta, S., and Balestri, S. 2018. Trust behind bars: Measuring change in inmates' prosocial preferences, *Journal of Economic Psychology 64*, 89–104. https://doi.org/10.1016/j.joep.2017.12.003

Maggioni, M. and Rossignoli, D. 2020. Clever little lies: Math performance and cheating in primary schools in Congo, *Journal of Economic Behavior & Organization 172*, 380–400. https://doi.org/10.1016/j.jebo.2019.12.021

Narayan, D., Chambers, R., Shah, M. K., and Petesch P. 2000. *Voices of the Poor: Crying Out for Change*, Oxford: Oxford University Press.

Péguy, C. 1911. *Les mystères de Jeanne d'Arc: le mystère des saints innocents*, Paris: Emile Paul Frères.

List of Illustrations

Chapter 1

Chapter 2

Chapter 3

Chapter 7

Chapter 8

Chapter 11

Chapter 12

List of Tables

Chapter 3

Chapter 6

Chapter 7

Chapter 8

Chapter 11

Index

agency (as a normative key driver of common good dynamics) 3, 10, 16–20, 54, 66, 71–76, 79, 84, 93–97, 104, 107–108, 115–120, 122, 125–127, 143–168, 170–172, 186, 188, 191–192, 194–196, 211, 221, 227, 232–233, 245, 247, 251, 257–259, 263–265, 267–271, 289, 300–301, 306–308, 310, 312–314, 317, 327–330, 336–337, 341, 343, 347–348, 357, 365, 367–369, 375

Arendt, Hannah 16, 33, 45

Aristotle 16, 30, 42, 47, 84–85, 298

Atlixco 3, 21, 114, 132, 275, 321, 331–343

basic common good 15, 27, 54, 73, 75, 80, 83–91, 104, 112–113, 116–120, 122–123, 130, 143, 180, 246, 323, 375

collective agency 3, 16–18, 66, 72, 74–76, 94–96, 104, 107, 115–120, 125–126, 144–146, 156–168, 170–172, 258–259, 267, 269, 368–369

common good dynamics 2–3, 14, 16–18, 20–21, 27–28, 53–54, 57–59, 63, 66–72, 74–75, 78–79, 84, 91, 93, 95–96, 103, 112, 127, 134, 136, 143, 145, 148, 156, 158, 179, 275, 303, 321–322, 326–328, 337, 367, 371, 375

common good matrix (common good metric) 4, 19, 21, 115, 160, 168, 244, 252

commoning 6, 11, 19, 58–59, 63, 66–68, 75, 86, 201–202, 208, 212, 214–215

commons 2, 6–7, 9–12, 14–16, 19, 28, 58–63, 66–68, 75, 77–78, 86, 105, 143–144, 165–166, 170, 196, 204, 206, 209, 275, 318, 322, 326

community-driven development (CDD) programs 11–12, 58, 63–68, 130

conflict 30–31, 36, 40, 46–47, 50–51, 53, 61, 67, 77, 83, 91–92, 122, 124, 128–129, 160, 169, 193, 210–212, 214, 220, 225, 232, 260, 300, 302, 304, 314, 342, 351, 358, 370, 372

conflict resolution mechanism 67, 122, 124, 342

cooperation 2, 4, 6–10, 30, 37–38, 45, 64, 67, 78, 92, 94, 127, 156, 160, 169, 209–212, 214, 261, 305, 326, 361, 370

corruption 64, 160, 183, 245, 304, 306, 312, 372–373

culture (as a basic common good) 27, 32, 54, 61, 82–83, 85–86, 88, 94, 103, 116, 119, 121, 123, 171, 192, 269, 308, 315, 374

democracy 5, 13, 28, 69, 94, 233, 258–259, 293, 299–300, 322, 325–326, 340

development policies 106, 238, 322, 333, 341

development process(es) 5, 8–9, 15, 27–28, 70, 107, 109, 134, 143, 148, 159–160, 171, 341

dignity 19, 31, 51, 86, 89, 92, 108–109, 120–121, 179–181, 187–189, 191–192, 194–197, 213, 283, 294, 325–326, 361, 370, 372

education (as a basic common good) 7–8, 10, 12, 15–17, 33, 36, 43, 49, 54, 57, 82, 85–87, 106, 108, 115–116, 119, 121, 123, 133, 180, 241, 243–246, 252, 255, 265, 280, 287, 303–305, 308, 337–338, 343, 358, 361, 364, 372

exclusion 68, 80, 120–121, 194, 204, 213, 224, 304–305, 374

flourishing 14, 51, 61, 69, 80–81, 84–85, 91, 94, 109, 179–181, 220, 230, 259,

About the Team

Alessandra Tosi was the managing editor for this book.

Melissa Purkiss performed the copy-editing, proofreading and indexing.

Anna Gatti designed the cover. The cover was produced in InDesign using the Fontin font.

Luca Baffa typeset the book in InDesign and produced the paperback and hardback editions. The text font is Tex Gyre Pagella; the heading font is Californian FB. Luca produced the EPUB, AZW3, PDF, HTML, and XML editions—the conversion is performed with open source software freely available on our GitHub page (https://github.com/OpenBook Publishers).

This book need not end here...

Share

All our books — including the one you have just read — are free to access online so that students, researchers and members of the public who can't afford a printed edition will have access to the same ideas. This title will be accessed online by hundreds of readers each month across the globe: why not share the link so that someone you know is one of them?

This book and additional content is available at:

https://doi.org/10.11647/OBP.0290

Donate

Open Book Publishers is an award-winning, scholar-led, not-for-profit press making knowledge freely available one book at a time. We don't charge authors to publish with us: instead, our work is supported by our library members and by donations from people who believe that research shouldn't be locked behind paywalls.

Why not join them in freeing knowledge by supporting us: https://www.openbookpublishers.com/section/104/1

Like Open Book Publishers

Follow @OpenBookPublish

Read more at the Open Book Publishers BLOG

You may also be interested in:

Wellbeing, Freedom and Social Justice
The Capability Approach Re-Examined
Ingrid Robeyns

https://doi.org/10.11647/OBP.0130

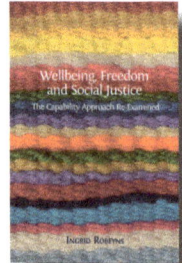

Democratising Participatory Research
Pathways to Social Justice from the South
Carmen Martinez-Vargas

https://doi.org/10.11647/OBP.0273

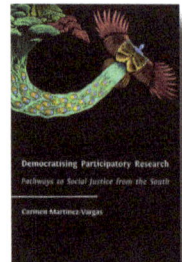

Peace and Democratic Society
Amartya Sen

https://doi.org/10.11647/OBP.0014

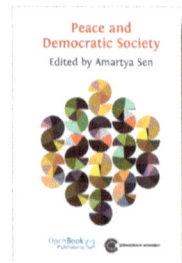

www.ingramcontent.com/pod-product-compliance
Lightning Source LLC
Chambersburg PA
CBHW051441270326
41932CB00025B/3391